# Law, Politics
# and the Judicial System
# in Canada

## Edited by F.L. Morton

The University of Calgary Press

# Dedication

This book is dedicated to Peter H. Russell, who introduced me to this subject ten years ago at the University of Toronto. For the past twenty years, Peter Russell has almost single-handedly enlightened his students and his colleagues about the political dimensions of the judicial process in Canada. This work is reflected in his numerous contributions to this volume. First as a teacher, and more recently as a colleague and friend, Peter Russell has been selfless in his assistance and helpful advice. I am happy to have the occasion to acknowledge it.

Copyright 1984 by F.L. Morton

ISBN 0-919813-03-8

Published by The University of Calgary Press
2500 University Drive N.W.
Calgary, Alberta T2N 1N4 Canada

Order from The University of Calgary Press

Price: $10.95

# Preface

Like many books, this one was born of necessity. When I arrived at the University of Calgary three years ago, there was no single text that presented an adequate political science treatment of the judicial process in Canada. This was a problem, as I was assigned to teach several sections of a "law and politics" course with enrollments of several hundred students annually. This book is the result.

The prior lack of a book on the Canadian judicial process is not that surprising. Constitutional law and judicial process have never constituted a separate sub-field of Canadian political science, for the simple reason that the Canadian courts have never had as high a political profile as their American counterparts. With a few notable exceptions, the study of law, courts, and judges in Canada has been left almost exclusively to the law schools. Their treatment, while often excellent from a practical perspective, has been predictably legalistic and methodologically uncritical. The subject has been something of an intellectual "no-mans land" — too political for law professors but too legal for political scientists.

The adoption of the Canadian Charter of Rights and Freedoms in 1982 has rendered this situation unacceptable, if it had not already become so. The Charter places new constitutional restrictions on both levels of government, explicitly authorizes judicial enforcement, and arms the judges with broad remedial powers. These changes will force the Canadian judiciary into a much more explicit political function than it had previously exercised. In deciding Charter of Rights cases, judges must make choices that have discernible impacts on public policy and that are not simply dictated by precedent or Charter wording. This expansion of the Canadian judiciary's political function requires that the same types of questions that have traditionally been asked about the other institutions that make up the governing process be asked about courts and judges.

The reader is forewarned that the focus of this book is tilted toward constitutional law and appellate courts, especially the Supreme Court of Canada. This is not meant to deny the political significance of trial courts or other areas of law. Rather it simply reflects the fact that constitutional law is the most political kind of law, and the practical limits of time and space. There should have been a chapter on administrative law, but alas there is not. That will have to wait for a second edition.

The structure of this book was largely modeled after the excellent American reader edited by Walter Murphy and C. Herman Pritchett, *Courts, Judges, and Politics — An Introduction to the Judicial Process* (New York: Random House, 1979). For the past three years I have used this book to teach a comparative course on Canadian and American judicial process. Its topical organization covers the major issues of the judicial process, and I was able to adapt its structure to the Canadian experience with only several alterations. I have found that the comparative perspective enriches the learning experience by forcing the realization that "our way" is not necessarily the only way, and would recommend it to others.

I am indebted to a number of people who helped to produce this book. I would like to thank the contributors, especially Peter Russell, Paul Weiler, and the family of the late Chief Justice, Bora Laskin. All were most generous in allowing me to use and to edit their works. I am indebted to the staff of the University of Calgary Press for their assistance, especially Sandy Buker, Shirley Onn, Tari Forrest, and Marcy Laufer. My colleague Tom Flanagan encouraged me in this project from the start, and he and Rainer Knopff were generous beyond the call of duty in proof-reading and offering helpful advice. Last but most of all, I want to thank my wonderful wife, who cheerfully tolerated my long absences and short memory during the final two months of preparing this manuscript.

F.L.M.

# Contents

\* Reprinted elsewhere in the book.

# 1

# The Rule of Law In the Canadian Constitution

On December 4, 1946, Frank Roncarelli was informed by the Quebec Liquor Commission that the liquor license for his Montreal restaurant had been revoked "forever." Mr. Roncarelli had not violated any Liquor Commission guidelines, nor had he been charged with or convicted of any criminal wrongdoing. The license was revoked because, as Mr. Roncarelli and indeed everyone else knew, Maurice Duplessis, the Premier of Quebec, wanted to punish him for his membership in and financial support of the Jehovah's Witnesses. The Jehovah's Witnesses are an evangelizing, fundamentalist protestant sect, who had outraged Duplessis and the French Catholic majority in Quebec through their outspoken criticisms of the Catholic Church and its priests. The Duplessis government had begun a campaign of legal harassment against the Witnesses, by arresting them for distributing their printed materials without a license. Roncarelli frustrated this plan by regularly providing bail money for his arrested fellow-believers, who would then return to the streets. Roncarelli thus became a special target of the harassment policies of the Quebec government.

After a thirteen-year legal battle, the Supreme Court of Canada finally ruled that the government of Quebec's treatment of Roncarelli had been arbitrary, wrong, and illegal. (Reading 1.1)

A majority of the Court held that in Canada there is a general right not to be punished by the arbitrary exercise of government power. A government, federal or provincial, can only move against an individual in accordance with known rules, and the Duplessis government had failed to meet this standard. In so ruling, the Supreme Court re-asserted one of the fundamental principles of the "unwritten constitution" of Canada — "the rule of law."

The Roncarelli case was just the most recent chapter in a living tradition that can be traced back through the nineteenth-century writings of A.V.C. Dicey (Reading 1.4); the American *Declaration of Independence* of 1776 (Reading 1.3); the political theory of the seventeenth-century philosopher John Locke (Reading 1.2); and back to the fields of Runnymede in June of

1215, when the English nobles forced King John to sign *Magna Carta* and to agree to rule *per legem terrae* — according to the laws of the land.[1]

If *Magna Carta* marked the beginning of the "rule of law" tradition, the next major event is the "Glorious Revolution of 1688," which deposed the Stuart kings and established the supremacy of Parliament over the Crown. This landmark event initiated the practice of government that we now take for granted (too much so!) — representative government, or government by consent of the governed. The second reading is from the writings of John Locke, often referred to as the "theorist of the Glorious Revolution." Locke's *Second Treatise on Government*, first published in 1690, has been the most influential defense and advocacy of "government by consent," or liberal democracy, ever written. In it, we find not only a defense of "government by consent of the governed," but also a restatement of the principle of *per legem terrae*. Locke explicitly declares that even the new sovereign, the legislature, must rule "by declared and received laws . . . interpreted by known authorized judges."

A careful reading of the passage from Locke reveals that in addition to these procedural restrictions, he imposes a second major restriction on the legislative, or "law-making," power of the state — "the law of Nature." This substantive restriction means that not only must laws be duly enacted and administered, but also that the laws themselves must not violate the "natural rights" of individuals that exist by the "law of Nature."

This double limitation on just government was given its most striking and memorable articulation in the American *Declaration of Independence* of 1776, written primarily by Thomas Jefferson. (Reading 1.3) The Americans justified their revolution, and subsequently founded their new republic, on the two fundamental principles of Locke's political theory: that "all men are by Nature equal," and that they possess "certain inalienable (i.e., natural) rights." There is a critical tension between these two fundamental concepts of equality and liberty. The principle of natural equality essentially means that no man is good enough to rule another without his consent. This banishes the traditional claims of priests, kings, and nobles to rule on the basis of their alleged natural superiority, and replaces it with government by consent of the governed. In practice, this has meant some form of "majority rule" democracy. The principle of natural rights means that a just government cannot violate these rights,

---

[1] The full text of s. 39 of *Magna Carta* reads as follows: "No freeman shall be taken or (and) imprisoned or disseised or outlawed or exiled or in any way destroyed, nor will we go upon him nor send upon him, except by the lawful judgement of his peers or (and) by the law of the land." This 700 year-old rule is the direct ancestor of the 1982 Charter of Rights and Freedoms, whose preamble declares: "Whereas Canada is founded upon principles that recognize the supremacy of God and the rule of law." Section 7 of the Charter essentially restates the modern formulation of *per legem terrae*, that no person can be deprived of his life, liberty, or security of the person, except according to the due process of law. Sections 8 through 15 then elaborate specific aspects of due process.

since the very purpose of government is to secure such rights. The tension arises from the fact that "majority rule" does not always produce laws that respect the rights of individuals or groups who are not part of the majority.

This tension is more of a practical problem than a theoretical one. Most of the time the combined practice of "government by consent" and "the rule of law" is a strong guarantee that the twin requirements of equality and liberty will both be met. It is unlikely that a governing majority will ever (knowingly) consent to policies that are destructive of their rights. The "rule of law" provides additional safeguards by detering rulers from pursuing ends and using means that "they would not like to have known by the people, and own not willingly."[2] But what happens when the majority consents to laws that are destructive of the natural rights of a minority? What happens when government by the "consent of the governed" no longer "secures these rights"? Neither Locke nor Jefferson answered this question. The practical problem of reconciling "majority rule" with "minority rights" was left to the founders of new liberal democracies such as the United States and Canada.

There have been two principal approaches to giving institutional expression to the principles of equality and liberty in modern liberal democracies: the British parliamentary or Westminster model, and the American "separation of powers" model. Because of two major differences in the Parliamentary and American systems, the courts in each system have very different functions and characteristics. The American model is ultimately based on and organized by a single basic document — a written constitution. This single document sets down in writing "the rules governing the composition, powers and methods of operation of the main institutions of government, and the general principles applicable to their relations to the citizens."[3] By contrast, the Westminster model is based on an "unwritten constitution" — a combination of historically important statutes, the common law, and numerous unwritten conventions and usages. The second difference is that the "written constitution" of the Americans includes an enumeration of the fundamental rights and liberties of the individual against government, known collectively as the *Bill of Rights*. (Reprinted in the Appendix) While individuals enjoy basically the same rights and freedoms under the British parliamentary model of democracy, they are not "spelled out" in any single, basic document of government, i.e., they are not "constitutionally entrenched."

The result of these two differences is that under the American model of democracy, the courts, and especially the Supreme Court, play a much more explicit and more influential political role. Ever since the 1803 case of *Marbury v. Madison*, American courts have assumed the function of interpreting and

---

[2] See Locke, *The Second Treatise*, ch. 11, Reading 1.2.

[3] Sir Ivor Jennings, *The Law and the Constitution*, 5th ed. (London: University of London Press, 1959), p. 33.

enforcing ''constitutional law'' just as they do all other law. This ''judicial review'' of legislative and executive actions is intended to ensure that they conform to the procedures and limitations laid down in the Constitution. If they do not conform, the court declares them to be ''unconstitutional,'' and therefore without legal effect.

It is easy to see how, in theory at least, combining the American practice of judicial review with an entrenched Bill of Rights resolves the tension between liberty and equality, majority rule and minority rights. If the majority enacts a law that infringes a constitutional right of an individual, he can go to court and ask the judges to strike down the law as unconstitutional. This approach to protecting civil liberties was particularly effective in promoting racial justice in American society during the 1950's and 1960's. While the more ''democratic'' (majoritarian) institutions of government refused to take action, the American Supreme Court used the Bill of Rights guarantee of ''equal protection of the laws'' to strike down the legal barriers of racial discrimination in American society. However, as the American Supreme Court expanded its ''judicial activism'' into more and more areas of public policy and local government, serious questions began to arise about the ''undemocratic'' character of its use of judicial review. In protecting the ''individual rights'' side of the liberal equation, the Court was perceived as neglecting and even violating the equality requirement of government by consent of the governed.[4]

The British model of parliamentary supremacy combined with ''the rule of law'' tradition avoids this problem. There are no written constitutional prohibitions for the British courts to enforce against Parliament, and the courts do not interpret or enforce constitutional conventions, the ''unwritten constitution.''[5] The critics of parliamentary democracy, however, contend that it is prone to the opposite problem — that there is no adequate mechanism to protect individuals or minorities from democratic majorities that violate their rights. While this may be true in theory, in practice it has not proven to be a serious problem in either Great Britain or Canada.

The key to the practical success of the British parliamentary system is conveyed in the reading from Dicey on ''the rule of law,'' and especially his quotation from Tocqueville. (Reading 1.4) Comparing the governments of England and Switzerland, Tocqueville observed that, ''In England there seems to be more liberty in the customs than in the laws of the people,'' while the opposite holds for Switzerland. For both Tocqueville and Dicey, the British condition is far preferable. For in the long run, the customs, habits, beliefs — in short, the public morality — of a society is a more dependable guarantee of

---

[4] This problem is the subject of chapter 13.

[5] The Canadian Supreme Court's decision in the 1981 *Constitutional Amendment Reference* was contrary to this generally accepted practice, and is probably best understood as an exception to an otherwise still valid rule.

just laws than the "paper barriers" of constitutional "guarantees." Put very simply, a written constitution cannot "guarantee" that the laws of a democratic society will be any more just or decent than the people who make up that society.

The government of Canada was basically modeled after the British parliamentary system. The one important exception is the federal form of the union of the Canadian provinces, and the defining of the forms and limits of this union in a single, written document — the British North America Act, now known as the Constitution Act, 1867. This aspect of Canadian government is especially important for the courts, because it has thrust upon them the function of judicial review, or "umpire" of the federal system.[6] Federalism aside, both levels of government in Canada were formed after the Westminster model, which meant parliamentary supremacy within their respective spheres of jurisdiction.

Accordingly, Canada has, until very recently, followed the British approach to the protection of civil liberty — parliamentary supremacy combined with "the rule of law," and a healthy self-confidence in the basic sense of fairness and toleration for diversity in the Canadian people. Inevitably the proximity of the United States has prompted constant comparisons. One of the most eloquent and forceful defenses of the Anglo-Canadian approach to protecting civil liberties was given by the dean of Canadian political science, R. MacGregor Dawson. In discussing the various components of Canada's unwritten constitution, Dawson argued:

> The mere fact that a constitutional doctrine is not explicitly enunciated and formally committed to writing may affect the external appearance but not disturb the genuineness or force of that doctrine. Thus the broad tolerance which will permit differences of opinion and will disapprove of punitive or repressive measures against the dissenters is of as great constitutional significance and may conceivably under some circumstances afford an even more assured protection than an explicit guarantee of freedom of speech, written into a constitution, yet with no solid conviction behind it.[7]

The force of Dawson's argument notwithstanding, Canadian political leaders have been increasingly attracted to the American approach to protecting civil liberties. In 1960 the Diefenbaker government enacted the Canadian Bill of Rights. It took the form of a statute, not a constitutional amendment, and applied only to the federal government and not to the provinces.[8] Partly because of dissatisfaction with this document and partly in response to political developments within Canada during the 1970's, the Trudeau government

---

[6] This is the subject of chapter 10.

[7] R. MacGregor Dawson, *The Government of Canada*, 4th ed. (Toronto: University of Toronto Press, 1963), p. 70.

[8] This is discussed in greater detail in chapter 11.

undertook a major program of constitutional reform in 1980. Prime Minister Trudeau's constitutional agenda included "patriating" the B.N.A. Act, an amending formula, and a new Charter of Rights that applied to both levels of Canadian government. After a year and a half of political maneuvering, confrontation, and finally compromise, all three objectives (or modified versions of them) were achieved.

The adoption of a constitutionally entrenched Charter of Rights (reproduced in Appendix) fundamentally altered the Canadian system of government by placing explicit limitations on the law-making power of both levels of government. Parliament was no longer supreme; the Constitution was. Or almost. Trudeau failed to have the Charter adopted in its original "pure" form. Attachment to the tradition of Parliamentary supremacy, combined with provincial suspicion and opposition, were too strong, and forced an important compromise. Added in the eleventh hour of constitutional negotiations between the federal government and the provinces, section 33 of the Charter allows both levels of government to ignore certain Charter provisions if they deem it necessary. Parliamentary supremacy was thus preserved, albeit in a qualified form.

As a result, Canada finds itself today almost equidistant between the British and American models of liberal democracy, with their differing approaches to civil liberties. As a result, the debate over which form of liberal democracy is best designed to protect the liberties of its citizens remains very much alive. The truth of this debate most probably lies somewhere between the two contending positions, for as Dawson pointed out:

> Written law and the conventions will normally complement one another, and each becomes necessary to the proper functioning of the other.[9]

While this debate is probably interminable, there is one undisputed fact about the effect of enumerating individual rights in a written constitution: it thrusts the courts, and the judges who constitute them, into a much more explicit and influential political role. This is the subject of the next chapter, while the details and consequences of this new role for Canadian judges and courts are elaborated in the remainder of the book.

---

[9] Dawson, *Government of Canada*, p. 71.

# 1.1

## RONCARELLI v. DUPLESSIS

Supreme Court of Canada (1959)

The judgment of Rand and Judson JJ. was delivered by

RAND J.: — The material facts from which my conclusion is drawn are these. The appellant was the proprietor of a restaurant in a busy section of Montreal which in 1946 through its transmission to him from his father had been continuously licensed for the sale of liquor for approximately 34 years; he is of good education and repute and the restaurant was of a superior class. On December 4 of that year, while his application for annual renewal was before the Liquor Commission, the existing license was cancelled and his application for renewal rejected, to which was added a declaration by the respondent that no future license would ever issue to him. These primary facts took place in the following circumstances.

For some years the appellant had been an adherent of a rather militant Christian religious sect known as the Witnesses of Jehovah. Their ideology condemns the established church institutions and stresses the absolute and exclusive personal relation of the individual to the Deity without human intermediation or intervention.

The first impact of their proselytizing zeal upon the Roman Catholic church and community in Quebec, as might be expected, produced a violent reaction. Meetings were forcibly broken up, property damaged, individuals ordered out of communities, in one case out of the province, and generally, within the cities and towns, bitter controversy aroused. The work of the Witnesses was carried on both by word of mouth and by the distribution of printed matter, the latter including two periodicals known as ''The Watch Tower'' and ''Awake,'' sold at a small price.

In 1945 the provincial authorities began to take steps to bring an end to what was considered insulting and offensive to the religious beliefs and feelings of the Roman Catholic population. Large scale arrests were made of young men and women, by whom the publications mentioned were being held out for sale, under local by-laws requiring a licence for peddling any kind of wares. Altogether almost one thousand of such charges were laid. The penalty involved in Montreal, where most of the arrests took place, was a fine of $40, and as the Witnesses disputed liability, bail was in all cases resorted to.

The appellant, being a person of some means, was accepted by the Recorder's Court as bail without question, and up to November 12, 1946, he had gone security in about 380 cases, some of the accused being involved in repeated offenses. Up to this time there had been no suggestion of impropriety; the security of the appellant was taken as so satisfactory that at times, to avoid delay when he was absent from the city, recognizances were signed by him in blank and kept ready for completion by the Court officials. The reason for the accumulation of charges was the doubt that they could be sustained in law. Apparently the legal officers of Montreal, acting in concert with those of the Province, had come to an agreement with the attorney for the Witnesses to have a test case proceeded with. Pending that, however, there was no stoppage of the sale of the tracts and this became the annoying circumstance that produced the volume of proceedings.

On or about November 12 it was decided to require bail in cash for Witnesses so arrested and the sum set ranged from $100 to $300. No such bail was furnished by the appellant; his connection with giving security ended with this change of practice; and in the result, all of the charges in relation to which he had become surety were dismissed.

At no time did he take any part in the distribution of the tracts: he was an adherent of the group but nothing more. It was shown that he had leased to another member premises in Sherbrooke which were used as a hall for carrying on religious meetings: but it is unnecessary to do more than mention that fact to reject it as having no bearing on the issues raised. Beyond the giving of bail and being an adherent, the appellant is free from any relation that could be tortured into a badge of character pertinent to his fitness or unfitness to hold a liquor licence.

The mounting resistance that stopped the surety bail sought other means of crushing the propagandist invasion and among the circumstances looked into was the situation of the appellant. Admittedly an adherent, he was enabling these protagonists to be at large to carry on their campaign of publishing what they believed to be the Christian truth as revealed by the Bible; he was also the holder of a liquor licence, a "privilege" granted by the Province, the profits from which, as it was seen by the authorities, he was using to promote the disturbance of settled beliefs and arouse community disaffection generally. Following discussions between the then Mr. Archambault, as the personality of the Liquor Commission, and the chief prosecuting officer in Montreal, the former, on or about November 21, telephoned to the respondent, advised him of those facts, and queried what should be done. Mr. Duplessis answered that the matter was serious and that the identity of the person furnishing bail and the liquor licensee should be put beyond doubt. A few days later, that identity being established through a private investigator, Mr. Archambault again communicated with the respondent and, as a result of what passed between them, the licence, as of December 4, 1946, was revoked.

In the meantime, about November 25, 1946, a blasting answer had come from the Witnesses. In an issue of one of the periodicals, under the heading "Quebec's Burning Hate," was a searing denunciation of what was alleged to be the savage persecution of Christian believers. Immediately instructions were sent out from the department of the Attorney-General ordering the confiscation of the issue and proceedings were taken against one Boucher charging him with publication of a seditious libel.

It is then wholly as a private citizen, an adherent of a religious group, holding a liquor licence and furnishing bail to arrested persons for no other purpose than to enable them to be released from detention pending the determination of the charges against them, and with no other relevant considerations to be taken into account, that he is involved in the issues of this controversy.

The complementary state of things is equally free from doubt. From the evidence of Mr. Duplessis and Mr. Archambault alone, it appears that the action taken by the latter as the general manager and sole member of the Commission was dictated by Mr. Duplessis as Attorney-General and Prime Minister of the province; that that step was taken as a means of bringing to a halt the activities of the Witnesses, to punish the appellant for the part he had played not only by revoking the existing licence but in declaring him barred from one "forever," and to warn others that they similarly would be stripped of provincial "privileges" if they persisted in any activity directly or indirectly related to the Witnesses and to the objectionable campaign. The respondent felt that action to be his duty, something which his conscience demanded of him; and as representing the provincial government his decision became automatically that of Mr. Archambault and the Commission. . . .

. . . In these circumstances, when the *de facto* power of the Executive over its appointees at will to such a statutory public function is exercised deliberately and intentionally to destroy the vital business interests of a citizen, is there legal redress by him against the person so acting? This calls for an examination of the statutory provisions governing the issue, renewal and revocation of liquor licences and the scope of authority entrusted by law to the Attorney-General and the government in relation to the administration of the Act. . . .

. . . The provisions of the statute, which may be supplemented by detailed regulations, furnish a code for the complete administration of the sale and distribution of alcoholic liquors directed by the commission as a public service, for all legitimate purposes of the populace. It recognizes the association of wines and liquors as embellishments of food and its ritual and as an interest of the public. As put in Macbeth, the "sauce to meat is ceremony," and so we have restaurants, cafes, hotels and other places of serving food, specifically provided for in that association.

At the same time the issue of permits has a complementary interest in those so catering to the public. The continuance of the permit over the years, as in this case, not only recognizes its virtual necessity to a superior class restaurant but also its identification with the business carried on. The provisions for assignment of the permit are to this most pertinent and they were exemplified in the continuity of the business here. As its exercise continues, the economic life of the holder becomes progressively more deeply implicated with the privilege while at the same time his vocation becomes correspondingly dependent on it.

The field of licensed occupations and businesses of this nature is steadily becoming of greater concern to citizens generally. It is a matter of vital importance that a public administration that can refuse to allow a person to enter or continue a calling which, in the absence of regulation, would be free and legitimate, should be conducted with complete impartiality and integrity; and that the grounds for refusing or cancelling a permit should unquestionably be such and such only as are incompatible with the purposes envisaged by the statute: the duty of a Commission is to serve those purposes and those only. A decision to deny or cancel such a privilege lies within the "discretion" of the Commission; but that means that decision is to be based upon a weighing of considerations pertinent to the object of the administration.

In public regulation of this sort there is no such thing as absolute and untrammelled "discretion," that is that action can be taken on any ground or for any reason that can be suggested to the mind of the administrator; no legislative Act can, without express language, be taken to contemplate an unlimited arbitrary power exercisable for any purpose, however capricious or irrelevant, regardless of the nature or purpose of the statute. Fraud and corruption in the Commission may not be mentioned in such statutes but they are always implied as exceptions. "Discretion" necessarily implies good faith in discharging public duty; there is always a perspective within which a statute is intended to operate; and any clear departure from its line or objects is just as objectionable as fraud or corruption. Could an applicant be refused a permit because he had been born in another province, or because of the colour of his hair? The ordinary language of the legislature cannot be so distorted.

To deny or revoke a permit because a citizen exercises an unchallengeable right totally irrelevant to the sale of liquor in a restaurant is equally beyond the scope of the discretion conferred. There was here not only revocation of the existing permit but a declaration of a future, definitive disqualification of the appellant to obtain one: it was to be "forever." This purports to divest his citizenship status of its incident of membership in the class of those of the public to whom such a privilege could be extended. Under the statutory language here, that is not competent to the Commission and a fortiori to the government or the respondent: *McGillivray v. Kimber.* There is here an administrative tribunal which, in certain respects, is to act in a judicial manner; and even on the view of the dissenting justices in *McGillivray,* there is liability: what could be more malicious than to punish this licensee for having done what he had an absolute right to do in a matter utterly irrelevant to the *Liquor Act?* Malice in the proper sense is simply acting for a reason and purpose knowingly foreign to the administration, to which was added here the element of intentional punishment by what was virtually vocation outlawry.

It may be difficult if not impossible in cases generally to demonstrate a breach of this public duty in the illegal purpose served; there may be no means, even if proceedings against the Commission were permitted by the Attorney-General, as here they were refused, of compelling the Commission to justify a refusal or revocation or to give reasons for its action; on these questions I make no observation; but in the case before us that difficulty is not present: the reasons are openly avowed.

The act of the respondent through the instrumentality of the Commission brought about a breach of an implied public statutory duty toward the appellant; it was a gross abuse of legal power expressly intended to punish him for an act wholly irrelevant to the statute, a punishment which inflicted on him, as it was intended to do, the destruction of his economic life as a restaurant keeper within the province. Whatever may be the immunity of the Commission or its member from an action for damages, there is none in the respondent. He was under no duty in relation to the appellant and his act was an intrusion upon the functions of a statutory body. The injury done by him was a fault engaging liability within the principles of the underlying public law of Quebec: *Mostyn v. Fabrigas*, and under art. 1053 of the *Civil Code*. That, in the presence of expanding administrative regulation of economic activities, such a step and its consequences are to be suffered by the victim without recourse or remedy, that an administration according to law is to be superseded by action dictated by and according to the arbitrary likes, dislikes and irrelevant purposes of public officers acting beyond their duty, would signal the beginning of disintegration of the rule of law as a fundamental postulate of our constitutional structure. An administration of licences on the highest level of fair and impartial treatment to all may be forced to follow the practice of "first come, first served," which makes the strictest observance of equal responsibility to all of even greater importance; at this stage of developing government it would be a danger of high consequence to tolerate such a departure from good faith in executing the legislative purpose. It should be added, however, that that principle is not, by this language, intended to be extended to ordinary governmental employment: with that we are not here concerned.

It was urged by Mr. Beaulieu that the respondent, as the incumbent of an office of state, so long as he was proceeding in "good faith," was free to act in a matter of this kind virtually as he pleased. The office of Attorney-General traditionally and by statute carries duties that relate to advising the Executive, including here, administrative bodies, enforcing the public law and directing the administration of justice. In any decision of the statutory body in this case, he had no part to play beyond giving advice on legal questions arising. In that role his action should have been limited to advice on the validity of a revocation for such a reason or purpose and what that advice should have been does not seem to me to admit of any doubt. To pass from this limited scope of action to that of bringing about a step by the Commission beyond the bounds prescribed by the legislature for its exclusive action converted what was done into his personal act.

"Good faith" in this context, applicable both to the respondent and the general manager, means carrying out the statute according to its intent and for its purpose; it means good faith in acting with a rational appreciation of that intent and purpose and not with an improper intent and for an alien purpose; it does not mean for the purposes of punishing a person for exercising an unchallengeable right; it does not mean arbitrarily and illegally attempting to divest a citizen of an incident of his civil status. . . .

# 1.2

## OF THE EXTENT OF LEGISLATIVE POWER

John Locke, *The Second Treatise* (1690)

The great end of Mens entring into Society, being the enjoyment of their Properties in Peace and Safety, and the great instrument and means of that being the Laws establish'd in that Society; the first and fundamental positive Law of all Commonwealths, is the establishing of the Legislative Power; as the first and fundamental natural Law, which is to govern even the Legislative itself, is the preservation of the Society, and (as far as will consist with the publik good) of every person in it. This Legislative is not only the supream power of the Commonwealth, but sacred and unalterable in the hands where the Community have once placed it; . . .

. . . Though the Legislative, whether placed in one or more, whether it be always in being, or only by intervals, tho' it be the Supream Power in every Common-wealth; yet,

First, It is not, nor can possibly be absolutely Arbitrary over the Lives and Fortunes of the People. For it being but the joynt power of every Member of the Society given up to that Person, or Assembly, which is Legislator, it can be no more than those persons had in a State of Nature before they enter'd into Society, and gave up to the Community. . . . Their Power in the utmost Bounds of it, is limited to the publik good of the Society. It is a Power, that hath no other end but preservation, and therefore can never have a right to destroy, enslave, or designedly to impoverish the Subjects. The Obligations of the Law of Nature, cease not in Society but only in many Cases are drawn closer, and have by Humane Laws known Penalties annexed to them, to inforce their observation. Thus the Law of Nature stands as an Eternal Rule to all Men, Legislators as well as others. . . .

. . . Secondly, The Legislative, or Supream Authority, cannot assume to its self a power to Rule by extemporary Arbitrary Decrees, but is bound to dispense Justice, and decide the Rights of the Subject by promulgated stand-ing Laws, and known Authoris'd Judges. For the Law of Nature being unwritten, and so no where to be found but in the minds of Men, they who through Passion or Interest shall mis-cite, or misapply it, cannot so easily be con-vinced of their mistake where there is no establish'd Judge: And so it serves not, as it ought, to determine the Rights, and fence the Properties of those that live under it, especially where every one is Judge, Interpreter, and Execu-

Cambridge and New York: Cambridge University Press, 1960. Edited by Peter Laslett. Reprinted with permission.

tioner of it too, and that in his own Case: And he that has right on his side, having ordinarily but his own single strength, hath not force enough to defend himself from Injuries, or to punish Delinquents. To avoid these Inconveniencies which disorder Mens Properties in the state of Nature, Men unite into Societies, that they may have the united strength of the whole Society to secure and defend their Properties, and may have standing Rules to bound it, by which every one may know what is his. To this end it is that Men give up all their Natural Power to the Society which they enter into, and the Community put the Legislative Power into such hands as they think fit, with this trust, that they shall be govern'd by declared Laws, or else their Peace, Quiet, and Property will still be at the same uncertainty, as it was in the state of Nature.

Absolute Arbitrary Power, or Governing without settled standing Laws, can neither of them consist with the ends of Society and Government, which Men would not quit the freedom of the state of Nature for, and tie themselves up under, were it not to preserve their Lives, Liberties and Fortunes; and by stated Rules of Right and Property to secure their Peace and Quiet. . . . And therefore whatever Form the Common-wealth is under, the Ruling Power ought to govern by declared and received Laws, and not by extemporary Dictates and undetermined Resolutions. For then Mankind will be in a far worse condition, than in the State of Nature, if they shall have armed one or a few Men with the joynt power of a Multitude, to force them to obey at pleasure the exorbitant and unlimited Decrees of their sudden thoughts, or unrestrain'd, and till that moment unknown Wills without having any mea- sures set down which may guide and justifie their actions. For all the power the Government has, being only for the good of the Society, as it ought not to be *Arbitrary* and at Pleasure, so it ought to be exercised by *established and promulagated Laws*: that both the People may know their Duty, and be safe and secure within the limits of the Law, and the Rulers too kept within their due bounds, and not to be tempted, by the Power they have in their hands, to imploy it to such purposes, and by such measures, as they would not have known, and own not willingly.

. . . Thirdly, The Supream Power cannot take from any Man any part of his Property without his own consent. . . .

. . . Fourthly, The Legislative cannot transfer the Power of Making Laws to any other hands. For it being but a delegated Power from the People, they, who have it, cannot pass it over to others. The People alone can appoint the Form of the Commonwealth, which is by Constituting the Legislative, and appointing in whose hands that shall be. . . .

. . . These are the Bounds which the trust that is put in them by the Society, and the Law of God and Nature, have set to the Legislative Power of every Commonwealth, in all Forms of Government.

First, They are to govern, by promulgated establish'd Laws, not to be varied in particular Cases, but to have one Rule for Rich and Poor, for the Favourite at Court, and the Country Man at Plough.

Secondly, These Laws also ought to be designed for no other end ultimately but the good of the People.

Thirdly, they must not raise Taxes on the Property of the People, without the Consent of the People, given by themselves, or their Deputies. And this properly concerns only such Governments where the Legislative is always in being, or at least where the People have not reserv'd any part of the Legislative to Deputies, to be from time to time chosen by themselves.

Fourthly, The Legislative neither must nor can transfer the Power of making Laws to any Body else, or place it anywhere but where the People have.

# 1.3

# THE DECLARATION OF INDEPENDENCE
Thomas Jefferson (1776)

When in the course of human events, it becomes necessary for one people to dissolve the political bands which have connected them with another, and to assume among the Powers of the earth, the separate and equal station to which the Laws of Nature and of Nature's God entitle them, a decent respect to the opinions of mankind requires that they should declare the causes which impell them to the separation.

We hold these truths to be self-evident, that all men are created equal, that they are endowed by their Creator with certain unalienable Rights, that among these are Life, Liberty and the pursuit of Happiness. That to secure these rights, Governments are instituted among Men, deriving their just powers from the consent of the governed, that whenever any Form of Government becomes destructive of these ends, it is the Right of the People to alter or to abolish it, and to institute new Government, laying its foundation on such principles and organizing its powers in such form, as to them shall seem most likely to effect their Safety and Happiness. Prudence, indeed, will dictate that Governments long established should not be changed for light and transient causes; and accordingly all experience hath shown, that mankind are more disposed to suffer, while evils are sufferable, than to right themselves by abolishing the forms to which they are accustomed. But when a long train of abuses and usurpations, pursuing invariably the same Object evinces a design to reduce them under absolute Despotism, it is their right, it is their duty, to throw off such Government, and to provide new Guards for their future security. . . .

# 1.4

# THE RULE OF LAW

A.V. Dicey (1885)

Two features have at all times since the Norman Conquest characterised the political institutions of England.

The first of these features is the omnipotence or undisputed supremacy throughout the whole country of the central government. This authority of the state or the nation was during the earlier periods of our history represented by the power of the Crown. The King was the source of law and the maintainer of order. The maxim of the Courts, *tout fuit in luy et vient de lui al commencement*, was originally the expression of an actual and undoubted fact. This royal supremacy has now passed into that sovereignty of Parliament which has formed the main subject of the foregoing chapters.

The second of these features, which is closely connected with the first, is the rule or supremacy of law. This peculiarity of our polity is well expressed in the old saw of the Courts, "*La ley est le plus haute inheritance, que le roy ad; car par la ley il meme et toutes ses sujets sont rules, et si la ley ne fuit, nul roi, et nul inheritance sera.*"

This supremacy of the law, or the security given under the English constitution to the rights of individuals looked at from various points of view, forms the subject of this part of this treatise.

Foreign observers of English manners, such for example as Voltaire, De Lolme, Tocqueville, or Gneist, have been far more struck than have Englishmen themselves with the fact that England is a country governed, as is scarcely any other part of Europe, under the rule of law; and admiration or astonishment at the legality of English habits and feeling is nowhere better expressed than in a curious passage from Tocqueville's writings, which compares the Switzerland and the England of 1836 in respect of the spirit which pervades their laws and manners.

"I am not about," he writes, "to compare Switzerland with the United States, but with Great Britain. When you examine the two countries, or even if you only pass through them, you perceive, in my judgment, the most astonishing differences between them. Take it all in all, England seems to be much more republican than the Helvetic Republic. The principal differences are found in the institutions of the two countries, and especially in their customs (*moeurs*)." . . .

---

*The Law of the Constitution*, 7th ed. London: MacMillan, 1908, ch. 4. Reprinted with permission.

iv. The Swiss do not show the love of justice which is such a strong characteristic of the English. Their Courts have no place in the political arrangements of the country, and exert no influence on public opinion. The love of justice, the peaceful and legal introduction of the judge into the domain of politics, are perhaps the most standing characteristics of a free people.

v. Finally, and this really embraces all the rest, the Swiss do not show at bottom that respect for justice, that love of law, that dislike of using force, without which no free nation can exist, which strikes strangers so forcibly in England.

I sum up these impressions in a few words.

Whoever travels in the United States is involuntarily and instinctively so impressed with the fact that the spirit of liberty and the taste for it have pervaded all the habits of the American people, that he cannot conceive of them under any but a Republican government. In the same way it is impossible to think of the English as living under any but a free government. But if violence were to destroy the Republican institutions in most of the Swiss Cantons, it would be by no means certain that after rather a short state of transition the people would not grow accustomed to the loss of liberty. In the United States and in England there seems to be more liberty in the customs than in the laws of the people. In Switzerland there seems to be more liberty in the laws than in the customs of the country.''

Tocqueville's language has a twofold bearing on our present topic. His words point in the clearest manner to the rule, predominance, or supremacy of law as the distinguishing characteristic of English institutions. They further direct attention to the extreme vagueness of a trait of national character which is as noticeable as it is hard to portray. Tocqueville, we see, is clearly perplexed how to define a feature of English manners of which he at once recognises the existence; he mingles or confuses together the habit of self-government, the love of order, the respect for justice and a legal turn of mind. All these sentiments are intimately allied, but they cannot without confusion be identified with each other. If, however, a critic as acute as Tocqueville found a difficulty in describing one of the most marked peculiarities of English life, we may safely conclude that we ourselves, whenever we talk of Englishmen as loving the government of law, or of the supremacy of law as being a characteristic of the English constitution, are using words which, though they possess a real significance, are nevertheless to most persons who employ them full of vagueness and ambiguity. If therefore we are ever to appreciate the full import of the idea denoted by the term ''rule, supremacy, or predominance of law,'' we must first determine precisely what we mean by such expressions when we apply them to the British constitution.

When we say that the supremacy or the rule of law is a characteristic of the English constitution, we generally include under one expression at least three distinct though kindred conceptions. . . .

. . . It means, in the first place, the absolute supremacy or predominance of regular law as opposed to the influence of arbitrary power, and excludes the existence of arbitrariness, of prerogative, or even of wide discretionary authority on the part of the government. Englishmen are ruled by the law, and by the law alone; a man may with us be punished for a breach of law, but he can be punished for nothing else.

It means, again, equality before the law, or the equal subjection of all classes to the ordinary law of the land administered by the ordinary Law Courts; the "rule of law" in this sense excludes the idea of any exemption of officials or others from the the duty of obedience to the law which governs other citizens or from the jurisdiction of the ordinary tribunals; there can be with us nothing really corresponding to the "administrative law" (*droit administratif*) or the "administrative tribunals" (*tribunaux administratifs*) of France. The notion which lies at the bottom of the "administrative law" known to foreign countries is, that affairs or disputes in which the government or its servants are concerned are beyond the sphere of the civil Courts and must be dealt with by special and more or less official bodies. This idea is utterly unknown to the law of England, and indeed is fundamentally inconsistent with our traditions and customs.

The "rule of law," lastly, may be used as a formula for expressing the fact that with us the law of the constitution, the rules which in foreign countries naturally form part of a constitutional code, are not the source but the consequence of the rights of individuals, as defined and enforced by the Courts; that, in short, the principles of private law have with us been by the action of the Courts and Parliament so extended as to determine the position of the Crown and of its servants; thus the constitution is the result of the ordinary law of the land.

General propositions, however, as to the nature of the rule of law carry us but a very little way. If we want to understand what that principle in all its different aspects and developments really means, we must try to trace its influence throughout some of the main provisions of the constitution. The best mode of doing this is to examine with care the manner in which the law of England deals with the following topics, namely, the right to personal freedom; the right to freedom of discussion; the right of public meeting; the use of martial law; the rights and duties of the army; the collection and expenditure of the public revenue; and the responsibility of Ministers. The true nature further of the rule of law as it exists in England will be illustrated by contrast with the idea of *droit administratif*, or administrative law, which prevails in many continental countries. These topics will each be treated of in their due order. The object, however, of this treatise, as the reader should remember, is not to provide minute and full information, e.g. as to the *Habeas Corpus* Acts, or other enactments protecting the liberty of the subject; but simply to show that these leading heads of constitutional law, which have been enumerated, these "articles," so to speak, of the constitution, are both governed by, and afford illustrations of, the supremacy throughout English institutions of the law of the land. If at some future day the law of the constitution should be codified, each of the topics I have mentioned would be dealt with by the sections of the code.

# 1.5

# THE INDEPENDENCE OF THE JUDICIARY
W.R. Lederman

This article is reprinted as Reading 5.2

# 1.6

# KEYTERMS

### Concepts

"the rule of law"
per legem terrae
natural right theory of government
"All men are by nature equal"
"written constitution"
"limited government"
judicial review
"unwritten constitution"
Parliamentary or Westminster form of democracy
"Separation of powers" or American form of democracy
judicial independence

### *Institutions, Events and Documents*

*Magna Carta* (1215)
Habeas Corpus Act (1679)
''Glorious Revolution of 1688''
John Locke, *Second Treatise on Government* (1690)
Declaration of Independence (1776)
Constitution of the United States of American (1788)
U.S. Bill of Rights (1790)
British North American Act (1867)
A.V.C. Dicey, *The Law of the Constitution* (1885)
*Roncarelli v. Duplessis* (1959)
1960 Bill of Rights
Canadian Charter of Rights and Freedoms (1982)

# 2
# Political Jurisprudence

This chapter raises a deceptively simple set of questions. What do judges do? Do they just interpret and apply the law? Or in the process of interpreting and applying the law, do the judges also "make law"? If the answer to this second question is yes, then how do courts differ from legislatures? Ultimately these questions take on a normative character: Should judges limit themselves simply to declaring what the law is, as determined by statute and precedent? Or if a judge finds the relevant statutes and precedents inadequate or even "wrong," is he free to "make new law"?

These are old and much debated questions, and they have been given very different answers by scholars and judges. There is some truth in each of these conflicting answers, because the character of the judicial process varies from nation to nation, and even within a single nation. What is true of trial courts is not applicable to appeal courts, and what is true for torts and contracts does not apply to constitutional law.

Canadian legal and political thought has traditionally held that judges do not, and should not, "make law" in any significant sense. "The law" has been portrayed as something that already exists "out there," and the role of the judge is merely to "find" it and declare its meaning to the interested parties. This view of judicial decision-making is known as the "declaratory model," and is closely associated with the British common law tradition, from which it evolved. In both Britain and Canada, this view of the judges as exercising "neither force nor will, but only judgement," has been reinforced by the practice of parliamentary supremacy and the theory of legal positivism.

The parliamentary model of government stresses that only the representative legislature can "make law," because only the elected legislators have the consent of the people to govern. This understanding of just laws comes directly from the equality-consent dimension of Locke's political theory, discussed in the preceding chapter. According to its logic, it would be unjust and unjustifiable for judges to "make law," since judges are neither representative of nor responsible to the citizenry. This very precise and limiting understanding of the judicial function has been reinforced by the theory of legal positivism. Legal positivism defines law as "the command of the sovereign," in this case, the Queen in Parliament. This definition stresses the form and function of the law, not its content. Again the notion of judicial law-making is logically incompatible with this view.

It is important to remember that the "declaratory model" of judging is drawn from British experience. This explains both its original dominance of Canadian jurisprudence, and also its more recent decline. As we saw in chapter one, Canada differs from Great Britain by being a federal not a unitary state, and by having the boundaries of federalism defined in a "written constitution" — the Constitution Act, 1867.[1] Because of this difference, Canadian courts and judges have had to fulfill an important function unknown in British legal experience — judicial review. Since its creation in 1875, the Supreme Court of Canada has acted as the "neutral umpire" of the federal division of powers between Ottawa and the provinces.

A constitutional law of federalism is political in a way other kinds of law are not. It defines and therefore limits the law-making powers of rival levels of government. Questions of constitutional law often arise in the context of heated political struggles between Ottawa and one or more provinces. Political passions run high, and all of Canada awaits the Court's decision with interest. Major government policy often hangs in the balance. In such circumstances, the decision of the Supreme Court has an undeniably political impact, and institutions that make such decisions inevitably come to be regarded as political.

In view of this dimension of Canadian law, it is not surprising that Canadian jurists began to be attracted by the "legal realism" theory of judging that had developed in the United States in the early decades of this century. The Americans had lived with the practice of judicial review since 1803. Moreover, the American Supreme Court exercised judicial review not just over the boundaries of federalism, but also enforced the more absolute limitations of the Bill of Rights. By the end of the nineteenth century, the U.S. Supreme Court had come to play an influential role in the major political issues of the day. The traditional "declaratory model" of judging, inherited with the common law from Great Britain, seemed to provide a less and less satisfactory explanation of what American courts and judges were actually doing in the area of constitutional law. A new generation of American jurists began to rethink and reformulate the relationship between judges and law. Through the writings of men like Oliver Wendell Holmes, Benjamin Cardozo, and Roscoe Pound, the "legal realism" theory of judging was developed.

The legal realists stressed the creative and personal connection between judges and law. Holmes declared that the law is "the prophecies of what the courts will do in fact, and nothing more pretentious."[2] Pound and Cardozo extended Holmes's critique by elaborating the subjective, personal dimension of judging. The key to this analysis was the "unfinished" quality of law, and

---

[1] Originally known and still commonly referred to as the British North America Act.

[2] *Harvard Law Review*, 10 (1897), p. 39.

the resulting discretion and freedom of the judge to give the law its practical meaning when applied to a novel set of circumstances. The legal realists were unanimous in rejecting the traditional "declaratory model" of judging. While they disagreed amongst themselves on how much and why, they all agreed that in a very real sense judges "make law" — especially appeal court judges, and especially in the area of constitutional law.

Predictably, it was the constitutional law decisions of Canada's first final court of appeal — the Judicial Committee of the Privy Council — that provoked the first appearance of judicial realism in Canadian legal and political thought. Beginning in the 1890's, the Privy Council made a series of important constitutional decisions that progressively narrowed the scope of the legislative powers of the federal government. This trend reached a climax in the mid-thirties, when the Privy Council struck down a number of federal "New Deal" programs designed to cope with the economic and social devastation of the Great Depression. This provoked an angry reaction among some Canadian leaders, who began to call for the abolition of appeals to the Privy Council. They argued that questions of Canadian constitutional law could best be answered by Canadian judges, judges with first-hand familiarity with the political and economic realities of Canadian life. Implicit in this argument was a tacit acceptance of the legal realist view that the personal background of a judge is an important factor in his legal decision-making. Because the goal of this movement was to make the Supreme Court the final court of appeal "of and for Canadians," it came to be known as "judicial nationalism." (See Reading 2.2)

In 1949, appeals to the J.C.P.C. were abolished, and the Supreme Court of Canada became the final and exclusive court of appeal for Canada. But this has not stopped the debate over the nature of the judicial process in Canada. The adoption in 1960 of the Bill of Rights stimulated new debate on this old issue. The broadly worded prohibitions of the Bill of Rights — such as freedom of religion and equality before the law — seemed to invite and even require judicial choice and creativity in giving them practical application. By and large the Canadian judiciary declined this invitation. Stressing the statutory (as opposed to constitutional) character of the Bill of Rights, and the absence of any explicit qualification of the tradition of parliamentary supremacy, the Supreme Court gave a very limited and traditional interpretation to the Bill's major provisions. Partly in response to the courts' cautious use of the Bill of Rights, it was superceded in 1982 by the Charter of Rights and Freedoms. A constitutionally entrenched document that applies to both levels of government, the Charter raises the issue of proper judicial decision-making in an even more pointed and pressing manner.

The competing views of proper judicial conduct are the subject of Paul Weiler's 1967 article, "Two Models of Judicial Decision-Making." (Reading 2.1) One — the "adjudication of disputes" model — stresses the traditional understanding of the judicial function, and the institutional characteristics that distinguish the judicial process from the legislative process. This is essentially a modified version of the "declaratory model" of judging. Weiler's second model, the "policy-making" model, asserts that there is no essential difference between judges and legislators, that "they make policy, or legislate, through essentially the same mode of reasoning." This model represents judicial realism taken to its extreme.

Weiler provides a conceptual framework through which we can better understand the differences between Canadian, British, and American judicial process, and better evaluate current recommendations that Canadian judges adopt a more "policy-making" or American-style jurisprudence. The "two models" analysis also demonstrates that different institutional consequences follow from the two different conceptions of judging. Current Canadian practices regarding judicial recruitment, judicial independence, jurisdiction, access to the courts, judicial fact-finding, and modes of legal argument — were all originally premised on the understanding that judges do not, and should not, "make law." As Canadian judges have gradually moved away from the "adjudication of disputes" approach and toward a greater "policy-making" role, the continued adequacy of existing institutional practices has been questioned. This evolution will almost certainly accelerate under the new Charter of Rights.[3] Weiler's elaborations of the different institutional consequences of the two models are not included in this chapter, but are placed with the readings in subsequent chapters as appropriate. We can thus use Weiler's analytical framework to understand the traditional aspects of the judicial process and to evaluate the pros and cons of present proposals for change.

The last two readings demonstrate the contemporary character of the debate over the proper role of the judiciary in Canadian law and politics. Jules Deschenes, recently retired Chief Justice of the Superior Court of Quebec, is one of the most out-spoken advocates of a more explicit "law-making" role for Canadian judges. (Reading 2.3) In the 1976 case of *Harrison v. Carswell*, we find a sharp disagreement over proper judicial role between the past Chief Justice of Canada, the late Bora Laskin, and the new Chief Justice, Brian Dickson. (Reading 2.4) This case also shows that the issue is not merely of theoretical interest, but has very real practical consequences. The principal difference between Dickson's majority opinion and Laskin's dissent is not about the law but about the limits of the Supreme Court's responsibility. Both agree that there is a serious legal problem raised by the Harrison case. Laskin argues that the Supreme Court should solve it, while Dickson maintains that law reform is the business of the legislatures not the courts.

---

[3] See Peter Russell, "The Effect of the Charter of Rights on the Policy-Making Role of Canadian Courts," Reading 11.8.

# 2.1

# TWO MODELS OF JUDICIAL DECISION-MAKING

Paul Weiler

## I. Introduction

The philosophy of the judicial process will soon be of great practical significance for the Canadian legal scene. The traditional, inarticulate, legal positivism of Canadian lawyers and judges is rapidly becoming outmoded by recent developments. First, the determination of our new Prime Minister to achieve an entrenched Bill of Rights will, of necessity, confer on the courts the power and the duty to make fundamental value judgments which cannot flow mechanically and impersonally from the language of the document. Second, the British House of Lords has decided to change its long-standing rule that its earlier precedents could not be overruled. Presumably, and hopefully, the Canadian Supreme Court will continue to imitate slavishly its English counterpart by following this decision. Third, Canadian scholarship about the Supreme Court has begun to utilize some of the advanced techniques of the behavioural sciences in order to study judicial decision-making. Two related developments should follow. Our judges will grow increasingly conscious of the freedom and the responsibility they have to develop and alter the law. Both academics and the public will become aware of the fact of judicial power and then go on to question its legitimacy.

It is only too true that we will be decades behind the same course of developments in our neighbour to the south. There is a favourable cast to this situation. We have available to us a significant body of American experience, and of jurisprudential reflection concerning it, which we can use in intelligently understanding and evaluating the process of change that the Canadian judicial process is likely to undergo. Moreover we can choose between at least two, substantially different conceptions of judicial decision-making which have been elaborated in some detail in American legal thinking. One theory characterizes the judicial function as, essentially, the "adjudication of disputes" within the legal system. The other holds that at least some courts are primarily engaged in "policy-making," in a manner largely indistinguishable from the other political agencies in our society. It is my intention to draw together, in a systematic way, these two very sophisticated theories, to show the conclusions which flow from the insights that lie at the root of each "model," and to indicate the important problems which, as yet, detract from the adequacy of

*Canadian Bar Review*, 1968, p.406. Reprinted with permission.

each. In doing so, I shall also record the significance of many apparently unrelated phenomena within the Canadian judicial system.

What theoretical significance do I attach to the use of these models? Sociological theory tells us that the position of judge in any society carries with it a set of shared expectations about the type of conduct that is appropriate to that position. These expectations have reference not only the proper *physical* behaviour of one who occupies that position but also to the mode of reasoning to be used in making his judicial decisions. There are several possible decision-making roles that can be proposed by society for its judges, each having different supporting reasons for their acceptance. Two of these roles are the subject of this article, "adjudicator" and "policy-maker." Both embody fundamental value choices for the society which, presumably, are made after some consideration of these competing justifications. Once the choice is made, the expectations that are connected with this one role must be shared by at least a substantial majority of the participants within the system in order that it have some institutional stability. Finally, the institutional position of the judge is reciprocally connected with society's wishes about how they should behave in their decision-making capacity. It is this connexion between the role we give to our judges and the design of the structure within which they operate that the two models are intended to display.

Hence, the function of each model is to trace the institutional implications of each of these fundamental value judgments about the appropriate mission of the judge. One model is based on the value judgment that judges should make policy choices as a political actor; the other assumes it is desirable that judges confine their activity to the settlement of private disputes. As we shall see, there are real differences in the social arrangements which are most compatible with these two distinctive judgements about the appropriate judicial role. We should be able to verify the existence of these proposed differences in actual practice, or in recommendations about changes in the existing system. Moreover, not only do these theoretical models serve as a framework for explanations of how judges do behave, they also assist our appraisal of how judges ought to behave.

Finally, the use of these two schematic representations of the judicial process should serve to illuminate a significant moral problem that has surfaced recently in American legal discussion of the role of the judiciary. Once an institution has gained inertial force and power as a result of shared expectations about how it is and ought to operate, it is then available as an instrument for serving social purposes that are not compatible with the original model. Is it legitimate for those who believe in a alternative model of judicial behaviour to make covert use of the existing organization? To what extent will such "parasitic" utilization of one version of the judicial process induce actual changes in the existing system which make it more compatible with the form that naturally flows from a new conception of appropriate judicial decision-making? To these, and other problems, this article is addressed in a preliminary way.

## II. The Adjudication of Disputes Model

The two models whose traits I am going to describe both agree in rejecting the viability and the desirability of the traditional Anglo-Canadian model of judicial decision-making. The latter suggests that a judge decides his cases by the somewhat mechanical application of legal rules which he finds *established* in the legal system. They are, in this sense, *binding* on him completely apart from his own judgment as to their fitness of his purpose. This theory has an historical, if not a logical, relationship with the dictates of an Austinian, positivist conception of law and a rigid notion of the division of powers. The "adjudication of disputes" model shares, to some extent, the assumption that judges have a distinctive and limited function. However, it emphatically denies the conclusion that it is *possible* for a judge to be purely passive, and *desirable* that he makes decisions without a necessary exercise of his judgment about what the law ought to be.

As was stated earlier the purpose of the model is to show the necessary inter-relationship between the function which judicial decision-making is primarily intended to perform, the institutional characteristics which are implied by such a function, and the qualities in judicial decision-making which flow naturally from this institutional background. In short, the job we give judges to perform determines the design of the judicial process; the nature of the structure influences the manner in which judges carry out their tasks; the form of judicial action limits the issues judges may appropriately resolve. Hence the adjudication model rejects the tacit assumption, often made, of "institutional fungibility." The latter holds that the same substantive policies can and should be achieved in the same undifferentiated way, whatever be the organizational form in which various actors are allowed to strive for these ends. To the contrary, the specific institutional form of adjudication, by comparision with that of legislation, for instance, limits both the goals for which judges should strive and the means they should use for achieving these goals.

To summarize the model very briefly, it conceives of the judge as the adjudicator of specific, concrete disputes, who disposes of the problems within the latter by elaborating and applying a legal regime to facts, which he finds on the basis of evidence and argument presented to him in an adversary process. The body of rules and principles which are to govern the private conduct of the participants in the legal order are largely settled by forces outside adjudication, although the judge does play a collaborative role in articulating and elaborating these principles. However, the primary focus of adjudication is the settlement of disputes arising out of private line of conduct, by evaluating such conduct in the light of established rules and principles. As we shall see, the whole institutional structure of adjudication — its incidence, access to it, the mode of participation in it, the bases for decision, and the nature of the relief available in it — are all defined by and flow naturally from this function. The key elements within the adjudicative model are (1) settlement of disputes, (2) the adversary process and (3) an established system of standards which are utilized in the process to dispose of the disputes.

### Settlement of Concrete Disputes

The first characteristic of "adjudication" is that it has the function of settling disputes (between private individuals or groups, or the government and the individual). These disputes are not future-oriented debates over general policy questions, although, as we shall see, the latter can enter into the final resolution of the problem. Rather, the disputes which are necessary to set the process of adjudication in motion involve "controversies" arising out of a particular line of conduct which causes a collision of specific interests. There is no *logical* or *factual* necessity about this proposition. There can be exceptions and the question of defining the limits of the adjudicative function can be difficult and debatable in the marginal areas. . . .

. . . To summarize, a court should confine itself to settling concrete, private disputes between individuals who apply to the adjudicator for the resolution of their problem. . . .

### An Adversary Process

An adversary process is one which satisfies, more or less, this factual description: as a prelude to the dispute being solved, the interested parties have the opportunity of adducing evidence (or proof) and making arguments to a disinterested and impartial arbiter who decides the case on the basis of this evidence and these arguments. This is by contrast with the public processes of decision by "legitimated power" and "mediation-agreement", where the guaranteed private modes of participation are voting and negotiation respectively. Adjudication is distinctive because it guarantees to each of the parties who are affected the right to prepare for themselves the representations on the basis of which their dispute is to be resolved.
. . .

### The Need for Standards

. . . Why does the institution of adjudication require the existence of standards for decision? Of what type are these standards and what does it mean to say that they "exist"? Taking these questions in reverse order, in order that standards "exist," there must be a shared consensus between the adjudicator and the parties about what the standards are which the former is going to apply. Secondly, the parties must reasonably have expected, at the time they acted, that these standards would be used to evaluate their private conduct. Of course, some legal rules can be directed only to the arbiter himself dealing with purely remedial problems. We draw our standards from the legal order which regulates private conduct because a primary objective of the use of adjudication is to preserve the viability of this legal order by settling authoritatively the disputes arising within it. Successful adjudication requires that there be a shared consensus about these rules, especially insofar as they can be utilized to evaluate the conduct of the parties which gives rise to the dispute.

In order that adjudicative decisions be characterized by the quality of rationality which is a prerequisite for their moral force and acceptability, the arbiter must have some principles which he can utilize in explaining to himself and to the parties his reasons for deciding one way or the other. The arbiter is under a duty to articulate a reasoned basis for his decision (whether or not he writes an opinion), because he is not conceded the power of *enactment*. He is not considered to have a *legitimate* power to exercise a discretion to settle a matter just because it needs settling, and without giving reasons for deciding on the particular disposition he selects. Hence, he cannot merely confront an undifferentiated factual situation and decide by an intuitive "leap in the dark." He needs a set of ordering principles which enable him to make sense of the situation and abstract those relevent facets of it which can be organized into a reasoned argument.

Second, the adjudicative process can have the enhanced quality of rationality, which derives from its focusing on a specific, concrete dispute for decision, only if there are standards or principles which enable the adjudicator to single out the relevant, problematic facets of the situation on which he is going to concentrate his attention. If there is no framework of settled principles within which he can operate, and every aspect of every situation is always open to question, then the adjudicator will not be able to focus his attention on unresolved problems. Thus, he will not be able to attain a significantly higher quality of rationality in the solution which he produces for the problem.

Thirdly, to the extent that adjudication entails adversary participation, the presentation of proofs and arguments to the arbiter, the process is meaningless unless the parties can know before their preparation and presentation of the case the principles and standards which the arbiter is likely to find relevant to his disposition of the dispute. It is impossible to make an intelligent argument "in the air" and without any idea of which factors are considered relevant by the person whom one's argument is attempting to persuade. If a relatively passive attitude is necessarily conducive to impartiality (although this does not exclude some reciprocal clarification of views), and a high degree of rationality in result thus depends directly on the quality of the preparations and representation by each side, then a consensus of standards is needed in order that intelligent alternative positions are established and that an adequate "joinder of issue" results. . . .

## III. The Judicial-Policy-Maker Model: The Judge as Political Actor

A second distinctive model of the judicial process has been developed in recent years, largely by American political scientists. Of course, it is not original in recognizing the inescapable fact that judicial decisions must involve the creative exercise of a court's judgment. It builds on the work of American

Legal Realism, which showed that the mechanical application of rigid, automatic rules does not and cannot dispose of individual cases. Men, as judges, decide cases and this activity is one for which they are personally responsible.

However, as we have see, the "adjudication" model also begins with this assumption. Judges must collaborate with other bodies in society in the development and elaboration of the law "as it ought to be." Yet this collaborative role is institutionally distinctive. The creative articulation of new legal rules is limited and incremental; it is based on a moving background of established legal principles; it is related to the dispute-settling focus of courts because the new rule must be appropriate for retrospective application to the facts giving rise to the instant case; finally, the adoption of the new rule must be justified in a reasoned opinion which establishes the probable "rightness" of the new rule. This whole set of limitations on judicial law-making is necessary in order to *legitimate* the final product. However, this legitimacy does not require a mechanical deduction of the rule from legal premises in which it somehow pre-exists, as in a "brooding omnipresence in the sky." The reasoning in the opinion is not of a logical-deductive type. Yet, it is supposed to be sufficiently communicable that it is open, in principle at least, to prior vicarious participation by the parties in the adversary process.

Many political scientists, by contrast believe that judges should be perceived as political actors, continuously engaged in the formulation of policy for society. To say that judges are political actors is not simply to assert the truism that they are part of the governmental system, "authoritatively allocating values in society." Nor is it characteristic of only this model that judges exercise personal judgment in each decision they make and that no conclusions are automatic. What is distinctive is the thesis that judges make policy, or legislate, through essentially the same mode of reasoning as other actors in the governmental system. Moreover, at least for some courts, such political action is becoming, and is seen to be becoming, their primary concern, and adjudication of disputes is growing secondary.

Legislators have traditionally been contrasted with courts by the fact that society considers it acceptable for them to justify authoritative policy-making by reference to their own value preferences, or the interests of those who support or have access to them. Legislators do not feel institutionally committed to the formulation of new legal rules only if they can be justified by a reasoned opinion relating the development to accepted doctrinal premises. This model suggests that some courts also are not, and should not be, so institutionally committed.

The quality of political decision-making both influences and reflects the make-up of the institution within which it is carried on. If, as, and when judges become candid policy-makers, courts will take on a "political" character, and judges will be subjected to "political" pressures. The new orientation of the "policy-making" model should render appropriate for judges the same analysis that is applied to other political actors, as regards the recruitment of the men who make these decisions, the timing of their policy pronouncements, the influences brought to bear on the court, both internally and externally, and the success which attends its policy promulgation. The new model explains, in an illuminating way, many recent judicial phenomena that have followed the proposal and adoption of the new political role by some courts in some legal system. Moreover, it shows the linkage of the various components in the judicial system, as it becomes redesigned for its new institutional function. I shall compare the new model with the old, showing the changes we may expect in the existing system if and when judges turn from adjudication to concentrate on policy-making. I will not be interested in empirical proof, by scalogram analysis or otherwise, that courts do or do not make decisions based on "policy," rather than "law." Assuming that judges may internalize the role of "political actor" rather than "adjudicator," I hope to make clear the institutional significance of this fact. . . .

## IV. Conclusion

I do not believe it is possible yet to decide which of these models expresses a more appropriate role for judges in our society. Nor does either version furnish a type of litmus test for discovering the nature of our present system. Probably, the various judiciaries in the common law are based on different mixtures of each role, however contradictory they may appear in the abstract. Our models are "ideal types," furnishing us with distinctive angles of vision on the same judicial reality, thus allowing us a more profound understanding and evaluation of tendencies within the existing system. Moreover, these two artificial constructs of the judicial process show us the practical significance of two as yet unresolved problems in legal philosophy. Is rational and communicable decision-making possible in choosing between social values? Is judicial choice about values that favour one interest over another a fair institution within a democracy.

In conclusion, I should emphasize my belief that the judicial process in Canada fits neither model as regards the appropriate mode of reasoning, although it is organized more or less along adjudicative lines. In fact, common law judging in Canada has truly been a wasteland of arid legalism, one that is only beginning to be relieved by a profounder vision of the scope of judicial action. For this reason alone, I am just as dubious about the desirability of judicial review of legislative action as about the present review of administrative action. Perhaps the proposal for a Canadian Bill of Rights should await the advent of judges who are products of a different legal education. It seems safe to predict that they will have been schooled in some version of the philosophies of judicial decision-making which I have sketched.

# 2.2

# JUDICIAL POWER IN CANADA'S POLITICAL CULTURE

Peter Russell

Perhaps I am overly self-conscious, but I must confess to a certain sense of unease when I refer to "judicial power" in Canada. Such talk, I suspect, will be regarded by most of my political science colleagues as irrelevant or trivial, by members of the legal profession as misguided and ill-informed, and by at least some of our public leaders as socially dangerous (if not obscene). But as a political scientist I find it impossible to leave the subject alone. I have long been fascinated with the phenomenon of judicial power in different societies, but especially in our own. It is (or has been) such quiet power, so unacclaimed, so often denied. It is precisely the subtle, ironic, strength which our judiciary derives from its hidden nature that so fascinates me. . . .

. . . I can only offer this notion of the power that interests me: the initiation of significant changes in our customs, our laws, or institutions and the maintenance of some important features of the established order. Our judiciary clearly has the power to do these things. What I wish to discuss here is our changing perceptions of this power and the way in which these perceptions may influence that power.

I can think of no better place to begin a discussion of judicial power in Canada than at the point where it first struck me as such an intriguing element in our system of government. That is, when I came across the following words in a judicial opinion: "It is, in fact, a prime element in the self-government of the Dominion, that it should be able to secure through its own courts of justice that the law should be one and the same for all its citizens." Now these words would not raise an eyebrow if uttered in the context of a unitary state such as England. But they were not; the Dominion referred to, the Dominion through whose courts the law should "be one and the same for all its citizens," was Canada, a federal country.

The quoted words are Lord Jowitt's and they formed part of the Judicial Committee of the Privy Council's 1947 decision that upheld, as constitutionally valid, federal legislation making the Supreme Court of Canada the exclusive final Court of Appeal for all Canadian courts in all matters of Canadian law, federal and provincial. These words, in effect, declared that Canada must have a unitary judicial system. These words were, in fact, quite unnecessary

*Courts and Trials: A Multidisciplinary Approach.* Edited by M.L. Friedland. Toronto: University of Toronto Press, 1975, p.75. Reprinted with permission.

for the judgment at hand. But it is interesting that these words were uttered as such a light-hearted reference to the apparently self-evident fact that Canada must have a unitary judicial system. It is interesting because these words were uttered by the very court that for three-quarters of a century had presided with such tender, loving care over the division of legislative powers in Canadian federalism and in the process had done its level best (by upholding provincial legislation and striking down federal legislation) to ensure that the law would *not* be one and the same for all Canadians.

The question arises how a tribunal which cared so much about Canada's having a federal division of legislative powers could be so off-hand about its having a unitary judicial system? This question becomes more intriguing when one compares Canada with the United States, where the situation is almost completely reversed. There, the national Supreme Court, while promoting a centralization of legislative power, has, especially since *Erie Railroad v. Tompkins*, been careful to respect state judicial autonomy in legal matters subject to local legislative authority.

The key to the Canadian situation is, I think, the relative innocence about judicial power which prevailed here for so long. If courts do not in any significant sense legislate, then there is no reason why devotees of federalism should be concerned about the division of judicial power. For, in essence, courts have no power. To quote my own rendition of the logic of this thinking from an earlier article: "Courts administer justice — legislatures exercise power — federalism has to do with dividing power, not justice — *ergo*, the Supreme Court's jurisdiction need not be federalized." It may well have been a good thing that this innocence about judicial power (or this cunning disguise) prevailed in Canadian legal thought for so long. For it may be argued that it enabled the Supreme Court and the Judicial Committee of the Privy Council to have a unifying effect on Canadian law and thereby partially offset the centrifugal influence these courts had on legislative power in Canada.

But I am not concerned with that issue here. In the present context what interests me is that this innocence about judicial power has not continued to characterize legal thinking in Canada. In the quarter century since Lord Jowitt's words were uttered, the mask has been, at least in part, removed. The undermining of the legal intelligentsia's belief in the non-political, mechanistic nature of judicial decision-making was stimulated by the drive for judicial self-government in the thirties and forties. As is well known, this movement was sparked by Canadian criticism of the way in which their lordships of the Privy Council had interpreted the Canadian constitution, the BNA Act. At first, the criticism tended to take the line that the Judicial Committee had erred in a purely legal sense and, to use the language of the 1939 *O'Connor Report* to the Canadian Senate, charged that there had been "most serious and persistent deviation on the part of the Judicial Committee from the actual text of the Act." But fairly soon the argument shifted to more avowedly political contentions, emphasizing the need to have a final court of appeal which "would be a better agency of constitutional adaptation.'' Canadian judges would, it was claimed, display a greater sensitivity to the needs of the country in serving as the final judicial arbiters of its constitutional law.

But once the case for judicial self-government shifts to these grounds, it concedes that in the judicial application of laws men make a difference and judicial decisions are not mechanically deduced from previously established rules of law. Following the attainment of judicial autonomy in 1949, there was evidence that these new currents of judicial realism in Canada would not be confined to constitutional law. In the legal periodicals, writers such as Horace Read, Gilbert Kennedy, and Bora Laskin began to urge Canada's senior appellate courts to take a ''more Canadian'' approach to the common law and important facets of statutory interpretation. Canadian judicial nationalism began to evoke echoes of provincial judicial nationalism from Quebec. Just as nationalist Canadian jurists denounced the British judges for their insensitive interpretation of the Canadian constitution, nationalist lawyers in Quebec resumed their protest against the Supreme Court of Canada's insensitive interpretation of Quebec's Civil Code and Code of Procedure. . . .

. . . Quebec reaction to the new realism in Canadian legal thought is one indication that an increased acknowledgment of judicial power may lead to a lessening of judicial authority. Certainly Canadian legal scholars have been more diffident and cautious in their expressions of realism than their American counterparts. As with so many intellectual trends which originate south of the border, judicial realism arrived in Canada a decade or so after its emergence in the United States. This time lag at least has the advantage of enabling Canadians to avoid the excesses of enthusiasm for or opposition to these new intellectual trends. In this case there were few, if any, counterparts to American extremists who are inclined to treat the judiciary as simply a specialized branch of the legislature — as if appellate judges simply translate their whims into judicial findings. Writers such as Frank Scott, Wolfgang Friedmann, Bora Laskin, Mark MacGuigan, and Paul Weiler, while acknowledging the important ''policy-making'' role of appeal courts, have taken pains to emphasize the distinctive characteristics of this exercise of judicial discretion. This interpretation has emphasized that judicial lawmaking is interstitial, that it occurs, ideally, in the setting of the adjudicative process, so that the parties to the legal controversy rather than the judges raise the issues and develop the contending arguments, and that it takes the form of reasoned arguments based on legal doctrines and precedents.

Now, in all of this we can see, I think, a shrewd political instinct. For these writers and others who decry political analyses of judicial behaviour sense that the legitimacy of the courts, and in particular the legitimacy of our Supreme Court acting as the nation's highest constitutional arbiter, may depend to a large degree on a very unrealistic image of the judicial role. In a democratic age, recognized authority to make laws and initiate policy is not readily conferred on an appointed judiciary. As I have suggested elsewhere, the position of our judges is analogous "to that of the monarchy facing the advance of parliamentary democracy: they could best retain popular respect by denying that they exercised real power. But unlike monarchy, myth and reality in the judges' case have remained too far apart." It is unlikely that as the public becomes more sophisticated about the realities of the judicial process, judicial power can continue to shelter behind the mask of an ideology which denies the very existence of that power.

In the United States, with a constitutional doctrine emphasizing checks and balances rather than parliamentary supremacy, judicial realism has been more compatible with the popular political culture. In some states there is a tradition of elected judges which underlines the political power entailed in judging; the process of selecting Supreme Court judges has always been a highly visible political process, and the notion of "constitutionalism" in American political thought lends some legitimacy to the judiciary's role of upholding the more enduring will of the people as expressed in the constitution over the will of any transient majority. . . .

. . . In Canada there has been as much, if not even more, concern to find a basis for objectivity, for removing judicial subjectivity from judicial decision-making even in areas where policy issues are admittedly unavoidable. Thus, the first generation of Canadian judicial realists were apt to talk rather glibly about judges adapting the constitution to the needs of the country or discovering a national or social consensus, much as one might find the law. A later generation of judicial realists has shown more scepticism of the judge's capacity for discovering some sociological natural law. Mark MacGuigan, for instance, after identifying the objectivity which he feels is inherent in the judicial process, concludes that "this objectivity is unstable and incomplete, for the subjective element is inevitable, regardless of the jurisprudential theory invoked. We are thus in the last analysis compelled to accept even the subjectivity of judicial legislation, and seem to have only the choice of accepting it gratefully or grudgingly." Again, Paul Weiler, in prescribing an ideal model of judicial reasoning, admits that "there is almost always an element of fiat within the narrow interstices left by the reasoning process." . . .

. . . There are some tendencies in the Canadian legal system which are apt to increase the occasions on which the courts, especially the senior appeal courts, are required to deviate from a narrow adjudicative role and consequently become more politically exposed. One such tendency is the reference case procedure — the long established practice in Canada, whereby the executive branch of government (federal or provincial) can require that the courts answer highly political, abstract, and hypothetical questions which are not at all "ripe" for adjudication. Two of the most recent instances, the *Offshore Mineral Rights* reference and the *Chicken and Egg War* case, plunged the Supreme Court into federal-provincial controversies. The court cannot be blamed for the decision of politicians to use the advisory opinion process as a stratagem in their political struggles. But the court, in responding to these reference questions, did not perform in a manner calculated to enhance its legitimacy.

In the *Offshore Mineral Rights* case the court, in finding a positive base for federal jurisdiction, employed the inherent national importance test in a most unconvincing way. With a simple, and somewhat arrogant, nationalist flourish the court asserted that "the mineral resources of the lands underlying the territorial sea are of concern to Canada as a whole and go beyond local or provincial concern or interests." The political circumstances surrounding this case were already explosive enough without waving this particular red flag before the provinces. Several provinces had strenuously objected to referring this question to the court. Following the decision, the premier of Quebec, Mr. Lesage, stated that "if French-speaking Canadians' constitutional rights are to be protected, the Supreme Court of Canada — which rules on constitutional questions — must be either changed or replaced." . . .

. . . For the full implication of these decisions to be seen they should be placed in the context of the Supreme Court's over-all performance as our final constitutional umpire since 1949. During this period twenty-one provincial Acts have been found invalid (43 percent of those challenged), whereas in not one of the twenty cases challenging federal Acts on constitutional grounds has the Supreme Court ruled against the federal level of government. While centralists may applaud the Supreme Court's strengthening of federal legislative power, they should consider the possibility that this very process may have weakened the judicial power of the Supreme Court. It is not accidental that the lengthiest section of the proposed charter for constitutional reform which emerged from the Victoria Conference in June 1971 concerned appointments to the Supreme Court of Canada. Increasing provincial demands to participate in the appointment of Supreme Court justices indicate a decline in the court's legitimacy as an acceptable umpire of our federal system. The politicization of the appointment process to the point where a judge may be viewed as a legislative representative of a particular sectional interest will surely reduce the Supreme Court's capacity to perform its role of constitutional arbitration in a judicious manner.

Another feature of our contemporary legal system which tends to accelerate the politicization of our courts is the Bill of Rights. . . . The statutory Bill of Rights which we now have, even though it has no application to provincial governments, has already added significantly to the policy-making responsibilities of the courts. A constitutional Bill of Rights will take this process much further. I am not concerned here with the wisdom of making such a change in our system of government. What I wish to emphasize is the ironic way in which such a change might affect judicial power in Canada. The effect is likely to be ironic, for while increasing judicial power in one sense, this expansion of the court's power into sensitive areas of social policy may at the same time reduce judicial authority by eroding the popular image of our judiciary as the impartial arbiters of our legal disputes. . . .

# 2.3

## JUDGES SHOULD BE LEGISLATORS
Toronto *Globe and Mail*

A two-month-old controversy over how far judges can go in replacing the lawmakers surfaced again here yesterday in a meticulously documented speech by Chief Justice Jules Deschenes of the Quebec Superior Court.

Chief Justice Deschenes told a Chamber of Commerce meeting that on paper the legislative, executive and judicial sections of Government are distinct but in practice they overlap, and when the lawmakers don't pass laws that are in keeping with "changing social conditions" it is up to the judges to exercise their "legislative power" and change the law to suit the time.

Chief Justice Deschenes . . . heads what the province's legal fraternity calls "the revolt of the judges" against the provincial Government.

On Sept. 16, he refused to find guilty 1,600 Montreal subway and transit workers who disobeyed an earlier court injunction ordering them to end an illegal strike and return to work.

He based his historic ruling on two reasons. First, the case was really a criminal matter and should have come up before Court of Queen's Bench, not Superior Court. Second, the injunction law is "socially inopportune" because people don't respect it and because social conditions have changed.

Yesterday, Chief Justice Deschenes tried to explain to his audience of businessmen why judges should legislate at times.

He cited more than 40 cases in which courts changed the law or overruled provincial or federal laws they decided didn't apply any longer or were wrong. . . .

. . . He said that judges have "opened new roads and widened perspectives on the law as they sought modern solutions compatible with changing conditions in our society."

Chief Justice Deschenes said provincial labor laws are undergoing a "mini-revolution" in the courts because of recent court decisions. "Jurisprudence has more surprises in store for the citizens of our country."

"The first role of judges," he said, "is to apply the law as it exists and this is the task to which they put most of their efforts. More often than not, there is no doubt in the law. . . . However, sometimes the evolution of thinking or morals tends to create an imbalance between the law and the facts." . . .

"That's when the courts must take on, with a reflected audacity, the heavy burden of adapting the law to the new social realities which show up."

---

Toronto *Globe and Mail*. November, 1982. Reprinted with permission.

He said that if a judge were there only to apply the law he would be reduced to a robot.

"The defenders of such a view would become its victims and soon be among its most virulent critics."


# 2.4

# HARRISON v. CARSWELL

Supreme Court of Canada (1976)


In this case the Supreme Court was faced with a dispute between Harrison, the manager of a shopping centre in Winnipeg, and Carswell, a striking employee of one of the stores in the shopping centre. Carswell was participating in a lawful strike and was picketing on the sidewalk in front of her employer's store. Harrison informed her that picketing was not permitted in any area of the shopping centre, and asked her to leave. Carswell refused, and was arrested and convicted of petty trespass. The legal issue at stake in this case was the conflict between the traditional rights of private property (protected by the law of trespass) and the right to strike.

The judgment of Laskin C.J. and Spence and Beetz J.J. was delivered by

THE CHIEF JUSTICE (dissenting) — I would be content to adopt the reasons of Freedman C.J.M. and, accordingly, to dismiss this appeal without more if I did not feel compelled, in view of the course of argument, to add some observations bearing on the decision of this Court in *Peters v. The Queen* dismissing an appeal from the judgment of the Ontario Court of Appeal. The observations I am about to make about the *Peters* case carry into two areas of concern respecting the role of this Court as the final Court in this country in both civil and criminal causes. Those areas are, first, whether this Court must pay mechanical deference to *stare decisis* and, second, whether this Court has a balancing role to play, without yielding place to the Legislature, where an ancient doctrine, in this case trespass, is invoked in a new setting to suppress a lawful activity supported both by legislation and by a well-understood legislative policy. . . .

. . . This Court, above all others in this country, cannot be simply mechanistic about previous decisions, whatever be the respect it would pay to such decisions. What we would be doing here, if we were to say that the *Peters* case, because it was so recently decided, has concluded the present case for us, would be to take merely one side of a debatable issue and say that it concludes the debate without the need to hear the other side.

I do not have to call upon pronouncements of members of this Court that we are free to depart from previous decisions in order to support the pressing need to examine the present case on its merits.

The judgment of Martland, Judson, Ritchie, Pigeon, Dickson, and de Grandpré, J.J. was delivered by Dickson J. . . .

. . . The submission that this Court should weigh and determine the respective values to society of the right to property and the right to picket raises important and difficult political and socio-economic issues, the resolution of which must, by their very nature, be arbitrary and embody personal economic and social beliefs. It raises also fundamental questions as to the role of this Court under the Canadian constitution. The duty of the Court, as I envisage it, is to proceed in the discharge of its adjudicative function in a reasoned way from principled decision and established concepts. I do not for a moment doubt the power of the Court to act creatively — it has done so on countless occasions; but manifestly one must ask — what are the limits of the judicial function? There are many and varied answers to this question. Holmes J. said in *Southern Pacific Co. v. Jensen*, at p. 221: "I recognize without hesitation that judges do and must legislate, but they can do it only interstitially; they are confined from molar to molecular actions." Cardozo, *The Nature of the Judicial Process* (1921), p. 141, recognized that the freedom of the judge is not absolute in this expression of his review:

> This judge, even when he is free, is still not wholly free. He is not to innovate at pleasure. He is not a knight-errant, roaming at will in pursuit of his own ideal of beauty or of goodness. He is to draw his inspiration from consecrated principles.

The former Chief Justice of the Australian High Court, Sir Owen Dixon, in an address delivered at Yale University in September 1955, "Concerning Judicial Method," had this to say:

> But in our Australian High Court we have had as yet no deliberate innovators bent on express change of acknowledged doctrine. It is one thing for a court to seek to extend the application of accepted principles to new cases or to reason from the more fundamental of settled legal principles to new conclusions or to decide that a category is not closed against unforeseen instances which in reason might be subsumed thereunder. It is an entirely different thing for a judge, who is discontented with a result held to flow from a long accepted legal principle, deliberately to abandon the principle in the name of justice or of social necessity or of social convenience. The former accords with the technique of the common law and amounts to no more than an enlightened application of modes of reasoning traditionally respected in the courts. It is a process by the repeated use of which the law is developed, is adapted to new conditions, and is improved in content. The latter means an abrupt and almost arbitrary change.

Society has long since acknowledged that a public interest is served by permitting union members to bring economic pressure to bear upon their respective employers through peaceful picketing, but the right has been exercisable in some locations and not in others and to the extent that picketing has been permitted on private property the right hitherto has been accorded by statute. For example, s. 87 of the *Labour Code of British Columbia Act*, 1973 (B.C.)

(2nd Sess.), c. 122, provides that no action lies in respect of picketing permitted under the Act for trespass to real property to which a member of the public ordinarily has access.

Anglo-Canadian jurisprudence has traditionally recognized, as a fundamental freedom, the right of the individual to the enjoyment of property and the right not to be deprived thereof, or any interest therein, save by due process of law. The Legislature of Manitoba has declared in *The Petty Trespasses Act* that any person who trespasses upon land, the property of another, upon or through which he has been requested by the owner not to enter, is guilty of an offence. If there is to be any change in this statute law, if A is to be given the right to enter and remain on the land of B against the will of B, it would seem to me that such a change must be made by the enacting institution, the Legislature, which is representative of the people and designed to manifest the political will, and not by the Court.

# 2.5

# KEYTERMS

## *Concepts*

declaratory model of judging
legal positivism
legal realism
judicial nationalism
adjudication of disputes model of judging
policy-making model of judging
adversary process
power vs. authority

## *Institutions, Events and Documents*

Judicial Committee of the Privy Council
*O'Connor Report* (1939)
Abolition of Appeals to J.C.P.C. (1949)
*Off-Shore Mineral Rights Reference* (1967)
*Harrison v. Carswell* (1976)

# 3
# The Canadian Judicial System

A distinctive feature of the Canadian judicial system is its unitary character. This distinguishes it from other federal nations such as the United States, which has "dual court systems." A dual court system parallels the division of legislative powers along federal lines, by creating federal courts for federal law, and state courts for state law. While the Canadian Founders adopted the logic of federalism for the distribution of legislative authority, they did not apply it to the judiciary. They created a single judicial system to interpret and to apply both federal and provincial laws. The unitary character of the Canadian judicial system is effectively illustrated by the judicial flowchart (figure 2) in Reading 3.3. This diagram shows how both civil law, which is mainly provincial in origin, and criminal law, which is almost exclusively federal in origin, move from trial to appeal through the same system of courts. This unitary character of the Canadian judicial system is politically significant, because it can mitigate the centrifugal forces of federal-provincial politics. Rather than accentuating regional differences, it promotes a continuity and uniformity of legal policy across the nation.

The unitary character of the Canadian judicial system is reinforced by the fact that it is the shared responsibility of both levels of government. The legal framework for this joint-responsibility is laid out in sections 92(14) and 96 to 101 of the Constitution Act, 1867.[1] (Reading 3.2) Section 92 allocates to the provinces the powers to make laws that provide for the "constitution, maintenance, and organization of provincial courts." Section 96 provides that the federal government "shall appoint the judges of the superior, district, and county courts in each province." These provisions create the joint federal-provincial responsibility for the "section 96" courts, which are created and maintained by the provinces but whose judges are appointed by the federal government.

---

[1] Formerly the British North America Act.

In the judicial hierarchy there are two additional tiers of courts beside the "section 96" or superior courts. "Below" are the "section 92 courts," so-called because they are created, maintained, and staffed wholly by the provincial governments, pursuant to section 92(14) of the Constitution Act. In most provinces these courts are entitled "Provincial Courts," and are the modern day successors of the old Magistrates or Police courts. "Above" the "section 96" courts is the Supreme Court of Canada, which, pursuant to section 101 of the Constitution Act, is created, maintained, and staffed wholly by the federal government. This allocation of responsibility for the different tiers of the judicial system is illustrated in the diagram in Reading 3.3. (Figure 1).

### Section 92 Courts

The "section 92 courts" can be described as both the least important and the most important courts in Canada. Their lack of status stems from their position as the lowest rung in the Canadian judicial hierarchy. They serve principally as trial courts for less serious offenses and as courts of preliminary inquiry for more serious offenses. Their decisions are always subject to review and reversal by "higher" courts. On the other hand, these courts are critically important because of the high volume of litigation that they process each year. Described as the "workhorse" of the Canadian judicial system, the provincial courts handle over 90% of all criminal litigation. For most Canadians, "a day in court" means a day in provincial court. As a result, the quality of justice in Canada is directly affected by the quality of the provincial court system. As a result of the somewhat belated recognition of their importance, there has been a conscious effort in the past several decades to improve the salaries and training of provincial court judges, the efficiency of court administration, and even the physical setting of court rooms and court houses. The criminal law jurisdiction of the provincial courts is illustrated in the flowchart in Reading 3.4 (figure 4). Provincial courts hear all provincial offenses and summary conviction offenses, and conduct all preliminary inquiries. In addition they hear indictable offenses under section 483 of the Criminal Code, some indictable offenses of election, and cases under the Young Offenders Act. Their civil law jurisdiction includes issues of minor civil claims and family law.

### The "Section 96" Superior, County, and District Courts

Each province has a two-tier system of superior courts: a trial court of general criminal and civil jurisdiction and a corresponding appeal court.[2] The names of these courts vary from province to province, but their constitutional status is the same. In Alberta, Manitoba, and Saskatchewan these

---

[2] While Ontario still has County and District Courts, most provinces have amalgamated them with the trial division of the superior court, the Court of Queen's Bench in Alberta.

courts are the Court of Queen's Bench and the Court of Appeal. In Quebec they are called the Superior Court and the Court of Appeal. In most of the other provinces they are distinguished as the trial division and appellate division of the province's Supreme Court. The judges in both courts are appointed by the federal government.[3]

The Court of Queen's Bench (or Trial Division of the Supreme Court) is generally regarded as "the key to the Canadian court system."[4] Its prestige flows from its very broad criminal and civil jurisdiction, and the fact that it is derived from the English superior courts of common law and equity. W.R. Lederman argues that the independence of these courts is part of the "unwritten constitution" inherited from Great Britain, and that they could not be abolished or significantly altered without doing violence to the fundamental order of Canadian government.[5]

The criminal jurisdiction of the Court of Queen's Bench includes the trial of all indictable offenses under section 427 of the Criminal Code and indictable offenses by election. It also hears appeals from all summary conviction offenses. (See figure 4 in Reading 3.4). The Court of Queen's Bench is clearly the most important civil law court. It hears divorces, separations, and guardianship disputes, and all civil disputes whose monetary claims are too large for small claims courts. It also hears appeals from juvenile and family courts, and from some administrative boards and tribunals.

The Court of Appeal of the province (or Appellate Division of the Supreme Court) is the highest court in the province. It sits principally to hear appeals from the Court of Queen's Bench on questions of law, and its decisions are binding on all other courts within the province (unless overturned on appeal to the Supreme Court of Canada). Its chief justice is the chief justice of the province.

### Supreme Court of Canada

At the summit of the judicial pyramid sits the Supreme Court of Canada. Since appeals to the Judicial Committee of the Privy Council were abolished in 1949, the Supreme Court has served as the final court of appeal for all matters of Canadian law. Its creation was authorized but not required by section 101 of the Constitution Act, 1867. Parliament, after considerable debate, exercised that power and enacted the Supreme Court Act in 1875.[6]

---

[3] Prince Edward Island does not have a separate appeal court. Appeals are heard by the Chief Justice, and two judges who did not participate in the trial.

[4] S.M. Waddams, *Introduction to the Study of Law* (Toronto: Carswell-Methuen, 1979), p.157.

[5] See W.R. Lederman, "The Independence of the Judiciary," Reading 5.2.

[6] See Jennifer Smith, "The Origins of Judicial Review in Canada," Reading 10.1.

The Supreme Court has jurisdiction to hear appeals on all questions of criminal and civil law from the provincial courts of appeal, and also accepts appeals from the Federal Court. Since 1975 the Court grants "leave to appeal" in a civil case only if it raises an issue of national concern or public importance, so that the Court now has considerably more control over the content and size of its docket than before. In Reading 3.1, the late Chief Justice Bora Laskin argues that the increasingly discretionary character of the Supreme Court's appellate jurisdiction changes the nature of the Court's function from that of traditional appellate review to one of "supervisory review." This represents a change of emphasis from concern for the individual case to overseeing the consistent development of Canadian law, especially in issues of public importance and national concern. An important exception to this trend is the reference procedure, by which the federal government can ask the Court for an "advisory opinion" on any question of constitutional or statutory law. While the number of references has decreased as a proportion of the total number of cases heard annually by the Court, they frequently represent the most important cases.[7]

The original Supreme Court Act authorized the appointment of six judges, and required that two of the six be from Quebec. This was deemed necessary to accommodate civil law appeals from Quebec. Not to be outdone by her provincial rival, Ontario demanded equal treatment, and eventually a custom of having two Ontario judges on the Court came into being. In 1927 the size of the Court was increased to seven judges, and again in 1949 to nine. The number of Quebec and Ontario judges was increased to three, Quebec's by law and Ontario's by custom. Again by custom, the three remaining vacancies were to be filled by one judge each from the Maritime provinces, the Prairie provinces, and British Columbia. This *de facto* practice of regional representation on the Supreme Court attests to its perception as an important "political" institution in the process of national government.

The Supreme Court is presided over by a Chief Justice, the highest judicial officer of Canada. Over time, customs developed to govern the appointment of the Chief Justice. A pattern of alternating the position between English-Canadian and French-Canadian judges developed, and also of appointing the most senior judge in terms of service within each of these groups. Both of these customs have been broken by the last two appointments of Chief Justices, both by Prime Minister Trudeau. In 1973 he appointed Bora Laskin, who had served considerably less time on the court than several other anglophone members. In April of 1984, Trudeau again broke with tradition by appointing another anglophone, Brian Dickson, to succeed Laskin. These recent appointments cast serious doubt on the continued validity of either of these traditions.

Because the Supreme Court was not constitutionally entrenched, Parliament could technically have abolished it at any time. Many commentators

---

[7] See Barry Strayer, "Constitutional References," Reading 6.2.

argued that this impugned the independence and thus the status of the Court. This situation has been changed by the Constitution Act, 1981. Section 41(d) declares that the composition of the Supreme Court (presently 9 judges with three from Quebec) can only be changed by the unanimous consent of all the provinces and the federal government. Section 42 requires that any changes to the Supreme Court other than its composition be done according to the new amending formula. These changes seem to eliminate the Court's potential vulnerability to Parliament, but also confuse the situation by "constitutionalizing" an arrangement that exists only by statute, the Supreme Court Act. It is anticipated that Parliament will propose further amendments to eliminate this anomaly.

### Federal Court of Canada

In addition to authorizing the creation of the Supreme Court, section 101 of the Constitution Act, 1867, also allows "for the establishment of any additional courts for the better administration of the laws of Canada." If it chose to, Parliament could use this authority to create an entirely new tier of federal courts, similar to those of the United States. In practice it has not done so, creating instead only two federal courts of specialized jurisdiction. In 1875 Parliament created the Exchequer Court. In 1970 it was renamed the Federal Court and given an expanded jurisdiction. The original jurisdiction of the Exchequer Court consisted of a collection of specialized areas of federal law — admiralty law, copyright and trademark law, income and estate tax law, and citizenship and immigration law. It also heard civil claims against the Crown.

In 1970, the new Federal Court inherited this jurisdiction, and in addition was given the function of supervising federal administrative law. The Federal Court has both a trial and an appellate division. The top "wedge" of the flow chart in figure 2 illustrates how the federal administrative law area has been hived-off from the rest of the judicial system, and made the special responsibility of the Federal Court. There is the possibility of leave to appeal to the Supreme Court from all Federal Court decisions. In 1983, Parliament created a new section 101 court, the Tax Court of Canada. It hears appeals from Revenue Canada, and its decisions may be appealed to the Federal Court.

### Judicial Committee of the Privy Council

Prior to Confederation, the Judicial Committee of the Privy Council served as the final court of appeal for the courts of all the British colonies, including Canada. It continued in this capacity under section 129 of the Constitution Act, 1867. The Privy Council served as final court of appeal for the entire British Empire. It was not a part of the regular English court system, and did not hear appeals from English courts. It consisted of five judges drawn mainly from the law lords of the House of Lords.

Even after the Supreme Court was created in 1875, appeals to the Privy Council remained. In addition to appeals from Supreme Court decisions, there were also appeals from the Court of Appeal of each province. This latter possibility, known as a *per saltum* appeal, allowed parties to effectively bypass the Supreme Court of Canada, and reduced its prestige and influence. The decisions of the Privy Council played a major role in shaping the constitutional development of Canada. Its interpretations of the federal division of powers significantly diminished the authority of the federal government while expanding that of the provinces. As discussed in the preceding chapter, this trend reached a climax during the 1930's, and provoked a reaction against the continued role of the Privy Council in Canadian public affairs. This "judicial nationalism" movement culminated in the abolition of appeals to the Privy Council in 1949. However its pre-1949 decisions remain an important part of Canadian law, especially in the areas of federalism.

# 3.1

## THE ROLE AND FUNCTIONS OF FINAL APPELLATE COURTS: THE SUPREME COURT OF CANADA

Bora Laskin

### I

. . . I look upon the functions of the Supreme Court of Canada as those that arise out of its jurisdiction; the definition of its role depends on how that jurisdiction is exercised, how it uses its final appellate authority having regard to the kind and range of cases that come before it. The interaction between jurisdiction and role is obvious; and, inevitably, the judges' view of their role is bound to undergo definition and redefinition in the day-to-day grind of the court's business and in the periodic changes of its membership. One can envisage judges of the Supreme Court having some differences of opinion, probably slight ones, on the court's functions; any differences about its role are likely to be more serious.

### II

The starting point for any consideration of the Supreme Court's functions and its role is that fact, a surprising one I am sure to foreign students of

*Canadian Bar Review*, 53 (1975), p. 469. Reprinted with permission.

federalism, that the Supreme Court of Canada has no constitutional base. This marks it off immediately from such kindred courts as the Supreme Court of the United States and the High Court of Australia. The Supreme Court of Canada is a statutory creation of the Parliament of Canada under the power given that Parliament by section 101 of the British North America Act to constitute, maintain and organize "a general Court of Appeal for Canada." The size of the court, its jurisdiction, its procedure, indeed all questions touching its operation as a general court of appeal, an appellate court in short without any declared right to original jurisdiction, were left to the Government and Parliament of Canada to prescribe.

The size of the court, originally composed of six judges, with a seventh added in 1927 and two more added in 1949 upon the abolition of all appeals to the Privy Council from any appellate court in Canada, testifies both to population and regional growth in Canada, to the expansion of the business of the court and to its ultimate grave responsibility as a final appellate court. Of significance in its structure and operations was the provision of a quorum for sittings of the court, the number being fixed at five upon the creation of the court and remaining constant despite increase in its overall size. There could not, and even today there cannot be more than one Bench for the hearing of appeals; and I am thankful that this precludes having two Supreme Courts of Canada. Perhaps the only power a Chief Justice has is to assign the Bench for the hearing of appeals. Since my personal preference is to have the full court sit, and since the recent change in our jurisdiction enables the court to be selective in the cases that it will hear, I will not view with any regret the surrender of the power of assignment which, in any event, has been exercised with regard to the opinions of the other members of the court as to whether a panel of five or the full court should be assigned in any particular appeal.

The jurisdiction of the court, the scope of its appellate authority, was undoubtedly the most important matter that faced the Government and Parliament of Canada in creating the court in 1875. A number of models were available for consideration. There was the model of a national appellate court, functioning like an English appellate court, or like the House of Lords, with general jurisdiction (be it as of right or by leave) not limited to any class or classes of cases. There was, second, the model of a purely federal court, with an appellate jurisdiction limited to matters within or arising out of the exercise of federal legislative powers, including the validity of that exercise, but excluding constitutional issues arising under provincial legislation in view of the fact that appeals then lay directly to the Privy Council from provincial courts of appeal. There was, third, the model of a federal appellate court having also comprehensive appellate jurisdiction in all constitutional matters as ultimate Canadian expositor of the constitution, albeit there was a further appeal to the Privy Council. This was the model offered by the Supreme Court of the United States. There was, fourth, the model of a purely constitutional court and, fifth, the model of a federal and a constitutional court, with separate chambers for each of these functions, in adaptation of the chamber system found today in the *Cour de Cassation* of France.

Happily, in my view, the first model was chosen, thus adapting to federal Canada a system of appellate adjudication operative in unitary Great Britain but familiar to Canadians of Bench and Bar. To have adopted the federal model represented by the Supreme Court of the United States or some other such model, would have required at least consideration of, if not actual establishment of a system of federal courts of original jurisdiction. A dual court system such as obtains in the United States was resisted in Canada, save for the establishment of an Exchequer Court with a limited jurisdiction, and of Admirality Courts. It was in the character of concurrent appointment as Exchequer Court judges that the judges of the Supreme Court of Canada were invested with original jurisdiction but this ceased when the Exchequer Court was set up on a separate base in 1887, ending a short first life and beginning a second one with a judge wholly its own, but with more added over the succeeding years.

Although the jurisdiction of the Exchequer Court was extended considerably when it was translated into the Federal Court of Canada in 1970, the latter is still a court of limited jurisdiction in federal matters. A serious and, in my view, unfortunate as well as an unnecessary upheaval in our Canadian system of judicature would result if the Government and Parliament of Canada moved now to federalize it at the level of original and intermediate appellate jurisdiction by withdrawing such jurisdiction in all federal matters from the provincial courts and reposing it in a federal court structure.

The Parliament of Canada has power to that end under section 101 of the British North America Act, the same section which authorized the creation of the Supreme Court of Canada. In authorizing as well (in its words) "the establishment of any additional Courts for the better administration of the laws of Canada," the section may be said to reflect some incongruity. On the one hand, it enabled Parliament to establish a "general," a truly national court of appeal whose authority was not limited to federal matters — the telling word is "general" — and, on the other hand to establish federal courts limited to jurisdiction in federal matters. To have exercised both grants of authority to the full, in the light of the fact that at Confederation in 1867 there were developed provincial courts habituated to adjudicate on matters that after Confederation were in terms of legislative power distributed between the central and provincial legislatures, would have created, and would now certainly create great tensions in federal-provincial relations. We can do without adding to those that already exist, although I am bound to add that tension to some degree is a by-product of federalism.

Parliament did exercise its authority to the full in establishing the Supreme Court of Canada in 1875 and in reconstituting the court in 1949 upon the abolition of all appeals in Canadian causes to the Privy Council. This makes good sense to me so long as the provincial courts are left, as they now are, to administer federal law as well as provincial law, indeed federal common law as well as provincial common law, save to the limited extent that judicial jurisdiction in federal matters has been reposed in the Federal Court of Canada, which has both a trial division and an appeal division in respect of those matters.

If there was any thought-out rationale for investing the Supreme Court of Canada with appellate authority from all provincial appellate courts, and in respect of provincial as well as federal matters cognizable in those courts, it was posited and, in my view, may be said to rest today on the following factors. First, there was and is the fact that particular litigation frequently involves issues that engage both federal and provincial matters which provincial courts have continued to handle without difficulty, and forum problems are, in general, avoided notwithstanding the hived-off jurisdiction of the Federal Court. Its jurisdiction is, on the whole, fairly distinct and has hitherto not created any intractable difficulties in forum selection, although some such questions have arisen. Second, there was and is the fact that the common law is largely the same in all the provinces outside of Quebec and that, subject to legislative changes, it ought to have an uniform operation in all those provinces, thus avoiding some possible conflict of laws problems; and, moreover, even in Quebec there are branches of the common law, as for example in the field of public law, that were and are common to it and to the other provinces of Canada. Third, there was and is the fact that many important branches of law, such as the criminal law, the law of negotiable instruments, the law of bankruptcy, the law of shipping, railway law, the law of patents and copyright have a national operation because they fall within exclusive federal competence; and even though they may interact in some respects with some aspects of the common law their interpretation and application must necessarily be uniform, and perhaps all the more so because of the interaction. Fourth, constitutional adjudication, involving the resolution of disputes as to the scope and reach of federal and provincial legislative powers must necessarily end in a court that can speak authoritatively for the whole of Canada, and I may add here that there is equally a case to be made for final uniform resolution of questions touching the operation of public authorities.

Thus it was that upon the establishment of the Supreme Court of Canada we had in the main a one-stream two-tier system of appeals like that in Great Britain, although that country did not have to contend with federalism as we know it in Canada. To some extent, there is a three-tier system in respect of Ontario cases by reason of the recent establishment there of an intermediate appellate court, with a limited jurisdiction, operating between courts of first instance and the Ontario Court of Appeal. Should this innovation spread to other provinces it would not alter the force of the considerations which led to the establishment of the Supreme Court of Canada as a national court. Its character does not depend on the system of appeals within the judicial structure of any one or more provinces but, rather on how far beyond adjudication on federal matters and on constitutional matters its jurisdiction should extend.

The Government and the Parliament of Canada saw no need to water down the broad authority given to establish ''a general Court of appeal for Canada''; and Parliament emphasized the breadth of its power by generous scope, especially in civil cases, for appeals as of right, appeals which the Supreme Court of Canada was obliged to hear, however local or private were the issues that they raised. This was appellate review in a traditional sense as distinguished from what I would term supervisory control.

Until the beginning of this year when appellate review was replaced by supervisory control (leave now being required in all non-criminal cases and in most criminal cases before an appeal will be entertained on the merits), appeals as of right in civil cases formed a large part of the Supreme Court's case load. I think this was one of the factors that led some scholarly students of the Supreme Court's work to urge federalization of its jurisdiction. Other factors were also raised in support of this position, such as the virtue of allocating judicial power along the same lines as legislative power, and the merit of leaving to final adjudication in the provincial courts legal issues reflecting local conditions and those based on provincial or municipal legislation.

I think that the amendments recently made to the Supreme Court's jurisdiction, making a previous requirement of leave (whether from the Supreme Court or the provincial appellate court) the general rule, has blunted the case that could formerly have been made and was made for limiting the Supreme Court of Canada to federal and constitutional issues. The four-pronged rationale which I mentioned earlier in this address as supporting a final appellate court with a general national jurisdiction is not, in my opinion, cogently answered by those who would reduce the court to a federal and constitutional institution. Still less is it answerable now that the Supreme Court is a supervisory tribunal rather than an appellate tribunal in the traditional sense. As a supervisory tribunal, it is fully able and would be expected to resist interference in purely local or private issues, and it is in fact enjoined to do so by the statutory formula which prescribes the requirements that must be met in order to obtain leave. The case for leave must be one with respect to which ''the Supreme Court is of the opinion that any question involved therein is, by reason of its public importance or the importance of any issue of law or any issue of mixed law and fact involved in such question, one that ought to be decided by the Supreme Court or is, for any other reason, of such a nature or significance as to warrant decision by it.''

The discretion given to the court under the foregoing formula is obvious, but it is a necessary control over the flow of cases that have already been before two courts. Now, even more in its supervisory role than in its heretofore more traditional appellate role, the Supreme Court's main function is to oversee the development of the law in the courts of Canada, to give guidance in articulate reasons and, indeed, direction to the provincial courts and to the Federal Court of Canada on issues of national concern or of common concern

to several provinces, issues that may obtrude even though arising under different legislative regimes in different provinces. This is surely the paramount
obligation of an ultimate appellate court with national authority. It is only
under this umbrella that it can, in general, be expected to be sensitive to the
correctness of the decisions in particular cases, whether they be between
private litigants only or involve some government as a party.

I think I can risk saying that the mere fact that any level of government or
any government agency is involved in a particular case is no more telling in
favour of leave to appeal than the fact that litigation is private necessarily tells
against the granting of leave. The issues in contention and, indeed, the issues
which will be determinative of the appeal, however there may be others of
importance in the case, and not the character of the parties, will guide the
court in the exercise of its power to grant or refuse leave. Even where the
court may be disposed to grant leave, it may do so, not at large, but by
defining the specific question or question on which it is prepared to have the
case come forward.

### III

I turn now to more debatable questions respecting the Supreme Court's
exercise of its jurisdiction, questions going to its role as Canada's highest and
final court on all justiciable matters. Two considerations affect any assessment of that role. One has to do with the kind of business that comes and will
come before the court; the second has to do with the collegiality of the court,
with the blend of individual independence of the judges *inter se* and their
institutional responsibility. The bulk of the court's business is, and is likely to
continue to be, the interpretation and application of statutes, some of which,
as for example, parts of the Criminal Code and of the Quebec Civil Code, to
take two illustrations, have long ago taken on what I may term a common law
appearance. Two statutes, one, the British North America Act (and its
amendments), only formally of that character (since it is Canada's chief
written constitution), and the second, the Canadian Bill of Rights, a quasi-
constitutional enactment are not, for interpretative purposes "statutes like
other statutes" (to adopt well-known phraseology); and there is little doubt,
certainly none in my mind, that the judicial approach to them, compelled by
their character, has been different from that taken with respect to ordinary
legislation. The generality of their language and their operative effect compel
an approach from a wider perspective than is the case with ordinary legislation,
especially legislation that is more precisely formulated.

The collegiality of the court touches a matter that may have a greater
interest for the academic component of this assembly than for the practising
Bar or members of the judiciary. It is theoretically open to each member of the
Supreme Court of Canada, as it is theoretically open to each member of any
appellate court, to write reasons in every case in which the member sits.
Practical and institutional considerations militate against this; and so it is that

when bare concurrences are filed with reasons proposed by a colleague, they may suggest some shift of position by the concurring judge who does not choose to write separate reasons, a shift on some matter subsidiary to or connected with the disposition of the main issue to which the concurrence was given.

Bare concurrences ought not to be taken as representing unqualified endorsement of every sentence of the reasons concurred in. Contextual approval, yes; and approval of the result, of course. After all the scrutiny and conferring on a set of proposed reasons are over, and after changes have been made in language and organization by the writer so far as he is willing to accommodate himself to the views of his colleagues, there may still remain in some colleague some questions about some parts of the reasons. However, he may decide on balance that there is no point in writing his own. In short, it is far safer and surer, if one would assess how a judge discharges his duties and how he regards his role and the role of the court, to assess him on what he himself writes and not on all of what is written by a colleague with whom he concurs in some particular case or cases.

There is no question that seems to have been as continuously and as strenuously considered, in relation to all courts and judges, and more particularly in relation to judges and courts of ultimate authority, as their law-making role. The Supreme Court of Canada began life at about the time Langdell and his case-law approach to the discovery of the "true legal rule" revolutionized legal studies in the United States. On the English side, before the nineteenth century was out the House of Lords had sanctified its own position as the expositor of the one true rule which, once declared, was alterable only by legislation. A quarter of a century later Cardozo was to tell us that at its highest reaches the role of the judge lay in creation and not in mere discovery. In this country, and perhaps in England too, we were inclined to think that creativity applied to what had not been previously considered and determined but, that accomplished in the highest court, creativity was spent and change was only for the legislature or for the constitutional amending process, as the case might be. . . .

. . . Controversy has now ceased on the law-making role of judges, especially of judges of a final appellate court. Laymen may beg the question by consoling the dissenting judges of a divided court with the remark, "too bad the law was against you," but judges and lawyers know better. The late Lord Reid helped to bury the declaratory theory by remarking in a speech delivered in 1971 that law is not some known and defined entity secreted in Aladdin's cave and revealed if one uses the right password. We do not believe in fairy tales any more, said Lord Reid, and Lord Diplock did not doubt, when speaking for the Privy Council in an Australian appeal in 1974, that "when for the first time a court of final instance interprets [a statute] as bearing one of two or more possible meanings . . . the effect of the exercise of its interpretative role is to make law." Such controversy as there is today in judicial law-making in a final court concerns the appropriateness of the occasion or of the case for enunciating a new rule of law and, even more important, the appropriateness of the occasion or of the case for upsetting an existing rule and substituting a different one in its place.

Neither here nor in any of the countries whence come our distinguished guests is *stare decisis* now an inexorable rule for our respective final courts. In this country, what appeared to be at times an obsessiveness about it came partly at least from our link with English law which also involved the ascendancy of English courts, so that *stare decisis* amounted to a form of ancestor worship. We are now able to view it as simply an important element of the judicial process, a necessary consideration which should give pause to any but the most sober conclusion that a previous decision or line of authority is wrong and ought to be changed. Such a conclusion is not likely to be arrived at by any judge or number of judges without serious reflection on its conformity or consistency with other principles that are part of the institutional history or the institutional patterns of the court. None of us operates without constraints that are both personal and institutional, born of both training and experience and of traditions of the legal system of which the court is a part.

When everything considered relevant has been weighed and an overruling decision commends itself to a judge, he ought not at that stage to stay his opinion and call upon the legislature to implement it. This is particularly true in respect of those areas of the law which are judge-made, and to a degree true in respect of those areas where legislation is involved which is susceptible of a number of meanings. A final court must accept a superintending responsibility for what it or its predecessors have wrought, especially when it knows how little time legislatures today have (and also, perhaps, little inclination) to intrude into fields of law fashioned by the courts alone, although legislatures may, of course, under the prodding of law reform agencies and of other public influences, from time to time do.

The role of the courts, the role of a final court, in the interpretation of legislation, bringing into play the relation between the legislative and the judicial arms of government, is of a different dimension, in my view, than the role played in the promulgation of judge-made law. The dimension comes from the dominant political and legal principle under which our courts operate, which is that, constitutional issues apart, Parliament and the provincial legislatures are the supreme, certainly the superior law-making bodies. On constitutional issues, issues concerning the division of distribution of legislative power, the courts, and ultimately the Supreme Court of Canada, have the final word (subject to constitutional amendment). This is a critical role, so critical for exercises of legislative and governmental power at both the central and provincial level as to put every Supreme Court decision in this field, whatever it be, into the political mill. Yet it is a role which the court cannot eschew if we believe in constitutional order, any more than can any final court with constitutional jurisdiction in a federal state. There is no other instrument with final authority available for this role. It is of course possible (and indeed there are known examples) for the central and provincial governments to avoid constitutional determinations in the Supreme Court of Canada by entering into co-operative arrangements which do not call for any test of constitutional competence. In this way they may hold some the tensions in their relations in equilibrium, so long as those arrangements last. The fact that such arrangements exist at all underlines the delicate nature of the Supreme Court's constitutional jurisdiction. Of course, it must proceed with caution in that field but, that having been said, it brings the same independent judgment to bear on constitutional questions as on other matters that are brought before it, fully conscious, however, that there are no more important public issues submitted to its adjudication than those that arise out alleged conflicts of legislative authority.

The stakes in interpretation and application of ordinary legislation may not be as high because here the courts play not an ascendant role but rather more of a complementary one. The judges, no less than others in society, owe obedience to legislation which they may be called upon to interpret and apply; they have a duty to respect the legislative purpose or policy whatever be their view of its merit. Judges subscribe to this proposition, and then may be seen to proceed to differ on what the purpose or policy is, or to differ on whether the legislation or some part of it is apt to realize the purpose. This is not the time nor the place to enlarge on the variety of approaches to legislative interpretation which in close cases can lead to different results in respect of the same piece of legislation. In the majority of cases where legislation is a factor in the litigation, there is no such difficulty in interpretation as to require the particular expertise of a lawyer or a judge. Where that special competence is necessary, the judges owe it to the enacting legislature as well as to the litigants to expose the legal reasoning which underlies their decisions.

The public expectation is, I suspect, of a somewhat different order. Since so much of the legislation that comes before the courts and before the Supreme Court of Canada involves controls or limitation of the social conduct or business behaviour of persons or classes of persons or corporations, either by direct penal sanction or by supervision of administrative agencies, those affected may look to the courts for some wider exposition than a strict regard for legal issues would warrant. Is the policy a desirable or a workable one? Is the administrative structure fair? Is the procedure fair, are the decisions supported by reasons that are disclosed to the affected persons? There is no invariable stance that a court takes on these questions. Where it has deemed it proper to pronounce on policy (as it has on occasion) it has done so with prudence, and, generally, when prompted by difficulties that reside in the interpretation and application of the legislation. Fairness of administrative procedure is more confidently dealt with by the courts because what is compendiously called "natural justice" has long been regarded as involving legal issues for their consideration.

Natural justice, embracing the right to notice of possibly adverse action, the right to be heard or to make representations before being adversely affected, and the right to be judged by an impartial tribunal, is a central feature of an evolved political and legal tradition which sees the courts as wielders of protective authority against an invasion of the liberty of the individual by government or its agencies. Text books, periodical literature and the every-day press reinforce this tradition, and thus strengthen the public expectation that the courts, and especially the Supreme Court of Canada, will speak out on the matter. The enactment of the Canadian Bill of Rights as a federal measure, and operative only at that level, has fed that expectation. It is well to recall that judges of Supreme Court spoke strongly on aspects of individual liberty in the *Alberta Press* case, the *Switzman* case, the *Roncarelli* case, and in other cases too, without the back-up or the direction of the Canadian Bill of Rights, which became effective only in 1960. It was able to do so because the avenues for recognizing individual rights or civil liberties had not been closed by competent legislation, nor did any relevant legislation as interpreted by the judges of the Supreme Court preclude them. Legislation may however appear to be preclusive in some areas of civil liberties, and if interpreted with that result the judicial duty of fidelity to legislation as superior law must be acknowledged whatever be the consequences, although the acknowledgment may be accompanied by an expression of regret or even of remonstrance that the legislation went so far.

The Canadian Bill of Rights has now provided a legislative measure and standard of protection of civil liberties but, in the generality of some of its language, it adds to the dilemmas of interpretation which are so often evident in civil liberties cases. Its direction may be clearer in some cases than it is in others, or clearer to some judges in some cases than to others. Each charts his own course here, as in the other roles that he is called upon to play in the discharge of his judicial duties and, indeed, in determing what roles he should take on.

This, however, is simply another aspect of the side discretion opens to a judge of a final appellate court. There may be differences about the scope of the discretion, but there cannot be any dispute about its existence. As I said at the beginning of my remarks, each judge puts his own questions and supplies his own answers and, in yielding ground to institutional considerations, he does so according to his own assessment of what they demand.

# 3.2

# CONSTITUTION ACT, 1867, SECTIONS 96-101

VII. — Judicature.

96. The Governor General shall appoint the Judges of the Superior, District, and County Courts in each Province, except those of the Courts of Probate in Nova Scotia and New Brunswick.

97. Until the laws relative to Property and Civil Rights in Ontario, Nova Scotia, and New Brunswick, and the Procedure of the Courts in those Provinces, are made uniform, the Judges of the Courts of those Provinces appointed by the Governor General shall be selected from the respective Bars of those Provinces.

98. The Judges of the Courts of Quebec shall be selected from the Bar of that Province.

99. (1) Subject to subsection two of this section, the Judges of the Superior Courts shall hold office during good behavior, but shall be removable by the Governor General on Address of the Senate and House of Commons.

(2) A Judge of a Superior Court, whether appointed before or after the coming into force of this section, shall cease to hold office upon attaining the age of seventy-five years, or upon the coming into force of this section if at that time he has already attained that age. (44A)

100. The Salaries, Allowances, and Pensions of the Judges of the Superior, District, and County Courts (except the Courts of Probate in Nova Scotia and New Brunswick), and of the Admiralty Courts in Cases where the Judges thereof are for the Time being paid by Salary, shall be fixed and provided by the Parliament of Canada. (45)

101. The Parliament of Canada may, notwithstanding anything in this Act, from Time to Time provide for the Constitution, Maintenance, and Organization of a General Court of Appeal for Canada, and for the Establishment of any additional Courts for the better Administration of the Laws of Canada. (46)

# 3.3

# THE CANADIAN JUDICIAL SYSTEM

The diagram in Table One represents the Canadian judicial system as it exists in Alberta. The names of the "section 92" and "section 96" courts vary from province to province. In Alberta they are called the Provincial Court and the Court of Queen's Bench, respectively. In Ontario, by contrast, the same courts are known as the High Court of Justice and the Court of Appeal. Together they constitute the trial and appellate divisions of the Supreme Court of Ontario. Also note that in Alberta there no longer are county and district courts, as they were amalgamated with the Court of Queen's Bench in 1979. The vertical arrows indicate the paths of appeal. The left-diagonal and right-diagonal hatch-marks indicate section 92 and section 101 courts, respectively. The cross-hatched area represents the section 96 courts and the joint responsibility of the two levels of government.

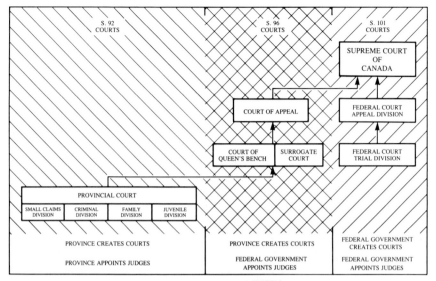

**THE CANADIAN JUDICIAL SYSTEM**

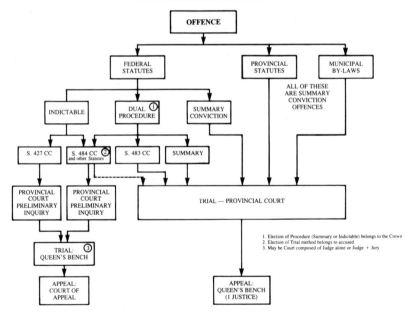

The second figure also represents the Canadian judicial system, but emphasizes the case flow pattern for the three principal areas of law: criminal, civil,
and administrative.

While each jurisdiction has its own courts, there are certain principles
which apply to all jurisdictions. The model on the following page illustrates
several of these principles.

**A General Overview of the Hierarchy, Procedural Flow
and Jurisdiction of the Courts of Canada, 1982**

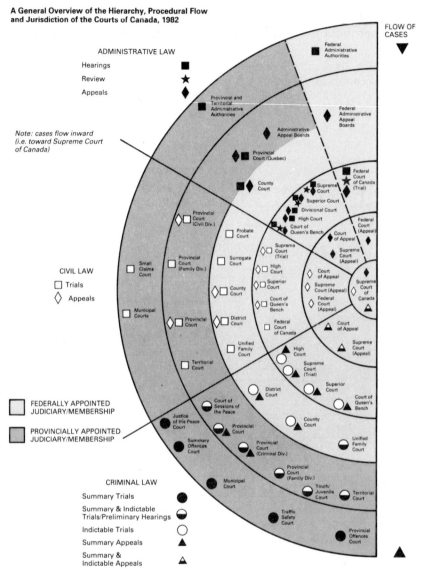

First, there is a structure which applies to each jurisdiction's court system. This is shown by the rings of the model focusing on the Supreme Court of Canada. Not all jurisdictions have a court in each of the rings (for example, some jurisdictions do not have a county or district court). The outside ring contains the courts that hear the less serious cases, and therefore these courts handle the higher volumes of cases. Appeals from a court decision always go to a court farther inwards, though not necessarily to a court in an adjacent ring. As one moves inward on the model, the trials and appeals heard generally increase in seriousness and complexity.

Secondly, the model reflects the distinction between courts with provincially appointed judges and those superior courts with federally appointed judges.

Thirdly, there are often special authorities, boards or tribunals set up to handle certain kinds of cases.

# 3.4

# THE CRIMINAL AND CIVIL COURT PROCESSES

**THE CIVIL COURT PROCESS**

TRIAL IN COURT OF
QUEEN'S BENCH
Judgement Registered

PRE-TRIAL CONFERENCE
Meeting between Judge & Parties'
Lawyers to clarify issues & shorten trial

EXAMINATION FOR DISCOVERY
Both parties questioned under oath
Disclosure of documents to be used
at trial by both parties

ASSESSMENT OF
DAMAGES & JUDGMENT
Where special damages must be
assessed by a judge

STATEMENT OF DEFENCE
Served on Plaintiff

DEFAULT JUDGEMENT
A judge can grant judgement by
default when defendant does not contest

STATEMENT OF DEFENCE
Defence of person or entity sued
Filed at office of Clerk of Court

STATEMENT OF CLAIM
Served on Defendant

STATEMENT OF CLAIM
Plaintiff's case
Filed in office of Clerk of the Court

CONSULTATION
With lawyer

CIVIL WRONG
Breach of Contract, Tort

THE CRIMINAL COURT PROCESS

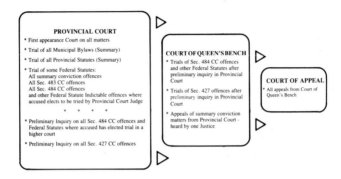

# 3.5

# KEYTERMS

### Concepts

unitary court system
dual court system
section 92 courts
section 96 courts
civil law
criminal law
administrative law
Common Law system
Civil Law system (Quebec)
indictable offense
summary conviction offense
preliminary inquiry
discretionary appellate jurisdiction

supervisory vs. appellate function
"per saltum appeal"

### Institutions, Events, and Documents

Provincial Court
Court of Queen's Bench
Court of Appeal
Supreme Court of Canada (1875)
Federal Court of Canada (1970)
Exchequer Court (1875-1970)
Judicial Committee of the Privy Council

# 4

# Judicial Recruitment and Selection

Under the Constitution Act, 1867,[1] judicial appointments are made by two different levels of government for three different levels of courts. Pursuant to section 101, the federal government is responsible for appointing all judges of the Supreme Court of Canada and the Federal Court. In addition, the federal government appoints all the judges of the "section 96 courts," even though the latter are created and maintained by the provinces. This is one of the distinctive features of Canada's unitary judicial system, and was originally intended to insure the independence of the provincial superior courts from local politics or prejudice. Finally, the provincial governments make all appointments to the provincial courts created pursuant to section 92 of the Constitution Act, 1867.

## Appointment Procedures

Federal judicial appointments are made by the Cabinet on the advice of the Minister of Justice, except for chief justices, who are recommended by the Prime Minster. An ongoing search for appropriate candidates is carried on by the Department of Justice. Through the Office of Special Advisor to the Minister of Justice, the Justice Department solicits suggestions from a nationwide network of contacts. Judges, bar associations, law schools, members of Parliament, and provincial office-holders are all encouraged to recommend individuals for judicial appointment. As judicial openings occur, the Justice Department contacts potential candidates to enquire if they would accept an appointment to a specified judgeship. If the response is positive, the government pursues its investigation into the qualifications of the candidate through additional phone calls and letters.

While political criteria inevitably have some influence in this process, it would be difficult to find a modern day equivalent of former Justice Frank Anglin's judicial ascent that culminated in his appointment to the Supreme

---

[1] Formerly the British North America Act, 1867.

Court in 1909. (See Reading 4.4) It is generally accepted that political patronage in judicial appointments has declined during recent decades. Individuals involved in the recruitment process have stressed their increased reliance on non-political criteria such as professional expertise, personal integrity, and work habits.[2] Once a tentative choice has been made, the candidate's name is submitted to the National Committee on the Judiciary of the Canadian Bar Association. Created in 1966 to provide a non-partisan source of advice to the federal government on judicial appointments, the Committee on the Judiciary reviews the candidate and his record. When this investigation is completed, the committee sends its final evaluation back to the Department of Justice, indicating that the candidate is well qualified, qualified, or not qualified. No candidates receiving an unqualified rating have been appointed.

While the criteria for judicial appointments to "section 92 courts" is similar, the actual process varies from province to province. The most important difference is the stage at which the government uses an independent, non-political body to assess potential candidates. Ontario's process is almost identical to the federal government's. The Attorney-General compiles and updates a list of potential candidates, and then refers his nominations to the Ontario Judicial Council for evaluation. If the evaluation is positive, then the Ontario cabinet makes the appointment. By contrast, in Alberta the independent Alberta Judicial Council receives applications for provincial court judgeships. After reviewing the credentials of the applicants, the Judicial Council recommends individuals to the provincial Attorney-General. If he disagrees with the Council's recommendation, he is free to request another. If he concurs, he in turn recommends the candidate to the Cabinet, which then makes the appointment. (See Reading 4.2) The significance of the difference between these approaches lies in the extent to which they allow political influence. The Alberta government can only make appointments from a pool of candidates who have already been screened by an independent body, while the Ontario government is initially unrestricted, and only uses the independent Judicial Council to review the decisions that the Attorney-General has already made. The latter procedure clearly gives the party that forms the government a much freer hand to favour party members and supporters when making appointments to the bench.

### Politics versus Professionalism

The judicial selection process in all common law nations manifests a concern to increase the influence of judicial expertise and to reduce the degree of political influence. The most obvious and important manifestation of this is the practice of appointing rather than electing judges. The potential for undue political influence is also limited by review of nominations by independent

---

[2] See the remarks of Ed Ratushny, former Special Assistant to the then Minister of Judice, Otto Lang, in Allan Linden, ed., *The Canadian Judiciary* (Toronto: Osgoode Hall Law School), 1976, chapter 2.

bodies such as the Canadian Bar Association, and reduced still further by merit selection nominating committees such as exist in Alberta.

This emphasis on insulating judicial selection from partisan politics is premised on the assumption that judges and judging are not "political" in the way legislators and legislating are, and therefore that judges need not be politically accountable. Impartiality is an essential ingredient of judicial authority, and the selection process must be carefully structured to preserve the perception of the judges as impartial arbiters. A non-political selection process assumes a non-political court. While this assumption was certainly true in the common law tradition out of which Canada's legal system evolved, it became strained with the introduction of written constitutional law and its corollary, judicial review. For reasons discussed in chapters one and two, appellate courts charged with interpreting constitutionally entrenched restrictions on democratic legislatures affect public policy more directly, than do courts whose functions are limited to interpreting common law and statutes. To the extent that this occurs, the original rationale for excluding political considerations from the selection process is weakened. Not surprisingly, the politicization of judicial selection has developed the furthest in the United States, where judicial review first arose and where the fact of judicial "law-making" has long been acknowledged. In some Western states judges are actually selected through public elections. Even though American federal judges are still appointed, strong political forces shape these appointments, especially appointments to the Supreme Court. While these practices may seem unacceptable and even shocking by Canadian standards, they are consistent with a more "political" judicial function. It seems inevitable that courts that act politically will come to be treated politically. (See Reading 4.1)

The tensions between the policy-making and adjudicatory functions of judges are reflected in the different recruitment and selection processes for the three levels of courts in Canada. As trial courts concerned primarily with questions of fact, the "section 92 courts" do not allow for significant judicial discretion in the interpretation and enforcement of the law. Their function is almost exclusively the adjudication of disputes in the traditional sense. Accordingly, the judicial selection process for these courts is the least political in an ideological sense. (See Reading 4.2) Political patronage, however, still plays a role. A recent study of sentencing in Ontario found that after 25 years of Progressive Conservative rule, most "section 92" provincial court magistrates were past or present supporters of the Progressive Conservative party.[3]

In appointments to the "section 96 courts," there is less consensus on where to strike the balance. (See Reading 4.3) While everyone agrees that legal expertise and moral rectitude are prerequisites, there is still disagree-

---

[3] John Hogarth, *Sentencing as a Human Process* (Toronto: University of Toronto Press, 1971), p. 64.

ment over how to structure the selection process. Some advocate more reform in the direction of professionalism by expanding the role of the Canadian Bar Association (or some other "neutral" agency) from that of reviewing candidates already chosen by the government, to the actual recruitment of candidates. Critics question whether the Canadian Bar Association is sufficiently representative of Canadian society to be given such authority, and stress the importance of political accountability for bad as well as good appointments.

More importantly, considerations of judicial patronage are still a part of Canada's political system. While the degree of patronage considerations have varied from one Minister of Justice to the next, the Liberal Party has continued to use its judicial appointments to "section 96 courts" to reward its members and supporters. In 1982 this practice provoked an angry reaction by the newly elected Progressive Conservative party of Premier Grant Devine in Saskatchewan. Provincial Justice Minister Gary Lane was reported as accusing Ottawa of "stacking the courts with partisan appointees," and saying that he "wants more consultation on appointments, not just a phone call after the fact."[4]  To protest the Liberal's alleged abuse of patronage in judicial appointments in Saskatchewan, the Devine government has been reducing the number of section 96 judgeships by eliminating positions as they become vacant through death or retirement. By May, 1984, 10 judgeships had been eliminated in this manner, thus denying Ottawa the opportunity to make appointments. Because of these kinds of tensions, there have been occasional recommendations that the Constitutions be amended to return "section 96" appointments to the provinces. However, no one gives these proposals any serious chance of being adopted. The patronage benefits of "section 96 court" appointments are too valuable a political asset for the federal government to give up.

The trade-offs between professionalism and politics become even more pronounced in the appointment process for the Supreme Court of Canada. The politics of regionalism and dualism have helped to shape Supreme Court appointments from its beginning. Ontario has successfully insisted on equal "representation" with Quebec, even though it lacks any equivalent to Quebec's unique civil law system, which is the technical basis for Quebec's special status. The other major regions of the nation have followed suit, so that the Prairie Provinces, the Maritimes, and British Columbia each have an unwritten but recognized claim to one of three seats remaining after Quebec and Ontario are satisfied. The French-English dualism of Canadian political experience has manifested itself in the tradition of alternating the appointment of the Chief Justice between an anglophone and a francophone.[5]

---

[4] *Calgary Herald*, April 11, 1984.

[5] Prime Minister Trudeau's appointment of Brian Dickson as Chief Justice in March, 1984 violated this tradition, and may mark its end.

In addition to reflecting "the politics of federalism," appointments to the Supreme Court have also begun to be influenced by the "politics of rights," This development can be traced back to the appointment of Bora Laskin as Chief Justice in 1973. At this time the Supreme Court was being widely criticized by civil libertarian lawyers and law professors for its narrow and cautious interpretation of the 1960 Bill of Rights. Laskin had proven himself as the Court's leading civil libertarian and judicial activist since his appointment in 1970, but tradition dictated that the most senior judge in terms of service on the Court be chosen Chief Justice. Trudeau broke with this tradition and chose Laskin, much to the delight of the Court's civil libertarian critics. There were rumours that several of the more senior judges who had been passed over might resign in protest, but this never materialized. Subsequent appointments to the Supreme Court have been increasingly analyzed and interpreted on the appointee's "civil liberties record," and the enactment of the Charter of Rights in 1982 can only accelerate this trend.

Since the Victoria Charter of 1971, a majority of the provinces have been lobbying for increased provincial participation in the appointment process and constitutional entrenchment of the convention of regional representation. (See Reading 4.6) The wisdom of either of these proposals is not self-evident. While their advocates argue that these changes would guarantee a more "representative" court, critics have pointed out the disturbing implication to this argument. According to one, a provincial veto over Supreme Court appointments would amount to the rejection of "the basic principle of the judicial process: that Judges are judges of the issue, not partisans of the parties to the issue."[6] Such criticisms notwithstanding, the federal government seems prepared to accept these changes in the hope that they will increase the legitimacy and authority of the Supreme Court, thus making it a more effective vehicle of "intrastate federalism."

These conflicting trends in judicial selection in Canada during recent decades make it difficult to predict future developments. Based on the apparent decline in patronage appointments, Sir Robert Megarry has predicted further depoliticizaton of judicial selection in Canada along the lines of the British experience that he describes. (See Reading 4.3) But then British judges have never exercised judicial review of a federal constitution nor interpreted an entrenched Charter of Rights. British judges have thus never become embroiled in the "constitutional politics" or "politics of rights" that are indirectly encouraged by judicial review. These are the kind of considerations that lay behind Peter Russell's prediction that a principal effect of the Charter will be "its tendency to judicialize politics and to politicize the judiciary."[7] If events prove Rus-

---

[6] See the remarks of E.D. Fulton in Reading 4.3.

[7] See Reading 11.8.

sell right, political patronage considerations might well be replaced by political considerations of a more ideological nature.

# 4.1

## TWO MODELS: JUDICIAL RECRUITMENT
Paul Weiler

If our model of the judicial process is to be built around the assumption that the judge is primarily a policy-maker, a "legislator," the first problem that arises concerns the manner in which he gains access to the institutional position within which he acts, and the manner in which he can be held accountable for his actions in this position. The corresponding implications of the "adjudication" model can be stated very briefly: the most necessary prerequisite for judicial office is legal training which must be accompanied by some degree of moral probity and respectability; the judge does not campaign for office on the basis of a policy programme, but rather is selected for his legal ability, as adjudged primarily by his peers in the profession; once in office the judge has tenure for life until retirement age, subject only to removal for misbehaviour: the latter ground for "impeachment" should never include substantive results in particular decisions.

None of these propositions is at all self-evident, and, in fact, actual systems of judicial recruitment vary more or less from this ideal type. It should be evident, though, that the policy-making model of the judicial role logically demands a radical recasting of the system. First of all the process of preliminary recruitment must undergo substantial change. The reason is that the recruitment system that is generally used will substantially influence the type of candidates who come forward. For instance, a system oriented towards, and dominated by, lawyers will result in a different product than one oriented towards and run by politicians. This is so because the different practices operate at the conclusion of different "socialization processes," (whose development in turn they foster), affecting the values and viewpoints of the judges they recruit.

Rather than focusing on legal ability and training as the key elements in judicial qualifications, the policy-making model holds that a person's political programme and abilities should be most important. In fact, the logic of the

---

*Canadian Bar Review*, 1968, p.406. Reprinted with permission.

system demands that these be evaluated in some manner other than an apoliti-
cal appointment process. Instead, judges should either be directly elected, or
the various groups whose interests are affected by the judges' decisions should
have some more formalized and legitimized form of participation in the making of the selection. For instance, appointments to a body which decides
questions of constitutionality, in particular distribution of powers between
federal and provincial governments, should not be made by only one side of
this conflict of interests. In Canada, as the personal judgment of the members
of the Supreme Court is perceived as highly important in federalism cases,
there have been demands that the federal government share its exclusive
appointing power, at least for cases of this type. Indeed, there is no real
reason why judges on such a body should be legally trained at all (however
helpful this may be), since other abilities may be just as relevant (as, for
instance, is the case in Parliament). Perhaps a type of senatorial, second
chamber may be the best avenue for taking a second look at legislation and
evaluating its proper impact on federalism.

It is interesting, though, that while a more explicit theory of the policy-
making role of judges has led to open consideration of how their backgrounds
and attitudes will affect various interests in society, there have been important
countervailing forces at work. In the first place there have been strong pressures to overturn the traditional confinement of judicial appointment to members of the party having the choice. It has been suggested that this is inconsistent with the traditional "impartiality" of the judge, and in any event results
in the overlooking of much talent for legal craftsmanship. No attention is paid
to the fact that legislative policy-making is necessarily partisan and largely
unrelated to skilled legal technique. Of course, there is a big difference
between political service as a reason for appointment and political values and
programme as the criterion.

Secondly, there has been increased effort in recent years to bring the
organized bar into a position of strong influence in the appointment process.
This is designed to ensure an informed judgment of legal craftsmanship by a
prospective appointee's peers and thence, perhaps, to "depoliticize" completely the selection of judges. The analogy is drawn between judges and
scientists and it is claimed that only a lawyer's professional peers can evaluate
his technical ability. Yet this is not true if judges, unlike scientists, are
policy-makers who do not decide on the basis of objective, communicable,
neutral criteria. If so, a different role must be afforded to organized groups
such as the Canadian Bar Association, in order that it be legitimate. Both
"legalism" and close connexions with positions of power in the organized bar
have strong substantive (and usually conservative) policy overtones. Even
where the epitome of bar influence is achieved, through the "Missouri Plan,"
one can perceive the return of politics in organized group efforts to reach
positions of influence within its operations.

# 4.2

# PROVINCIAL JUDGE APPOINTMENTS

Wayne Kondro

In legal circles, an appointment to the bench — and the gossip over who the new judge will be — is taken as seriously as skiers take snow. Within weeks, another provincial judge will likely be appointed for Calgary. This has, of course, stirred the imaginations of local lawyers. One lawyer jokes that the appointments are a matter of throwing darts at a list of names posted on the wall. In fact, a far more formal, more complicated selection procedure is involved.

Unlike appointments to the Court Queen's Bench, which are made from Ottawa, the first step towards becoming a provincial judge is no different than the first step in becoming a short-order cook — filling out an application. But beyond this lie interviews, recommendations and the task of assessing a candidate's "judicial temperament." Only purists believe the character of a judge has no effect on the number of years a convicted person spends in jail or whether he walks.

Selections are made by the Judicial Council, which is comprised of Alberta's top three judges, the president of the Law Society and two lay (but political) appointees. The Council recommends an applicant to the attorney general, who in turn interviews the nominee. Finally, the provincial cabinet meets to ratify the selection.

The application seems to be a hazy, indistinct step in the procedure. In practice, the appointees have generally been earmarked for some time. The most recent appointee, Robert Dinkel, Calgary lawyer and campaign manager for the Tories in the 1975 and 1979 provincial elections, was singled out for judicial robes long before a tailor took his measurements. Dinkel has since astonished the community, establishing himself in a few months as a conscientious judge who "does his homework."

Lawyers say provincial appointments, generally, are not political. "Appointments at Queen's Bench are a lot more political than provincial court," say John James. Why? For a start, Alberta has been a one-party province for 50 years. Who is political if everyone is formerly Social Credit turned Tory? But the major factor is the reputation of provincial court itself. "Don't think for a moment that the judiciary is held in the highest esteem," one lawyer says.

In part, this is because provincial court is where 90 percent of all criminal cases are handled, and most are dispatched in a few minutes. Few participants lack at least one bitter memory of a case gone awry. For judges, the cases must soon resemble one another. As lawyer Don W. Macleod says: "After a

*Calgary Herald.* May 8, 1982, p.A7. Reprinted with permission.

while, there's not much they have not seen before.'' ''It's a rat race down there,'' another lawyer says. ''It's fine for the first 12 years, but when you've done it for 15 years it's got to be pretty soul-destroying.''

In the legal eye, provincial judges do not have the ''prestige'' accorded justices at higher levels like the Court of Queen's Bench. ''Law firms treat it as a court of secondary importance,'' James says. Calgary's top provincial judge, Hubert Oliver, says that the primary reason for this disrespect is probably the history of provincial court itself, which evolved from magistrate's court.

''We're still magistrates in the backrooms,'' Oliver says, ''We don't have the prestige, I don't think we ever will.''

This lack of prestige, some say, is a stumbling block to finding high-calibre judges. No one wants to be consigned to oblivion. ''There's nowhere to go beyond provincial court,'' one lawyer says, pointing out that only two judges, Frank Quigley and Allan Cawsey, have been able to ''escape'' to the Court of Queen's Bench.

But perhaps the biggest road-block to those considering an appointment has been the indifference of the provincial government. ''The government doesn't give them the money to properly run the courts or pay the judges,'' one lawyer says. The provincial judges recently received a pay hike — from $51,000 to $62,000, annually — but even now their wage falls well below that of Queen's Bench justice, which is around $82,000. In highly-paid Calgary, a ''good'' lawyer will draw $100,000-plus yearly. Lawyers being what they are, few are willing to slash their income and take a bench appointment. And as one judge notes, ''we don't have a pension plan.'' Judges are government employees. A secretary who began working for the province when she was 18 receives a far better pension than a judge appointed at 40.

Being underpaid and overworked leads to ''burnout,'' one source says, and after a while sickness and heart attacks increase. These many factors mitigate against a large number of high calibre applicants. ''In Calgary,'' says chief provincial judge Robert Kosowan, ''we might have difficulty in getting a quality application. They're not too interested.'' And picking a judge is difficult because ''everyone has a different idea of what makes a good judge,'' he adds.

Most believe a judge should have a background in criminal law. ''You don't like him learning at the bench at the expense of the poor bastards crawling out of the remand centre,'' one lawyer explains. But because of the effect a judge's character has on justice it is the more intangible qualities that many find the more important in determining who should be a judge. A judge ''always has to be a gentleman,'' lawyer Tony Managh says, or the court is reduced to ''day-to-day blood and guts and loses its ability to do what it's supposed to do — find the truth.''

. . . It would probably be impossibile for the Judicial Council to find a candidate with all these ideal qualities, especially when the bench is overworked, underpaid, and often treated with indifference. "But you never know," Park says, "until you see them on the bench. You can be pleasantly surprised or mildly disappointed." It's sort of like playing darts.

# 4.3

# A SYMPOSIUM ON THE APPOINTMENT OF JUDGES

G.M. Stirling

## I. The Chairman - D.C. McDonald

My own serious interest in the subject before us today arose several years ago when I was president of a provincial political association being that of the party in power federally. Those of us in Edmonton who wielded apparent power were determined to ensure that, within the existing system, such recommendations for appointments as flowed to the Minister of Justice from any responsible party officials did so after due and often detailed consideration by a co-ordinating committee of constituency association presidents and the like. It was not a bad attempt to sift and channel opinions through people who had, after all, been elected to positions of responsibility within the party, and it represented an attempt to operate the system democratically. During that period our views were remarkably effective with Ministers who preceded Mr. Turner as Justice Minister, because they were an attempt at rationality, given the rules of the game. At least one unsavoury experience during that period caused me to resolve to make an effort at some time in the future to further the cause of reform of the system of selection.

Around that time the longstanding struggle of some prominent figures in the Canadian Bar Association bore fruit with the creation in 1966 of the National Committee on the Judiciary and the announcement in 1967 by Mr. Trudeau, then Minister of Justice, that he had been consulting the Committee. Mr. Turner has continued this practice and deserves full credit for doing so. However, the manner in which that Committee works in practice and even its membership have, for five years, been a mystery. This mystery will be removed today, most informatively, by Mr. Stirling.

After five years I do not consider it unreasonable to provoke this Association, and our political leaders, into considering further reform. Let us not stand still

*Alberta Law Review*, 2 (1973), p. 279. Reprinted with permission.

in the search for better justice in all respects. Another reason, for keeping the spotlight on the question of selection of judges is that, if there is in the future to be a constitutionally entrenched Bill of Rights, the influence of judges on our politico-social development will be even more significant than it has been in the past, and therefore their qualifications are even more important. When word of this panel reached certain quarters it was suggested to me that matters of this kind ought not to be discussed in public, but only between gentlemen, in private. I disagree — the more so because laymen are prepared to discuss these matters publicly. . . .

## II. Remarks by G.M. Stirling, Q.C.

There is still some misunderstanding in the minds of some members of the Association as to the function of the National Committee on the Judiciary and I should make it clear to them at the outset that we have no part whatever in the selection or appointment of judges. By an arrangement made between the Association and the then Minister of Justice, this Committee was set up with the sole function of advising the Minister as to whether or not, in our opinion, a nominee was qualified for appointment to the Bench. I wish to make it quite clear that I have no authority to speak for the National Committee. Any views I may express are entirely my own.

I should explain the method of operation: The Minister submits to our Chairman the names of the parties that he is considering for appointment and these are circulated in a personal, confidential manner to each member of our Committee. I cannot, of course, inform you as to the manner in which the other members operate, but I assume that they adopt the same procedure that I do — that is, that I contact, by long distance telephone, friends or acquaintances in the particular locality where the nominee practices — and they, in a confidential manner, give me their opinion as to the qualifications of that particular nominee. On the basis of the information that I receive, I then notify the Chairman that, as far as I can ascertain, the party in question is well qualified, qualified, or not qualified, as the case may be, for judicial appointment. In most instances, I enlarge a little upon the report that is made in respect of each individual. Where there is a serious divergence of views expressed by the members of the Committee, the Chairman invariably requests a reassessment. The chairman then correlates the information that he receives and advises the Minister.

As you will appreciate, the Minister is not bound to be guided by the advice of our Committee, although I believe in all but one or two cases he has done so. To the best of my knowledge, there was only one instance in which the Minister was not prepared to accept the views of our Committee, and in another case, an appointment was made without reference to us. In both of these instances, the Chairman brought the views of our Committee firmly to the attention of the Minister with, I believe, a salutary effect. Whether or not our Committee is serving a useful purpose may best be judged by the results to date. There may be conflicting views in this regard but, as far as I can ascertain, the Minister has been very happy to have the assistance and support of the Committee and it seems to me it must be of great assistance to him in reaching his conclusion, independently, without having to submit entirely to political or other pressures.

The members of the Committee have endeavoured to act carefully and dispassionately in obtaining their reports and have not been influenced by local or regional pressures. If the existence of the Committee does not prove to be a deterrent to unwarranted or frivolous nominations, I firmly believe that, at the very least, the Minister must realize that every submission will be fearlessly scrutinized and reported upon, and that, if he should persist in disregarding the views of the Committee, he would be open to serious criticism from this Association — which we persist in claiming to be a very influential body. None of us would be naive enough to think that the names that are submitted are not prompted, in most instances, by some political consideration. However, as far as we have been able to ascertain, most of the appointments made by the present Minister of Justice and his predecessor have been very favourably received.

Those of us who have had the opportunity of reading some of the material that has been published in the United States dealing with this same problem have, I am sure, been impressed by the success of what is known as the "Missouri plan" and it seems to me that a modified form of this procedure could very well be followed in Canada. It might be desirable to suggest that, in every province, a standing independent commission should be set up composed of a Judge of the Superior Court, as Chairman, with reputable senior lawyers and representative laymen forming the membership, who would screen all qualified available lawyers in the province and submit a limited number of names to the Minister of Justice, and that the Minister would have the final selection, but would be bound to appoint one of the men named by the Commission. This would not prevent the Minister from requesting the Commission to consider the parties that he would wish to appoint, for political reasons, but it would have to be definitely provided and understood that no judge would be appointed who was not on the final slate submitted by the Commission, or subsequently approved by it. . . .

The National Committee on the Judiciary was a step in the right direction and, I trust, has now proved its worth — but, it is only a beginning — a first step — and the Association should now press on to inaugurate the setting up of Provincial Commissions for the purposes that I have outlined. The prerogative of appointment still rests with the Crown, as represented by the Minister of Justice, but the "Missouri-type plan" should prove to be the best method of securing the most competent and highly qualified judges.

### III. Remarks by W.H. Hurlburt, Q.C.

"The quality of our judges is the quality of our justice."

The quality of the legal profession, the police, the law and even the quality of our Court houses also affect the quality of justice. But it is true that the quality of our justice depends upon the quality of our judges. We should, therefore, do everything possible to see that the person who becomes a judge is the one who will best perform the judicial function. The propositon here advanced is that the qualifications of those available should be investigated carefully and that the investigation should not be affected by any consideration other than fitness for the judicial function.

In practice, judges are appointed to the superior, district and county courts in the expectation that they will perform the judicial function well. The evidence, however, is that extraneous factors are also considered. It is an advantage to have deserved well of the political party which forms the Government of the day. It is an advantage to have the support of the right members of that party. It is not clear that the standards of the Minister of Justice and of the Cabinet have always been and will always remain as high as they are today. It should not be difficult to choose between a system of appointments which has regard only to merit and a system which has regard to merit and something else. . . .

I propose that in each Province a nominating commission be established to suggest names to be considered for appointment by the appointing authority to the superior, district and county courts. I submit that the establishment of independent nominating commisssions to submit names to the appointing authority would be a major and significant reform in the interest of the public, the Bench and the Bar. . . .

## IV. Remarks by F.C. Muldoon, Q.C.

I think, in addressing myself to the topic of this panel discussion, that if no other panelist has been assigned or voluntarily undertaken the role of *bête noire*, it ought to be mine.

First then to be negative for a few minutes. There are a couple of relatively inarticulate, rather major premises which I think I perceive on the part of our profession, with which I fundamentally disagree. One of these premises is that when it comes to advising on matters of the judiciary, this voluntary association of the Canadian Bar, and the governing bodies of the provinces have some of the consecrated attributes of a kind of royal priesthood. I would not wish to belittle the voluntary good works of the bar, especially in advancing the work of law reform; but I sense still much of a kind of elitist euphoria which takes a heavy toll of our credibility when we purport to advise on the selection and appointment of judges. It was long ago that Mr. Justice Trueman of the Manitoba Court of Appeal said:

> . . . Lawyers in Canada are born in the purple and bred in the great traditions of the English Bar and Bench. Nothing of a lesser mould will content us.

One would think that such an attitude would long since have evaporated. I must state candidly that . . . our profession does manage to communicate such an impression to the general public. Before the Bar can make any influential and persuasive proposals about the selection and appointment of judges, without attracting the deepest suspicion of motives, it must first rid itself of the pomposity of elitism.

The other disagreeable major premise which becomes all too articulate when we speak or write of the judicial appointments in this land is that there is something sinister or scandalous about political partisanship. Perhaps the inefficiency (as that word is understood in a commercial or industrial sense) — the inherent inefficiency of democracy bothers us. However, unless we were to subvert it, the great hallmark of democratic government is the right of the people to select, from among contending partisan political adversaries, who shall govern. I assume that I am in the company of many fellow-lawyers who, from time to time, bear the worry or even the fear about how much popular affection and support our civilized and still useful democratic institutions ultimately would enjoy in time of dire crisis. I think most of us have recently pondered that from time to time. Without politicians engaged in partisan competition, we should have no democratic institutions — or else they would be blighted, bland ones of extremely short half-life. And yet, when it comes to the sensitive subject of judicial appointments, we of the Bar seem to join in the all too general distaste for, and even mockery of, politicians and political processes, including political appointments. This, it seems to me is very counter-productive in practice, in theory, and in ethic.

One of the arguments presented against the political input to the selection of judicial personnages is a strained analogy to government seeking and retaining the services of eminent scientists. In obtaining the best scientific talent, government casts about for the opinions of other scientists, and politicians recognize that they themselves are not particularly qualified to assess scientific merit. One does not devalue the imagination, innovativeness and intellect necessary in scientific pursuits, when one observes that judicial performance is perforce different. A judge leads, in his proper sphere, a very public life indeed, and exercises his judicial functions and powers in, and on behalf of the body politic. In this sense the judge is, and must be, a kind of politician even though he does not campaign to remain in office and he must always and everywhere be scrupulously non-partisan. I think that we, as a profession, have manifested disdain toward the political selection and appointment of judges, not because the appointments have been universally bad — they haven't been that way at all. Most are, I think, quite felicitous — but it is because we as an organization constitute a kind of establishment without as much influence as it desires. As a well known lawyer-politician recently said whimsically, but indicating a deep appreciation of human behaviour: "Lack of power corrupts, and absolute lack of power corrupts absolutely." The majority of appointments are then, perhaps surprisingly, apt because, in Canadian society, there is probably no more broadly based institution than a political party in power. It is surely a much more broadly representative institution than the Canadian Bar Association can ever hope to be. In my view, political input to the process is proper and ought not to be eliminated, even if it could be eliminated. . . .

## V. Remarks by the Honourable E.D. Fulton, P.C., Q.C.

My remarks will be confined to the method and problems of appointment of judges by the federal authority only, since this is the field with which I am familiar; and, whatever may be agreed as the method or principles governing selection and appointment by one level of government will be capable, at least in principle, of application to an exercise by, the other. Within that context, I should like to deal with three aspects of the problem:

1. The problems inherent in the proposals for a system of nomination by other than the responsible political authority.

2. Current proposals as to the method of selection and appointment to the Supreme Court of Canada.

### 1. Responsibility for Selection and Appointment

The issue here seems to be the following:

(a) Should the initial responsibility for selecting appointees to the Bench be transferred to a formally appointed non-governmental body who will select and submit a panel or panels of names of persons considered qualified, from amongst whom the Minister should appoint one?

(b) Or should the initial responsibility continue to rest with the Minister, to canvass the field of qualified persons, and to discuss the names of the proposed appointee with a non-governmental body for advice as to whether or not he is in fact well-qualified?. . . .

One of the back ground papers to which we have been referred speaks of the "faceless mask of the Cabinet confronting the public in judicial selection." This is in the context of the desirability of a more direct responsibility or accountability for the quality of judicial appointments — particularly if they are bad. How much more faceless the mask would be, and how much less accountable the Minster or the Cabinet would be, if there were interposed a mechanism by means of which he or she would say: "But we had no responsibility in the matter — we simply acted on recommendations that were made to us, and which we were bound to accept." Those who advocate the system of nominations by an outside *independent, non-political* body, from which nominations the appointments must be made, say, "the only way to avoid the imposition of political considerations is to have such a non-political organization submit lists of eligible appointees."

In reply, we may ask: "Is it really to be supposed that politics is confined to governments and to political parties?" There is politics in every organization that has elected officers and an elected executive. So is there an "establishment" in every organization. The establishment can be changed — and is changed every so often — by the votes of the members of the organization. That is the process of politics. In this sense there is politics in the Bar Assocaition, there is politics in the Law Society; there is also an establishment in each of them. There has to be, because again by its very nature there is politics in every organization that has an elected executive.

But in our system of democracy there is only one organization that is responsible to all the people — that is the Government, through Parliament. And it is the country generally, not just the lawyers, that suffers if bad appointments are made. Of what benefit then is it to substitute the politics of a non-responsible body — that is, not responsible to the general electorate — for that of a body that is so responsible? What penalties will attach to the Canadian Bar Association or the Law Society or any other "non-political" organization or body — if an appointment they have initiated turns out to be wrong?

So I suggest that unless and until we decide to change the system of responsible Parliamentary democracy, under which the Government is responsible through Parliament to the people for all its actions, the responsibility for judicial appointments should be left where it now lies. . . .

### 2. Appointments to the Supreme Court of Canada

The third matter which I want to put before you is the proposal, placed before the last session of the Federal-Provincial conference on the Constitution of the Prime Minister and provincial Premiers, as to a new method of appointing judges of the Supreme Court of Canada. While no legislation has yet been introduced or even forecast, it appears that this proposal was accepted in principle at the Conference and it is a matter to which I believe this Association should give very serious and urgent consideration. If I understand the proposal correctly, it can be summarized by saying that first, there would be a formal requirement that every future appointment to the Supreme Court of Canada would require the approval of the Government of the province from the Bar of which the appointment is made; second, that this approval would have to be formally sought and formally given; and third, that in the event of disagreement there would be a formal but fantastic process of arbitration (which has been described as a ping-pong process) by which the disagreement may be resolved.

Now this is not an application of the principle of consultation, which was discussed earlier. In my view, it is not even a mere extension of it. It is a radical change in the power of, and responsibility for, appointment; for under this system no appointment could be made without, in effect, the formal approval and sanction of the Government of the Province, obtained either directly in the first instance or indirectly through the arbitration process. I will not do more than mention one or two of the obvious questionable features of this suggestion. One is the matter of the dignity of the Bench: What is to be the lot and position of a Judge appointed after formal objection to his qualifications or suitability has been made by one of the parties to his appointment, resolved only by a process of arbitration? And it should be noted that this goes further than the United States system, where the President appoints and the Senate may or may not ratify; here the Province would become an appointing power. Another is the question of further erosion of the Federal power; but that may perhaps be more probably debated in the purely constitutional forum, rather than in one concerned with the quality and integrity of the judiciary.

The main point which I wish to raise here is one which concerns the basic principle of the judicial process; that judges are judges of the issue, not partisans of the parties to the issue. It seems inescapable that the imposition of such a system as outlined would, by necessary implication if not by direct enactment, involve acceptance of the principle that judges of the highest court in Canada are chosen not because they are expected to be good judges of the law, but because they are acceptable as partisans or representatives of a position or interest.

Admittedly, it is necessary to ensure fair representation of all regions of Canada on the Supreme Court. There are omissions, now; if desired, this can be rectified by a simple amendment increasing the number of judges — perhaps the workload alone would justify this. Admittedly also, it is essential to ensure a proper proportion of judges to deal with issues involving the Civil Law arising in the Province of Quebec. There is provision now for a minimum number of Judges of the Supreme Court of Canada from that Province; if it is felt to be insufficient, this can be rectified by a simple amendment increasing the number of Judges in the Supreme Court of Canada who are required to be — or have been — members of the Bar of that province trained in the Civil Law. Admittedly also, the Supreme Court of Canada will be increasingly concerned with constitutional issues, but if it is felt that the Court does not now contain a sufficient number of Judges trained and experienced in constitutional law, that weakness, if there be one, can be rectified by the process of insuring the appointment of those trained in constitution law.

By a combination of all or some of these methods if there are felt to be present weaknesses in these regards, due assurance could be given of a sufficiency of judges familiar with the regional, legal, and cultural problems peculiar to the areas from which they come, which are indeed a part of the very fabric of the kind of issues which arise in our country. But surely the basic principle is important, and worth maintaining, that they approach these issues, whether arising by way of private litigation or constitutional dispute, as judges of the law and Constitution, not as spokesman for, or representatives of, a particular region or interest. . . .

## VI. Remarks by the Honourable Sir Robert Megarry

. . . First, I must make a brief disclaimer. Naturally I shall say nothing that comes from any confidential source; I merely recount what is generally known or believed by the English Bar, or is the public domain. That said, I may begin with the formal details of appointment to the Bench in England. It is briefly told. There are three main categories of judges, and I give the figures in round numbers. First, there is the High Court and above (Court of Appeal and House of Lords), with a total of 100. Second, there are 125 county court judges; and third, there are 50 stipendiary magistrates. That makes a total of 275. All are appointed by the Crown on the Advice of the Lord Chancellor or, in the case of the Court of Appeal and House of Lords, the Prime Minister. The responsibility for this advice is individual and not collective; it is not a Cabinet matter. The Prime Minister is generally believed to consult closely with the Lord Chancellor before making his recommendations, and so it is the Lord Chancellor who in substance is the great appointer to the Bench.

The Judicature Act, 1925, s.12, replacing provisions in the Judicature Act, 1873, and the Act of Settlement, 1700, provides that judges of the Supreme Court (that is, the High Court and Court of Appeal) hold office "during good behaviour, subject to a power of removal by the Crown" on an address presented to His Majesty by both Houses of Parliament." No English judge has ever been removed under these provisions, but in 1830 Sir Jonah Barrington, a judge of the Court of Admiralty in Ireland, was removed for misconduct and malversation in office. That is all. County court judges and stipendiary magistrates are in effect removable by the Lord Chancellor for inability or misbehaviour. I know of only one such removal. In 1851 Judge Ramshay had become very eccentric indeed, and after a hearing he was removed from office. From his chambers in the Temple he continued to send letters to court officials asserting that he was still the judge, and adjourning the court, but all to no avail; and quo warranto proceedings against his successor failed. . . . So we have little experience in this field that would assist you. At the same time, it is said that there have been some instances — a very few — in which the Lord Chancellor and others have encouraged a resignation; but that is a little different. Other and more subtle forces, and not least, association with the Bar, and the influence of the Inns of Court, do much to sustain the judge in England on the difficulties of his office.

Retirement? This is now mandatory at 75 for High Court judges and above, at 72 for county court judges, and at 70 for stipendiary magistrates. Machinery for discipline? Nil. Training? Nil. And so on that I seem to be of very little use to you. Yet I think that we have been merely looking at the tip of the iceberg. We must look a little below the surface if we want to get a balanced picture. Let me mention, as briefly as may be, seven factors which help to show the realities.

1. There are relatively few appointments to be made. With a population for England and Wales approaching 50 million, there are a little less than 100 judges of High Court level and above to do all the trial and appellate work; and that comes to two judges per million of population. At the same level, Canada had roughly five and half times as many judges per million population, and about three times as many at the county court level; if one ignores the size of the population and takes absolute figures, yours are of the order of 250 and 160 as compared with our 100 and 125. . . .

2. The field from which appointments are made is much smaller in England than in Canada. Three main factors play their part; specialization of function, specialization of subject-matter, and age. The first lead primarily refers to the division of our legal profession into barristers and solicitors. Of a total legal profession of some 28,000 or 29,000, less than about 2,600 are practising barristers. With certain exceptions at the lower levels, all appointments are made from the Bar, the branch of the profession that lives out its professional life in the courts. There is then the further division of barristers into Q.C.'s and juniors. Of the 2,600 practising barristers, rather less than 300 are Q.C's; and appointments to the High Court are nearly always made from among practising Q.C.'s. In fact, the field of choice is smaller than that, because after discounting those who are approaching retirement or have not been very successful, probably there are some 150 or 200 who do the great bulk of the work; and it is from them that the appointments will be made.

In England, of course, silk is a reality and not merely an honour. A junior who takes silk takes his professional life in his hands, for he has to give up all his smaller work, including settling pleadings, and, being unable to appear in court without a junior, must confine himself to the bigger cases; and the number of these is limited. A junior does not lightly apply for silk, and silk is not to be had for the asking. It is believed that something like four out of five applications fail. Solicitors play an important part in this field. Nobody will be appointed a Q.C. unless many solicitors, on a basis of trial and error, have acquired a faith in his abilities as an advocate; and no Q.C. will get much work unless many more solicitors have faith in his forensic abilities at the higher level of silk. The collective judgment of solicitors thus plays a large part in selecting the field of possible candidates for the Bench. Solicitors judge from knowledge and experience, too; unlike the lay client, they will not confuse a flashy but incompetent display with a restrained but skilled performance.

I need say little about specializaton of subject-matter. Barristers tend to specialize in work which usually finds its way into one or other of the three Divisions of the High Court, Chancery, Queen's Bench, and Probate, Divorce and Admiralty (soon to become the Family Division); and within those broad divisions there are often specialist sub-divisions. This, of course, narrows the field. A Queen's Bench judge dies; who will be appointed in his place? You may be sure that it will not be a Q.C. who normally practises in the Chancery Division.

As for age, there is in practice a limited range for appointment. Looking at recent years, the average age for appointment to the High Court comes out at about 52 for the Probate, Divorce and Admiralty Division, 53 or 54 for the Queen's Bench Division, and 55 or 56 for the Chancery Division. The youngest age at which anyone has been appointed to the High Court this century is 42 and the oldest 65 (though I cannot forbear from mentioning that Sir Salathiel Lovell began his five years in the Court of Exchequer when he was 89; but that was in 1708). The normal effective range of ages is from the late forties to the late fifties. Again, this restricts the field of choice.

Let me take a melancholy but practical example. Suppose that, overwhelmed by the hospitality that I have been receiving here (and that is far from a remote possibility), I keel over and die before your eyes. A successor to my seat in the Chancery Division will then have to be appointed. Well, this does not look very difficult. In the *Law List* there is a list of the Q.C.'s who practise specially in the Chancery Division. There are 28 names there. Some of the more senior are over the age at which appointment is probable; others are too young or too inexperienced. There are other considerations, too, and in the end probably most lawyers who have any familiarity with the Chancery Division would agree upon the handful of names, perhaps two, three or even four, from which the appointment would almost certainly be made. The Chancery Division is small, with only ten judges, and the field is more open in the Queen's Bench Division, with some 45 judges. But even so, in most cases the question must come down to one of choosing from a very small number of possibilities; and this must usually make the process of appointment far less complex than it must be in some other jurisdictions.

3. Most judges have had some trial runs on the Bench before being appointed. Your chairman touched on this a short while ago when he mentioned what Henry Cecil had said in his book. It is common for a potential judge to be appointed a Commissioner of Assize for a period of four, six or eight weeks at a time; and during this period he has the temporary status of a High Court judge. Again, many a barrister sits three or four times a year as a Recorder, or Chairman or Deputy Chairman of Quarter Sessions, spending perhaps some twenty days a year as a judge in criminal cases too serious for the magistrates and not serious enough for a High Court judge. Although the prime purpose of these activities is to get the work done, there is great value in the incidental result that it becomes known what sort of a judge the barrister is likely to make if he is appointed to the Bench. Nobody can really tell how anyone will behave as judge until he has been seen performing as a judge. Being a judge is so different from being an advocate, not least in that the advocate knows which side he is on. There have been many instances of Commissioners of Assize demonstrating their suitability for judicial office, and in other instances demonstrating just the opposite, for a wide variety of reasons. Men react to the stresses of the Bench in remarkably different ways. Like the elephant, the judicial quality is easily recognizable but very difficult to define; and so this is one of the fields in which "Try it and see" becomes an important adage. By way of footnote, I may add that until 1933 Scotland even had a trial run for each newly appointed judge of the Court of Session *after* his appointment; but this had become a mere formality.

I would attach very little value to any formal training for judicial office. I do not see how you can effectually train a man to be a judge. You can, of course, teach a man the technique of driving a car; but it is the man and not his training that predominantly determines whether he uses wisely and tolerantly the skills that he has acquired, or whether he is a foolish and aggressive driver. The judicial quality is something that the man has or has not got; and whatever training may do to improve the native quality, it cannot graft a judicial temperament on to barren stock.

4. The Lord Chancellor, the great appointer of judges, is an active judge himself. He is a Cabinet Minister, of course, but he is far from being that alone. He is necessarily someone of a sufficient judicial stature to enable him to preside over the House of Lords, and command the respect of the other law lords. He does not merely sit in an office and in Parliament, but lives and moves in the world of law. He has long known many of the senior members of the Bar, and of course in the House of Lords he listens to many arguments. There is, therefore, much that he can decide upon his own first-hand knowledge, and not merely upon report.

5. Judges live and work with the Bar. If you are near the Inns of Court in London at lunch-time on any day during term, you will see that at about 1 p.m. most of the judges of the High Court and Court of Appeal and many of the practising members of the Bar are on their way to the halls of their Inns of Court for lunch. Each judge will be a bencher of his Inn, and the senior Q.C.'s and some of the senior juniors (you will know what I mean) will also be benchers. All lunch together on a basis of equality, whether judge, silk or junior. Seniority as a bencher depends on seniority of election, and is unaffected by judicial office. The atmosphere is one of ease and friendliness; and informal though this is, it has a constitutional importance. It is in these regular and informal contacts that we find so much of value rubbing off on each other. It tends to prevent the judges from becoming pompous and overbearing; and not only is the judge constantly reminded of his own days at the Bar, but also the silk or junior find himself absorbing overtones of the Bench. A civilizing atmosphere spills over into the courts, and sweetens the acerbities of the contest. This association contributes towards a firmness of moral tone throughout the administration of the law, and provides a nursery for the future judge.

6. It is rare for an appointment to the High Court to be refused. The prevailing tone is that it is of paramount importance to the country that the standard of the Bench should be maintained at the highest possible level, and that if a barrister is offered an appointment to the Bench, this shows that the Lord Chancellor thinks him the most suitable person to be appointed. Whatever, the individual feelings may be, the need to maintain the standard of the Bench impels acceptance. . . .

7. Last, and in some ways the most important, is the fact that 25 years ago politics dropped almost completely out of appointment to the English Bench. The effect of political considerations in making judicial appointments is certainly not something to be exclusively attributed to Lord Halsbury while he was Lord Chancellor, interesting though some of his appointments were. Long before his time, and for many years after it, the general belief was that a career in Parliament was a powerful aid to appointment to the Bench; and there were many appointments that gave colour to this belief. The normal road to many of the highest offices in the law, too, was not by successful service as a puisne judge but by becoming Attorney-General or Solicitor-General. The

Attorney-General of the day was regarded as having something of a right to the Chief Justiceship of the Common Pleas when it fell vacant. It was his "pillow," and when in 1880 that office in effect became merged in the Chief Justiceship of the Queen's Bench as the Lord Chief Justiceship of England, some regarded that office as having become the pillow. Later events tended to support that view; and although the emphasis on politics was probably lessening, down to the war of 1939-45 the position was substantially unaltered.

The change can almost be pinpointed. On January 21, 1946, Viscount Caldecote, C.J., a former Solicitor-General, Attorney-General and Lord Chancellor, resigned, and Lord Goddary, a law lord, was appointed Chief Justice in his place. Lord Goddard was a lawyer through and through, with no more than a faint brush with politics in his youth; and he had moved steadily up from the King's Bench to the Court of Appeal and then to the House of Lords. Within a fortnight, on February 1, 1946, Sir Donald Somervell, a former Tory Attorney-General, was appointed to a seat in the Court of Appeal, even though the Government in power from 1945 to 1951 was a Labour government. These two appointments seem to have set the seal on the change. Politics were out, and such politics as were in were bi-partisan. During the six years of the Labour government, Lord Jowitt, as Lord Chancellor, was responsible for the appointment of over half the entire Bench; and yet not until towards the end of the time did he make any appointment to the High Court from the M.P.'s supporting his own party, and then only one. In 1958 Lord Goddard retired as Chief Justice, and despite political contenders, the appointment made was of Lord Parker, a Lord Justice with no political career. When Lord Parker retired this year, again the appointment as Chief Justice went to a non-political member of the Court of Appeal, Lord Widgery; and each of these appointments was made while a Tory government was in power. With that unanimity of performance, there is good reason to believe that each of the two major political parties is at least agreed on the proper approach to judicial appointment today.

I am not saying that to have been in politics is today an actual disqualification for appointment to the Bench; but I do say that to be an active supporter of the party in power no longer seems to be an asset of any real weight. Experience in public affairs, especially in Parliament, may be a factor of great value in moulding a man's character and giving him breadth of vision; the Bench would be the poorer without some who have this background. But it has ceased to matter much whether the candidate for appointment is a supporter or opponent of the party in power. With the withering of partisan claims to appointment has come another change. For over twenty years nearly all appointments to the Court of Appeal and House of Lords have been by way of promotion from the High Court, and not *per saltum* from the Bar. A vacancy in the Court of Appeal will be filled from the ranks of the High Court judges whose judicial abilities are known. No longer is there the problem of trying to guess the probable performance of a giant of the Bar as a Lord Justice of Appeal, and trying to compare that guess with a reasoned estimate, based on experience of how a High Court judge of, say, five years standing would do in the Court of Appeal.

Those, then, are the seven factors that I wanted to put before you. Perhaps I may add some comments on two final matters. First, there is the actual process of appointment to the Bench. On this, I speak with no certain knowledge, but on guesses which I hope are intelligent. The Lord Chancellor's Office is in effect a small government department, with a staff of some two dozen lawyers. By a mysterious system of osmosis and grape-vines, I would expect the Lord Chancellor and his staff to have a pretty good idea about all that is going on in the legal world. If at any given moment you were to ask the Lord Chancellor whether X or Y or Z is likely to appointed a judge when a vacancy occurs, and he were willing to answer, I should expect him to be able to say, then and there, that X is a strong candidate, that Y is a possible, and that Z is a nonstarter. You will remember how small the English Bar is, how few English silks there are, and how small the country is. Only a very small part of the population lives more than 250 miles from London.

Despite the background of knowledge of the Bar, the Lord Chancellor may be expected to consult the Chief Justice and the Master of The Rolls (who presides over the Court of Appeal) when a vacancy occurs; and if it is in the Chancery Division or the Probate, Divorce and Admiralty Division, he may well consult the head of that Division as well. Whether those consulted ever have or take the initiative, suggesting that A or B is better than X and Y who are under consideration, I cannot say. I should doubt if there are rules or even conventions; I should expect everything to be highly informal or, if you like, very English. When the Courts Act, 1971, comes into force there will be many changes, some of them important; but I do not think that they will alter the essence of what I have been saying.

Secondly, perhaps I may be mildly historical. On at least some views it is possible to discern four stages in the part played by politics in appointments to the Bench, each stage merging into the next. In the first stage, party politics may play so large a part that some of those appointed fall short of the standards that the office demands. In the second stage, political claims do no more than give some preference amongst those who are fully qualified for appointment; of three candidates with not much to choose between them, the supporter of the party in power will be preferred to the political opponent or the politically inert. Without being unduly cynical, it is possible to observe that there are times when a government may prefer the sight of a political opponent sitting non-politically on the Bench to the sight of him in vigorous opposition in the legislature. The third stage comes when the political opponent has prospects of appointment which, other things being equal, are on a par with those of a political supporter, or nearly so. At the fourth stage politics have ceased to play any real part. Appointments are made very largely from the ranks of those who have made law and not politics their life.

As I indicated, England seems to have reached this fourth stage in 1946. Where Canada is I must leave you to say; if I had to guess, from what I have read and heard recently my surmise would be that it is somewhere about the third stage, or not far short of it. I repeat that I would not suggest that politics should disqualify. In considering suitability for the Bench a strong case can be made for the wide-ranging span of a statesman's career as against the restricted vision of a technically superb lawyer; the old jibe is that law sharpens the mind by narrowing it. But not all politicians are statesmen, nor do all fine lawyers have minds that are closed to the wider issues of life — not by a long chalk. In the end, the question, as in so many fields, is one of balance, within the national genius. . . .

# 4.4

# FRANK ANGLIN JOINS THE BENCH: A STUDY OF JUDICIAL PATRONAGE, 1897-1904

James G. Snell

Though of intrinsic interest and importance, historical evidence of the process of judicial appointment in Canada is often difficult to uncover. However, in the case of Frank Anglin, who eventually became Chief Justice of Canada (1924-1933), there is a good deal of material in some of the country's archives. The story that these records reveal is one of interest, involving a Toronto lawyer with a powerful compulsion to become a judge, an important minority group that was able to voice effectively its demands and by whose needs Anglin was able to profit, and a federal government coping with various pressures and claims as it dealt with the requirements of the judicial system and of the Liberal Party. After appointment to the Supreme Court of Ontario in 1904 and to the Supreme Court of Canada in 1909, Anglin J.'s service on the bench was noteworthy. Yet it is the process by which Anglin joined the judiciary that is fascinating, in its revelation of both the strength of his own ambition and the complexity of pressures and criteria by which such appointments were made.

Frank Anglin was the oldest son of a middle-rank member of the federal Liberal Party. His father, Timothy Warren Anglin, had been a Member of the Legislative Assembly in New Brunswick (1861-1882), a Speaker of the House of Commons, and had largely based his political career on being a representa-

*Osgoode Hall Law Journal*, 18:4 (1980), p. 664. Reprinted with permission.

tive of Irish Catholics in Canada. It is not surprising, therefore, that Frank Anglin became interested in following in his father's footsteps, both as a politician and as a ethno-religious representative. In fact, the young Anglin was quick to begin acting as a spokesman in Irish Catholic issues. As early as 1889 he spoke out publicly about Irish Catholic needs and it was not long before the young Toronto lawyer was addressing the public and the leaders of the Liberal Party concerning the Irish Catholic perspective of the Manitoba schools question and other matters. . . .

. . . In a period when political partisanship was rampant and when patronage consideration dominated government appointments in all spheres, Anglin could not hope to be named to a judgeship on the basis of merit alone. In fact, of twenty-one extant letters from Anglin discussing the prospects of a position on the bench, not one mentions any qualifications which might be described by "merit." Instead, two arguments were put forward as the grounds for his expectations of an appointment. The first, Anglin's claims on the basis of his past services to the Liberal Party, was not frequently mentioned but seems always to have been understood. What Anglin concentrated on, and what he hoped would make his insistent requests stronger than those of others, was his standing as a leader within the Irish Catholic community of Ontario. In September 1897, at age thirty-two, he warned the Prime Minister about the "strong attempt that is being made at present and will be kept up, to inflame the minds of Irish Catholics in this Province against the Liberal Party upon the ground of discrimination against Catholics by the Governments both here and in Ottawa in the matter of appointments." Of the sixty-four junior and district County Court judgeships, only five were held by Roman Catholics, and only one Catholic held a Superior Court judgeship. Such underrepresentation of Catholics should clearly be rectified, the lawyer advised, if the Government wished to calm discontent among Irish Catholics and to retain their electoral support.

As proof of his claims to be a representative of the Irish Catholic community, Anglin summoned the support of a large number of clerical and lay leaders. At various times the Archbishops of Toronto, Ottawa and Kingston wrote to the Prime Minister and the Minister of Justice on Anglin's behalf; so too did the members of Parliament for Wellington North, Hastings East and Huron West, the Bishops of Alexandria, Peterborough and Pembroke, and parish priests. Even Anglin's mother added her support to the cause, by writing her late husband's colleague, David Mills, who was at that time the Attorney-General of Canada. Time and time again during the several years following 1897 Frank Anglin and his friends voiced their demands for greater representation of Roman Catholics on the bench.

As much as the support for Anglin came from all sections of Ontario, so too did the specific judgeships being sought. First, the Toronto barrister applied for an anticipated vacancy on the Carleton County Court. When this opening did not materialize as soon as expected, Anglin (while carefully maintaining his claims to such a position) turned his attention to the Perth County Court. . . .

Despite such efforts the Toronto lawyer must have been frustrated to see both the Stratford and Ottawa posts go to others.

Yet, perseverence was clearly one of Frank Anglin's more developed traits. Tactfully acknowledging that the Carleton and Perth appointments had been wise he proceeded to advance his aspirations for a prospective vacancy in Cornwall. . . .

It is an indication of how much Anglin was attracted to the bench that early in 1898, while asserting his claims to the Cornwall post, he diverted his attention briefly to British Columbia. The existing opening on the Supreme Court of that province could be ably filled by himself, he suggested to cabinet members. There were no Roman Catholics on the British Columbia bench, where formerly there had been two; there were no English-speaking Catholics on any Superior Court west of Toronto (except one in the Klondike). Furthermore, the Government clearly had the power to name an outsider to such a post (Anglin sent a memorandum to the Solicitor General on this point) and while the British Columbia bar was opposed to an outsider as Chief Justice, the same was not true of a puisne judge. Here, he suggested, was an easy way to deal with Ontario Catholic resentment regarding discrimination. Anglin's daydreams about the west coast were quickly shattered when the Justice Minister reported ''insuperable difficulties.''. . . .

. . . A year later, in mid-1899, Anglin returned to the fray. His hopes for the County Court judgeship in Cornwall were again brought to the Prime Minister's attention and several letters of clerical support from across the province were forwarded to Ottawa. Anglin also hastened to advise Laurier that if the persistent rumours of John Costigan's appointment to the post were accurate, many Liberal supporters would be alienated and no strength would be added to the Party. The Prime Minister replied by informing the applicant that no further letters from clerics were needed — what Anglin lacked was local suppprt. Quickly, the Toronto lawyer responded that such backing was difficult for an outsider and that there were political advantages to meeting the wishes of Anglin's allies, since their influence extended across Ontario and was more important than that of a few local politicians.

Meanwhile, Anglin adopted a new tactic. If the Government could be persuaded to bring in a measure providing County Court judges with a liberal pension on retirement at age seventy-five, a number of vacancies would be created; voluntary retirement could not be anticipated otherwise. He found it necessary to add that he expected to benefit directly from the proposed retirements.

No such legislation was forthcoming, and the Toronto barrister was soon back to familiar themes although the setting was new. . . .

If Anglin was willing to bow out of the competition in Lincoln County, he clung tenaciously to his dreams of the Cornwall bench. When he heard of rumours to name [J.R.] O'Reilly to the United Counties Court, the Toronto lawyer reacted in a proprietary fashion. The Cornwall judgeship had been promised to Anglin and any appointment other than his own would solidify his feeling and conviction of being badly treated in the matter. The Prime Minister was plainly apprised of Anglin's sense of indignation.

As the Toronto lawyer's missives became more emotional, so too did Sir Wilfrid Laurier's. Declaring complete ignorance of anything touching on the Cornwall appointment, the Prime Minister retaliated, complaining of "a peremptory tone" and "a stand and deliver attitude" on the part of the aspiring judge. When letters of support for Anglin's appointment (this time to the High Court) flowed in during the summer of 1900, the Prime Minister's exasperation became particularly evident. To one of Anglin's Toronto backers, Laurier said:

> If you really want Mr. Anglin to be appointed a judge of the High Court, and if you are a friend of his, I would advise you to tell him that if he continues to badger me with letters from all parts of the province, I will refuse point blank to appoint him.

The message was certainly plain.

Moreover, the nature of the message must have reached Frank Anglin soon after, for the correspondence from and about the Toronto barrister began to change quite noticeably. Within days he had offered to help in any way during the election campaign, asking for nothing in return. He also hastened to point out that while letters of recommendation had been written favouring Anglin's nomination to the High Court, he himself had refrained from applying. He had informed the Prime Minister of recent proposals to lead Ontario Catholic Liberals away from the Party and of his own refusal to head such a movement. Nevertheless, Anglin reminded both Laurier and the Minister of Justice that English-speaking Catholic Liberals in Ontario and the West were dissatisfied with the Government. . . .

By fall of 1901 the barrage of Anglin's claims for consideration and letters of support had ceased. It was three more long years before he finally received his reward. In 1904 Anglin, at the age of thirty-nine, was named to the High Court of Ontario (Exchequer Division), where he performed quite ably before moving on in 1909 to the Supreme Court of Canada. . . . Frank Anglin himself enjoyed such praise, but in 1909 he seemed at least as pleased by what he assumed to be his appointment as an English-speaking Catholic representative. He thanked the Prime Minister on behalf of "our people" and pointed out that his promotion had broken the constraints of the previous tradition that only Quebec Catholics were named to the Supreme Court of Canada.

While the records reveal no evidence of the Government's reasoning behind Anglin's promotion in 1909, there is no doubt that his earlier pleas as an Irish Catholic spokesman were accepted by members of the Laurier Government. David Mills, Minister of Justice 1897-1902, in particular was quite sympathetic to complaints of Roman Catholic underrepresentation on the bench, and on several occasions he expressed his opinion both about the general problem and about Anglin's desire for appointment.

Soon after becoming Minister of Justice, Mills was warned about those who presented themselves as "professional Irish Catholics," but he professed a belief that such men were few in number. A true liberal philosophically, Mills proclaimed that no man would be barred from the public service because of his religion and hoped that ultimately religious differences would ultimately fade away as grounds for selection. He was quickly ensnared, however, in the standard dilemma of reverse discrimination: in order to prove that religious denominations were treated equally and fairly, it would be necessary to single out those churches which were underrepresented and to appoint several of their members.

> I am certainly very anxious to see that the Liberals of the Catholic faith are treated with perfect fairness, and I shall do my best to bring about this result, and I am sure that in this aim I shall have the support of my colleagues, but to make it the subject of frequent discussions in the newspapers certainly will not facilitate the work . . . . It will be singularly unfortunate to have any class of a community feel that their religion was a barrier to personal promotion, and the action of every party ought to be such as to put an end to any suspicion of this sort, but it certainly would have a very bad effect upon the Liberal party if they were to go into the ranks of their political opponents to choose candidates for appointment on account of their religion. A man ought to be a Liberal: he ought to be competent: he ought to be a man of good reputation: and having these qualities his religion ought not to stand in the way of perfectly fair treatment. If time is given us, I think in the end there will be no ground of complaint in this regard.

Yet in practice Mills found it not easy to balance religious affiliation with other criteria for nomination to the bench. "I must keep in view the religious complexion of the localities in which they [Roman Catholics] are appointed," he informed one correspondent, "so that, where one of that faith is to be appointed it may be as far as possible amongst those of his own religion."

By early 1898 the Minster of Justice had a short list of three qualified English-speaking Catholic barristers in Ontario, including Anglin and O'Reilly, and he intended to appoint these men to the judiciary as suitable opportunities arose. More specifically, Mills advised George Ross, the powerful Ontario Minister of Education, that Frank Anglin was being considered for a post in eastern Ontario, "and I do not think it would at all do to disappoint him." To a Liberal colleague Mills underlined the political advantages in such an appointment:

> One of the parties whose names have been pressed upon this Department for appointment is F. Anglin of Toronto, for whom I hope a position may be found either as a senior or junior Judge in some county where there [are] a fair number of his co-religionists, and I am the more anxious to do something for him because I think his appointment would give satisfaction in certain quarters, and I shall be glad to hear from you any suggestion which you make. . . .

. . . Frank Anglin's campaign for a place within the judiciary is revealing of the process of elite accommodation. He was a member of a family already recognized as forming part of the elite among Irish Catholics in Canada; his father had maintained a political career through that role. By supporting Anglin's demands for access to the bench, the Irish Catholic leaders of Ontario were helping to perpetuate the influence of a fellow member of the elite leaders of Ontario were helping to perpetuate the influence of a fellow member of the elite. Consciously or otherwise, in securing a position in the judiciary Frank Anglin was also entrenching his role as a leader of that important social group within Canadian society. As well, in allowing Irish Catholic leaders access to the bench, the existing federal political elite was accommodating the political structure to Irish Catholics as an interest group and was further legitimizing people like Anglin as that group's elite.

The details of Anglin's quest for the bench are more revealing of the process of judicial appointment at the turn of the century. Evidence of religious discrimination in Protestant Ontario comes as no surprise, but it is interesting to watch the government trying to deal with that factor balanced against several others. The Minister of Justice's genuine attempts to give Roman Catholics more appropriate representation on the bench were important in opening up the judiciary. Just as meaningful was Mills's concern to work with the legal profession in determining judicial selections. At the same time, his emphasis on proven political affiliation should not be forgotten. It was to Frank Anglin's undoubted advantage that he had solid Liberal credentials as well as standing as a leader of an influential minority.

# 4.5

# THE JUDICIAL ELITE

John Porter

As far as the senior judiciary selected are concerned, there were 5 who held other political elite roles during 1940 to 1960, 4 former federal cabinet ministers and one former provincial premier. A further 3 had been provincial premiers before 1940, one of whom had also been a federal cabinet minister. Thus the overlaps during the careers of the 44 senior judiciary number 8, less than one-fifth.

There are, however, other political roles from which individuals move into the judiciary, provincial cabinet ministers, for example. Of the 44 judges, 25 had known political affiliations, and 22 of the 25 had held elected political positions, many of which were in provincial cabinets. It is likely, however, that the number with political affiliations is greater because it is recognized

*Canada: The Vertical Mosaic.* Toronto: University of Toronto Press, 1965, p.415. Reprinted with permission.

that appointment to the bench are patronage appointments, although in most cases persons are appointed after some consultation with the law societies of the provinces concerned. There is the constitutional requirement also that 3 members of the Supreme Court of Canada come from Quebec.

Of the 44, 21 were appointed to their high judicial office without previous judicial experience. There is no pattern of moving up a judicial hierarchy. Of the 23 who did have previous judicial experience the pattern was one mainly of moving from the trial division to the appellate division of the provincial supreme court and from there to the provincial chief justiceship or to the Supreme Court of Canada. Seventeen of the 44 had served on the Supreme Court of Canada. Ten of the 17 went directly to the Supreme Court without previous judicial experience while the remaining 7 served for a time on the provincial courts.

The judiciary is the end of the line for a political career. There was no case of a judge giving up his job to enter or return to political life. All political careers of course do not end up on the bench because there is a limited number of judicial appointments (there are more than formerly because judges must now retire at seventy-five), and not all politicians are lawyers who qualify for judicial appointments. The extent to which the bench at all levels constitutes the culmination of the political career is indicated by the proportion of those who were federal cabinet ministers or provincial premiers during their careers and who went to the bench. In the elite 121 individuals were federal cabinet ministers or provincial premiers at some time in their careers (some were both). If we subtract the 30 still serving (1962) in these positions, there are 91 who have left these two offices. Of the 91, 15 that is one-sixth, went to the bench. Although these interchanges take place in the political system, they are not a major aspect of the political career. Where they do take place, however, they constitute what must be one of the most curious of occupational systems, one in which a person whose political role is marked by partiality, irrationality, and opinion-expressing assumes a judicial role marked by impartiality, rational inquiry, and attention to fact.

# 4.6

# CONSTITUTIONAL REFORM OF THE JUDICIAL BRANCH

Peter Russell

In negotiating Supreme Court reform, Canada's political leaders have been far more concerned about where the judges come from and how they are appointed than with what the Court does. Provincial politicians have been anxious to secure an appropriate distribution of Supreme Court judgeships from the various regions of the country as well as a voice for provincial governments in the selection of judges. Federal politicians have been concerned to strengthen the legitimacy of the Court as a national institution. These concerns have produced a convergence of interest in achieving a common goal in Supreme Court reform: strengthening the Court's capacity to serve as a vehicle of "intrastate federalism." While interstate federalism refers to the division of power between the two levels of governments, intrastate federalism, in the words of Donald Smiley, refers to "the reflection of provincial/regional aspirations and interests in the structure and operations of the central government."

Throughout the Court's history the composition of its bench has reflected both dualist and regional precepts. Dualism has been manifest at the statutory level in the provisions of the Supreme Court Act requiring that a minimum number of the Court's members come from Quebec — two out of six from 1875 to 1927, two out of seven from 1927 to 1949 and three out of nine since 1949. This statutory requirement is designed to ensure that some judges have a background in Quebec's distinctive Civil Law system. Given that Civil Law appeals are nearly always heard by a panel of five judges, the three out of nine requirement means that Quebec judges can form the majority in these cases. Regionalism, on the other hand, has been observed only at the informal level of custom or convention in the practice of appointing judges from the various regions of common law Canada. Since 1949 the pattern of three from Ontario, two from the West and one from the Atlantic Provinces has been observed with only one short deviation from 1979 to 1982 when Ontario had two and the western provinces three.

Until quite recently constitutional proposals relating to the Supreme Court proposed simply to entrench the existing statutory provisions — namely that the Court be composed of nine judges, three of whom must be from Quebec.

*Canadian Journal of Political Science*, 17:2 (1984). Reprinted with permission.

But in the last few years this position has been challenged by proposals to expand the Court's bench to 11 judges and to entrench some pattern or principle of regional representation. In 1978 the federal government's Bill C-60 called for an 11-judge Supreme Court with four judges from Quebec and a requirement that ''as nearly as reasonably may be'' the remaining seven be drawn from the Atlantic provinces, Ontario, the prairie provinces and British Columbia. British Columbia's proposal for a 11-judge court, not surprisingly, dropped the entrenchment of Quebec's special status but followed the federal proposal in recognizing B.C. as one of Canada's five regions. B.C. recommended that at least one judge come from each of the five regions. The Pepin-Robarts Task Force, endeavouring to achieve a reconciliation of dualism and regionalism, proposed an 11-judge court with five from Quebec and a ''regional distribution'' of the other six.

The motivation behind these proposals to expand the Court is not to obtain additional judges for a increased caseload but to increase the opportunities for regional representation. Such proposals are a good example of symbolic goals being pursued at the expense of operational consequences. Regional representation on the Supreme Court must be essentially a matter of symbolic gratification. Here it is important to understand the difference between the Supreme Court and the Senate as instruments of intrastate federalism. Intrastate federalism made some operational sense in the context of Senate reform for it is reasonable to envisage the members of a reconstituted federal upper house usefully and properly examining federal government policies in such fields as agriculture, energy, regional developemnt, tax transfers, trade and transportation in terms of their impact on the interests of the regions they represent. But when we consider both the issues which the Supreme Court is called upon to decide as well as the nature of the adjudicative process, it is difficult to accept that the representation of regional interests either could be or should be prominent in the work of the Supreme Court. It seems very doubtful that there is a Western, or Atlantic or Ontario or Quebec position which must be articulated in the Court's deliberations if it is to make sound decisions on the subjects that are coming to dominate the Court's docket — namely, review of the federal administrative process, the interpretation of the Criminal Code and other federal statutes and disputes arising under the Constitution, including the Charter of Rights and the division of powers. On the other hand, from an operational point of view, expansion of the Court has some distinctly negative implications. Collegiality, that elusive but highly desirable quality of appellate courts, would be watered down with 11 judges. Such an expansion of the Court would encumber the interaction of judges that takes place in conference, through the circulation of draft opinions and by participating in the same cases. Such interaction improves the quality of the Court's work by illuminating and clarifying points of agreement and disagreement. Moreover, expansion to 11 judges might make it more difficult to make further progress toward having the full court hear important cases. Failure to make progress in this regard means that the Court is increasingly exposed to the criticism that the outcome of cases, expecially those with a high political profile, is influenced by the selection of judges to hear particular cases. Certainly the workload of the Court in terms of requests for leave to appeal have been increasing and will increase further as a result of the Charter of Rights. But the strains on our 9-judge Canadian court are still a long way from those with which the the 9-judge U.S. Supreme Court has been coping for a great many years. The Court will have to become more efficient and more selective in screening requests for leave to appeal. This is greatly to be preferred to increasing the number of cases to be decided on the merits and in the process diluting the quality of the jurisprudence produced by the Court.

In terms of both operational and symbolic consequences, the wisest course of action would appear to be simply to put the existing statutory requirement — three out of nine from Quebec — in the formal constitution. Operationally this makes sense providing the Court remains the court of last resort for cases dealing with Quebec's distinctive Civil Law system. Symbolically, such a measure would represent a very modest response to the aspirations of many Quebecois for greater recognition of Quebec's special place in Confederation. It is unlikely that a Canadian constitution which in the long run is to have legitimacy for all citizens can be built on a single conception of the federation, be it provincial equality, regionalism or dualism. While the principle of provincial equality is embodied in the new amending formula, and regionalism would appear to be the dominant concern in reforming the Senate, perhaps, as the Pepin-Robarts report suggests, the appropriate place for accommodating the dualist ideal in the restructuring of national institutions is to entrench the special status Quebec has traditionally enjoyed in the Supreme Court's composition.

Among federal and provincial political leaders there would appear to be a consensus on the need for a constitutional amendment modifying the federal executive's monopoly over the selection and appointment of Supreme Court judges. The logic behind this consensus is stated very clearly in the Province of British Columbia's 1978 *Constitutional Proposals*:

> British Columbia believes that the judges of the highest court in the land, whose chief role is the umpire of the federal system, should not be subject to unilateral appointment by one level of government. An umpire must not only be neutral, he must in all respects appear to be so. Appointments by one level of government, whichever it may be, compromise that neutrality in the eyes of the other level of government and in the eyes of the public.

The fact that the federal government has acceded to this logic indicates the extent to which umpiring the federal system has come to be accepted as a primary role of the Supreme Court. It also indicates the distrust which exists between the two levels of government.

At the level of performance the evidence does not suggest that the federal government, at least in the modern period, has taken advantage of its control over Supreme Court appointments to appoint individuals biased in its favor. There has been a marked trend in the pattern of Supreme Court appointments away from persons with a political background. Most appointees have had no discernible constitutional orientation. As Professor Hogg has pointed out, of the three justices appointed in recent years — Laskin, Pigeon and Beetz — who had written on the constitution before their appointment, two — Pigeon and Beetz — were sympathetic to the preservation of provincial rights. Although disgruntled provincial premiers have given a great deal of publicity to Supreme Court decisions adverse to their interests, the record of the Supreme Court in constitutional adjudication demonstrates an almost exquisite balance. Indeed, it could be argued that symbolic assurance of their neutrality in the constitution might ease the pressure on the judges to reach outcomes calculated to preserve their credibility as federal umpires.

But what arrangement for appointing Supreme Court judges will meet the symbolic need and at the same time be acceptable at the operational level? Two basic proposal have been put forward over the years — sometimes separately, sometimes in combination. In both, the federal executive retains the power of appointment, but the appointment requires, in one, approval of one or more provincial governments and, in the other, ratification by a federal upper house reconstituted to serve as a more credible representative of regional interests.

An advantage of the latter is that it exposes the appointment process to public scrutiny. The case for such scrutiny is now even stronger given the Court's responsiblity of reviewing the legislation and executive actions of federal and provincial governments under the Charter of Rights. But the viability of this option depends on Senate reform. The approach to Senate reform which responds most directly to the desire of provincial governments to participate in the selection of Supreme Court judges is the Bundesrat model in which the upper house is constituted by delegates of the constituent units. It would seem most unlikely that this approach to Senate reform will be acceptable to the federal government.

Upper house ratification is, at best, likely to supplement the more characteristically Canadian method of "executive federalism" — decision by federal and provincial ministers behind closed doors. Among the federations, Canada has been a pioneer in designing procedures for facilitating the formal participation of provincial governments in Supreme Court appointments. The latest model is to be found in "The Best Efforts Draft" which emerged from the Continuing Conference of Ministers on the Constitution in the summer of 1980. It reads as follows:

(1) Where a vacancy in the Supreme Court occurs, the Minister of Justice of Canada shall consult with the Attorneys General of all of the provinces and shall secure the consent of the Attorney General of the province of the person being considered for appointment as to the appointment of that person.

(2) Where consent is not forthcoming, the Minister of Justice of Canada and the appropriate provincial Attorney General shall, together with a person chosen by them or if they do not agree a person chosen by the Chief of Justice of Canada, determine the person to be recommended for appointment.

A distinct advantage of this proposal — perhaps its greatest — is that it takes up only about two inches of text whereas its predecessor generally ran to a foot or more! One measure of the distrust which exists among our federal and provincial politicians is the lengths to which they have gone in designing mechanisms for the worst case scenario in which the two levels of government persist in disagreeing on how to fill a court vacancy. Here at least the complication of two alternative "nominating commissions" for breaking deadlocks has been eliminated. At the same time there is now a requirement, missing in earlier proposals, for consultation with all the provinces. Presumably one purpose of such consultations, in the case of non-Quebec appointments, would be to determine the province from whose bench or bar the vacancy should be filled. Most importantly the federal government's monopoly of the right to submit names for consideration has been dropped.

While this 1980 model is a distinct improvement over earlier proposals, and may represent the approach that is most acceptable to political leaders, still from an operational point of view it may be inferior to the federal-provincial multi-partisan, nominating commission proposed by Professor Lederman. If the first priority of our political leaders in the selection of Supreme Court judges is professional merit, then they should be willing to accept Professor Lederman's model and turn over the selection of candidates to a true nominating commission constituted by both levels of government and representatives of all political parties. This would strengthen the quality control that has been developed through the Office of Special Advisor to the Minister of Justice and considerably widen the recruitment process. However, there seem to be little likelihood of the contemporary political elite's agreeing to the sacrifice of personal political power which such a proposal entails.

# 4.7

# KEYTERMS

*Concepts*

judicial independence
impartiality
political patronage
merit selection nominating committees

*Institutions, Events, and Documents*

National Committee on the Judiciary (1966)
Office of Special Advisor to the Minister of Justice
The Victoria Charter (1971)
Alberta Judicial Council
Ontario Judicial Council

# 5

# Judicial Independence, Ethics, and Discipline

Disputes are a fact of life in political communities. In the course of their personal and commercial interactions, individuals become involved in disputes over what happened (questions of fact) and what the law is that governs their situation (questions of law). Typically neither party is willing to allow the other to unilaterally answer these questions, for fear that an adversary will exploit any ambiguity of fact or law to his own advantage. The self-interest of both parties prevents either from serving as arbiter of the dispute. What is needed is an outside third party who is independent of both disputants, and thus can be counted on to render an impartial inquiry and resolution of the dispute.

While the need for a mechanism of dispute resolution is common to all societies, different cultures have met this need in different ways. In the Western European tradition, the institutions that have evolved to perform this function are what we know today as courts. Historically speaking, Canada is a very recent part of the Western European tradition, and our legal system (like the rest of our culture) is in large part inherited and adapted from this tradition. The authority of contemporary Canadian courts still rests on the ancient requirement of impartiality. We are willing to submit our disputes to judges and to obey their decisions voluntarily, even if we lose, only because we believe that they provide an unbiased and reasoned application of the laws to the facts of our particular dispute. In order to insure impartiality, we expect a judge to be independent of our adversary. In the area of criminal law and other types of disputes between individuals and the state, this means that judicial independence from the Crown is an essential prerequisite for the proper functioning of our legal system.

Canada's legal system did not evolve from the Western European tradition at large, but rather from the distinctive British common law tradition.[1] This

---

[1] Except for Quebec, whose Civil Law originated in France. Note, however, that since criminal law and procedure are matters of federal jurisdiction, the criminal law process in Quebec is based on the same common law practices as the rest of Canada.

means that Canada has been fortunate enough to inherit the British institutional practices and safeguards of judicial independence that for centuries have made Great Britain an exemplary model for the protection of individual freedom.[2]

While the tradition of judicial independence is much older, it became an official part of Britain's "unwritten constitution" as part of the Act of Settlement in 1701. During the seventeenth century, the Stuart Kings had flagrantly violated the independence of the British courts. After Charles II was deposed in the "Glorious Revolution of 1688," Parliament and the English bar were eager to provide more certain guarantees for judicial independence in the future. As part of the Act of Settlement, they forced the new king, William III, to agree to legal provisions securing the independence of the judiciary. Judicial tenure of office was established on the principle of *quamdiu se bene nesserint* — "during good behaviour" — and henceforth judges could be removed only by address of both houses of Parliament. In addition, judicial salaries had to be ascertained and established by law, and were no longer set by royal decree.

Having established judicial independence at home, the British Parliament was somewhat reluctant to introduce it in British North America. Originally colonial judges served only "at pleasure." This practice inevitably lead to abuses by colonial governors, and these abuses were one of the grievances enumerated in the Declaration of Independence by the American revolutionaries in 1776.[3] Significantly, no sooner had the American successfully thrown off British political rule, than they entrenched the British provisions for judicial independence in their new state and federal constitutions.[4] It was not until the 1830's and 1840's that similar provisions for judicial independence were made for the rest of British North America.

At Confederation in 1867, the now familiar terms of judicial independence were written into the Constitution Act. Section 99 provides that "judges of the superior courts shall hold office during good behaviour, but shall be removable by the Governor General on address of the Senate and House of Commons." In 1960 this was amended to require mandatory retirement at the age of 75. Section 100 requires that the "salaries, allowances and pensions of

---

[2] See the admiration of the nineteenth century French political thinker Alexis de Tocqueville, quoted by A.V.C. Dicey in Reading 1.4.

[3] "He has made judges dependent on his will alone, for the tenure of their offices, and the amount and payment of their salaries."

[4] Note that there was no national judiciary under the first American constitution, The Article of Confederation. The more centralist Constitution of 1788 created a national Supreme Court, and provided for judicial independence in essentially the same terms as the Act of Settlement. The practice of electing judges in some American states, referred to in chapter four, dates from a much later period in American history.

the judges of the Superior, District, and County Courts . . . be fixed and provided by the Parliament of Canada.''

It should be noted that the tenure provisions apply explicitly only to the superior courts created pursuant to section 96. This has raised the question of whether the judges of the Supreme Court and Federal Court of Canada, County and District Court judges, and the judges of the ''section 92'' provincial courts enjoy less independence than their superior court brethren. Lederman argues that although the independence of these courts is not constitutionally entrenched in explicit, written provisions, it remains part of Canada's ''unwritten constitution.'' While tenure of office in these courts is provided for only by ordinary statute, Lederman declares that these provisions are ''ordinary' in form only, because they are declaratory of basic constitutional principles and traditions.'' (See Reading 5.2) The constitutional reforms of 1982 appear to further reinforce the independence of the Supreme Court of Canada by entrenching its present size and composition.[5]

In recent years this old issue of judicial independence has taken on a new dimension: the administrative independence of the judges collectively from the executive branch of government. Historically the Departments of Justice, at both the federal and provincial levels, have been responsible for administering their respective judicial systems. This has resulted in multiple roles for the respective Attorney-Generals and Ministers of Justice, who are also responsible for arguing the Crown's position in cases before these same courts. An increased sense of the potential for conflict of interest in this situation has resulted in a series of reforms. In 1977 the federal government created the Commissioner for Federal Judicial Affairs to administer federal judicial business independently of the Minister of Justice. British Columbia, Manitoba, New Brunswick, and Ontario also have created professional court administrators. In 1981 Justice Jules Deschenes and Professor Carl Barr completed a study commissioned by the Canadian Judicial Council investigating the problem of the administrative independence of the courts. (Reading 5.5) They concluded that the problem was sufficiently serious to merit complete judicial control of court administration. However in September, 1982 the Canadian Judicial Council rejected complete administrative autonomy, at least for the present, and called instead for more and better consultation and decision-sharing between court administrators and judges.

No matter is more critical to the maintenance of judicial independence than the procedure for removing judges guilty of serious misconduct or gross incompetence. While such exigencies must be provided for, the removal procedure must be structured so as to minimize the potential for political abuse. While requiring address by both houses of Parliament is a solid guarantee of judicial independence, the federal government recently took additional steps to further reform the removal process.

---

[5] See additional comments in the Introduction to chapter three.

In 1971, the Judges Act was amended to authorize the creation of the Canadian Judicial Council, consisting of the chief justices and associate chief justices of all the superior courts, and chaired by the Chief Justice of the Supreme Court of Canada. The Judicial Council is authorized to supervise judicial conduct and to investigate allegations of judicial misconduct. If the Council discovers sufficiently serious misconduct on the part of a judge, it can direct the removal of county and district court judges, and recommend to Parliament the removal of superior court judges. By transferring the responsibility for investigating allegations of judicial misconduct from the executive branch to the judges themselves, the potential for political abuse is reduced, and the independence of the judiciary enhanced.

The Canadian Judicial Council came close to exercising its new powers in 1982 at the conclusion of its investigation into allegations of misconduct by then Justice Thomas Berger of the British Columbia Court of Appeal. On November 5, 1981, the federal government and all the provinces except Quebec reached a compromise agreement on the proposed constitutional reforms of the Trudeau government. One of the compromises was the federal government's agreement to delete those sections that dealt with the protection of the ''aboriginal rights'' of Native peoples. In the weeks following, Justice Berger publicly criticized Canadian political leaders for this action on at least two occasions. These criticisms were reported in the press, and a justice of the Federal Court, upon reading these reports, lodged a complaint of judicial misconduct with the Canadian Judicial Council. (Reading 5.3) The Judicial Council appointed a committee of investigation, and invited Justice Berger to testify in his own defense. He refused, but sent two letters defending his actions as a matter of conscience and a question of principle. (Reading 5.3) The Committee of Investigation's final report concluded that Justice Berger was guilty of judicial misconduct, and stated that they would have recommended removal from office, had it not been for the unique circumstances of the incident. (Reading 5.3) The Judicial Council modified the Investigation Committee's report. Its final report to the Minister of Justice declared that Justice Berger's actions had been ''indiscrete,'' but that they did not constitute grounds for removal from office. In the event, Justice Berger announced his intention to resign anyhow, and did so several months later.

The Canadian press gave the ''Berger affair'' considerable publicity, and some editorials criticized the Canadian Judicial Council for trying to censor or punish Justice Berger for exercising his ''freedom of speech.'' The late Chief Justice, Bora Laskin, was sufficiently upset with what he considered to be a gross misunderstanding of these events to publicly address the issue in a speech to the Canadian Bar Association in September, 1982. (Reading 5.4) The late Chief Justice's remarks are important because they demonstrate that judicial independence cuts both ways. Not only does it prohibit politicians from interfering in the judicial process, but it also prohibits judges from interfering in the political process. In response to Berger's appeal to individual conscience, Laskin argued that a judge's ''abstention from political involvement is one of the guarantees of his impartiality, his integrity, his independence.''

Greater judicial involvement in politics and policy-making is also the subject of Paul Weiler's analysis of ''judicial accountability.'' (Reading 5.1) Weiler reminds us that the reason judges are purposely made ''unaccountable,'' unlike other high ranking officials of state, is that the judges' function is perceived as non-political. To the extent that courts openly and explicitly engage in policy-making, the justification of judicial independence is eroded. Weiler argues persuasively that a court which actually resembled his hypothetical ''policy-making model'' could not logically lay claim to judicial independence. The ''judges'' of such a court would be much more like administrative executives, who serve ''at pleasure'' of the executive, and can be changed with the change of political party control of the House of Commons. In light of Lederman's generally shared assumption that judicial independence is a prerequisite of the ''rule of law,'' the implications of Weiler's analysis are disturbing indeed. At a minimum, they should force us to assess the potential costs (and not just the potential benefits) of a greater policy-making role for Canadian courts.

# 5.1

## TWO MODELS: JUDICIAL ACCOUNTABILITY

Paul Weiler

. . . What is even more interesting, perhaps, than the question of appointments, is the problem of accountability. It is basic to the theory of political democracy that responsibility of policy-makers to those whom they affect by their decisions is ensured by making them submit themselves to an electorate (or else making them accountable to those who do submit themselves). Yet it is interesting to note the empirical findings that judicial elections are traditionally rare, or pro forma, or non-partisan. Even where there is a real contest, it is inconsistent with society's symbolic image of the judiciary to make the subject of campaigning an incumbent's decisional record. One can safely assume that greater concentration on, and amplification of, a judge's policy-making role will quickly erode this sentiment.

---

*Canadian Bar Review*, 1968, p.406. Reprinted with permission.

Even those most insistent on the judge's free, creative policy choices (and the implication thereof for the appointment process), find it difficult to "think the unthinkable" and face the problem of impeachment. One of the reasons, obviously, is the connotation of punishment inherent in the term, which stems from its historical identification with moral misbehaviour. There is no reason at all why judges should not be subject to the process of removal (perhaps under a new name), not because of their moral shortcomings, or even because of negligent work, but simply because the representative organs of society (or the electorate itself) disagrees with the substantive content of their policy decisions. There are obvious reasons why this is undesirable in the case of adjudicative decisions primarily designed to dispose of concrete disputes between specific individuals. The moral quality of the latter stems largely from the belief that the decision-maker is completely impartial and that his decision is influenced by no considerations other than those relevant to the specific dispute. He must not be, or seem to be, concerned about an unpopular decision's effect on his continuance in office. Obviously, however, if the prime focus of judicial decisions is the creation of legislative policy for society, then this function is inherently partisan. As such it should be subject to the same type of influence as other subordinate arms of the elected bodies in our system of government. Perhaps judges should hold office "at pleasure," and change with administration, as do department heads, for instance. In other words, judicial policy-making entails the same type of problem as does administrative policy-making and the "tenured" judiciary should be no more sacrosanct than the independent administrative agency.

It has been hypothesized that the Supreme Court of the United States, which makes policy from a supposedly sheltered, independent position, is really subject to control by the popularly-elected branches of government. This is so because the power of appointment is exercised sufficiently often to allow for changes in popular attitudes to be reflected in the composition of the court. The President, with the advice of the Senate, can appoint judges who are responsive to the majority will. The logic of the policy-making model of the court leads to the conclusion that this fact should be legitimized and that the existing system should be greatly rationalized so as to make accountability much more effective, in the ways suggested above. Does this logic lead to a further conclusion? Insofar as a court is considered primarily a policy-maker (for instance, the United States Supreme Court), should its adjudicative functions be stripped from it and bestowed elsewhere? Perhaps it should be subject to the same type of differentiation which overtook the English House of Lords in the nineteenth century, when it divided itself into "lay" and "judicial" branches. This, of course, does not mean that an adjudicative supreme court should consider itself bound to accept the mode of reasoning which characterized the judicial House of Lords soon thereafter.

# 5.2

# THE INDEPENDENCE OF THE JUDICIARY

W.R. Lederman

## Introduction

An independent judiciary has long been an established feature of our Constitution in Canada, coming to us as a primary part of our great inheritance of English public law and governmental institutions. My purpose here is an ambitious one — to explain the essential *positive* functions of an independent judiciary as an integral part of our total constitutional system. This involves examining the relations between the judiciary on the one hand, and parliaments and cabinets on the other, as they play their respective parts in making and applying laws for our country, at both the provincial and the federal levels. Also, of course, this task requires some examination of the institutional arrangements that are the basis of judicial independence, and some assessment of the relevance of such independence to the needs of our time for good government under law . . . . What I have to say falls under three main headings:

1. Our English Constitutional Inheritance,
2. Essential Operational Elements of Judicial Independence, and
3. Judicial Independence, Democracy, and The Rule of Law.

## 1. *Our English Constitutional Inheritance*

Sir Arthur Goodhart has told us, in his distinguished lectures on "English Law and the Moral Law," that the English are not as much without a constitution as they frequently profess to be. He gives four principles which he maintains are equally basic as first or original principles of the English constitution. They are briefly as follows: (1) "That no man is above the law" (among other things, this means that all official persons, the Queen, the judges and members of Parliament included, must look to the law for the definition of their respective positions and powers). (2) "That those who govern Great Britain do so in a representative capacity and are subject to change . . . . The Free election of the members of the House of Commons is a basic principle of English constitutional law." (3) That there shall be freedom of speech, of thought and of assembly. (4) That there shall be an independent judiciary. "The fourth and final principle which is a basic part of the English constitu-

Linden, A.M. *The Canadian Judiciary.* Toronto: Osgoode Hall, 1976, p.1. Reprinted with permission.

tion is the independence of the judiciary. It would be inconceivable that Parliament should today regard itself as free to abolish the principle which has been accepted as a cornerstone of freedom ever since the Act of Settlement in 1701. It has been recognized as axiomatic that if the judiciary are placed under the authority of either the legislative or the executive branches of the Government then the administration of the law might no longer have that impartiality which is essential if justice is to prevail.'' Sir William Holdsworth expressed a very similar view on the status of the judiciary. He said:

> The judges hold an office to which is annexed the function of guarding the supremacy of the law. It is because they are the holders of an office to which the guardianship of this fundamental constitutional principle is entrusted, that the judiciary forms one of the three great divisions into which the power of the State is divided. The Judiciary has separate and autonomous powers just as truly as the King or Parliament; and, in the exercise of those powers, its members are no more in the position of servants than the King or Parliament in the exercise of their powers . . . it is quite beside the mark to say that modern legislation often bestows undivided executive, legislative and judicial powers on the same person or body of persons. The separation of powers in the British Constitution has never been complete. But some of the powers in the constitution were, and still are, so separated that their holders have autonomous powers, that is, powers which they can exercise independently, subject only to the law enacted or unenacted. The judges have powers of this nature because, being entrusted with the maintenance of the supremacy of the law, they are and always have been regarded as a separate and independent part of the constitution. It is true that this view of the law was contested by the Stuart kings; but the result of the Great Rebellion and the Revolution was to affirm it.

. . . For present purposes, two things are noteworthy about the Canadian judicial system. First, while it is true that the guarantee of removal from office only by joint address of the Parliament of Canada is explicitly specified by the B.N.A. Act just for the Superior courts of the Provinces, this most emphatically does not mean that there is no constitutional protection for the security of tenure in office of other judges in the total judicial system just described. The same point applies concerning the explicit guarantee of salaries in the B.N.A. Act, which mentions only the Superior, District and County courts of the Provinces. The position in my view is that the Superior Courts, by virtue of the explicit provisions for them in the B.N.A. Act afford the prototype — the model — which should be followed for all other Canadian courts.

In other words, I am saying that security of tenure and salary for judges in Canada, as a matter of basic constitutional law and tradition, is not limited to the strictly literal reach of sections 99 and 100 of the B.N.A. Act, I remind you of the words of Goodhart and Holdsworth. They make it clear that essential provision for the independence of the judiciary generally has long been deeply rooted as an original principle in the basic customary law of the constitution. In Britain herself, the explicit provisions about judicial security are in the ordinary statutes — but these ordinary statutes, including the Act of Settlement itself, manifest the more fundamental unwritten constitutional principle I have described, as Goodhart and Holdsworth insist. The same point can and should be made about the status of Canadian judges. In Canadian

Federal statutes we have provisions ensuring the independence of the County and District Court judges, the judges of the Federal Court of Canada and the judges of the Supreme Court of Canada itself. In various Provincial statutes, security is likewise provided for provincially-appointed judges, for example the Provincial Criminal Court judges in Ontario. My point is that though these are ordinary statutory provisions, they are "ordinary" in form only because they are declaratory of basic constitutional principles and traditions.

Now of course, for the judges who depend on ordinary statute in this respect, there is room for variations in just how their basic constitutional independence is to be implemented. But, provided they are guaranteed security of tenure in office until a reasonable retirement age, subject only to earlier removal for grave misconduct or infirmity, after full due process by way of enquiry, then the basic constitutional mandate for their independence is satisfied. I am not arguing that all judges are, or have to be, under the parliamentary joint address procedure in order to be secure and independent. Adequate due process leading to removal for cause may take several forms. In this respect, we should note the recent advent of the Canadian Judicial Council, under which the federally-appointed judges as a group themselves apply due process and self-discipline concerning any of their own members against whom complaints may have been entered. This is a progressive step in safeguarding the independence of the judiciary that is quite in harmony with the concept of independence. . . .

## 2. *Essential Operational Elements of Judicial Independence*

What I have said so far implies that the elements of judicial independence fall into two groups, individual elements and collective ones.

The individual elements may be stated in these terms. A judge is not a civil servant, rather he is a primary autonomous officer of state in the judicial realm, just as cabinet ministers and members of parliament are the primary official persons in the executive and legislative realms respectively. No minister of the Crown, federal or provincial, and no parliament, federal or provincial, has any power to instruct a judge how to decide any one of the cases that comes before him. If a parliamentary body does not like the judicial interpretation of one of its statutes in a particular case, then it can amend the statute, use different words, and hope that this will cause a different judicial interpretation when next the statute is before a court. But that is all a parliamentary body can do or should attempt to do under the constitution. As for ministers of the Crown, when the government is an interested party in litigation or prosecution before the courts, then the minister can instruct counsel to appear and argue in court for the result the executive government would prefer, but that is all a minister can do or should attempt to do under the constitution. The judge remains autonomous, both as to his determinations of fact and his interpretations of the applicable law. As Chief Justice Laskin said recently, the judge must supply his own answers from his own resources, and thus there is something of the loneliness of the long distance runner in every judge. Long term security of tenure in office with the corresponding guarantee of salary ensures that the judge can maintain this position, especially as he is not allowed to hold any other office concurrently with his judicial office.

The reason for this individual independence of judges is best explained in the words of the late Robert MacGregor Dawson, as follows:

> The judge must be made independent of most of the restraints, checks and punishments which are usually called into play against other public officials . . . . He is thus protected against some of the most potent weapons which a democracy has at its command: he receives almost complete protection against criticism; he is given civil and criminal immunity for acts committed in the discharge of his duties; he cannot be removed from office for any ordinary offence, but only for misbehaviour of a flagrant kind; and he can never be removed simply because his decisions happen to be disliked by the Cabinet, the Parliament, or the people. Such independence is unquestionably dangerous, and if this freedom and power were indiscriminately granted the results would certainly prove to be disastrous. The desired protection is found by picking with especial care the men who are to be entrusted with these responsibilities, and then paradoxically heaping more privileges upon them to stimulate their sense of moral responsibility, which is called in as a substitute for the political responsibility which has been removed. The judge is placed in a position where he has nothing to lose by doing what is right and little to gain by doing what is wrong; and there is therefore every reason to hope that his best efforts will be devoted to the conscientious performance of his duty. . . .

. . . But, assuming the appointment of able people to judicial office, this is not in itself enough to ensure that the judicial system functions well as a whole and in all its parts. There are problems of the whole system of courts that have an important bearing on the independence of the judiciary. . . .

. . . First, my outline of the many parts that make up the unitary Canadian judicial system shows that responsibility for necessary appointments and legislation is shared between the federal and provincial levels of government. Accordingly, for the solution of these system problems, there must be a great deal of federal-provincial consultation and collaboration at the cabinet and parliamentary levels. This applies also to the provision of adequate financial support for the judicial system. Generally speaking, the administration of justice in Canada has been seriously under-financed, and both levels of government are to blame for this.

In the second place, in certain vital respects, collective responsibility for the effective operation of the judicial system should be invested in the judges themselves. Here the role of the Chief Justices and the Chief Judges is very important, as spokesmen for themselves and their brother judges. This refers particularly to the assignment of judges to case lists, and to determination of priorities for the grouping and hearing of cases. In my view, to safeguard the basic independence of the judiciary, the Chief Justices and the Chief Judges should be in operational control of these matters for their respective courts, with adequate administrative staff responding to their directions.

I have now spoken of the individual and the collective elements that go to make up an independent judiciary. But there is a final question that remains to be answered. What, in the end, is the main purpose of maintaining an independent judiciary? Sir William Holdsworth said, "The judges hold an office to which is annexed the function of guarding the supremacy of the law." My third and final topic is an attempt to explain why he said this.

### 3. *Judicial Independence, Democracy, and the Rule of Law*

At this point I return with particular emphasis to the special importance of our superior courts of general jurisdiction. We say that we have the rule of laws rather than of men, but this has a special dependence on the men who are the superior court judges. Constitutionally they have the last word on what the laws mean, so, does this not really mean the personal supremacy of superior court judges? I deny this for the following reasons. It is basic to the rule of law that doctrines, ideas and and principles are supreme, not persons. The great case of *Roncarelli v. Duplessis* confirmed this as the position in Canada. In aid of this supremacy, we find that the superior courts possess under the constitution a final supervisory review function over lesser courts, and over officials, boards and tribunals of all kinds, to ensure that they stay within the limits of the powers respectively given them by the constitution, or by statute, or by common law. The superior courts have power to nullify decisions of other officials and tribunals for excess of jurisdiction or breach of natural justice in procedure. But here we encounter that basic constitutional dilemma — Who watches the watchman? Who checks the superior courts themselves for excess of jurisdiction or breach of natural justice in procedure? The answer is that, at this primary level of constitutional responsibility, the superior court judges must be trusted to obey the laws defining their own functions, and to check themselves. Believing in the supremacy of law, they must themselves scrupulously obey it. They must be all the more careful about this precisely because there is no one to review their powers, as they review the powers of others. Judicial restraint on these terms at the superior court level is the ultimate safeguard of the supremacy of the law, enacted and unenacted, to use Holdsworth's terms. Remember too that at the intermediate and final levels of judicial appeal you have a plural bench, so that a majority of several judges is necessary to reach a decision. Several heads are better than one, and in the process purely personal peculiarities are likely to be cancelled out. It seems to me that this is as close as we can get to the rule of laws rather than of men.

There are further reasons for confidence in the independent judiciary, and I am speaking now of all judges, both provincially-appointed and federally-appointed. The conditions on which they hold office mean that they have a personal career interest to be served by the way they go in deciding cases that come before them. The laws to be interpreted and applied must be expressed in words, and words are not perfect vehicles of meaning. Hence there is frequently room for partisan interpretation, and that is precisely what you would get if one of the interested parties was in a position to make his interpretation prevail. At least the judges have no such personal interest in biased interpretation one way or the other, hence, in the words of Sir Arthur Goodhart, they are able to bring to the administration of the law that impartiality which is essential if justice is to prevail.

Finally, I assert that the power of the independent appointed judiciary is neither undemocratic nor anti-democratic. The statutes of our popularly elected legislatures do have priority, and will be made to prevail by the courts, if the parliamentarians speak plainly enough.[6] But often their statutes speak only in general terms that must be further particularized by someone else, or they speak in ambiguities that must be resolved by someone else. These tasks fall to interpretative tribunals, especially the courts at all levels of the judicial system. Judicial procedure respects the individual by giving him a fair hearing and allowing him and his counsel to argue that the reason of the law is in their favour. This is as much a feature of democracy as it is to give the same citizen a vote, as a means of influencing his own fate. As for judicial law making, the judicial tasks just referred to do involve discretions that are at times legislative in character. But I must stop here, for the judge as lawmaker is another large subject, with its own place later in this book.

---

[6] This was written in 1976, before the adoption of the Chamber of Rights and Freedoms in 1982. The Charter now has higher priority than ordinary statutes.

# 5.3

## THE BERGER AFFAIR
## BERGER BLASTS "MEAN-SPIRITED" MINISTERS

Ottawa *Advocate Citizen*

Justice Tom Berger said Monday the decision of all Canadian first ministers to abandon native rights as one of the prices for agreement on the constitution was "mean-spirited and unbelievable."

The B.C. Supreme Court justice also said the compromise provincial override clauses on major parts of the charter of rights is a cause for grave concern in the light of the treatment of minorities by all Canadian governments.

Berger was head of the Royal commission on the MacKenzie Valley pipeline, which heard the concerns of native people about industrial development in the North.

---

Ottawa *Advocate Citizen*. November 10, 1981. Reprinted with permission.

"Last week our leaders felt it was in the national interest to sacrifice the rights because they felt they were serving the greater good in reaching an agreement."

"It was mean-spirited. There are a million and more natives in Canada: Indians, Inuit and Metis and for the most part they are poor and powerless. They were the people who were sacrificed in this deal."

"That is the whole point of minority rights, that they should not be taken away for any reason."

Berger said "I can still hardly believe that it has happened. We have had 10 years of increasing consciousness of native rights and land claims."

"It has had an impact on many people but not on Canadian statesmen. It passed right by them."

Berger said the blame lies with all first ministers including Rene Levesque since he did not point to the denial of native rights as a reason for his refusal to sign the agreement.

Berger said Canadians, concerned about the protection of unpopular minorities, can take little comfort from the fact that the federal government insisted on a five-year renewal of every action to override the fundamental, legal and equality rights in the Charter of Rights.

Berger said the problem is always "the first time when an inflamed majority wants to strike at a defenceless minority not, five years later when it is irrelevant."

# REPORT OF THE COMMITTEE OF INVESTIGATION TO THE CANADIAN JUDICIAL COUNCIL

May 31, 1982

From the material annexed it can be seen that Mr. Justice Berger intervened in a matter of serious political concern and division when that division or controversy was at its height. His office and his experience as a Royal Commissioner (appointments made because of his office and his competence), obviously made his comments newsworthy. He described the decision of the first ministers to "abandon" native rights to be "mean-spirited and unbelievable." In his article he criticized the loss of Quebec's veto and argued for one amending formula in preference to another. He again attacked the first ministers for "repudiating" native rights and argued for the restoration of s. 34 "for the recognition and confirmation of aboriginal and treaty rights of Indians, Inuit and Metis."

Justice Berger, while agreeing that what he did may be unconventional, argues that the issues he discussed transcended partisan politics. Because the resolution of the issues in his opinion bore directly on how we were to be governed for the next 100 years, he felt obliged to speak out publicly. He refers to the late Mr. Justice Thorson and Chief Justice Freedman speaking on public issues. We do not have the facts with relation to those matters and are not in a position to comment on them.

Justice Berger also notes that no complaint was made to the Judicial Council about his address to the Canadian Bar Association. It is true that it appears that judges, in speaking to legal bodies, are accorded somewhat greater leeway in expressing their views than they are in speaking to the general public. However, it should be noted that a great part of the address seems to be a thoughtful philosophical discussion of the nature of Canada and its parts and the importance of its preservation. It may be, on reflection, that some of the statements made in this address, although not of as strident a nature as the material complained of, were inappropriate for a judge. It may also be that because he was speaking to an audience of lawyers and judges, the media and others took no notice of his remarks.

Justice Berger's views, which he eloquently defends in his letter to Chief Justice Laskin, are not in issue. What is in issue is his use of his office as a platform from which to express those views publicly on a matter of great political sensitivity. It is possible that other members of the judiciary held opposing views, as obviously elected representatives did, with equal conviction. Justice Berger makes reference to the Honourable Mr. Martland's statements with regard to the *Charter of Rights* after he retired from the bench. The analogy is not a helpful one except to underline the principle that judges do not speak out on political issues while holding office. Mr. Martland at the time he gave his interview was no longer a judge. His franchise had been restored and there was no longer any possibility that he would be called on to determine issues as an impartial judge. In our view, Justice Berger completely misses the mark when he says "does it make all the difference that nothing was said until he (Mr. Martland) retired?" It makes the greatest of difference. Politically controversial statements by a citizen who is no longer a judge and who can never again be called on to be a judge, do not destroy the necessary public confidence in the impartiality of judges.

Not only must judges be impartial, the appearance of impartiality, as Lord Devlin pointed out, must be maintained for the fair and proper administration of justice. If a judge feels compelled by his conscience to enter the political arena, he has, of course, the option of removing himself from office. By doing so, he is no longer in a position to abuse that office by using it as a political platform. One would not have expected Justice Berger's views to have been given the media attention they were given if he had not been a judge but merely a politician expressing his views in opposition to other politicians.

Judges, of necessity, must be divorced from all politics. That does not prevent them from holding strong views on matters of great national importance but they are gagged by the very nature of their independent office, difficult as that may seem. It can be argued that the separation of powers is even more emphatic here than in England. In England, High Court judges have the right to vote. Here, federally appointed judges are denied the right to vote in federal elections and in a number of provinces they have been deprived by statute of a right to vote in provincial elections, and in some cases, even in municipal elections.

It is apparent that some of the native peoples are unhappy with s. 35 of the Canadian Charter of Rights and Freedoms. If Justice Berger should be called on to interpret that section, for example, the meaning to be given to the word "existing" in the phrase "the existing aboriginal and treaty rights of the aboriginal peoples of Canada," would the general public have confidence now in his impartiality? After Justice Berger spoke publicly on the necessity for Quebec retaining a veto, his brother judges in Quebec were called on to determine whether such a right existed.

## Conclusion

In our view it was unwise and inappropriate for Justice Berger to embroil himself in a matter of great political controversy in the manner and at the time he did. We are prepared to accept that he had the best interests of Canada in mind when he spoke, but a judge's conscience is not an acceptable excuse for contravening a fundamental rule so important to the existence of a parliamentary democracy and judicial independence. To say that not all judges are cast in the same mold, as does Justice Berger, is only to state the obvious. On every great matter of political concern it would be probable that judges would hold opposing views privately and, if Justice Berger's view is acceptable, it would be possible to have judges speaking out in conflict one with the other because they hold those opposing views from a sense of deep conviction.

We say again if a judge becomes so moved by conscience to speak out on a matter of great importance, on which there are opposing and conflicting political views, then he should not speak with the trappings and from the platform of a judge but rather resign and enter the arena where he, and not the judiciary, becomes not only the exponent of those views but also the target of those who oppose them.

This is not a question, as Mr. Justice Berger suggests, which each judge must decide for himself. That question has been answered for him from the moment he accepts the Queen's Patent as a judge.

So far as the material before us reveals, Justice Berger's impropriety has been an isolated instance. Chief Justice McEachern also advised us in his Submission that Justice Berger had disengaged himself from the constitutional debate as soon as the Chief Justice spoke to him. Nevertheless, we view his conduct seriously and are of the view that it would support a recommendation for removal from office. There are, however, in addition to those already noted, special circumstances which make this case unique. As far as we are aware, this is the first time this issue has arisen for determination in Canada. It is certainly the first time the Council has been called on to deal with it. It is possible that Justice Berger, and other judges too, have been under a misapprehension as to the nature of the constraints imposed upon judges. That should not be so in the future. We do not, however, think it would be fair to set standards *ex post facto* to support a recommendation for removal in this case.

The judicial office is one which confers important privileges, obligations and protections necessary to the carrying out of the duties of one of Her Majesty's judges. A judge must accept the duty to protect that office, his fellow judges and the public from political controversy as the best way of maintaining "the historic personal independence" of judges.

We conclude that the complaint *non se bene gesserit* is well founded but, for the reasons stated, we do not make a recommendation that Justice Berger be removed from office.

# A MATTER OF CONSCIENCE

Justice Thomas R. Berger Letter to Canadian Judicial Council
December 3, 1981

*CONFIDENTIAL*                                          3rd December, 1981.

The Honourable Chief Justice Bora Laskin,
c/o Canadian Judicial Council
130 Albert Street
Ottawa, Ontario, K1A 0W8

Dear Chief Justice:

I understand that you and your colleagues on the Judicial Council are concerned by my intervention in the constitutional debate. I spoke at Guelph University on November 10th. The following week the Globe and Mail published an article of mine on the constitutional accord of November 5th. I enclose copies of both the speech and the article. The Prime Minister has accused me of making a foray into politics.

What I have done may be unconventional. But it was not a venture into politics in any ordinary sense. It is not as if I had discussed the ordinary stuff of political debate — inflation, interest rates, the budget, or the nationalization of the Asbestos Corporation. The issues which I discussed transcended partisan politics. In fact, when the vote on the constitutional resolution was taken this week, there were dissenting votes by members of all parties in the House.

This was, after all, a moment of constitutional renewal, unique in our country's history. The First Ministers (except Premier Levesque) had signed a constitutional accord. I felt a sense of great dismay about the accord. My remarks were directed not to the Prime Minister or any one of the premiers, nor to any political party, but to our leaders collectively.

While these are questions that rise above narrow partisanship, they are nevertheless political questions in the broad sense. Indeed, they bear directly on the question of how we are to be governed for the next 100 years. It was for this reason that I felt obliged to speak out publicly.

What I did is not without precedent. Mr. Justice Thorson used to participate in the campaign for nuclear disarmament. Chief Justice Freedman went on television in October, 1970, to declare his support for the invoking of the War Measures Act. On the occasion of his visit to Vancouver to open the new Court House in September, 1979, Lord Denning told us that the trade unions in England were a threat to the freedom of that country. No doubt each of these judges felt compelled to speak out. It may be said that it would undermine the independence of the judiciary if judges were constantly engaged in such activity. But they are not. These interventions by judges are infrequent, even rare.

I enclose a copy of the Prime Minister's remarks made here in B.C. He taxes me for not supporting him at an earlier stage of the debate (he had also done this at a press conference a week earlier) and then goes on to urge that my conduct has been offensive. In fact, I did support his Charter before he abandoned it. I enclose a speech I made to the annual meeting of the Canadian Bar Association in Vancouver in September, to an audience of 1,000 or more lawyers and judges, presenting the case for the Charter. (I remind you that Lord Scarman is one of the leading figures in England who has publicly urged the adoption of a Charter of Rights in that country). I was, I am afraid, outspoken. Yet none of the lawyers, judges or politicians there present complained. I do not understand why what was opportune before November 5th became "inopportune" after November 5th. The views I expressed had not changed (though couched, perhaps, in more forceful language after November 5th).

What I did was done after considering carefully what I should do, and with the best interests of my country in mind. I do not believe that anything I have done has impaired the independence of the judiciary.

The Prime Minister has, with respect to my intervention, urged the judges to "do something about it." I believe it is a mistake to think it is possible to place fences around a judge's conscience. These are matters that no tidy scheme of rules and regulations can encompass, for all judges are not cast from the same mould.

Mr. Justice Addy's letters have arrived. I do not think anything that he has said calls for a reply beyond what I have already written in this letter. It is a question of principle. Should the Judicial Council issue edicts on matters of conscience? If you and your colleagues agree with Mr. Justice Addy, there is nothing more to be said. I believe, however, that these are matters that individual judges must decide for themselves.

Yours sincerely,

Thomas R. Berger

cc: The Hon. Chief Justice McEachern

# OUTSPOKEN B.C. JUDGE RESIGNING

*Calgary Herald*, May 15, 1982.

VANCOUVER (CP) — Justice Thomas Berger, an outspoken champion of minority rights who refused to accept that his judicial robes include a gag, will be stepping down from the B.C. Supreme Court this summer.

And when he departs on August 27, he will leave an imprint that, flouting tradition, endorses the concept of judges defending minorities against parliamentary incursions.

"I believe a judge has the right, a duty, in fact, to speak out on an appropriate occasion on questions of human rights and fundamental freedoms," Berger said last year.

On Wednesday, Berger resigned from the bench, citing differences between himself and Supreme Court of Canada Chief Justice Bora Laskin and the Canadian Judicial Council over constraints imposed on public speaking by judges.

Starting in September, Berger will teach constitutional law and civil liberties at the University of B.C. two days a week and resume a limited law practice . . . .

. . . In a letter addressed to Justice Minister Mark MacGuigan, he said his differences with Laskin and the Judicial Council are well known.

He said this extended beyond the dispute over his intervention in a constitutional debate in November, 1981, when he said that on rare occasions a judge may have an obligation to speak out on human rights. Berger said his departure also concerns Laskin's views on judicial involvement in royal commissions.

MacGuigan said Thursday he has no qualms about accepting Berger's resignation, but he was unhappy that Berger made public his letter of resignation now when he plans to remain a judge until August 27.

MacGuigan said judges should avoid public controversies.

# 5.4

# THE MEANING AND SCOPE OF JUDICIAL INDEPENDENCE

Bora Laskin

. . . I hope I do not abuse this privilege if I strike a serious note in this address. It would please me better if I could banter and amuse, which I may assure you is not beyond my capacity. But special reasons, to which I will come shortly, impel me to speak more soberly on a subject of fundamental importance to the judicial office. That subject is the meaning and scope of judicial independence. I would have thought that its meaning would have been well understood over the years in which the Judges have exercised their judicial roles. I would have thought that there was a clear public understanding that Judges cannot be measured in the same way as other holders of public office or any members of the public. In my understanding, and in that of most of the members of the legal profession and members of the Bench, Judges are expected to abstain from participation in political controversy. Obviously, considering the storm that has brewed early this year on the Berger affair, I was somewhat mistaken. The limited public role of the Judge, one perfectly

Address to the Annual Meeting of the Canadian Bar Association, September 2, 1982. Reprinted with permission.

clear to me, seems to have been misunderstood or forgotten, even by lawyers, let alone by members of the press and of the public.

A fundamental principle has pervaded the judicial role since it took root in the reign of Queen Anne. It was established — not without fits and starts — that Judges would no longer hold office at the pleasure of the Crown, at the pleasure of the government. They would have security of tenure, once assigned to their position, and would hold office during good behaviour to the age of retirement. Their duration in judicial office would no longer depend on governmental whim, and they could be removed only for judicial misbehaviour.

What this imported, as it evolved over the years, was the separation of the executive and the judiciary; no admixture of the one with the other; no mixture of the judiciary in politics or political controversy; correspondingly, no intermeddling of the executive with the judiciary; each branch was to be independent of the other, left alone to carry on its separate duties. For the Judges, they had utmost freedom of speech in the discharge of their judicial functions. Unbelievably, some members of the press and some in public office in this country, seem to think that freedom of speech for the Judges gave them the full scope of participation and comment on current political controversies, on current social and political issues. Was there ever such ignorance of history and of principle?

A Judge, upon appointment — and I am speaking here of appointments which cover all members of our provincial and federal superior courts as well as the Supreme Court of Canada — takes a prescribed oath of office. It is a short oath which is common to all superior court Judges, being as follows:

> I do solemnly and sincerely promise and swear that I will duly and faithfully, and to the best of my skill and knowledge, execute the powers and trust reposed in me as . . .
> So help me God.

But it is invested with all the authority and surrounded by all the limitations that are imported by the principle of judicial independence and that are spelled out in the *Judges Act*, the federal statute which defines the judicial office.

What does the *Judges Act* say about the judicial office? It says quite clearly that a Judge may not, directly or indirectly, engage in any occupation or business other than his judicial duties. There is a limited exception for him or her to act as commissioner or arbitrator or adjudicator or referee or conciliator or mediator, if so appointed in respect of a federal matter by the federal Government; and similarly, if so appointed by the provincial government in respect of a provincial matter. These are short-term, temporary assignments not intended to give a Judge a regular assignment to carry out a non-judicial role. Two recent illustrations of the distinction may be mentioned. A few years ago, the Government of Canada wished to appoint a Judge as a Deputy Minister of an executive department. He was unwilling to accept the position unless he retained his security as Judge. The Government was prepared to go along. I felt it my duty as Chief Justice to protest and did so vigorously, pointing out that it was either the one position or the other, but not both.

A Judge who wishes to accept an executive appointment could not remain Judge at the same time. In the case I mentioned, the Judge put more store on his judicial position than on the proposed executive position. The matter was accordingly dropped. The same thing happened a little later in Ontario when the provincial government wished to appoint an Ontario Supreme Court Judge as Chairman of the provincial Workmen's Compensation Board. Again, I protested; if the Judge wished to accept the provincial appointment, he should resign from the Bench; he could not be both Judge and non-judicial or executive functionary. The principle was accepted and the matter was abandoned.

These instances concerned permanent appointments to governmental positions. The authorized exceptions to allow governments to appoint Judges to special assignments as, for example, by order-in-council or by a limited inquiry, do not involve Judges in executive government or in governmental operations. They are asked to perform a particular service, with generally a short-term duration, although some inquiries like the MacKenzie Valley Pipeline and the McDonald Inquiry into the R.C.M.P. did go on for some years.

I am myself not a great supporter of the use of Judges to carry out short-term assignments at the behest of a government, federal or provincial. Apart from anything else, it is not always convenient to spare a particular Judge, given the ever increasing workload of all Courts. Moreover, there is always the likelihood that the Judge will be required to pass on policy, which is not within the scope of the regular judicial function. But I recognize that governments will continue to ask Judges (generally with the consent of their Chief Justice) to perform these limited tasks. The important thing to remember is that these short-term assignments are not intended to establish a career for the Judge in the work he or she carried out. The Judge is expected to make his or her report to the particular government and to regard the assignment as completed without any supplementary comment. Any comment or action is for the government; the Judge himself or herself is *functus*, done with the matter. This has been the general behaviour of Judges who have accepted and carried out special or particular governmental assignments. Whatever has been the value of the inquiry must rest in what it says — the Judge is certainly not intended to be a protagonist, however enamored he or she may become of the work. Nor is the Judge intended to make a career of the special assignment.

There has been a large increase in the number of federally-appointed Judges in the last decade. Indeed, there are now 466 superior court Judges throughout Canada and 232 county and district court Judges. I do not take account of provincial court Judges who are appointed by provincial governments. The increase in the number of federally-appointed Judges increased the burden of judicial administration, the need to monitor complaints (which are inevitable, even if in most cases misconceived) and the need also to provide outlets for judicial conferences. It was beyond the capacity of Parliament to provide for these matters and they also raised sensitive matters engaging the independent position of the Judges.

In 1971, a new policy was introduced by Parliament to govern supervision of judicial behaviour or, I should say, alleged misbehaviour. . . .

. . . The Canadian Judicial Council came into being in October, 1971 and has had a considerable amount of business in the past decade. It has exercised its powers of inquiry and investigation with great care, seeking on the one hand to satisfy complaints against alleged judicial misbehaviour and on the other hand to protect the reputation of the Judge against unfounded allegations. The most common type of complaint received against Judges has to do with objections to their judgments. Laymen have misconceived the role of the Council: it is not a court of appeal to rectify decisions alleged to be in error; for that there are established appeal courts, and the Council repeatly has to tell complainants that the recourse is an appeal, not an invocation of the powers of the Canadian Judicial Council.

Since the Canadian Judicial Council has a statutory mandate to conduct inquiries into alleged judicial misbehaviour, it can hardly ignore a responsible complaint. In the Berger case, the complaint was made by a long-serving superior court Judge. Was the Canadian Judicial Council to ignore it? At least, it had the obligation to consider whether the complaint merited investigation, that it was not merely frivolous. Those members of the press who became engaged with the complaint in Justice Berger's support seemed entirely ignorant of the mandate of the Canadian Judicial Council. They appeared to be of the view that a Judge's behaviour was for him to measure, that it was not open to the Canadian Judicial Council to investigate, let alone admonish a Judge in respect of a complaint against objectionable behaviour. This was clearly wrong and could have been established by some modest inquiry.

My mention of the Berger case is not to reopen an issue which is closed. It is only to set the record straight on the statutory function and duty of the Canadian Judicial Council, whoever be the subject of a complaint to it. In view of the obvious misunderstanding to which the Berger incident gave rise, it seemed important to me that I, as Chairman, should underline the role and duty of the Canadian Judicial Council, however distasteful it may be to assess the behaviour of a fellow Judge. I would have welcomed, as I always do, the balance provided by the media, by the press, and I regret that it was unfortunate that they did not discharge that responsibility on this occasion.

There was one respect in which members of the press, and indeed some public "bodies" and members of Parliament, showed their ignorance of judicial propriety. It was said that pursuit of the complaint against Justice Berger was an interference with his freedom of speech. Plain nonsense! A Judge has no freedom of speech to address political issues which have nothing to do with his judicial duties. His abstention from political involvement is one of the guarantees of his impartiality, his integrity, his independence. Does it matter that his political intervention supports what many, including the press, think is a desirable stance? Would the same support be offered to a Judge who intervenes in a political matter in an opposite way? Surely there must be one standard, and that is absolute abstention, except possibly where the role of a

Court is itself brought into question. Otherwise, a Judge who feels so strongly on political issues that he must speak out is best advised to resign from the Bench. He cannot be allowed to speak from the shelter of a Judgeship.

In the Berger case, the Judge's intervention was on critical political and constitutional issues then under examination by the entire Canadian ministerial establishment. No Judge had a warrant to interfere, in a public way, and his conviction, however well intended, could not justify political intervention simply because he felt himself impelled to speak. To a large degree, Judge Berger was reactivating his McKenzie Valley Pipeline inquiry, a matter which was years behind him and should properly be left dormant for a political decision, if any, and not for his initiative in the midst of a sensitive political controversy.

The Canadian Judicial Council — one member of Parliament accused us of being engaged in a witch hunt — was badly served by those who, obviously, did no homework on the Council's role and on its obligation. There was another matter which seemed rather shabby, also the result of failure to do any homework. It was indicated, quite explicitly in some news quarters, that the Canadian Judicial Council acted because the Prime Minister had complained of the Judge's intrusion into the political sphere when the Prime Minister was giving a press interview in Vancouver. The record on this matter is quite clear. The written complaint against Justice Berger was addressed to me under dates of November 18 and 19, 1981 and delivered to me, from Ottawa, on those days. The next day, November 20, 1981, I sent a memorandum to the Executive Secretary of Council asking that the complaints — there were two successive ones — be referred for consideration by the Executive Committee. So far as the Canadian Judicial Council was concerned, the complaint had become part of our agenda. The interview of the Prime Minister did not take place until November 24, 1981. It is therefore mere mischief making to suggest that the Canadian Judicial Council was moved to action by the Prime Minister.

The Berger inquiry, as I have said, is behind us, and I regret that I found it necessary to say as much as I did about it. However, the Canadian Judicial Council, which does not and cannot reach out publicly to the media, deserves to have its record cleared. This would not have been necessary if we had been better served by the press throughout the whole affair. A matter like the Berger case is not likely to recur; the Canadian Judicial Council has signalled the danger of recommended removal from office if it should recur. As it was, the Council took a placating view and administered an admonishment in the following terms:

1. The Judicial Council is of the opinion that it was an indiscretion on the part of Mr. Justice Berger to express his views as to matters of a political nature, when such matters were in controversy.
2. While the Judicial Council is of the opinion that Mr. Justice Berger's actions were indiscreet, they constitute no basis for a recommendation that he be removed from office.

3. The Judicial Council is of the opinion that members of the judiciary should avoid taking part in controversial political discussions except only in respect of matters that directly affect the operation of the Courts.

In view of the obfuscation that surrounded the Berger case, there are a number of propositions that must be plainly stated. First, however personally compelled a Judge may feel to speak on a political issue, however knowledgeable the Judge may be or think he or she be on such an issue, it is forbidden territory. The Judge must remain and be seen to remain impartial. Compromise which would impair judicial independence and integrity is out, if the Judge is to remain in judicial office. Second, no federally-appointed Judge can claim immunity from the examination by the Canadian Judicial Council of complaints (unless obviously frivolous) lodged against the Judge; nor against the decision of the Canadian Judicial Council to investigate the complaints through a formal inquiry. Third, the Canadian Judicial Council is not limited to recommending removal or dismissal; it may attach a reprimand or admonishment without either recommending removal or abandoning the complaint. Only if it gets to removal does it become necessary, in the case of a superior court Judge, to engage the Minister of Justice and Parliament, whose approval on a recommended removal must be sought. Fourth, Judges who are objects or subjects of a complaint are entitled to a fair hearing, to appear before the Council or before an appointed committee or to refuse to appear (as Justice Berger did refuse). Refusal to appear does not paralyze the Council, and did not in the Case under discussion . . . .

# 5.5

## ADMINISTRATIVE INDEPENDENCE: CONCERNS OF THE CANADIAN JUDICIARY

Jules Deschenes and Carl Baar

Although, at least by tradition, the Canadian judiciary is independent in the exercise of its judicial prerogatives, it does not enjoy, generally speaking, the same independence in the administration of the Courts.

Everywhere across Canada, it is basically the provincial Ministers of Justice who are responsible for this administration and in turn they call upon

---

*Masters in their own House: A Study of the Independent Judicial Administration of the Courts.* Ottawa: The Canadian Judicial Council, 1981, p.19. Reprinted with permission.

various other departments: Public Works, Supply, Public Service, Social Affairs, Communications, the Treasury Board, and so on.

This administrative subordination of the judicial to the executive causes a great deal of friction. However, as might be expected, the friction has not attained a uniform level throughout the country.

On the contrary, judges of all jurisdictions in Alberta and Manitoba, and judges of the Ontario and British Columbia courts of superior jurisdiction seemed generally satisfied with their relations with the executive.

But as I was told over and over again, whether relations between the judicial and the executive are good or poor depends very often on the personalities of the parties involved; no system can be based on such a flimsy and unstable foundation.

Indeed, it would seem that this factor is responsible for the surprising turnover of the judicial personnel in the Territorial Court of the Yukon: five of its judges in succession have resigned since 1968, while the Deputy Minister of Justice remains.

Leaving aside these difference between regions, there are two questions which profoundly disturb the judiciary at all jurisdictional levels from one end of the country to the other.

The first general cause for concern results from the multiple role played by Ministers of Justice or Attorneys Generals. Everywhere except in the Northwest Territories, where the federal Minister of Justice sees to public prosecution, the same minister:

a. acts daily before the courts personally or, more often, through his substitutes, as attorney for public prosecution;

b. provides the courts with the support staff and services needed for them to operate; and

c. defends the budgets of the courts in Parliament.

This means that the courts hear the minister submit the conclusions which he feels are necessary in the public interest, and they must impartially adjudicate in the light of the law.

But it is on this same minister that the courts must rely for their financial support; and it is to this same minister that the courts must apply for the staff and services they need. The conflict is obvious and the dangers it conceals are ever present. Both the British and the Americans clearly understood this point.

Forty years ago, when the question of the administrative independence of the courts was being discussed in the United States, Attorney General Homer S. Cummings himself sharply criticized a situation which he described in these terms:

> The Attorney General presently fixes the numbers and salaries of the court clerks, the deputies, the judges' secretaries, and the amount and character of equipment for judges and clerks. It controls the travel arrangements, the accommodation in federal buildings, the payment of salaries of judges, clerks, and deputies, and the travel expenses for judges and

clerks. It controls even the power of judges and their law clerks and the secretaries to travel on official business. It prepares and presents to the Bureau of the Budget the estimates for the expenses of the courts, and it is with all of this power over the affairs of the court, the principle (*sic*) litigant before them.

In 1971, Lord Hailsham, Lord Chancellor of England, expressed the same point of view during the debate on the reform of the British Courts:

Many Ministers of Justice not merely appoint judges, but also look after prisons, and start prosecutions. To my mind, this would be something altogether dreadful in the British system and I would fight that in the last ditch.

Consequently it is not surprising that in 1976 Professor Watson concluded:

Yet in Canada. the current trend is for provincial departments which are heavily involved in litigation before the courts to assume increasing and broad roles in court administration. This would appear to be an unsatisfactory state of affairs.

This problem falls outside the competence of the courts: it can only be solved politically.

Now, while in certain provinces such as Quebec, the difficulty is recognized, in others such as Ontario or Nova Scotia many officials are satisfied with a system which "may not be logical, but it works," and seem to fear that the cure might be worse than the disease. There are even other provinces where it is considered offensive merely to raise the question at all!

One thing is certain: it is the unanimous wish of the Canadian judiciary to see this ambiguity eliminated and the functions of attorney for public prosecution and provider of court services separated. Therefore, I recommend that:

4. *The political authorities should realize the ambiguity in the present position of Minister of Justice or Attorney General and separate the function of attorney for public prosecution from that of provider of court services.*

The second general cause for concern within the judiciary has to do with the ambivalent relations existing between court staff and judiciary.

The staff is composed of people who are appointed under different provincial statutes and who are answerable to the Minister of Justice. Essentially, their training, job descriptions, annual evaluations, promotions and salaries depend on the minister. Therefore it is from him that they will expect to receive their instructions. As well, except for management, they are usually members of a union within the public service and thereby have still another allegiance.

At the same time, however, by the very nature of their duties, members of any court support staff are called upon to cooperate daily with the judiciary; and by the very nature of the institution, Chief Justices are required to give the staff directions which they expect to be respected.

Thus the support staff may well find itself torn between conflicting loyalties: one to the minister and the other to the courts. Some have tried to alleviate the problem, or to ignore it, or even to dispute that it exists; but I saw it in various regions of the country: in Prince Edward Island as in Quebec, in Ontario as in Alberta. For example:

a) a judge gave employees of a registry instructions that they found diffi-cult to reconcile with directions from the Attorney General's Department; they decided to give priority to the departmental directions;

b) a registrar stated that he didn't have to take orders from Chief Justices and didn't have to answer to them either;

c) a clerk refused in open court to make certain entries the judge dictated to him in the minutes of the hearing; the clerk justified his refusal by citing instructions to the contrary that he had been given by the registrar in order to save time;

d) a registrar agreed to a request from a Chief Justice, although he knew it would be refused; then he did not forward the request to the department so as to avoid the negative reply he anticipated; a futile attempt to curry favour with both parties;

e) another registrar stated that he works in a world full of mental reserva-tions where nothing is ever straightforward.

Therefore there is nothing surprising in the avowal of one Chief Justice: he is always concerned that his directions will be interfered with by people who have a hierarchical authority over those to whom he gives directions.

It is obvious that this unhealthy situation cannot be allowed to continue, even among those who seem able to adapt to it. This implies a reorganization of the line of authority within the court administration system. I will study how this reorganization may be achieved in theoretical and practical terms later. For the moment, I recommend that:

> 5. *The Executive should adopt suitable measures to ensure that the support staff give faithful allegiance to the courts which it is engaged to assist.*

Over and above these two general causes for concern, the administrative subordination of the judicial to the executive — bad in principle — spawns a host of difficulties, as the list below, which is by no means complete, will show:

a) difficulty in obtaining the necessary staff (throughout the country and on all jurisdictional levels);

b) inadequate premises (in many places);

c) problems with office supplies, photocopies;

d) inadequate security;

e) problems related to transportation and travelling expenses;

f) no prior consultation concerning
   i) changes in registry office hours;
   ii) changes in forms prescribed in the rules of practice;
   iii) legislation affecting the judiciary;

g) indirect or covert amassing of statistics on judges;

h)  budgetary subordination of various judicial councils;

i)  fear on the part of certain judges that the administration will transfer them to a remote region.

In Quebec, the *Courts of Justice Act* even goes so far as to make the code of Ethics of the judiciary subject to Government approval (sec. 261) and to make it the Government's prerogative to decide whether the Judicial Council's head office is to be in Quebec City or in Montreal (sec. 252)!

All these worries, great and small, of the Canadian judiciary result from its administrative subordination to the executive power. In turn, this subordination is rooted in the executive's overt intention to take, exercise and keep total control — except for a few recent timid innovations — of the management, particularly the financial management, of the courts.

Now the public's perception of justice cannot help but be adversely affected by this situation where judges must entreat permission and beg for resources from the executive. One Chief Justice avowed frankly: "There is no longer even a resemblance of independence."

One incident will help convey more clearly the breadth of the gulf separating the political and judicial positions. I had just pointed out to an Attorney General that the judicial is subordinated to the executive: "What you call the weakness of the system," he replied, "is precisely what constitutes its strength."

We must therefore study appropriate measures to loosen the grasp of the executive on the judicial: the public interest would be all the better protected.

# 5.6

# KEYTERMS

*Concepts*

impartiality
judicial independence
"tenure for good behaviour"
administrative independence

*Institutions, Events, and Documents*

Act of Settlement (1701)
Canadian Judicial Council (1971)
Commissioner for Federal Judicial Affairs (1978)

# 6

# Access to Judicial Power

Traditionally, access to the courts has been strictly limited to individuals who meet the threshold requirements of "standing," the right to bring a case before a court. In order to establish standing, a would-be litigant must usually prove the existence of a *lis*, or legal dispute. Not all disputes raise legal issues, and not all legal issues arise in the context of real life disputes. In the realm of constitutional law, mere distaste for or opposition to a particular statute or government policy does not constitute a dispute. A legally recognizable dispute requires the existence of a specific legal interest and an injury or a demonstrable threat of injury to that interest. Finally, a case must not become moot during the course of litigation. If the original dispute that gave rise to the case ceases to exist, a judge will normally refuse to answer the legal issues raised and terminate the judicial hearing.

These restrictions on access to the courts can be traced back to the original common law purpose of courts as adjudicators of real life disputes between individuals. Like other aspects of the judicial process, these strict restrictions on access to the courts were well adapted to adjudicatory purposes, but are subject to criticism in the area of modern public law, where significant policy impact is often implicit in a judicial decision. As Weiler points out, other policy-making institutions are not restricted in these ways. If courts are, or should be, policy-makers, then why should an interest group have to wait for a dispute involving one of its members in order to bring its policy issue into court? (Reading 6.1)

Given the attachment of Canadian judges to the adjudicatory view of the judicial process, one would expect the rules governing standing in Canadian constitutional law to be much more strict than their American counterparts. While this was true historically, a recent series of Supreme Court decisions has dramatically reversed this situation.[1] In the last of these, the *Borowski* Case, (Reading 6.4) the opinion for the majority ruled that:

---

[1] *Thorson v. A.-G. Canada*, (1975) 1 S.C.R. 138; *Nova Scotia Board of Censors v. McNeil*, (1976) 2 S.C.R. 265; and *Minister of Justice of Canada v. Borowski*, (1981) 2 S.C.R. 575.

> [To] establish status as a plaintiff in a suit seeking a declaration that legislation is invalid, a person need only to show that he is affected by it directly or that he has a genuine interest as a citizen in the validity of the legislation and that there is no other reasonable and effective manner in which the issue may be brought before the court.

The *Borowski* decision seems to remove the traditional requirement that a would-be litigant demonstrate a concrete personal interest that is affected by the legal issue raised, and creates instead a very broad right for all citizens to go to the courts and demand that the judges force the government to "behave constitutionally." In effect it now seems that almost any person or group can go to the courts and raise any issue of constitutional law at any time. This may partly explain then Chief Justice Laskin's dissent in *Borowski*, which warned that "the result would be to set up a battle between parties who do not have a direct interest, to wage it in a judicial arena."

The Charter of Rights has further broadened access to the courts. Section 24(1) of the Charter creates a general right for anyone who thinks one of his new Charter rights has been violated to apply to "a court of competent jurisdiction to obtain such remedy as the court considers appropriate and just in the circumstances." The probable effect of section 24(1) is to transform what was still a discretionary privilege — albeit a very broad one — in *Borowski*, into a constitutional right. Section 24 appears to allow a person to litigate any Charter issue he chooses without demonstrating any "personal interest" distinct from the public at large. This interpretation of section 24(1) was confirmed by the Federal Court of Appeal's decision in the *Cruise Missile Test* case in 1983.

The net effect of the *Thorson, McNeil*, and *Borowski* decisions, combined with the new Charter of Rights, has been to increase dramatically the potential for judicial policy-making by Canadian judges. There would appear to be no remaining legal barriers to prevent the litigation of the constitutionality of almost any government decision or policy. If American practice is any guide, the "losers" in the legislative arenas are almost certain to take advantage of this new forum to challenge government policy that they oppose. It will thus be difficult for the courts to avoid becoming entangled in the major political controversies of the day.

An important exception to the traditional requirement of a *lis* is the reference procedure. Starting with the original Supreme Court Act of 1875, the federal government has given itself the authority to "refer" questions of law to the Supreme Court of Canada for answering. A reference procedure is not really a case in the true sense, as there is no real dispute involved, but only a request for an advisory opinion on a hypothetical legal issue. This distinctive characteristic of the Canadian judicial process is not found in American jurisprudence. Article III of the American Constitution spells out the requirement of a *lis* by limiting the federal courts to hearing only "cases or controversies." At a very early stage this "case or controversy" requirement was interpreted as preventing the Supreme Court from providing "advisory opinions" to the federal government.

The fact that reference cases are technically "advisory opinions" on hypothetical questions of law should not lead one to underestimate their importance in Canadian law and politics. Approximately one quarter of all final appellate court decisions involving constitutional law have been references. Since 1949, this figure has declined to sixteen percent. Among these are many of Canada's most important and politically influential constitutional law decisions. Predictably, governments almost never refer questions to the courts in a political vacuum. References tend to be very timely politically, either anticipating a political problem that is on the horizon or, in some cases, already being litigated in a lower court. Finally, while judicial decisions in references are not technically binding on anyone (since there are no real parties), they have been regarded as authoritative nonetheless.

The reference procedure has generated ongoing controversy in Canadian jurisprudence. In the original Supreme Court Act of 1875, some provincial leaders perceived it as suspiciously resembling the much disliked disallowance power of the federal government, and opposed the entire Supreme Court Act for this reason.[2] This suspicion was nurtured by the rather non-judicial characteristics of the original reference procedure. Only the federal government could refer questions of law to the Supreme Court, but these could be questions concerning the validity of provincial laws. Once the question was referred, there was no opportunity for affected parties — including provinces — to present oral or written arguments in defense of their interests. When the Supreme Court decided a reference, it did not provide any written opinion to support or explain its decision.

In response to continued provincial criticism of the reference procedure, it was substantially reformed in 1891 to make it more closely resemble a normal judicial proceeding. The 1891 amendments require that interested parties be given the opportunity to submit oral and written arguments to the Court, and that the Court hand down a written opinion with its final decision. While the federal government did not give provinces the authority to refer questions to the Supreme Court, during the next decade most provinces gave themselves a reference power to their own courts of appeal. Even after these reforms, the question remained whether answering reference questions from the executive branch was a proper judicial function. This question was put to rest in 1912, when the Judicial Committee of the Privy Council decided a provincial challenge to the constitutionality of the federal government's reference procedure. The J.C.P.C. ruled that although answering references was a "non-judicial function," it could nonetheless be imposed on the courts by statute. It also noted in passing that similar provincial practices implicitly supported the legitimacy of the federal reference procedure.

The advantages and disadvantages of the reference procedure are ably discussed by Justice Barry Strayer in Reading 6.2. One of the alleged advantages,

---

[2] See Jennifer Smith, "The Origins of Judicial Review in Canada," Reading 10.1.

however, deserves further comment. The reference procedure, Strayer and others have argued, is a practical device for each level of government to police the constitutional excesses of the other. While no doubt this is true in theory, in practice there has been a strong tendency for both levels of government to abuse the reference device as a political weapon to attack policies of the other.

The federal government's *Off-Shore Mineral Rights Reference* in 1967 is commonly cited as an example of a bad-faith effort of the federal government to seize through the reference procedure what it could not get through political negotiation. The Supreme Court's decision in favour of the federal government in this case seriously harmed the Court's image as an impartial arbiter of federal-provincial disputes, and thus its long-term authority.[3] More recent examples include Newfoundland Premier Brian Peckford's use of the reference procedure to improve his bargaining position on the issue of who has the legal authority to control the development of the Hibernia oil reserves. Although Peckford's gamble backfired miserably,[4] he had made it clear from the start that he would not accept the "moral authority" of a Supreme Court decision that went against him. In so doing, Peckford was taking a page out of the book of Quebec premiers, who have repeatedly responded to Supreme Court decisions in a politically self-serving manner. If they win, they can claim that they were right all along, and declare that this is yet another example of Ottawa's overreaching its legitimate jurisdiction. If they lose, they can claim that it is yet another example of how the Supreme Court "always" takes the side of the federal government, and cannot be trusted to look out for provincial rights.

This type of political maneuvering places the Supreme Court in an almost "no win" situation, where the justices are "damned if they do, and damned if they don't." The cumulative effect of this sort of political abuse of the reference procedure is to diminish the authority of the courts. Strayer concedes this as a potential problem, but seems to suggest that it can be minimized by the self-restraint of political leaders, both federal and provincial. This seems doubtful. Can elected political leaders be relied upon to put the long-term institutional interests of the courts ahead of their own short-term political interests? Past experience suggests not.[5]

---

[3] See Reading 2.2.

[4] The federal government referred the same issue to the Supreme Court of Canada before the Newfoundland Court of Appeal made a decision, and the Supreme Court ruled in favour of the federal government. This decision effectively destroyed any legal support for Newfoundland's position on Hibernia development.

[5] The problem of "executive self-restraint," or the lack thereof, during the 1970's is insightfully elaborated by Edward McWhinney, *Quebec and the Constitution, 1960-1978* (Toronto: University of Toronto Press, 1979), ch. 8.

# 6.1

# TWO MODELS:
# OCCASIONS FOR JUDICIAL ACTION
Paul Weiler

. . . The theory of the judge as a policy-maker gives one a fresh point of view not only on the question of who becomes such a "political actor," and how, but also on the question of when and how he is able to act, or be induced to act. The classic theory of the court as adjudicator indicates that the judge's function is to settle disputes when requested by one of the parties. Unlike most other political actors, he remains passive and is unable to seize the initiative to make his decision when he feels the time is propitious. Only if there exists a specific "case and controversy" which is still extant at the time of decision is the latter permissible. On the other hand, once the judge is requested to act by a party to a dispute, then the judge is obliged to decide one way or the other. He cannot take the position (at least in a fully-developed legal system) that he can find no answer or solution to the disputed question. All this of course flows naturally from the theory that the primary goal of judicial activity is dispute-settling, rather than policy-settling.

It should be apparent that such an account of "when" a judge engages in political action is highly anomalous to one who believes the latter to be the prime focus of judicial activity. According to this theory, the courts are merely another branch of government to which various interest groups seek access in order to have their political desires satisfied. As such, courts have certain institutional characteristics which render them peculiarly suited to satisfying better certain interests and to giving greater protection to particular groups (especially those which may be under-represented elsewhere). The courts tend to develop a specific clientele group which becomes adept at bringing relevant influence to bear on the courts, and which probably acts in a reciprocal fashion to protect the interests of the judicial institution and to preserve its effectiveness and power.

In the context of such a systematic political explanation of the courts' work, the classic theory of the occasion for judicial action just does not make sense. In the first place, there is no reason why the development of a group interest in a particular policy decision (which can be obtained only from a court) should coincide with the occurence of a specific dispute in which a representative of the group is involved. This creates a preliminary problem of obtaining access

*Canadian Bar Review*, 1968, p.406. Reprinted with permission.

to the court. Even this is probably overshadowed by the difficulty of obtaining access in a specific suit which raises in an especially favourable way an issue whose resolution will constitute the desired political decision. The group must be able to manage effectively the source of litigation so as to preclude the court being required to make the policy decision in a unfavourable context, in order to decide a case which, by the rules of the game, must be adjudicated.

In Canada there are several recent phenomena which the two models help illuminate. In a recent decision, the Canadian Supreme Court rejected the attempt by the Jehovah Witnesses to get a favourable policy response to the actions of the Quebec Government directly aimed at them. The court applied the classic adjudication requirement of a "lis" to frustrate the efforts of a group which had inspired most of the Supreme Court doctrines in the previous decade, favourable to political freedoms. On the other hand, in a politically charged context, the federal government used the Reference device to obtain from the court a policy ruling that measurably improved its bargaining position in the dispute over offshore mineral rights. This case clearly showed the political desirability to a policy-making court of having discretionary control over its own jurisdiction. It needs this power so that it can protect its institutional resources and legitimacy by choosing the strategic time and occasion for its policy initiatives. Just as in the case of judicial appointments, arguments in favour of reform of the courts' jurisdiction, based on technical considerations of efficiency, do have political significance when viewed through the "policy-making" model.

# 6.2

# CONSTITUTIONAL REFERENCES

Barry Strayer

One of the most distinctive features of Canadian judicial review is its frequent resort to the constitutional reference. This frequency can be demonstrated by a survey of the leading cases: those reaching the Privy Council up to 1949, the Supreme Court of Canada thereafter, decided from 1867 to 1981. Of 282 cases involving the constitutional issues, 77 had their origins in a constitutional reference while 205 involved concrete cases. Nor does the fact

*The Canadian Constitution and the Courts: The Function and Scope of Judicial Review.* 2nd ed. Toronto: Butterworths, 1983, p.271. Reprinted with permission.

that over a quarter of the leading decisions were given in such proceedings reveal the full significance of constitutional references. In terms of impact on the political, social, and economic affairs of the country the decisions in these cases have had an effect far beyond their numerical proportion. It is therefore essential in any study of judicial review of legislation in Canada to give some particular attention to this device. . . .

### Advantages

To the extent that problems of standing can still prevent judicial review on constitutional grounds, references provide a means whereby constitutional issues may be placed before the courts.

. . . Rules of standing in constitutional cases have largely depended in the past on the requirements of particular remedies and . . . as a result certain remedies were available for judicial review only to persons with an ''interest'' distinct from that of the general public. At best the applicant for a declaration, injunction, *certiorari* or prohibition, who does not have such a specific interest, will be subject to the discretionary power of the court to grant or withhold standing, and in the case of *mandamus* he will not be able to proceed. There may be certain constitutional norms, such as the requirements for distribution of constituencies or of periodic elections, in which no individual would be regarded as having a sufficient interest in such judicial review. There may be issues, such as the validity of the federal spending power when used in areas of provincial legislative jurisdiction, or the propriety of constitutional amending procedures, where no individual could persuade a court to grant him standing.

It must be recognized, however, that if the recent trend continues with respect to the discretionary grant of standing in declaratory actions for judicial review, the resort to references to overcome standing problems in constitutional cases may be of marginal importance.

As well as permitting initial judicial review where it would not otherwise be available, a reference may be used to obtain the opinion of a higher court where an appeal would not lie. It is improbable that this precise type of situation would arise now with respect to an appeal from the highest court of a province to the Supreme Court of Canada. Since 1949 the *Supreme Court Act* has permitted appeals without limitation in any matter where either the provincial appellate court or the Supreme Court gives leave. In a constitutional case leave would no doubt be forthcoming from either court. Yet the reference will still be a good substitute for an appeal in some cases. In some provinces there may be situations where an appeal to the highest court is not available, and a reference may be used. Or the parties to the original litigation may not wish to carry a case to the Court of Appeal or the Supreme Court and the provincial or federal Attorney General may be powerless to do so. There is also the possibility that the courts may refuse leave to appeal a case which the Government feels should be appealed. While the Government's power should not be used lightly in such circumstances, the court could be forced by a reference to deal with the issue on which they had refused leave to appeal. Or a reference could be used instead of an appeal to raise related issues not involved in the lower court.

In cases where judicial review will be ultimately possible through private litigation, a reference may nevertheless be desirable to hasten the process. To facilitate public or private planning it may be very valuable to have a judicial opinion in advance with respect to the legality of a particular course of action. For example, the Government may wish to have clarified the constitutionality of a nation-wide unemployment insurance scheme or a marketing scheme before establishing elaborate machinery for its operation. A vivid example of this kind of situation may be found in *Reference re Anti-Inflation Act.* In order to move swiftly to combat a high rate of inflation Parliament had passed this Act on December 15, 1975, effective October 14, 1975 directly imposing wage and price controls in the federal public and private sectors, and providing for the imposition of similar controls in the provincial sector where any province entered into an agreement to have those controls apply along with federal administration thereof. All provinces except Quebec entered into such agreements and Quebec established parallel controls. Questions were soon raised as to the validity of the federal law, and its application by agreement to the Ontario provincial domain was being challenged in an action commenced in the courts of that province. Other cases were contemplated elsewhere in Canada. Since the application of the law would disrupt a myriad of transactions throughout the country it was urgent that the constitutional position be clarified. It was referred to the Supreme Court on March 11, 1976, argued on May 31-June 4, 1976, and judgment was given on July 12, 1976, generally upholding the validity of these arrangements. Thus within seven months of the passage of the Act a definitive ruling of the highest court had been obtained as to its validity. The disruptive effect of continuing uncertainty, and the probability of much longer delays before all the issues would otherwise have reached the Supreme Court by ordinary appeal, made the reference device a valuable means of clarifying the situation.

It may be important to businessmen to know under which level of Government they are to operate, and speed of clarification of this issue may be useful in encouraging economic development. This justification has been used, for example, in connection with references to the courts to seek judicial opinions on questions of jurisdiction and ownership over offshore resources.

There will also be situations where speedy determination is more of a necessity than a convenience. Emergency conditions such as war make it imperative that the Government be assured at once of the validity of proposed action. For example, if it wishes to create a regulatory system to ensure the maintenance of vital supplies and the prevention of waste, it cannot afford the luxury of waiting for chance litigation to uphold or strike down the scheme.

A reference may also provide relief where a private citizen would not find it convenient to take a constitutional case to the higher courts. A litigant may have grave doubts about the validity of a statute applied against him, but it may be less expensive for him to drop his objection than to carry the case to an appeal. Yet such a statute applied similarly to dozens or hundreds of people may collectively cause great expense or injustice. In addition, various lower courts may hold conflicting views as to the validity of the law, some upholding it and other deeming it invalid. If no affected individual is prepared to undertake the expense and trouble of appeal, the enforcement of the statute will fall into chaos and the law itself into discredit. A reference to an appellate court may provide the authoritative decision required to restore order. If the statute is held invalid, numerous citizens will be relieved from compliance with legislation which it was not practical for them to contest individually.

With respect to issues which the courts usually regard as non-justiciable a reference might be used to permit judicial determination. There are obviously many non-justiciable issues where the decision ought not to be made by the judiciary, in any form of procedure, because a policy determination is required and there are no objective criteria for guidance. But there are other areas, such as the propriety of parliamentary procedure, where pre-established norms are available for application. It is not certain that a court would review a federal statute on the basis that it was passed by a procedure not in accordance with the *Constitution Act.* Yet the directions of the Act in this regard are as clear as those of sections 91 and 92 which the courts constantly apply.

Finally, references provide a flexible means for each level of Government to challenge the constitutional authority of the other level of Government. The federal Government was given this power in another form through the disallowance procedure. But federal disallowance of provincial legislation on the sole grounds that it was *ultra vires* fell into disfavour and by 1935 was expressly abandoned. Even where the power was exercised on this ground, it was common for the Federal Government first to refer the question of validity to the Supreme Court and be guided by its advice. The reference is now the principal means for the Government of Canada to challenge the validity of provincial legislation. It may of course refer such legislation on its own initiative or at the request of the province concerned. Equally, the provinces may challenge the validity of federal legislation or even a parliamentary resolution by referring it to a provincial court, in this way ensuring that it will ultimately reach the highest tribunals. In Ontario the Attorney General may, in the alternative, seek a declaration that an Act of Parliament is invalid, but presumably the reference procedure would be speedier.

The essential advantage of the reference system thus appears to be facilitation of judicial review. In some cases it makes the impossible possible, in others it speeds the process where time is of the essence. To those for whom enforced judicial activism poses no threat, the constitutional reference may appear as an unmixed benefit. But it is also essential to consider some of the problems which arise out of its use.

### Disadvantages

Two principal disadvantages of references can be identified: they may foster abstract jurisprudence because they require an opinion from the court without the benefit of an adequate factual context; and they may cause the court to decide issues which are not really justiciable because Governments are seemingly unlimited in the questions they can refer. These difficulties flow from the very nature of references: that is, they do not arise out of a specific controversy between parties where legal rights are in issue.

The first problem mentioned, the lack of an adequate factual basis, has been thought not only to hinder sound characterization of laws, but also to lead more frequently to a finding of invalidity.

The suspicion that they favour findings of invalidity cannot be clearly confirmed on a statistical basis. A survey of leading constitutional cases from 1867 through 1981, those reaching the highest tribunal available, either the Privy Council or the Supreme Court, shows that the results in the courts for each level of Government were not dramatically different as between references and ordinary litigation. Of cases involving provincial competence, in 42 references provincial authority was upheld in 22 cases and found lacking in 20 cases — a failure rate of about 50%. In ordinary litigation, in 138 cases the provinces succeeded in 82 and lost in 55, a failure rate of about 40%. For the federal authority, in 38 references there was a finding of invalidity in 11 cases, a loss rate of about 29% whereas the loss rate in ordinary litigation was 13 of 68 cases, or about 20%. So the contrasts are far from marked as between results achieved in references and ordinary litigation. The statistical results are unreliable because of the relatively small numbers and the probable existence of other factors involved as between references and litigation and as between federal and provincial results.

It is interesting, however, to look at some of the most abstract and influential reference decisions in our constitutional history to understand the nature of this problem. One need only look at a few examples. In the 1916 *Reference re Insurance Act* the Supreme Court was asked for an opinion as to the validity of certain sections of the federal *Insurance Act, 1910.* This legislation required the federal registration of insurance companies before they could carry on business. It was broad enough to cover provincially incorporated companies carrying on business in Canada outside the province of incorporation. A majority of the Supreme Court confined itself to an exercise in semantics, holding that the federal power to regulate "trade and commerce" could not include "a trade." The insurance business was regarded as "a trade," hence not susceptible to federal control. One of the dissenting judges, Davies J., took a more functional approach. He took judicial notice of the national significance of the insurance business, the mobility of insured persons, and the possible national repercussions of the failure of a major company. This enabled him to find that the business of insurance was clearly a matter of national trade and commerce. But the Privy Council on appeal sided with the majority below, Viscount Haldane at his dogmatic best holding that

. . . it must now be taken that the authority to legislate for the regulation of trade and commerce does not extend to the regulation by a licensing system of a particular trade in which Canadians would otherwise be free to engage in the provinces.

Here was a reference involving the bare question, "Are sections 40 and 70 of the 'Insurance Act, 1910,' or any or what part or parts of the said sections, *ultra vires* of the Parliament of Canada?" No factual information was included with the reference, nor apparently was any otherwise presented to the court. Without consideration of the factual context in which the legislation would operate, the majority of the Supreme Court and the Privy Council set aside the legislation on a conceptual analysis of the word "trade". The net result was to bar the Parliament of Canada from regulating businesses which were interprovincial in scope, because their operations could be analytically dismembered into a collection of "particular trades" carried on in particular provinces. . . .

. . . This examination of a few major reference decisions of historic importance illustrates their potential for creating abstract jurisprudence. There are, however, several mitigating factors which should be recognized in assessing the merits of the reference system in this respect.

First it should be recognized that while such decisions were conceptual rather than functional, this was also true of contemporary decisions in normal litigation. There were many concrete cases where facts were probably available but not relied on. In defence of the Privy Council decisions of this period, whether on references or in litigation, it has been argued that, whatever their economic validity, they were politically realistic.

Secondly, there are situations where there is no need for a factual study of legislative effect or administrative action. This arises where the issue is solely that of an interpretation of a section of the constitution where no legislation is involved and no official action is being questioned. These cases will be rare, and the decision therein may be of limited use. But occasionally they will be valuable, where the issue in question is sufficiently narrow. For example in *Edwards v. A.G. Can.* the question was whether the word "persons" in section 24 of the B.N.A. Act included women, thus making the latter eligible for appointment to the Senate. The answer turned completely on internal evidence in the Act. The effect of each possible interpretation was readily apparent. . . .

. . . Thirdly the remedy for abstract reference decisions should not be total abandonment of this sometimes useful device, but rather a more selective use of it accompanied by adequate fact-introduction. . . . It has been demonstrated that the Supreme Court has led the way in emphasizing the importance of facts in references and the trend appears to be for counsel to meet these judicial expectations. What we are seeing in reality is a rather unsteady movement from the conceptual jurisprudence so beloved by the Judicial Committee and its followers to a more functional jurisprudence in which facts are all important. Therefore much of this particular problem traditionally associated with the reference process may disappear, although the inherent nature of the device is a reminder that constant care must be exercised in its use. There should be a careful framing of questions so that issues may be raised as precisely as possible. Courts should refuse to answer questions which are too general or which require a factual context if none is provided. They should also avoid answering questions not clearly included in the reference order. If these principles are faithfully applied in reference cases, there will be far less complaint of abstractness.

The second major problem with references noted above is that they may call upon a court to answer questions that are not justiciable. Reference statutes at both the federal and provincial level allow Governments to refer any "matter" to the courts. This would appear on its face to include any question not only of law, but also of politics, science, or taste. It has recently been held, however, by a majority of seven in the Supreme Court in the *Re Resolution to Amend the Constitution* that such a provincial statute

> . . . is wide enough to saddle the respective courts with the determination of questions which may not be justiciable and there is no doubt that those courts, and this Court on appeal, have a discretion to refuse to answer such questions.

Given the lack of a clear separation of powers in our system it is perhaps not surprising that the court did not deny itself the right to decide non-justiciable questions by only asserted a power to decline to do so at its discretion. It is encouraging to know that the courts will not feel obliged to decide questions which functionally belong elsewhere. But at the same time it must be noted that, having asserted the right to refuse to answer, the court in this same case proceeded to answer questions posed by provincial Governments to their courts and appealed to the Supreme Court as to the existence and nature of a political convention concerning the sue of legal powers.

While Legislatures have thus authorized Government to refer non-justiciable questions to the courts, normally they do not do so nor, it is submitted, should they do so if they wish to protect the court from undue political controversy and resulting hazards to their legitimacy. The federal Government has in fact articulated such a principle in the course of resisting pressures for references to the Supreme Court.

When governments do not exercise self-restraint in this respect, it is open to the courts to do so and to decline to decide such issues. When these safeguards are not employed, the reference system does thrust the courts into the decision of non-justiciable issues that may in the long term impair their effectiveness.

Lesser criticisms of the reference system include that of possible interference with private rights. Judges have occasionally hesitated to answer a referred question because, though worded generally, it may include issues on which the rights of specific individuals may turn. It is thought unfair to render such decisions where individuals who may be seriously affected are not represented before the court. As previously noted, this criticism appears specious for the same may be said of almost any decision. . . .

. . . The real fault lies, not in the initial reference decision having possible implications for private individuals, but rather in the misplaced fidelity with which such decisions are subsequently followed. This is part of the broader complaint that reference decisions have generally been given undue precedential value. In other words, what were originally intended to be opinions only have been treated as judgments.

When the *Supreme Court Act* was amended in 1891 reference opinions were described as "advisory only." This was soon ignored and the Privy Council and Supreme Court expressly followed the decisions in earlier federal references with undiscriminating zeal. Not until 1957, after the "advisory only" provision had actually been dropped from the *Supreme Court Act* did the Supreme Court suggest the possibility that it would ignore earlier reference decisions, even those of the Judicial Committee. It then stated that it was not bound by a decision of the Judicial Committee rendered in a reference involving some of the same issues and parties now before it in a concrete case. It may be noted, however, that this was *obiter dicta*, for the Supreme Court accepted the opinion of the Privy Council.

It is to be hoped that this judicial declaration of independence will not be forgotten by its authors. Uncritical following of reference decisions brings discredit on the whole reference system. The rendering of opinions on hypothetical questions or on issues affecting private rights would create few problems if they were not subsequently treated as conclusive. An opinion on an abstract question should be regarded as of limited value, valid only in relation to the assumptions and facts on which it was rendered. . . .

. . . Combined with the abandonment of *stare decisis* with respect to reference opinions, there should be a more discriminating use of such opinions when invoked for persuasive purposes. In analyzing what a reference actually "decided," the opinion should be carefully examined in relation to the precise hypotheses put to the court and the facts, if any, before it. Such analysis may reveal that the opinion decided very little, in which case it ought not to be an embarrassment in subsequent cases.

In sum, it is suggested that if references have created premature or overly broad precedents the fault lies more in judicial practice than in the reference system. Judicial reform would remove the substance of this complaint.

### Conclusion

The controversy over references is really an aspect of the larger controversy with respect to the role of the judiciary in interpreting and applying the constitution. Judicial activists will generally approve of a system which overcomes obstacles to judicial review. Those who take a more restricted view of the role of the judiciary will see it as a hazardous procedure, burdening the courts with hypothetical questions and producing premature decisions with mischievous consequences.

On balance the case for the use of references seems more supportable. If one accepts the courts as the best arbiters of constitutional rules, one should favour a system which facilitates judicial review. There are some situations where a reference will be justified in the interests of speed, clarification for the benefit of many individuals who would not readily be able to seek judicial review, or the elimination of technical barriers to bringing actions or taking appeals.

Several caveats must be entered, however. In the first place, some of the justifications for the use of references have been attenuated by developments of the last decade. The obstacles to standing for individuals to seek declarations on constitutional issues, the nearest substitute for a reference, have largely disappeared. With almost universal legal aid for the individual and numerous special interest groups able to undertake or support litigation, Government initiatives by way of a constitutional reference are now not as necessary to ensure judicial review. At the same time the development of a more functional jurisprudence with greater emphasis on the factual context tends to militate against the use of the reference which often lacks factual substance. So although there is still a role for the reference it has been somewhat reduced by events.

Where there are reasons for resorting to a reference, Governments should still avoid doing so if the issue to be referred is not justiciable in the sense that it is one better left to another branch of Government or one which lacks objective criteria for its determination. The principal danger to be avoided here is the reference of essentially a political issue to the courts: where there are few, if any, genuinely legal criteria to which courts can resort for a rationale for their decision, they may be perceived as making a political judgment which may impair their long-term credibility.

Once the decision is taken to refer a constitutional question, then care should be taken in its framing so that the issues are precisely defined. The referring Government and counsel on all sides should make every effort to ensure that all relevant facts are placed before the court.

As for the courts, they should be astute enough to refuse answers to questions that are non-justiciable, or too vague to be effectively answered. They should have regard to gleaning all relevant evidence, including an active resort to judicial notice. They should also examine critically earlier opinions and be prepared to disregard or distinguish those which were too general, too vague, or too abstract.

Even a carefully constructed reference system must play a secondary role in judicial review, however. A decision based on complete facts and real issues is to be preferred to one based on incomplete facts, or hypothetical problems, and a binding authority is likely to be more reliable than an advisory opinion. Thus, if other circumstances are equal and judicial review through a concrete case is feasible, it should be preferred. The reference should be seen as a useful supplement to our judicial review system, but one to be resorted to with caution and perhaps, in the future, with diminishing frequency. The second century of Confederation has so far seen a sharply reduced rate of references in comparison to the volume of ordinary constitutional litigation, and this trend is likely to continue.


# 6.3

## THE CHICKEN AND EGG REFERENCE

Paul Weiler


I shall begin my analysis by a sketch of a case study-our recent constitutional *cause célèbre* arising out of the "chicken and egg war." This was primarily an engagement fought by the bordering provinces of Ontario and Quebec. Ontario farmers produced an abundance of cheap eggs and Quebec farmers an abundance of cheap chickens. The surplus producers were naturally interested in the market of the consumers in the neighbouring jurisdiction. Equally naturally, the somewhat less efficient producers of each product were not so enamoured of competition within their own bailiwick. When they went to their own government for protection, the response was legislation facilitating the creation of marketing schemes. These provided for the controlled marketing, at fixed prices, of all the chickens sold in Ontario and all the eggs in Quebec, whatever the source. Unfortunately, it appears that the marketing boards became a little greedy and went even further, giving undue preference in marketing to those products coming from within the province. This had particularly adverse effects on farmers in other provinces such as Manitoba, which, as a consistent producer of agricultural surpluses, was the classic innocent and injured bystander in the "chicken and egg war."

On the surface, I find it rather hard to see what the courts have to contribute to the resolution of this essentially political and economic conflict. There certainly was ample scope for bargaining and negotiating terms of settlement which might offer at least something to everyone. One could understand that the federal government, which represented producers and consumers from all affected jurisdictions, might have been an appropriate arbiter. Unfortunately, earlier judicial decisions of the twenties and the thirties had themselves created the very institutional gaps which fostered such interprovincial marketing conflicts. At this very time, the federal government was attempting to shepherd through Parliament a new Farm Products Marketing Act which would

*In the Last Resort: A Critical Study of the Supreme Court of Canada.* Toronto: Carswell-Methuen, 1974, p.156. Reprinted with permission.

endeavour to solve these problems through a complicated process of inter-administrative delegation. Though there appeared to be substantial consensus in favour of the general scheme of the Bill by both federal and provincial ministers of agriculture, it was being delayed by opposition members who largely represented western farming interests. In the interim, the federal government had carefully resisted many calls to refer the "political" dispute to the Supreme Court of Canada for immediate "legal" resolution.

Unfortunately, Manitoba, which was understandably loath to wait for a political decision on the larger question, devised a scheme for circumventing the reluctance of the federal Justice Minister. The provincial government manufactured a controversy by initiating a carbon copy of the Quebec scheme, a proposed Order-in-Council which provided for Manitoba control of the marketing of extraprovincial eggs in Manitoba. It then referred these regulations to the Manitoba Court of Appeal for a decision about their constitutionality, under its own provincial reference legislation. When the Manitoba Court of Appeal decided against the constitutional validity of the scheme, the Manitoba government was entitled as of right to appeal this "loss" to the Supreme Court of Canada. In this way, it could achieve a binding decision as to all such schemes which would be authoritative in all the provinces.

Some may be troubled by this apparent subversion of the adversary process. Manitoba purported to argue for, and then appeal on behalf of, laws which it was proposing to enact for the sole purpose of having the Supreme Court declare them unconstitutional. I am more concerned by the general deficiencies of the "reference" procedure which made this ploy possible. A direct reference of a legal question to the courts is a means of overcoming the limitations of adjudication in having constitutional policy settled quickly. For that reason, it enjoys some favour among lawyers. Unfortunately, while we may get the law established quickly, we may also get it wrong. Many of our worst constitutional decisions have come from references and this case did not prove an exception to that rule.

The point of a reference is to bring a legal problem before the courts without having to wait for litigation about a situation in which the legal issue is important. This changes only one factor in a complex institutional equation without considering the unhappy effect on the other elements. We are still relying on the courts for the right answer to the constitutional question. What mainly qualifies a judge to reach an intelligent conclusion is that he acts as an impartial arbiter of a dispute arising in a concrete setting. Because a specific fact situation triggers the litigation which requires a constitutional ruling, the judge has the benefit of seeing the real-life implications of his decision and he can carefully tailor the reach of his conclusion as he sees fit. His judicial neutrality is preserved by an adversary process which allows the interested parties to bring all the relevant factual background before him, depicted in as favourable a light as possible from each point of view.

In the *Manitoba Egg Reference*, both of these advantages to adjudication were dissipated. There was no concrete focus around which the reasoning of the Supreme Court could be organized nor was the factual economic background to the statute presented. The Manitoba government conspicuously omitted to set out in the Reference the relevant economic evidence which might well have supported the reasonability of provincial action in the area. Ontario and Quebec, both of which were vitally interested in sustaining this kind of legislation, did not have an opportunity to present this factual support. Indeed, the questions which the Manitoba government posed to the Court did not focus on what appears to have been the real character of the dispute — the discriminatory application of provincial marketing quotas against out-of-province producers — and instead required the Court to make a blanket decision about the legality of any such marketing scheme, no matter how favourably it might be applied to extraprovincial products. In my opinion, the most sensible response would have been a forthright refusal to answer the question on the grounds that the dispute was not appropriate for judicial resolution. One senses that Mr. Justice Laskin, who was especially critical of the abstract character of the Reference, was drawn in this direction, but eventually the legal mystique surrounding issues of federalism overcame his reluctance. The majority opinion proceeded blithely ahead, without any apparent concern for the complex and inter-related political or economic interests involved in the dispute, and the Court gave Manitoba the broad legal weapon it wanted.

Are there any inadequacies in the substantive reasoning and results of the Court which may have reflected some of thse procedural deficiencies? A casual reading of the opinion certainly indicates the truth of Hughes' dictum that "the Constitution is what the judges say it is." In the first place, the Supreme Court is attempting to work out a distinction between regulation of interprovincial and intraprovincial trade. However, this is a purely judicial gloss on the text of the BNA Act, which has become constitutional dogma with little real assessment of the reasons for it. It began with *Citizens Ins. Co. of Can. v. Parsons*, [1881], a Privy Council decision which upheld the validity of fairly innocuous provincial legislation regulating the terms of insurance contracts. In order to do so, the Court excluded provincial intervention from the economy only when it amounted to "regulation of trade in matters of interprovincial concern." Soon this formula became constitutional doctrine for the converse problem — determining the ambit of valid dominion legislation. Because there has never been any real assessment of the reasons why we should have such a judge-made allocation of legislative authority, it is not surprising that the courts have never discovered how to apply it in anything but a wooden and legalistic way.

The underlying functional problem is that consumers of farm products, who are making purchases through a national currency and credit system, cannot effectively be regulated by a legislative body which has jurisdiction over a portion only of the undifferentiated products which are being marketed to them. If the federal government alone can control the marketing of extraprovincial products or trade, and the provincial government alone can control intraprovincial products or transactions, then there will have to be substantial identity in the content of co-ordinated legislation if the regulatory goals of either are to be achieved. Otherwise, the supply of unregulated goods will frustrate the orderly marketing and price supports which are the major thrust of current farm policy. Yet, the attainment of co-operation always faces the obstacle of possible federal disinterest in a relatively localized problem or a parochial local veto of legislation desired by the federal government and a majority of the provinces. Hence, the requirement of co-operative action is always risky, time consuming and in the interests of those who do not want to be regulated (and who win from a governmental decision not to intervene whether it comes on the merits or not). . . .

[A number of precedents are reviewed that support the constitutionality of the Manitoba regulations.]

. . . In the face of this course of decision, it would seem very difficult to legally invalidate the proposed Manitoba Egg scheme. In order to do so, the Court would have to make and justify a very substantial change in the direction of Canadian constitutional law. Of course, the two older cases — *Shannon and Home Oil* — were directly on point and firmly in favour of provincial jurisdiction. Whatever hints to the contrary we might have seen in the 1957 *Reference*, dealing with an analogous situation, seemed put to rest by the *Carnation* case. Yet the Court, without a suggestion that it was doing any more than follow a long unbroken line of decisions, turned around and held the Manitoba scheme invalid. The opinion for the Court majority was again written by Mr. Justice Martland. The sum total of his reasoning to this conclusion is contained in the following passage:

> It is my opinion that the plan now in issue not only affects interprovincial trade in eggs, but that it aims at the regulation of such trade. It is an essential part of this scheme, the purpose of which is to obtain for Manitoba producers the most advantageous marketing conditions for eggs, specifically to control and regulate the sale in Manitoba of imported eggs. It is designed to restrict or limit the free flow of trade between provinces as such. Because of that, it constitutes an invasion of the exclusive legislative authority of the Parliament of Canada over the matter of the regulation of trade and commerce.

I suggest that this argument is question-begging as a response to the legal authority of the *Carnation* case decided less than three years before (let alone the older but more direct precedents of *Shannon* and *Home Oil*). No doubt there are factual distinctions between the two marketing schemes, but I do not believe that there are meaningful economic differences relevant to the central legal issue — should one province have the power to control agricultural marketing inside its boundaries when this necessarily affects or "concerns" the interests of citizens in other provinces? I will indicate my reasons for this judgment, but I should first point out that even if I am wrong there is not one sentence in the majority opinion which purports to show why one scheme is valid, but the other is not. Instead, we are given only labels — *affects* interprovincial trade or *aims at the regulation* of such a trade. We have met other instances of the same tendency in earlier chapters; the reader may remember the notion of "unusual danger." Constitutional law is shot through with such verbal formulae masquerading as legal guidelines. These the individual judges apply in some mysterious fashion to produce a result which they tell us is the law, or at least the law for the time being. . . .

. . . There are some observers who will not be troubled by this, and will believe that what the Court says is law, and must be followed, and that is the end of that. Unfortunately, others, especially those adversely affected by this "law," will ask why they should accept the intuitive judgements of the Court as final. Ontario and Quebec may simply say that they believe their legislation is somewhat different from that involved in the *Manitoba Egg Reference* and one can find no principle or reasoning in the latter case which would indicate whether or not the distinction is specious. In any event, it seems that shortly afterwards the affected governments met and engaged in some serious bargaining which was directed towards the real conflicts and problems in the area. This was to be expected because it is hard to see how the "winner take all" kind of judicial decision could be an acceptable basis for resolving a very complex problem involving not only a conflict between different groups of producers, but an equally vital conflict between producers and consumers who vote in the same province. The most intriguing comment made just before the meeting of the ministers of agriculture was that they were all agreed then on just one thing — that the Supreme Court decision would *not* be the basis of their final settlement.

# 6.4

# MINISTER OF JUSTICE OF CANADA v. BOROWSKI

Supreme Court of Canada (1981)

Laskin C.J.C. (dissenting): — This appeal, which is here by leave of this Court given on terms as to costs, arises out of a taxpayer's action brought in the Court of Queen's Bench of Saskatchewan. The purpose of the action was to obtain a declaration against the appellants, the Minister of Justice of Canada and the Minister of Finance of Canada, that the so-called abortion provisions of *Criminal Code*, s. 251(4), (5) and (6) are inoperative as offending ss. 1(a) and 2(e) and (g) of the *Canadian Bill of Rights* and that any expenditure of public money to support therapeutic abortions under the aforesaid provisions of the *Criminal Code* is consequently illegal. Issue was taken by the defendants appellants as to the jurisdiction of the Court of Queen's Bench to entertain the action. . . . . In their statement of defence, the defendants also challenged the standing of the plaintiff to maintain the action, regardless, apparently, of the appropriateness of the forum.

I start with the proposition that, as a general rule, it is not open to a person, simply because he is a citizen and a taxpayer or is either the one or the other, to invoke the jurisdiction of a competent Court to obtain a ruling on the interpretation or application of legislation or on its validity, when that person is not either directly affected by the legislation or is not threatened by sanction for an alleged violation of the legislation. Mere distaste has never been a ground upon which to seek the assistance of a Court. Unless the legislation itself provides for a challenge to its meaning or application or validity by any citizen or taxpayer, the prevailing policy is that a challenger must show some special interest in the operation of the legislation beyond the general interest that is common to all members of the relevant society. This is especially true of the criminal law. For example, however passionately a person may believe that it is wrong to provide for compulsory breathalyzer tests or wrong to make mere possession of marijuana an offence against the criminal law, the Courts are not open to such a believer, not himself or herself charged or even threatened with a charge, to seek a declaration against the enforcement of such criminal laws.

The *rationale* of this policy is based on the purpose served by Courts. They are dispute-resolving tribunals, established to determine contested rights or claims between or against persons or to determine their penal or criminal liability when charged with offences prosecuted by agents of the Crown. Courts do not normally deal with purely hypothetical matters where no concrete legal issues are involved, where there is no *lis* that engages their processes or where they are asked to answer questions in the abstract merely to satisfy a person's curiosity or perhaps his or her obsessiveness with a perceived injustice in the existing law. Special legislative provisions for references to the Courts to answer particular questions (which may be of a hypothetical nature) give that authority to Governments alone and not to citizens or taxpayers. Merely because a Government may refuse a citizen's or taxpayer's request to refer to the Courts a question of interest to the taxpayer does not *per se* create a right in the citizen or taxpayer to invoke the Court's process on his or her own, or by way of a class action on behalf of all citizens or taxpayers with the same interest.

There are exceptions to the general rule and to the policy. One of the earliest recognized has been a municipal taxpayer action to restrain an allegedly illegal municipal expenditure . . . . An explanation of this exception is that it involved a public right to see that municipal expenditures were lawfully made, being expenditures which were limited by considerations that do not apply to a Province or to Canada. No municipal taxpayer could raise a *lis* in the ordinary sense or court a penalty or other sanction in respect of an allegedly illegal municipal expenditure and, hence, unless a taxpayer action was permitted the illegality would go unchallenged and unchallengeable.

In the provincial and federal field, the issue of an illegal, or perhaps unconstitutional, expenditure would not likely arise *per se* but, in the main, only (as is alleged in this case) in connection with the operation of challenged legislation: the challenge to the expenditure would thus depend on the outcome of the challenge to the legislation.

Another exception (but a more limited one in view of the discretion associated with it) is shown in the judgment of this Court in *Thorson v. A.G. Can. et al. (No. 2)* (1974). . . . That case involved a taxpayer's class action to obtain a declaration of the invalidity of the *Official Languages Act*, now R.S.C. 1970, c. 0-2, and of the illegality of the appropriation of money to administer it. It was clear that a justiciable question was raised to the claim of invalidity, namely, whether Parliament had respected the limits of its legislative authority under the *British North America Act, 1867*. Again, the *Official Languages Act* was not a regulatory type of statute nor a penal one but rather, uniquely, a declaratory and directory statute, a statute which created no offences and imposed no penalties. Unless, therefore, a citizen or taxpayer action was permitted to question its validity, there would be no way in which its validity could be tested unless the federal Attorney-General did so through a reference and a request to this end had been denied. . . .

. . . There is, in this respect, in the permissive provisions of s. 251(4), (5) and (6), some similarity perhaps to the directory features of the legislation in the *Thorson* case. However, these provisions are part of a scheme which embraces sanctions as well, and I do not find the similarity to be sufficient to put the legislation here on the same level as the statute involved in the *Thorson* case. Indeed, to borrow from the words of this Court in the *Thorson* case, the present case is not one where all members of the public are affected alike. This, in my view, is a central consideration in the exericse of the Court's discretion against giving standing here to the plaintiff respondent.

It is contended on the plaintiff's behalf that if he cannot bring himself within the *Thorson* case, his position as to standing is as strong as that of the respondent in this Court's follow-up decision to *Thorson* in *Nova Scotia Board of Censors v. McNeil* (1975). . . . That was also a case where a taxpayer action challenging the validity of legislation, provincial legislation in that case, was held to be maintainable. . . . The *Theatres and Amusements Act* of Nova Scotia, whose validity was challenged in the *McNeil* case, was a regulatory statute directed to film exchanges, theatre owners and cinematograph operators and apprentices. It also provided for the appointment of a Board, empowered to permit or prohibit the use or exhibition in Nova Scotia, for public entertainment, of any film or any performance in any theatre. Licensing regulations were provided for in respect of theatres and film exchanges, in respect of cinematograph operators and apprentices and in respect of theatre performances. Unfettered discretion to suspend or revoke any licence was vested in the Board. It had, to put it shortly, complete control over the exhibition of films and over theatres in the Province. Although there was a statutory right of appeal to the Lieutenant-Governor in Council, it was not open to a member of the public.

The Nova Scotia Courts, before whom the question of standing came, and this Court on appeal construed the challenged statute as involving members of the public in so far as the Board had the power to determine what members of the public were entitled to view in theatres and other places of public entertainment. This Court assessed the matter as follows:

> Since the issue of validity does not fall for determination here and, indeed, has not even been argued in relation to the question of standing I would not, in this case, go beyond the tentative conclusion that there is an arguable case under the terms of the challenged legislation that members of the Nova Scotia public are directly affected in what they may view in a Nova Scotia theatre, albeit there is a more direct effect on the business enterprises which are regulated by the legislation. The challenged legislation does not appear to me to be legislation directed only to the regulation of operators and film distributors. It strikes at the members of the public in one of its central aspects.
>
> In my view, this is enough, in the light of the fact that there appears to be no other way, practically speaking, to subject the challenged Act to judicial review, to support the claim of the respondent to have the discretion of the Court exercised in his favour to give him standing.

This passage underlines at least one important difference between the situation in *McNeil* and the present case. In *McNeil*, the plaintiff could legitimately complain (on this Court's construction of the challenged statute) that he was a person within its terms who was being deprived of a right to view a film because of an allegedly unconstitutional exercise of legislative and administrative power. In the present case, there is no deprivation under or by reason of the challenged legislation of which the plaintiff can complain. In short, the plaintiff here is not in the same position under the legislation which he challenges as was McNeil in his case. There he was a person within the compass of the enactment that he was challenging; the plaintiff is outside the *Criminal Code* provisions that he is attacking.

I am of the opinion that the plaintiff in this case cannot bring himself within the *McNeil* case nor within the *Thorson* case, so far as concerns the character of the legislation involved here as compared with the legislation in those cases. . . .

. . . The present case lacks concreteness despite the fact that it raises a highly charged issue. Moreover, it appears to me that to permit the issue to be litigated in as abstract a manner as would be the case in having the plaintiff alone carry it against two Ministers of the Crown would hardly do justice to it, absent even any intervenors who might, with the same obsessiveness on the opposite side of the issue, argue for the valid operation of the challenged provisions. Even accepting, as is probable, that if standing was accorded to the plaintiff, other persons with an opposite point of view might seek to intervene and would be allowed to do so, the result would be to set up a battle between parties who do not have a direct interest, to wage it in a judicial arena.

I would hold, therefore, that not only has the plaintiff failed to establish any judicially cognizable interest in the matter he raises but, on any view of this case, the discretion of the Court should be exercised to deny him standing. It follows that his action should be dismissed. . . .

Martland, J. (for the Court):

. . . The issue raised is a difficult and important one, involving the question as to whether the human rights declared in the *Canadian Bill of Rights* protect a human foetus.

In his statement of claim, the respondent states that he is a citizen of Canada and a taxpayer to the Government of Canada. He goes on to state in the following paragraphs of the statement of claim:

3. On February 20, 1969 the Plaintiff was elected by the voters of the provincial constituency of Thompson, Manitoba to represent them in the Legislative Assembly of Manitoba, a position he maintained until June 28, 1973. In his capacity as taxpayer, elected representative of the people in the Legislative Assembly, a member of the governing party in the Legislative Assembly of Manitoba and Minister of and adviser to Her Majesty the Queen in Right of the Province of Manitoba, the Plaintiff has continuously promoted and defended the rights of individual human foetuses, including their right to life.

4. The Plaintiff has canvassed all practicable means to invoke action on the part of both Provincial and Federal Governments to repeal or to impugn the validity of the abortion sections of the *Criminal Law Amendment Act*, Statutes of Canada, 1968-69, chapter 38, section 18, (now section 251, subsections (4), (5) and (6), of the *Criminal Code of Canada*, hereinafter referred to as "the abortion section of the *Criminal Code*") and to cease and desist from spending public funds to abort and destroy individual human foetuses.

5. The steps taken by the Plaintiff included:

   (a) His resignation, on or about September 5, 1971, *inter alia*, because as Minister of and adviser to Her Majesty the Queen, he "could not be a party to, or accept, child-destroying legislation in which we (are) involved";

   (b) His address in the Legislative Assembly of Manitoba, on May 4, 1973, opposing adoption of the budget presented by the Provincial Treasurer that proposed to finance the abortion and destruction of individual human foetuses by the expenditure of public funds;

   (c) His continuous objection over a term of years to payment of his personal income tax to the Federal Government to protest its expenditures of public moneys collected by personal income taxes, to finance and to promote the abortion and destruction of individual human foetuses, and his conviction and sentence to terms in jail for his stand;

   (d) His personal correspondence with the Premier and Cabinet of the Province of Manitoba, with the Prime Minister of Canada and with Members of his Cabinet including the Minister of Justice, the Minister of Finance, and the Solicitor-General of Canada requesting that they take appropriate legal action to protect the rights of individual human foetuses;

   (e) His request addressed to the Official Guardian of Manitoba in the year 1977, to take legal proceedings on behalf of individual human foetuses to prevent their abortion and destruction, and to protect their right to life.

In every instance, the efforts of the Plaintiff to move public official to impugn the validity of the abortion provisions referred to in paragraph 4 hereof by judicial proceedings met with negative response. No one undertook to subject these provisions, of great public importance, to judicial review.

For the purpose of these proceedings, all of these statements must be accepted as being true. . . .

In both the *Thorson* and *McNeil* cases, the challenge to the legislation in question was founded upon their alleged constitutional invalidity. In the present case, the challenge is based upon the operation of the *Canadian Bill of Rights*. I agree with the view expressed by the Chief Justice that no distinction should be made between a declaratory action to obtain a decision on validity under the *British North America Act, 1867* and a declaratory action to obtain a decision on the operative effect in the face of the *Canadian Bill of Rights*.

The legislation under attack here is not declaratory or directory as in the case of the *Official Languages Act* nor is it regulatory as in the case of the *Theatres and Amusements Act*. It is exculpatory in nature. It provides that in certain specified circumstances conduct which otherwise would be criminal is permissible. It does not impose duties, but instead provides exemption from criminal liability. That being so, it is difficult to find any class of person directly affected or exceptionally prejudiced by it who would have cause to attack the legislation.

Doctors who perform therapeutic abortions are protected by the legislation and would have no reason to attack it. Doctors who do not perform therapeutic abortions have no direct interest to protect by attacking it, and, consequently, an attack by a doctor in that category would be no different from that made by any other concerned citizen. The same thing applies to hospitals. A hospital which appoints a therapeutic abortion committee has no reason to attack the legislation. A hospital which does not appoint such a committee has no direct reason to attack the legislation.

There is no reason why a pregnant woman desirous of obtaining an abortion should challenge the legislation which is for her benefit. The husband of a pregnant wife who desires to prevent an abortion which she desires may be said to be directly affected by the legislation in issue in the sense that by reason of the legislation she might obtain a certificate permitting the abortion if her continued pregnancy would be likely to endanger her life or health and thus prevent the abortion from constituting a crime. However, the possibility of the husband bringing proceedings to attack the legislation is illusory. The progress of the pregnancy would not await the inevitable lengthy lapse of time involved in Court proceedings leading to a final judgment. The abortion would have occurred, or a child would have been born long before the case had been finally terminated, perhaps in this Court.

The legislation proposed to be attacked has direct impact upon the unborn human foetuses whose existences may be terminated by legalized abortions. They obviously cannot be parties to proceedings in Court and yet the issue as to the scope of the *Canadian Bill of Rights* in the protection of the human right to life is a matter of considerable importance. There is no reasonable way in which that issue can be brought into Court unless proceedings are launched by some interested citizen.

In the light of the *Thorson* and *McNeil* cases, it is my opinion that the respondent should be recognized as having legal standing to continue with his action. In the *Thorson* case, the plaintiff, as an interested citizen, challenged the constitutional validity of the *Official Languages Act*. The legislation did not directly affect him, save in his position as a taxpayer. He had sought, without avail, to have the constitutional issue raised by other means. He was recognized to have status. The position is the same in the present case. The respondent is a concerned citizen and a taxpayer. He has sought unsuccessfully to have the issue determined by other means.

In the *McNeil* case, the plaintiff was concerned about censorship of films in Nova Scotia. He had sought by other means to have the validity of the *Theatres and Amusements Act* tested, but without success. In that case there were other classes of persons directly affected by the legislation who might have challenged it. None the less, he was recognized as having legal standing because it also affected the rights of the public. The position of the respondent in this case is at least as strong. There are in this case no persons directly affected who could effectively challenge the legislation.

I interpret these cases as deciding that to establish status as a plaintiff in a suit seeking a declaration that legislation is invalid, if there is a serious issue as to its invalidity, a person need only to show that he is affected by it directly or that he has a genuine interest as a citizen in the validity of the legislation and that there is no other reasonable and effective manner in which the issue may be brought before the Court. In my opinion, the respondent has met this test and should be permitted to proceed with his action.

# 6.5

## KEYTERMS

### Concepts

standing
*lis*
"case or controversy" requirement
taxpayer's suit
declaratory judgement
moot case
reference case
advisory opinion

### Institutions, Events, and Documents

The Supreme Court Act (1875)
The Chicken and Egg Reference (1971)
*Minister of Justice of Canada v. Borowski* (1981)

# 7

# Interest Groups and Litigation

One of the important developments in American law and politics during the past thirty years has been the strategic use of constitutional litigation by organized interest groups to achieve public policy objectives. This new form of political action was successfully pioneered by the National Association for the Advancement of Colored People, the leading Black civil rights group, in its fight against racial segregation in the American South. Politically stymied in both the national Congress and in the Southern state legislatures, the NAACP turned to the federal courts for help. The success of the NAACP inspired other interest groups to adopt similar strategies to change existing public policies on such issues as capital punishment, abortion, censorship of pornography, and women's rights. Almost all of the most important and most controversial decisions of the American Supreme Court since 1954 have been litigated directly or indirectly by organized interest groups.

A question of major political significance is whether the new Charter of Rights will act as a catalyst for litigation as an interest group activity in Canada. Historically, Canadians have not generally used litigation as a political tactic. As historian Kenneth McNaught reports, the courts, the press and the public have all tended to reject "any concept of the courts as positive instruments in the political process." (Reading 7.2) It seems that this tradition is going to be strongly challenged by the advent of the Charter of Rights. A variety of civil libertarian, feminist, and other "single issue" groups have high expectations about using Charter litigation as a vehicle for political change. According to one participant-observer of the politics of Charter-making, "The Charter was viewed as a redistributive tool."[1] On the second anniversary of the Charter, an article in the Toronto *Globe and Mail* summarized the principal effect of two years of Charter litigation as "helping Canadi-

---

[1] Sandra D. Burt, "Women and the Canadian Charter of Rights and Freedoms: A Case Study of Women's Groups and Canadian Public Policy," Paper presented at the 55th annual meeting of the Canadian Political Science Association, Vancouver, June 7, 1983, p. 10.

ans realize that they now have a platform from which to raise a variety of social justice issues.''[2]

As readings for this chapter indicate, these expectations are already being translated into action. ''Operation Dismantle,'' a coalition of peace groups, labour unions, and women's organizations, has challenged the federal Cabinet's decision to permit testing of the U.S. Cruise missile in Western Canada. (Reading 7.3) Both pro- and anti-abortion groups have initiated Charter challenges to the abortion sections of the Criminal Code. (Readings 7.4 and 7.5) The Canadian Advisory Council on the Status of Women is considering establishing a ''legal defense fund,'' modeled after the American experience, to monitor and to initiate Charter litigation related to feminist policy objectives. (Reading 7.6)

With the easy access created by section 24(1) of the Charter, Canadian interest groups face no legal barriers in turning their ''causes'' into cases.[3] How Canadian judges will respond to these invitations to undertake social and political reform is another question. The Supreme Court of Canada, which will have the final word in this matter, has not yet decided a sufficient number of Charter cases to support any conclusions or predictions. A study of first year Charter litigation found that individual litigants won approximately 25% of all Charter cases, but that provincial courts of appeal were much more ''pro-Crown'' than the trial courts.[4]

The significance of interest groups' use of the Charter does not just rest on their success in particular cases. Organized interest groups can significantly influence the Court's agenda during this critical formative period of Charter interpretation. The Supreme Court, like all courts, is essentially a passive institution: it must wait for litigants to come to it with cases. Although it is now free to choose which cases it will hear, it still must choose from cases initiated by others. Thus the type of cases it chooses from will be an important influence on the early judicial interpretation of the Charter.

Interest groups can also participate indirectly in politically important cases. The judicial decision of a case in constitutional law usually affects interests beyond those immediately represented by the parties to the case. A case involving an issue of federalism will determine which level of government may or may not pursue certain types of policies for the foreseeable future. A case that pits censorship of obscenity against the right to ''freedom of the press'' can affect the availability and extent of pornography in Canadian

---

[2] *Globe and Mail*, April 17, 1984.

[3] See Introduction to chapter six.

[4] F.L. Morton, ''Charting the Charter — Year One: A Statistical Analysis,'' Paper delivered at the 56th annual meeting of the Canadian Political Science Association, University of Guelph, June 10, 1984.

society. In both examples there would be many groups interested in and affected by the court's decisions who might not be actual parties to the case. This raises the question of whether "third parties" should be allowed to participate in a legal case, and if so, how?

By using Weiler's "two models" paradigm we can understand how different assumptions about the judicial function lead to different answers to these questions. (Reading 7.1) Under the "adjudication of disputes" model of judging, third parties should not be permitted. The focus of the judicial proceeding is on the unique dispute of the immediate parties to the case. Each party has a self-interest in developing the facts and arguments most favourable to his interest, and if this is poorly done, only the responsible litigant suffers. On the other hand, if the courts are essentially "policy-making" institutions, then all groups or individuals who are affected or even interested should be allowed to present evidence and argue their positions.

Canadian judicial practice falls somewhere between these two hypothetical extremes. Recognition of the broader policy impact of judicial decisions, especially in constitutional law, has led to the development of the "intervenor" and *amicus curiae* devices. These are procedures which allow interested third parties to participate in cases in which they are not a principal litigant. In cases challenging the constitutional validity of a statute, federal law and most provinces allow the Attorney-General of the interested government(s) to "intervene" to represent the government's position and to defend the impugned statute. In both federal and provincial reference procedures, courts are explicitly given the authority to notify "any person interested," and allow them to be heard. Under the federal reference procedure, the Supreme Court of Canada may even appoint and pay for counsel to represent interests that would not otherwise be heard.

The *amicus curiae* brief is a dicretionary device used by common law courts to allow third parties to participate in a proceeding. Its literal meaning of "friend of the court" connotes its non-partisan origins as a means of assisting courts in identifying relevant precedents. In American jurisprudence the *amicus* device has evolved into a tool of partisan advocacy in public law cases. In the 1976 *Bakke* case, more than 100 groups filed 59 *amicus curiae* briefs, taking different sides on the issue of whether "affirmative action" constitutes "reverse discrimination." One can see the resemblance of this procedure to a legislative committee accepting petitions or hearing testimony from interested parties. In Canada the courts have made very minimal use of the *amicus curiae* procedure in constitutional law. This can be partly attributed to the availability of the alternative device of "intervenor," and partly to judicial traditionalism and aversion to anything that appears to "politicize" the courts. Based on American experience, one can predict an increase in the number of intervenors and *amici curiae* under the Charter of Rights.

Yet another way interest groups can use litigation to achieve policy objectives is through the "class action suit." A class action is a lawsuit brought by an individual on behalf of himself and other similarly situated persons, who

have a common interest and a common grievance. It has been used extensively in the United States by environmental and other "citizens' action
groups" to force corporate and governmental compliance with regulatory
policies. Its use in Canada has been much more limited due to strict judicial
interpretation of what constitutes a "common interest" and to other procedural problems affecting expenses. (Reading 7.7) Recent developments suggest that this too may be changing. Quebec recently established a public fund
to pay the legal expenses of class action suits, and an Ontario Law Reform
Commission report has recommended legislative reforms that would facilitate
the bringing of class action suits in that province.

# 7.1

# TWO MODELS: ACCESS TO THE COURTS
Paul Weiler

. . . This shades into the related issue of allowing representation to groups
which are interested in a general policy result but are not involved in a
particular controversy that raises the issue of this policy before a court. The
adversary theory of adjudication assumes that parties interested in the specific
dispute will represent sufficiently the opposing general positions so as to put
adequately all the elements which make up a rational decision and, in any
event, if they do not make an effective case, only the interested parties really
suffer from an adverse judicial decision. Yet, if the essence of judicial decision-
making is the formulation of general policy for society, it is obvious that all
those whose positions are affected by the policy have an interest in the best
possible argument being made to the court. Since, in fact, it is unrealistic to
rely as a general matter on the specific parties to the case (if for no other
reason than that of finance), there is a tendency in such a theory to develop a
device for allowing interested groups representation in judicial policy-making
by allowing them to participate in the argument which influences the court.
Such a device, in fact, is available in Canada in the form of "intervention" or
the "amicus curiae." In constitutional matters, the federal and provincial
Attorneys General must be notified and allowed to appear and argue this
issue. In the case of references, the Supreme Court has power and has often

*Canadian Bar Review*, 1968, p.406. Reprinted with permission.

used it, to allow private groups to appear and even to appoint counsel to argue on behalf of such an interest.

These various considerations have contributed to the formulation of a new theory of "litigation as a form of pressure group activity," of interest groups "lobbying the Supreme Court." The theory is intended as a response to its analogue under the adjudication model, that judge-made law (or policy) emerges accidentally from the fortuitous circumstance of litigation which reaches the court for the purpose of obtaining a settlement of a specific dispute or controversy, a "trouble case." Now, as organized groups perceive the possibilities for social change inherent in litigation the quality of randomness to judicial policy-making becomes substantially diluted. A very valuable recent paper by Mr. Hakman has thrown substantial doubt on conclusions drawn from the work of Mr. Vose that such lobbying activity was a valid explanation for any significant part of the present judicial activity in the American Supreme Court. This is really irrelevant to a theoretical model which prescribes what ought to be, and what might well become the case in the near immediate future. Hence it is worth while to describe briefly some of the present evidence for the concept.

The most significant evidence stems from the activity of the National Association for the Advancement of the Coloured People (N.A.A.C.P.) in inducing the Supreme Court to develop doctrines favourable to the "integration" interest in the United States. Especially important was the gradual development of such doctrines from easy cases as deprivation of the right to vote in elections and then in primaries, through restrictive covenant litigation, to "separate but equal" public education, and finally anti-miscegenation statutes. Such a development shows the importance not only of a "conceptual bridge" in "legal" reasoning, but also a "political" Supreme Court awakening and educating the nation to the problem. The N.A.A.C.P. was faced with many tactical problems: finding specific cases for litigation and ensuring that they do not become moot; obtaining control over the litigation and thus ensuring expert development of the evidence (including policy facts) and argument for the court; gaining control over the course of litigation in this whole area to ensure that the best possible case reached the Supreme Court first; and then maintaining the initiative in the complete implementation of the favourable policy results obtained. The success of this whole effort is demonstrated not only in the substantive results sought but also in the development of the doctrine that this particular N.A.A.C.P. activity (and all others of its type) are protected by the constitutional value of freedom of association for political purposes. In a sense the latter result means that the courts have provisionally accepted the theory of litigation as a form of group political activity.

Yet Harlan J.'s dissent does show the problem of meshing the conception of litigation as a form of political lobbying with an institutional set-up designed for adjudication of disputes. There is always a possibility that a conflict of interest will arise between the nominal party to the case (who may be very concerned about the specific dispute) and the group which controls the litigation (which is concerned primarily with a favourable policy result). Suppose the lawyer hired by the latter gets an offer of a favourable settlement for the individual party which will deprive the court of a chance to speak? Suppose the individual case is not as favourable an avenue for the policy judgment as another piece of litigation being promoted by the same group that pays for the lawyer of the nominal party? The suggested remedy to the situation is a change in the rules of participation that allows a direct constitutional attack on legislation by affected groups or their members. The implication of this for the judicial process are obvious.

Other American examples can be given of phenomena that partially support the theory. Professor Paul Freund has decribed the competing efforts of the Roosevelt government and of private economic interests to formulate for (and get in front of) the courts the most favourable case (from each respective point of view) raising the issue of the constitutionality of New Deal legislation. Mr. Vose has shown that the original development of the Brandeis brief (which collects for the court policy facts showing the reasonability, and thus the constitutionality, of impugned social legislation) derived from the efforts of the National Consumers League to function as a pressure group which could more effectively put the argument in favour of constitutionality than the nominal party at interest in litigation.

The *amicus curiae* brief raises two further problems. First, it shows the conflict between the real interests present in the "private adjudication" and "public policy-making" models of judicial activity. If the focus of judicial decisions is on the settlement of private disputes, then too unrestricted a system of *amicus curiae* briefs will be unduly burdensome to the parties interested in the particular dispute. In this connexion, the United States Supreme Court rules requiring the consent of the parties to private briefs reflect the theory of the adversary nature and control of the judicial process. One might contrast the position of Mr. Justice Black which is a forerunner of a model that allows groups to lobby via their briefs, to bring policy information to the court, and to attract support for an activist role of the court. Secondly, since the *amicus curiae* brief is designed to influence the court by presenting it with data relevant to its formulation of policy with which to dispose of a particular dispute, it raises the question of what exactly are the available means for influencing a judicial decision and which of these are to be considered proper. The political actor model of the judicial process puts both of these problems in a new light.

# 7.2

# POLITICAL TRIALS AND THE CANADIAN POLITICAL TRADITION

Kenneth McNaught

An American Scholar, T. Becker, wrote recently that "in a sense, all trials are political. Since courts are governmental agencies and judges are part of the 'system' all judicial decisions can be considered political." This excessively commodious definition is less useful than one proffered by Professor Nathan Hakman when he suggests that courtroom participants act politically when their activities involve other members of society. Hakman then proposes that scholars can conceptualize conscious or unconscious use of court cases as (1) an instrument for securing private and personal remedies; or (2) an instrument for changing legal symbols (i.e., applicable rules of law); or (3) a means of organizing and/or suppressing movements for social and economic power and control. Even this approach to a definition casts a very wide net. Within it one could catch hundreds of "test cases" — from *Roncarelli* to the Bennett New Deal legislation.

I suspect that a Canadian attempt to define a political trial would result in more constrictive language. We have never been as ready as the Americans, for example, to view the courts as means for changing "legal symbols" — especially if such a process includes implementing significant social change. Thus, under Hakman's third rubric, our courts have seldom, if ever, been used to "organize movements for social and economic power and control"; they have, however, very often been used in attempts to suppress such movements. It may very well be because of this Canadian tradition that attempts to politicize some recent trials — such as the FLQ cases, the Quebec labour leaders' trial, and the lesser cases of student anti-war and "occupation" demonstrators — seem largely to have failed, at least by comparison with the Angela Davis case, the Black Panther cases, the Ellsburg case, or the Chicago trials in Judge Hoffman's court.

A preliminary survey of Canadian political trials strongly suggests that our judges and lawyers, supported by the press and public opinion, reject any concept of the courts as positive instruments in the political process. In Canada the positive aspects of politics seem more clearly to belong to the political parties, the legislatures, and the press. A corollary of this is that

---

*Courts and Trials: A Multidisciplinary Approach.* Edited by M.L. Friedland. Toronto: University of Toronto Press, 1975, p.137. Reprinted with permission.

political action outside the party-parliamentary structure tends automatically to be suspect — and not least because it smacks of Americanism. This deep-grained Canadian attitude of distinguishing amongst proper and improper methods of dealing with societal organization and problems reveals us as being, to some extent, what Walter Bagehot once called a "deferential society." We have certainly shown deference to the concept of *established* authority and procedures and even to the legal idea that valid authority flows downward from the crown.

Far from being merely medieval, such attitudes have often proven more liberal in their effect than those of radical or participatory democracy. In any event, the basically British belief that both liberty and justice are impossible without order lies at the heart of the Canadian political tradition and of the manner in which our judicial process has dealt with cases of a clearly political nature. . . .

. . . Conversely to the conventional wisdom of Canadian history, it may well be that our judicial history indicates that we have had somewhat more confidence in the validity of our institutions and our whole national experiment that have the Americans in theirs. Sir John A. Macdonald, with his talent for compression, summed up the purpose and the self-confidence of the Canadian experiment when he remarked during the 1864 Quebec Conference: "Thus we shall have a strong and lasting government under which we can work out constitutional liberty as opposed to democracy, and be able to protect the minority by having a strong central government." Constitutional liberty has remained the other side of the Canadian monarchical coin. . . .

. . . On the basis of this discussion it may be argued that our courts, in dealing with clearly political cases, have both reflected and expounded a confidence in the legitimacy of an evolving Canadian society and especially in the political-legal principles of that society. Thus they have firmly rejected the use of violence by any entity other than the state. So, too, they have resisted any effort to make them the agents of social change or to destroy the trial process by disruptive politicization. One result of these consistent attitudes has been positive encouragement of democratic party organization and, indeed, of a multi-party system which is distinctively Canadian. Judicial insistence on the legitimacy of established authority, nourished by retention of the symbols and precedents of constitutional monarchy, has often, of course, worked to the advantage of social-economic elites. But where this has been the case, changes in the structure of power and the distribution of wealth have been sought, often effectively, through democratic political action. Moreover, if the courts have been quick to lend support to established authority in real or alleged crisis situations and thus have appeared to be an arm of the executive, their severity has often been mitigated by executive-legislative policy — deciding, for example, who should actually be prosecuted, reprieved, or compensated.

Finally, although the courts have resisted any temptation to propound advanced ideas in social-economic policy, it would be absurd to argue that they have simply reflected a Canada that is a Lockean fragment frozen in unchanging political attiudes. What the courts *have* reflected is an unchanging Canadian belief in constitutionality against a background of political adaptation to the changing requirements of an increasingly industrial society. . . .

# 7.3

## ANTI-CRUISE CAMP WINS FIRST ROUND

*Calgary Herald*

The anti-cruise missile movement won a major legal victory Thursday to stop Canadian tests of the weapon when the Federal Court rejected a government move to toss their case out of court.

Justice Alex Cattanach gave government lawyers 30 days to file a defence statement setting out why the federal approval for testing the missile "is justifiable in a free and democratic society."

A full hearing will then be scheduled into the bid by a coalition of 26 peace, trade union and women's organizations for an interim injunction to block the unarmed missile tests starting early next year in Western Canada.

Lawrence Greenspon, lawyer for the coalition, was elated at the court win, calling it "the first time in Canada that the government's executive action and the matter of whether it is constitutional will come before the courts."

The cruise opponents are challenging the government approval for test-flying the cruise missile on the grounds it threatens guarantees of life, liberty and security set out in the Charter of Rights and Freedoms accompanying the Constitution.

James Stark, president of Operation Dismantle, said if they win the interim injunction, the next step will be to seek a permanent ban on the cruise tests. "Hopefully, the whole process can be completed before the tests begin, which is to say January or so in 1984."

Cruise opponents must still prove their case that cruise tests present a recognizable threat to Canadians' constitutional rights. If they succeed, Greenspon said, the government then must "demonstrably justify that violation as being a reasonable limit on the right to life, liberty and security of the person."

Garton [Crown counsel] argued unsuccessfully that the case against cruise-missile tests should never have been permitted to come to court.

---

*Calgary Herald*. September 16, 1983. Reprinted with permission.

"This matter does not belong in a court of law," he said early in the six-hour court proceeding, "It belongs in the Parliament."

Executive decisions, like that of the federal cabinet in July approving tests of American war weapons, could not be challenged in court before the Charter of Rights and Freedoms and should not be now, Garton said. It is "purely a matter of policy, of national defence."

Cattanach said he was persuaded the minimum requirement of "a scintilla" of justification for an injunction hearing had been successfully presented by the anti-cruise lawyers.

Greenspon argued that there is no reason why a federal cabinet decision shouldn't be subject to a court review if it violates the constitution. Otherwise, "they'd be professing to be above the law," he added, despite the fact that the Charter of Rights and Freedoms binds Parliament and the government of Canada just like ordinary citizens.

During the afternoon hearing, Greenspon said that permitting a full hearing will allow Canadians to hear expert opinions about the likelihood of personal or property damage from test-flying the unarmed missiles.

Garton protested that the only risk the cruise opponents mentioned in their legal challenge was the danger of an escalating international arms race. No one is worried about the risk of a test missile "falling on someone's head," he said.

"I am," Cattanach replied, prompting courtroom laughter.

# 7.4

# ABORTION LAW TEST BEGINS

*Calgary Herald*

More abortions were performed at the Regina General Hospital last year for "socio-economic reasons" than for medical reasons, Dr. Donald Carnduff said Monday.

Carnduff, medical care administrator of Saskatchewan's busiest hospital, made the statement during the first day of a case in Saskatchewan Court of Queen's Bench court in which Canada's abortion law is being challenged.

Joe Borowski, a former Manitoba cabinet minister, is attempting to have

---

*Calgary Herald.* May 10, 1983. Reprinted with permission.

the 1969 criminal code amendments, which made abortions legal in certain cases, declared invalid.

Carnduff, who has been with the Regina General Hospital since 1972, admitted he didn't have a percentage breakdown on the reasons for abortion or a clear definition for each.

He testified that therapeutic abortion committees generally classify the reason as: medical, psychological or soci-economic. He didn't know why.

While 447 abortions were approved by the Regina General Hospital's five-member committee in 1982 only 420 were performed, said Carnduff.

The balance, he said, had either changed their minds or had gone elsewhere.

Carnduff spent three hours on the witness stand describing how the hospital follows the Criminal Code of Canada instruction in performing therapeutic abortions. Borowski, wearing a pale-blue three-piece suit and a striped tie fastened near the collar with a silver cross, quietly sat behind his lawyer, Morris Shumiatcher, briskly taking notes.

A key objective for Borowski is to halt the use of taxpayers' money for abortion committees and therapeutic abortions.

Edward Sojonky, counsel for the federal government, objected repeatedly to Shumiatcher's line of attack and questioning.

He disagreed initially with Shumiatcher wanting to call nine expert witnesses.

But Justice W.R. Matheson, after hearing arguments for 75 minutes, ruled in favor of Shumiatcher.

Outside the courthouse during the luncheon break, Sojonky told reporters having experts testify "on the meaning of life" is irrevelant when a legal point is being argued.

Shumiatcher is basing his case on the principle that Section 7 of the new Charter of Rights prevails over Section 251 of the Criminal Code.

About 150 placard-carrying men, women and children demonstrated peace-fully outside the court house in favor of freedom of choice.

Some protesters took in the proceedings, including one woman who wore a button which read: "If men became pregnant, abortion would become a sacrament."

Carnduff testified there is no special fund to pay for abortions at the Regina General Hospital.

He told Shumiatcher that cost of staff and equipment are covered by the hospital budget, which is maintained through taxpayers' money grants from the Department of Health.

The doctor, under cross-examination from Sojonky was even more specific explaining that abortions are "lumped together" with other out-patient services in the hospital budget.

The case, described as the first real test of Canadian abortion law, is expected to last a month. . . .

# 7.5

## ABORTION LAW CHALLENGED

*Calgary Herald*

Canada's largest abortion rights group is using the Charter of Rights and Freedoms in a challenge launched this week against the federal abortion law.

In a writ issued in the Supreme Court of Ontario, the Canadian Abortion Rights Action League is seeking a declaration that the Criminal Code section on abortion is "of no force and effect" because it conflicts with the year-old Charter.

The Criminal Code section makes it illegal to perform an abortion in Canada unless it is done in an accredited hospital after a therapeutic abortion committee at the hospital has decided that continuing the pregnancy would be likely to endanger the woman's life or health.

The suit is being launched in the name of the abortion rights group and its president, Norma Scarborough.

---

*Calgary Herald.* April 29, 1983. Reprinted with permission.

# 7.6

## KEEPING EYE ON CHARTER

Toronto *Globe and Mail*

Women lawyers across Canada are keeping a vigil on the provinces as they review legislation suspected of discriminating against women and hence breaking the Charter of Rights.

Provincial laws dealing with housing, employment, and matrimonial and human rights have been identified as having some provisions that discriminate against women.

---

Toronto *Globe and Mail.* January 13, 1983. Reprinted with permission.

"We want to guard against the scenario where governments haven't brought into line legislation that is in conflict with the equality rights guaranteed in the Charter," Toronto lawyer Marilou McPhedran said.

Women law students at Osgoode Hall Law School in Toronto and the University of Windsor are doing their own audit of Ontario and federal laws on welfare and pensions, to identify those statutes that contravene the Charter.

The National Action Committee, which represents 220 women's organizations across the country, has established a Canadian Charter of Rights Committee responsible for monitoring the provincial reviews that will be ongoing until 1985 when the major equal-rights law comes into force. . . .

. . . NAC is also planning a national conference on the Charter for the fall of 1984, aimed at homemakers and working women. . . .

. . . The initiative to identify Charter issues of concern to women stems from a weekend think tank in Toronto last spring, when two dozen of the country's top female legal experts gathered to discuss the Charter and how to enhance public understanding of it.

Since then, they have begun the provincial monitoring, set up a trust fund to promote study days on the Charter for women lawyers and are organizing conferences to educate housewives and working women about their status under the Charter.

"What we're seeing is quite fascinating. It's a spinoff of the enormous groundswell of involvement of women's groups" when they mounted a strong federal and provincial lobby in 1981 to get section 28 of the Charter (which guarantees equality between the sexes) excluded from the override clause, according to Susan Vander Voet, national co-ordinator of the Canadian Council on Learning Opportunities for Women.

Joining the public education and watchdog role are the National Association of Women and the Law and the Canadian Advisory Council on the Status of Women.

Concerned with women's rights that will be challenged in the courts under the Charter, the council has commissioned three Toronto women lawyers — Elizabeth Atcheson, Mary Eberts and Beth Symes — to study the idea of establishing a legal defence fund that would litigate test cases.

NAWL is having a conference next month in Victoria that will focus on pensions and imposed and mandatory affirmative action, including how they are affected by the Charter.

Miss McPhedran agreed that women cannot afford to take a wait-and-see attitude until 1985 — they must pressure governments now to change legislation that is in conflict with the Charter. . . .

# 7.7

## CLASS ACTIONS AS A REGULATORY INSTRUMENT

D.N. Dewees, J.R.S. Prichard, & M.J. Trebilcock

Regulation may take many forms, but it is usually a means by which society, through government agencies, alters the behaviour of individuals, groups, or organizations. There are other ways to alter behaviour than direct regulation. Private lawsuits are a means of both redressing some grievances and controlling behaviour — deterring behaviour that might subject one to a lawsuit. The private lawsuit can therefore substitute in some ways for direct regulation. . . . One special form of private lawsuit, the class action, is examined in this paper as, among other things, a means of affecting behaviour in place of direct regulation. . . .

. . . A class action is a lawsuit brought by an individual, the class representative, on behalf of himself and all other persons similarly situated, who constitute the class. The class members must have a common interest and a common grievance. . . .

. . . In many areas of law we rely upon both public enforcement and private litigation to limit in the public interest wrongful activity that falls short of traditionally criminal acts. The laws governing these areas may be classified as public welfare legislation or "social regulation," since they deal with acts that are prohibited for the improvement of social welfare generally but are not inherently criminal. For example, the Ontario *Environmental Protection Act* prohibits the discharge of certain pollutants in excess of specified amounts, and the Crown can prosecute violators of this Act. In addition, a private citizen who is harmed by a pollution discharge can in some cases bring a civil action seeking compensation for the damage he has suffered and perhaps an injunction against further harmful emissions. If a firm produces a sufficiently hazardous product it may be in violation of laws governing product safety and subject to public prosecution for this activity. It may also be liable in a civil suit to those injured as a result of the product's hazardous design. The threats of both public prosecution and private civil litigation act as deterrents to wrongful activity in a wide variety of fields, such as environmental protection, product safety and quality, occupational health, restrictive trade practices, and securities regulation.

Toronto: Ontario Economic Council, 1980. Reprinted with permission.

Thus there are two procedures for attacking wrongful activity. The first is public prosecution, in which the Crown prosecutes the wrongdoer for violation of a specific statute or regulation. If the prosecution is successful a fine is imposed on the wrongdoer to be paid to the state, and further wrongdoing may be prohibited. The second procedure is a private civil suit in which the victim of the wrongful activity sues the wrongdoer for the damages he suffered and perhaps for an injunction against further wrongdoing. A variation of the civil suit is a class action in which a private citizen brings a suit against the wrongdoer on behalf of himself and all other victims similarly situated. A successful class action results in damages paid by the wrongdoer and distributed to the members of the class who can be identified and contacted. An injunction prohibiting further wrongful activity may also be granted. . . .

### Barriers to suit

The major economic disincentives facing a class representative in deciding whether to lend his name to a potential suit all involve some form of transaction cost, just as in the case of non-class litigation. If litigation were truly costless for any plaintiff, he would in theory bring a suit in respect of a 10-cent claim with only a 10 per cent probability of success. But of course litigating is not costless, and apart from the personal time and effort entailed in lending one's name to a suit as a class representative other costs or potential costs are incurred. Some of these are out-of-pocket expenses or disbursements associated with meeting procedural requirements, such as providing notice to other class members of the pendency of the suit and the right to opt out. Individual class members may also face distribution costs in proving a right to a share in a common class recovery. Other possible costs faced by the class representative relate to the expense entailed in hiring a lawyer for the class and the risk of having to pay his legal costs if the suit fails.

1. Notice costs

   Perhaps surprisingly, present Anglo-Canadian law on class actions does not require a class representative to give notice to other class members of the pendency of the suit on their behalf and their right to opt out if they wish. . . . In contrast to the Anglo-Canadian notice rule, U.S. class action law requires notice to class members, although there has been debate over the appropriate scope and financing of this requirement. The notice issue is clearly one of the major design issues to be resolved in the reform of class action procedures. . . .

2. Distribution costs

   Assuming that a class action has been successful and a judgment for compensation given in favour of a class, class members will still face the costs of coming forward individually to prove a claim to a share in the common recovery. Present Canadian class action rules regard this as the only permissible form of distribution of a common class recovery.

   The existing rules prevent class actions being brought in many cases because of the difficulty of proving individual claims to a share in the common recovery. . . .

3. Legal fees

Legal costs pose special problems for class actions. Existing Anglo-Canadian rules produce the following results. If a class action succeeds, the class representative, while of course not liable for the other side's legal costs, remains liable for that portion of the legal costs of the class not indemnified by the defendant (i.e., the difference between solicitor and client costs and party and party costs) and is not entitled to a contribution from other members of the class. If his own claim is relatively small it will not be worth pursuing in the face of this prospect. If the class action fails the class representative will become liable for two sets of costs: the legal costs incurred by the class and the legal costs of the defendant. These rules operate as daunting disincentives to the bringing of class actions. . . .

Two alternative "private" (non-subsidized) solutions, both involving contingent fee components, might be considered. The first would be to retain the traditional two-way costs rule, which is economically sound because it ensures that the losing party bears the full costs inflicted by his conduct on the other party, but with the following modifications. If a class action succeeded, the class would recover its damages and its lawyer his costs from the defendant, those costs reflecting the value of his time invested in the suit multiplied by a factor to compensate him for the risk of non-compensation in the event of the suit's having failed. If the suit instead failed, the lawyer for the class would have no claim for costs against the class or its representative, and he might be made personally liable for the defendant's costs (to discourage unmeritorious suits), thus freeing the class or its representatives from any such liability. The compensation received by the lawyer for the class in successful suits must of course reflect the risk of this liability.

The second alternative would be to adopt the no-way costs rule proposed in Bill C-13 but provide for compensation to the lawyer from the class fund in successful suits on a basis which reflects the risk of non-compensation in the event of an unsuccessful suit, where no costs would be recoverable (to discourage unmeritorious suits). This is essentially the present American rule. . . .

. . . It has been shown that both of the alternatives just described can significantly lower a barrier to class litigation without unleashing a flood of non-meritorious claims.

Contingent fee arrangements are at present prohibited in Ontario. The subject arouses strong passions. On one hand it can be argued that throughout our economy there exist specialized risk-bearers, such as insurance companies, mutual funds, and manufacturers through product warranties, offering to assume risks — at a price — that other people would prefer not to bear. By specializing in risk-bearing these firms are able to diversify away some of the risks assumed in a way that the individual risk-bearer is commonly unable to do. The lawyer under a contingent fee arrangement is performing much the same function. In return for the prospect of a higher fee in the event of a successful suit, he agrees to absorb all his own costs (and possibly the defendant's cost and notice costs) in a losing suit and absolve his client from them. On the other hand it is argued that contingent fee arrangements are open to abuse. For example, lawyers may have stronger incentives to settle suits so undertaken on terms very favourable to themselves but highly disadvantageous to their clients. Also, lawyers will typically be much better placed than their clients to assess the risks entailed in bringing suit and to take advantage of their clients' relative ignorance in entering a contingent fee arrangement. Judicial supervision of settlements or fee levels may be at best an imperfect check on such abuse. However, the weak incentives for class representatives and class members to monitor their lawyers' performance pose problems not peculiar to contingent fee arrangements.

If a contingent fee approach to the problem of overcoming legal cost disincentives to bringing class actions were unacceptable, the broad alternative approach would be a "public," subsidized, response to the cost barriers. This is the direction followed in the Quebec *Class Action Bill* (Bill 39, 1978), where a special public fund is set up out of which class actions may be subsidized. While this approach might be an improvement over the current system, it does present difficulties. First, the funding agency is given a very poorly chartered discretion, the exercise of which is likely to involve it in considerable controversy (the spectre of a trial within a trial), because very often its decisions will mean life or death to a proposed class action. Second, there is no clearly articulated theory of why public subsidization of this class of non-means-tested litigant can be socially justified.

### Class actions as "legalized blackmail"

One of the most persistent and trenchant criticisms of class actions is that they are a form of "legalized blackmail" allowing class representatives and class lawyers to exact unjustified settlements from class defendants.

Though the charge has typically been loosely made, there appears to be some substance to it. First, to the extent that class actions promoted purely deterrent and not compensatory objectives (i.e., non-viable suits), critics who believe such an objective is inappropriate for a private law suit may view such actions as an illegitimate form of private coercion. Second, to the extent that class members or class lawyers are able to manipulate the selection of a class representative to ensure that he is judgment-proof in the event of a losing suit and an adverse costs award, parties bringing at unmeritorious class action may have an ability to inflict, or threaten to inflict, substantial and non-recoverable legal costs on the defendant, the desire to avoid which may induce unjustified settlements. Third, the combination of the large amounts of money involved and the large number of allegedly aggrieved parties entailed in many class actions may generate false signals to the public by inducing unjustified identification or association with the grievances asserted by the class. In view of the extensive coverage the media are often likely to attach to large lawsuits, corporate defendants will often feel under pressure to settle in order to fore-close flow of adverse publicity that may well continue throughout the typi-cally lengthy course of most class action litigation. Fourth, all other things equal, class actions may be more likely to involve claims with a lower proba-bility of success than individual suits for the same aggregate amount. In the latter case litigants will often tend to be business or institutional parties engaged in continuous dealings, where litigation is invoked only as a last resort in dispute resolution. The constraint of continuous dealing will apply less frequently to most types of class actions. . . .

. . . The concern over class actions as blackmail has arisen primarily under the U.S. rules allowing contingent percentage fees. It has been shown that under certain circumstances this fee arrangement may lead both the class representative and his lawyer to be willing to sue even though they have a very small chance of winning: sometimes less than 10 per cent. . . .

### The lawyer as an entrepreneur of law enforcement

The traditional model of the lawyer-client relationship depicts the lawyer as an agent sought out, retained, instructed, and monitored by a client who has recognized for himself that he faces an existing or potential legal problem. However, this model is not an accurate description of the relationship between a lawyer and his client in a class action involving a large number of relatively small claims. It is not plausible that an individual with a claim of $100 will hire a lawyer and bring a $2 million class action simply to recover his $100. The lawyer, not the class representative, has the real economic interest here.

A change to an entrepreneurial role for lawyers is inherent in a private enforcement mechanism for cases in which the potential recovery of individ-ual plaintiffs or class members is small in relation to the legal costs. If policy seeks to promote class actions of this kind the incentive structure facing a prospective lawyer for the class becomes a critical issue. In many class action situations the class lawyer can only realistically expect to be paid if the suit succeeds. It is unlikely that he will be able to look to the class representative for payment if the suit fails, and he has no right at present to seek payment from the class members at large. Moreover, such a right would often be of little value because of the transaction costs entailed in enforcing a costs claim against individual members of a large class. Thus, for better or worse, class actions in many cases must be undertaken if at all, on a contingent fee basis, giving the lawyer a direct stake in the outcome of the action.

Beyond fee arrangements, the entrepreneurial role played by lawyers in much class action litigation has other implications. In particular, present prohibitions against maintenance and champerty (''fomenting'' or financing litigation) would need to be abrogated in situations where this form of private enforcement was desired. Also, current prohibitions against advertising and other forms of solicitation of clients by lawyers would require modification in a class action context. If law enforcement policy contemplates a positive role for private law enforcement through the class action mechanism, those persons most capable of identifying violations of the law should be encouraged to do so and to take action to prevent the offensive conduct. . . .

### Private versus public enforcement

. . . Besides seeing the class action as an instrument of regulation, this paper analyzes it as an alternative to public enforcement of regulatory standards. That is, even when a collective decision sets appropriate rules of conduct, the issue whether these rules should be enforced by public or private prosecutions remains. In this context the private class action is a variant of private prosecution that merits consideration as an alternative to public enforcement actions. . .

. . . 1. An assessment of private and public enforcement reveals that the primary advantages of private enforcement are the sometimes superior ability to detect offences, the change from criminal to civil liability with a consequent lessening of the standard of proof, the potential compensatory contributions of a civil action in cases involving significant individual losses whether they are recovered in individual or class form, a check, though not a costless one, on abuses of the public prosecutor's discretion, the possibility of relief from systematic public underenforcement of regulatory statutes.

2. Private prosecution should not be looked to as a panacea for achieving optimal levels of enforcement, because it faces a number of difficulties. The determination of the damages payable in a civil suit is likely to be more complex than the assessment of a fine. The "perverse incentive" problem limits the desirability of using multiple levels of damages to reflect the fact that the probability of enforcement is often less than certain. Fluid class recovery schemes may cause inequities and inefficiency. Finally, cases of both underenforcement and overenforcement may rise where the incentive structure facing private enforcers is relied on to achieve optimal levels of enforcement. . . .

# 7.8

## KEYTERMS

*Concepts*

''litigation as a form of interest group activity''
test case
*amicus curiae*
intervenor
class action suit
political trial

# 8
# Fact Finding in the Courts

All informed decisions must be based on an adequate knowledge of relevant facts, and different kinds of decisions require different kinds of facts. Accordingly, decision-making institutions have developed different fact-finding procedures designed to suit their distinctive needs.

The original adjudicatory function of courts has strongly influenced the procedures and rules governing judicial fact-finding. In order to determine guilt or innocence — "what really happened" (or "historical facts") — common law courts developed special rules to guard against biased or false evidence. The judge assumed a neutral and passive role. The parties to the dispute were responsible for developing all the relevant facts and legal arguments. Hearsay evidence was excluded altogether, and first-hand testimony had to be given under oath, subject to cross-examination and the introduction of contradictory evidence by one's adversary. The giving of false information under these circumstances, perjury, was itself made criminal. These rules and procedures are known collectively as the adversary process, and they constitute the core of the judicial process in all common law countries.

Precisely because it is well suited to its original purpose, the adversary process is much less adept at collecting the kind of facts relevant to public policy-making decisions. Policy-makers want to know about general patterns of human behaviour — what Horowitz calls "social facts" — in order to formulate public policy. (Reading 8.2) To get these facts, legislators and administrators may consult past studies of the problem, commission new studies to provide current socio-economic information, and conduct extensive hearings to gather additional information, including indications of political support and opposition. Under the traditional rules of the adversary process, judges can do none of this.

The advent of written constitutional law and judicial review placed serious strains on the common law courts' fact-finding procedures. While the inevitable policy impact of constitutional law decisions created a felt need among judges for additional factual information, their procedures were inadequate and even hostile toward such information. There was also a strong sense that it was inconsistent with the adjudicatory function of courts to base a decision on "social facts." This was perceived as more a legislative than a judicial activity. As Weiler points out, this perception was not, and is not, simply an old-fashioned attachment to traditional ways. If a judge makes unanticipated use of non-traditional factual materials, is this fair to unsuspecting litigants who presented facts and arguments along traditional lines? In some cases the relevant "historical facts" and the "social facts" may actually suggest conflicting solutions. Should judges ignore the plight of the individual plaintiff in the name of making policy for the many? In short, when it comes to collecting and using facts, there are serious and real tensions between the adjudicatory and policy-making functions of courts. (Reading 8.1)

Historically, Canadian judges have used extrinsic evidence (the proper legal term for "social facts") very sparingly. The adjudicatory view of the judicial function, the influence of the decisions and style of the British Privy Council, and a deference to the tradition of parliamentary supremacy have all led Canadian judges to use a textually oriented form of judicial reasoning. The written opinions accompanying the Court's decisions have tended to be highly conceptual and poorly grounded in the socio-economic contexts which gave rise to the cases. This problem is further aggravated in reference procedures, where there are not even any "historical facts" to guide the judges' reasoning. The *Chicken and Egg Reference* is a notorious example of what can happen in these circumstances. (See Reading 8.3)

This "interpretivist" approach has been especially criticized in the area of constitutional law as too "legalistic." There have been calls for a more sociological jurisprudence, a kind of judicial reasoning "which insists that constitutional words and statutory words must be carefully linked by judicially noticed knowledge and by evidence to the ongoing life of society."[1] This type of jurisprudence requires more extensive use of extrinsic evidence than Canadian judges have thus far been willing to accept.

For similar reasons, American judges also refused to allow "social facts" into court until 1908. In that year a young lawyer (later to become a Supreme Court justice) named Louis Brandeis successfully defended the state of Oregon's maximum hour labour laws by submitting studies showing a higher incidence of serious maternal health problems for women working long hours in certain occupations. He asked the judges to accept these studies as proof that the legislators had a "reasonable basis" for enacting the mandatory restrictions on freedom of contract. The Supreme Court agreed, and thus began the American practice of the "Brandeis brief," or judicial use of pertinent socio-

---

[1] W.R. Lederman, "Thoughts on Reform of the Supreme Court of Canada," *The Confederation Challenge*, Ontario Advisory Committee on Confederation, Vol. II (Toronto: Queen's Printer, 1970), p.295.

economic facts.[2] This practice is consistent with the greater policy-making role of the American Supreme Court, and distinguishes it from other final appellate courts.[3]

The Canadian Supreme Court's 1976 decision in the *Anti-Inflation Reference* suggests that the Canadian aversion to extrinsic evidence may be changing. (Reading 8.4) The question of the validity of the federal government's wage and price control legislation was referred to the Supreme Court. The mandatory restraint policies clearly were being applied to sectors of the economy that were normally under provincial jurisdiction, and could not be supported by the federal government's normal section 91 power to regulate "trade and commerce." Based on existing precedents, there were only two possible legal justifications for the mandatory wage and price controls: the "national emergency" test or the "inherent national importance" test. Both of these tests seemed to pose an essentially empirical question: had inflation become so serious in Canada by the mid-1970's as to constitute a "national emergency" or an issue of "inherent national importance"?

Recognizing the inadequacy of the traditional factum and oral argument procedures to deal with this dimension of the case, then Chief Justice Bora Laskin summoned the counsel for the various governments and private intervenors involved in the case. After several private meetings, the late Chief Justice announced a two-stage procedure for the submission of factual evidence and an opportunity to rebut evidence prior to oral argument. The result was a new chapter in Canadian judicial process.

The federal government submitted its "white paper" on inflation, the documentary basis of its legislative policy, and also a Statistics Canada bulletin showing changes in the monthly consumer price index. The Canadian Labour Congress, one of the intervenors opposed to the wage and price controls, submitted a 64-page economic study of inflation in Canada, which had been especially commissioned for the occasion. It was later supported by telegrams from 38 Canadian economists. On the "rebuttal date," the federal government and Ontario made additional submissions responding to the economic arguments advanced in the CLC's original submission.

In the end the Supreme Court made minimal use of the extrinsic evidence that had been submitted. Laskin's opinion noted that the extrinsic material supported the contention that the government had a "rational basis for the legislation," while Ritchie's opinion cited the "white paper" as proof of the existence of an "emergency." More importantly, the *Anti-Inflation Reference*

---

[2] *Muller v. Oregon*, 208 U.S. 412 (1908).

[3] The High Court of Australia does not even receive a written factum or brief before oral argument, thus precluding any "brandeis brief" presentation of "social facts." The same is true of courts in Great Britain and New Zealand. The refusal to use written factums in these courts is an implicit commentary on their self-perception as adjudicators not policy-makers.

set a new precedent for the use of "social science" briefs in Canadian constitutional law. Henceforth, the Supreme Court may resurrect the procedures elaborated by Laskin whenever it deems it appropriate to the case at hand.

There are other less dramatic devices that judges can use to import "social facts" into a judicial proceeding. One is the traditional practice of "judicial notice." Judicial notice is a technique through which a judge may unilaterally take notice of factual matters that he deems relevant to the legal questions that he must answer. A recent example was the late Chief Justice Laskin's opinion for the majority in a 1972 "breathalyzer" case brought under the 1960 Bill of Rights. In finding that the "breathalyzer" requirement did not violate "due process of law," Laskin declared,

> I am, moreover, of the opinion that it is within the scope of judicial notice to recognize that Parliament has acted in a matter that is of great social concern, that is the human and economic costs of highway accidents arising from drunk driving, in enacting s. 223 and related provisions of the Criminal Code.[4]

A judge may not "take notice" of extrinsic facts that are highly technical or not well-known. As the preceding example illustrates, "judicial notice" is limited to facts that are generally known and accepted, or at least easily demonstrated. While it is thus an effective vehicle for introducing common sense into judicial proceedings, it has much more limited value in cases involving complex policy issues.

Yet another device for the introduction of "social facts" into judicial proceedings is the use of the "expert witness." Under the *Canada Evidence Act* each party can call up to five "expert witnesses" to testify on a subject at issue before the court. One restriction is that the subject must be sufficiently complex that specialized study is required to become an "expert" on it. For this reason an Ontario judge refused to allow Father Philip Berrigan, an American "peace activist," to testify at the trial of the 63 persons charged with trespassing during an anti-nuclear demonstration at a Litton Systems Canada plant in November, 1983. The judge ruled that Berrigan's testimony was not relevant to the trespassing charge. By contrast, a recent Charter of Rights case in Calgary saw a total of four "expert witnesses" called to testify on the issue of whether Canada's election law violates the "freedom of speech" provision of the Charter. These included a Canadian and an American political scientist, a Canadian constitutional historian, and Canada's Chief Electoral Officer.[5] The use of "expert witnesses" has the disadvantages pointed out by Horowitz. They are hired and paid by the parties to the case, so

---

[4] *Curr v. the Queen*, (1972) S.C.R. 889.

[5] This is the National Citizen's Coalition challenge to Bill C-169, which effectively eliminates "political action committees," or "pacs," from directly participating in federal elections. No decision has been made.

they are inevitably partisan. Nor is there any guarantee that the "experts'" definition of the relevant facts and issues is adequate.

A related matter is the judicial use of "legislative history" in determining the constitutional validity of a statute. While "legislative history" is not the same as "social facts," it can serve a similar purpose of situating a case in the real-world context from which it comes. Historically no common law courts permitted themselves to go beyond the actual text of a statute in interpreting its meaning. With the advent of ever increasing government social and economic regulation, courts have felt the need to go beyond the texts of statutes to discover their legislative purposes. American courts began to use legislative history in constitutional cases during the 1920's, and now do so extensively. Legislative history has usually been held inadmissable in Canada, but again the 1976 *Anti-Inflation Reference*, and the use of the government "white paper," marks a departure from past practice. Since then, the Supreme Court has made extensive use of Hansard and other historical sources in the *Senate Reference* of 1980 and the *Constitutional Patriation Reference* of 1981.

While historically Canadian courts have been very reluctant to admit, much less use "social facts," recent developments suggest a change. This new trend is likely to be accelerated by the large number of Charter of Rights cases now working their way through the judicial system.[6] Several Charter sections seem to require some presentation of "social facts." Section 1, for example, declares that the subsequently enumerated rights are not absolute, but subject to "such reasonable limitations prescribed by law as can be demonstrably justified in a free and democratic society." The last element of this test suggests that it may be appropriate to compare challenged Canadian practices with practices of other "free and democratic societies." A similar need for comparative factual data seems implicit in the section 15 right to "equal benefit of the law" and the section 23 right to minority language education "where numbers merit." If this is the case, there will increasing pressure on Canadian judges both to allow and to use more extrinsic evidence and "social facts" than they have in the past.

---

[6] Because of the hierarchical structure of the judicial system and the large number of cases, it usually takes several years for a case to reach the Supreme Court. While no Charter cases reached the Supreme Court during the first two years, at the beginning of the third year — May, 1984 — there were 31 Charter cases in which leave to appeal had been granted.

# 8.1

# TWO MODELS: INFLUENCING JUDICIAL POLICY-MAKING

Paul Weiler

. . . One necessary conclusion is that the adversary process will become increasingly unsuited for the judicial process as it becomes more and more concerned with overt policy-making. When the court administers a relatively well-defined set of rules and principles, and applies them to settle private disputes, it makes sense to confine the bases of decision to a record prepared for it by the parties during an adversary hearing. Because "ex parte" communications to the adjudicator are traditionally prohibited, due to their incompatibility with this process, the *amicus curiae* device is necessary to get before the court those considerations that are relevant to the interests of other affected parties. Such devices as telegrams, or picketing, or parading are so unthinkable as means of influencing courts that they can be criminally prohibited in the face of a constitutional value for freedom of speech.

Still, the second model of the judicial process holds the prime function of the judge to be general policy-making, rather than adjudication. None of the aforementioned techniques for making a group position known, and influencing a policy decision, would be considered highly offensive to a legislature. Judges of the United States Supreme Court have expressed distaste at *amicus* briefs which do no more than indicate the position of an affected interest group to possible decisions. The attitude appears equally anomalous within the policy-making model. A problem that perhaps is more important than the responsiveness of the court to affected interests is its access to the type of "policy" facts which enhance the quality of the decision it will make. The viability of the adversary process for this purpose is extremely doubtful.

One suggested means is the famous Brandeis brief, which presented to the courts a summary of the legal and extra-legal literature that was relevant to a constitutional problem. However, the purpose of this brief was merely to demonstrate the existence of a body of informed opinion supporting the *reasonableness* of the *legislative* rule of law. What the judicial policy-maker is concerned with are studies of policy facts supporting the *soundness* of a *judicial* rule of law (now to be created). The unchallenged Brandeis brief is as inapt for this purpose as is the adversary production of evidence for the record. This may not justify the action of the Supreme Court of Canada in the

*Canadian Bar Review*, 1968, p.406. Reprinted with permission.

*Saumur* case in prohibiting payment of costs to the victorious party for preparation of a Brandeis-type brief, so as to discourage its use. Perhaps it does justify a rule of self-restraint which prohibits judicial policy-making that depends on the resolution of conflicting versions of substantial, informed opinions about the reasons for a new legal rule. Only if the parties to the dispute could not reasonably claim unfair surprise at "judicial notice" of a social consensus concerning the desirability of a new rule is its judicial adoption warranted. Absent such a principle of judicial self-restraint, there will be continually-growing tension between the demands of rational policy-making and the limitation of the adversary process.

One method by which a solution to the problem may be sought is the increased use of legal periodical literature, by judicial notice or otherwise. Presumably the Canadian Supreme Court will consign its earlier prohibition of the citation of *Canadian Bar Review* articles to the oblivion it deserves. We must then face the issues raised by their use, especially when the problem is enhanced by articles that deal with a case which is in process of being brought before a particular tribunal, and suggest and defend certain proposed decisions. This would not appear to be inconsistent with the adjudicative model, which envisages "the collaborative articulation of shared purposes" as the proper mode of judicial-legal reasoning. However, it would be highly improper if it were thought that the article was not written solely in the spirit of purely disinterested scholarship, but rather was "planted" by one of the parties in an effort to influence judges by showing them the "weight" of scholarly opinion. Yet would our attitude be the same if writers were commissioned to write articles in popular journals which support one position, and which then are used to help try to convince (or force) legislators to agree with this position. If the primary focus of judicial activity becomes policy-making, it will become less intelligible to condemn use of partisan materials written by those "with an axe to grind."

# 8.2

# FACT FINDING IN ADJUDICATION

Donald C. Horowitz

The fact that judges function at some distance from the social milieu from which their cases spring puts them at an initial disadvantage in understanding

---

*The Courts and Social Policy.* Washington, D.C.: The Brookings Institute, 1977, p.45. Reprinted with permission.

the dimensions of social policy problems. The focused, piecemeal quality of adjudication implies that judicial decisions tend to be abstracted from social contexts broader than the immediate setting in which the litigation arises, and, as already indicated, the potentially unrepresentative character of the litigants makes it hazardous to generalize from their situation to the wider context.

The judicial fact-finding process carries forward this abstraction of the case from its more general social context. To make this clear, it is necessary to distinguish between two kinds of facts: historical facts and social facts. Historical facts are the events that have transpired between the parties to a lawsuit. Social facts are the recurrent patterns of behavior on which policy must be based. Historical facts, as I use the term, have occasionally been called "adjudicative facts" by lawyers, and social facts have also been called "legislative facts." I avoid these terms because of the preconceptions they carry and the division of labor they imply. Nonetheless, by whatever designation they are known, these are two distinct kinds of facts, and a process set up to establish the one is not necessarily adequate to ascertain the other.

Social facts are nothing new in litigation. Courts have always had to make assumptions or inferences about general conditions that would guide their decisions. The broader the issue, the more such imponderables there are. The breadth of the issues in constitutional law has always made it a fertile field for empirical speculation. Does a civil service law barring alleged subversives from public employment have a "chilling effect" on free speech? Is the use of third-degree methods by the police sufficiently widespread to justify a prophylactic rule that would exclude from evidence even some confessions that are not coerced? Does pornography stimulate the commission of sex crimes, or does it provide cathartic release for those who might otherwise commit such crimes?

Constitutional law is a fertile field, but it is not the only field in which such questions arise. If a court refuses to enforce against a bankrupt corporation an "unconscionable contract" for the repayment of borrowed money, will that make it more difficult for firms needing credit to obtain it and perhaps precipitate more such bankruptcies? Does it encourage carelessness and thus undercut a prime purpose of the law of negligence if an automobile driver, a shopkeeper, or a theater owner is permitted to insure himself against liability inflicted as a result of his own fault?

These are, all of them, behavioral questions. They share an important characteristic: no amount of proof about the conduct of the individual litigants involved in a civil service, confession, obscenity, bankruptcy, or negligence case can provide answers to these probabilistic questions about the behavior of whole categories of people. As a matter of fact, proof of one kind of fact can be misleading about the other. What is true in the individual case may be false in the generality of cases, and vice versa. The judicial process, however, makes it much easier to learn reliably about the individual case than about the run of cases.

The increasing involvement of the courts in social policy questions has increased the number and importance of social fact questions in litigation. As the courts move into new, specialized, unfamiliar policy areas, they are confronted by a plethora of questions about human behavior that are beyond their ability to answer on the basis of common experience or the usual modicum of expert testimony. A few examples, drawn from a social science manual for lawyers, will make the point:

> Do the attrition rates for different racial groups applying for admission to a union apprenticeship program suggest a pattern of racial discrimination?
> How would the elimination of a local bus system through bankruptcy affect low income people and the elderly poor in particular?
> How are different income groups and communities of varying sizes differentially affected by the formula allocation of General Revenue Sharing funds?

Obtaining answers to such behavioral questions has become exigent, and not only because the interstices in which courts make fresh policy keep expanding. If a judge or a jury makes a mistake of fact relating only to the case before it, "the effects of the mistake are quarantined." But if the factual materials form the foundation for a general policy, the consequences cannot be so confined.

Traditionally, the courts have been modest about their competence to ascertain social facts and have tried to leave this function primarily to other agencies. They have shielded themselves by applying doctrines that have the effect of deferring to the fact-finding abilities of legislatures and administrative bodies, to avoid having to establish social facts in the course of litigation.

The reasons for this general modesty are well grounded. There is tension between two different judicial responsibilities: deciding the particular case and formulating a general policy. Two different kinds of fact-finding processes are required for these two different functions. The adversary system of presentation and the rules of evidence were both developed for the former, and they leave much to be desired for the latter.

In general, the parties can be depended upon to elicit all of the relevant historical facts, through the ordinary use of testimony and documentary evidence, and the judge or jury can be presumed competent to evaluate that evidence. Social facts, on the other hand, may not be elicited at all by the parties, almost surely not fully, and the competence of the decision-maker in this field cannot be taken for granted.

These deficiencies of the adversary process have led to proposals for the employment of outside experts as consultants to the courts. So far, relatively few impartial experts have been appointed, and the proof of social facts has largely been left to the traditional adversary method.

Expert testimony is the conventional way for the litigants to prove social facts, but its deficiencies are considerable. The experts are usually partisans, employed by the parties, and their conclusions tend to reflect that status. If the parties provide a skewed picture of the problem they purport to represent, their expert witness may do the same. Finally, reliance on expert witnesses hired by the parties makes the judge the prisoner of the parties' definition of the issues of social facts that are involved.

The rules of evidence are equally inapt for the verification of social facts. They are geared to the search for truth between the parties, not to the search for truth in general. Understandably, there is a prohibition on the introduction of hearsay evidence. Courts must act on what happened, not on what someone said happened. The emphasis in judicial fact-finding on choosing between conflicting versions of events by assessing the credibility of witnesses also places a premium on requiring witness to have firsthand knowledge of the events about which they testify. Sensible though the hearsay rule may be, however, it makes the ascertainment of scientific facts of all kinds including social science, very difficult. Books and articles constitute inadmissible hearsay; they are not alive and cannot be cross-examined. Consequently, when behavioral materials are introduced into evidence, it is usually pursuant to some exception to the hearsay rule. . . .

. . . The use of expert testimony involves another kind of exception. Duly qualified experts, unlike ordinary witnesses, need not confine themselves to testifying about facts. They may also state their opinion, which may be nothing more than a guess or a bias. Yet the studies on which their opinion may be based remain inadmissible as hearsay (though they may be introduced to impeach an expert's opinion).

All of these cumbersome devices tend to make the judge dependent on secondary interpretations of the relevant empirical material and to discourage him from going directly to the material itself. As we shall see in later chapters, filtered knowledge has its problems.

If new rules and mechanisms do develop to aid in informing the courts about social facts, further problems will arise. The courts may have to administer a dual system of evidence — one part for historical facts, another for social facts — and there is the problem of what might be called contamination. Evidence introduced for one purpose may, as it often does, spill over to infect the other set of issues. Compartmentalization to prevent contamination is one of the hardest jobs a judge must perform. This particular problem suggests again the underlying tension between deciding the litigants' case and making general policy.

How have social fact issues been handled by the courts in practice? They have been handled in much the same way that the rules of evidence and the adversary system have been adapted to accommodate social facts: by neglect or by improvisation.

A first, quite common way is to ignore them or to assume, sometimes rightly, sometimes wrongly, that the litigants' case is representative. This is patently inadequate. . . .

. . . A third way of dealing with social facts is to go outside the record of the case in search of information. This is what Mr. Justice Murphy did when he sent questionnaires to police forces in thirty-eight cities in order to determine the relationship between the admissibility of illegally obtained evidence and police training in the law of search and seizure. The same impulse has sometimes moved other judges, restless in their ignorance of behavioral fact, to consult experts of their acquaintance, as Judge Charles Clark, then former Dean of the Yale Law School, consulted the Yale University organist about a music copyright case that was pending before him. These attempts, primitive as they are, show the existence of a deeply felt need rather than a method of satisfying it.

What these examples also suggest is that the need for empirical data is often not even sensed until the case is on appeal. The traditional formulation of causes of action rarely incorporates social facts as an element of proof. When behavioral facts are implicitly incorporated (for example, "reasonable care of a prudent man under the circumstances"), these standards are often not met by evidence but left to the decision-maker to judge from his own experience.

The law thus tends to slight the need for behavioral material in a number of ways. In practice, this means that the option of utilizing such material falls on counsel. Generally, public-interest lawyers have been much more assiduous about introducing evidence of social facts than have other lawyers, and it is they who have often compiled voluminous records of expert testimony and memoranda. . . .

That the process of adjudication places the emphasis heavily on the accurate ascertainment of historical facts, while it neglects and renders it difficult to prove social facts, is, of course, exactly what might be expected from its traditional responsibilities. This is to say, the fact-finding capability of the courts is likely to lag behind the functions they are increasingly required to perform.

To argue that this problem of capability exists is still to say nothing of the materials on which proof of social facts might be based. The problems here are considerable. There may be no studies that cast light on the issue in litigation. If there are, the behavioral issue may be framed in a way quite inappropriate for litigation. Studies may, of course, be specially commissioned for the purposes of the lawsuit. Even if the potential bias of such studies is overcome, the constraints of time and resources may dictate research methods much less than satisfying. On large issues, existing data are likely to be fragmentary. Then the question becomes one of generalization from partial or tentative findings, or one of drawing inferences from proxies. This is no place for a full-scale consideration of the imperfect fit between law and social science. It is enough to say here that the problems of social science do not disappear in litigation, but are instead compounded by the litigation setting, the different ways in which lawyers and social scientists ask questions, and the time constraint.

This last point needs to be underscored. As I have said earlier, litigation is, for the most part, a mandatory decision process. Courts do not choose their cases; cases choose their courts. With certain exceptions, a case properly brought must be decided. Whereas a legislator or administrator has some freedom to shy away from issues on which his quantum of ignorance is too great to give him confidence that he can act sensibly, courts are not afforded quite the same latitude. That courts have difficulty finding and absorbing social facts in the context of a largely mandatory decision process that puts them at a comparative disadvantage in social policymaking.

# 8.3

## THE CHICKEN AND EGG REFERENCE
Paul Weiler

This article is reprinted as reading 6.3.

# 8.4

## THE ANTI-INFLATION REFERENCE: THE ANATOMY OF A CONSTITUTIONAL DECISION
Peter H. Russell

This article is reprinted as reading 10.4.

# 8.5

# KEYTERMS

*Concepts*

historical/adjudicative facts
social/legislative facts
adversary process
rule of hearsay evidence
perjury
extrinsic evidence
"Brandeis brief"
judicial notice
expert witness
legislative history

*Institutions, Events, and Documents*

The *Chicken and Egg Reference* (1971)
The *Anti-Inflation Reference* (1976)

# 9
# Precedents, Statutes, and Legal Reasoning

One of the most distinctive characteristics of the judicial process is its formalized method of reasoning. Because their authority flows from the public perception that they are "merely" applying pre-existing rules to resolve new disputes, judges are not permitted the broad prerogative enjoyed by the legislative and the executive branches. Unlike the latter, courts are not supposed to create new policies to deal with new problems. In their oral or written judgements, judges must explain where and how they derived the "rule" used to settle a case. There are three principal sources for these "rules": a written constitution, legislative statutes (including administrative regulations), and prior judicial decisions, known as precedents. Constitutional interpretation is the subject of the following two chapters. This chapter is concerned with the role of precedent and statutory interpretation in judicial reasoning.

Until the middle of the nineteenth century, most internal or domestic law in English-speaking societies was common law. Common law originated in the judicial recognition and enforcement of traditional usages and customs of the Anglo-Saxon and later Norman peoples in the British Isles. As these judicial decisions were made, they in turn became part of the common law. The common law in contemporary Canadian society consists of all previous judicial decisions by Canadian and British courts, as they are recorded in the case reports of these nations. The common law system is distinguished from the civil law system by its basis in precedent rather than legislative enactment. The civil law system originated in ancient Roman law, developed on the European continent, and was imported into Quebec by the French. It is based on a single, comprehensive code, enacted by the legislature.

The law of precedent, or *stare decisis*, is a self-imposed judicial rule that "like cases be decided alike." As Gordon Post explains, the law of precedent is essentially a formalization of the common sense use of past experience as a guide to present conduct. (Reading 9.1) The value of judicial adherence to *stare decisis* is two-fold. First, continuity and certainty in the law is a prerequisite of civilized human activity. If there is no reasonable guarantee that what is valid law today will still be valid law tomorrow, personal, economic, and political intercourse would grind to a halt. In each of these spheres of human activity, present day decisions and activities are predicated on expectations about the future. Ensuring a high degree of predictablity and continuity between the present and the future is one of the primary purposes of a political regime. As the institutions charged with interpreting and adapting the laws over time, the courts are responsible for maintaining continuity and certainty. As Dicey said, "A law which was not certain would in reality be no law at all." (Reading 9.2) Adherence to the rule of precedent — "deciding like cases alike" — is the mechanism that provides this certainty.

The rule of precedent also contributes to guaranteeing the "rule of law, not of men." One of the ideals of the Western tradition's conception of justice is that the laws be applied equally and impartially to all persons. This ideal precludes any *ad hoc* application of the laws, and demands instead that laws be applied uniformly, or that any deviation from the rule be justified on principle — that is, by another rule. The idiosyncracies or personal preferences of a judge are not permissible grounds for judicial decisions. This would re-introduce the "rule of men" rather than the "rule of law." By minimizing the discretion or freedom of individual judges, *stare decisis* preserves the "rule of law."

It should be emphasized that *stare decisis* minimizes but does not eliminate the element of judicial discretion or creativity. While legal reasoning presents itself as a deductive process, the reality is a more subtle blend of both inductive and deductive reasoning. Legal reasoning is accurately described as "reasoning by example."[1] The judges are essentially asking, "Whether the present case resembles the plain case 'sufficiently' and in the 'relevant' aspects."[2] In determining what is "sufficient" and what is "relevant," the judge must ultimately make certain choices. Because of this element of choice, a judge is responsible for striking the balance between continuity and innovation. The central thrust of the theory of legal realism (discussed in chapter two) has been to emphasize this element of choice and judicial discretion, and the ensuing responsibility of the judge for his choice.

Weiler's analysis of the Supreme Court's responsibility for the development of tort law is based on this legal realist perspective. (Reading 9.3) Weiler argues that judges can no longer claim that precedent "dictates" nonsensical or patently unfair legal conclusions. Judges must be critical in their use of precedent, and go beyond the surface "rule" to discover the animating "principle." The proper function of the common law judge, according the Weiler, is to derive specific rules from more general principles, as the

---

[1] Edward H. Levi, *An Introduction to Legal Reasoning* (Chicago: University of Chicago Press, 1949), p.1.

[2] H.L.A. Hart, *The Concept of Law* (Oxford: Oxford University Press, 1961), p. 124.

situation demands. Since situations change, rules must change also. While the "cattle trespass" exemption to normal tort law responsibility may have been appropriate to the rural, agricultural society of eighteenth century England, it had become a dangerous anachronism in twentieth century Canada. (Reading 9.3) Similarly in *Boucher v. the King*, the Court was faced with a conflict between the definition of "seditious libel" developed in nineteenth century, homogeneous, protestant Britain, and the norms of freedom of religion and speech in twentieth century, pluralistic Canada. (Reading 9.4) Appeal court judges have a duty, says Weiler, to adapt the common law to the changing needs and circumstances of contemporary society.

Strict adherence to *stare decisis* is yet another aspect of the "adjudication of disputes" function of courts that poses problems for judicial policy-making. Refusal to disavow or change past decisions plays no constructive role in a policy-making institution, as the examples of legislative and executive practice make clear. While certainty and continuity are legal virtues, adaptability and innovation are more important in the policy-making process. The case for abandoning a strict adherence to precedent is especially strong in constitutional law. Not only is policy-impact more probable, but constitutional law lacks the flexibility of common law and statutes. If the courts make a "mistake" in the latter areas, it can be corrected by remedial legislation. But if the Supreme Court makes a constitutional decision with undesirable policy consequences, the only direct way to correct the damage is through formal constitutional amendment, an extremely cumbersome and difficult process.[3] Predictably, the U.S. Supreme Court was the first court of appeal in a common law nation to abandon *stare decisis* as an absolute requirement. The demotion of *stare decisis* from a binding rule to a guiding principle is another index of a court's evolution toward a greater policy-making role.

The recent advent of judicial realism in Canadian jurisprudence has brought with it a decline in the status of the rule of *stare decisis*. Long after the American Supreme Court had abandoned absolute adherence to precedent, the Canadian Supreme Court continued to perceive itself as bound to adhere not only to its own previous decisions but those of the British House of Lords as well. This latter restriction is attributable to the role of the Judicial Committee of the Privy Council as Canada's final court of appeal until 1949. Ten years after the abolition of that role, the Supreme Court declared its independence from British precedents as well. (Reading 9.3) In 1966 the British House of Lords officially declared that, when appropriate, it would no longer follow its own prior decisions. However, the Supreme Court of Canada continued to profess strict adherence to its prior decisions until the 1970's. Under the leadership of Bora Laskin, the Canadian Supreme Court began to move in the

---

[3] This is not true of judicial decisions based on sections 2 and 7 through 15 of the Charter of Rights, which are subject to the section 33 "legislative override" provision.

same direction. In 1972, before his appointment as chief justice, Laskin had written that *stare decisis* was "no long an article of faith in the Supreme Court of Canada, but it still remains a cogent principle."[4] Speaking as the new Chief Justice at the Centennial Symposium of the Supreme Court in 1975, Laskin repeated that *stare decisis* was no long "an inexorable rule," but rather,

> simply an important element of the judicial process, a necessary consideration which should give pause to any but the most sober conclusion that a previous decision or line of authority is wrong and ought to be changed.[5]

Practicing what he preached, Laskin led the Supreme Court to overturn three precedents during the next three years, including an old Privy Council decision dealing with the federal division of powers.[6] This abandoning of strict adherence to *stare decisis* is yet another indicator of the Supreme Court's institutional evolution toward more of a policy-making court.

The second principal source of law is legislative statutes. Beginning in the nineteenth century, legislatures in Great Britain, Canada, and the United States began to codify large portions of the common law. In large part this was a democratic reaction against the perceived elitism of the "judge-made" character of the common law. By reducing the confusing maze of common law precedent to clearly worded, legislative statutes, it was thought that the law would be made easier for "the people" to understand, and that the democratic authority of "government by consent" would be enhanced.

In 1892 the Canadian Parliament abolished all criminal offenses at common law, and replaced them with a comprehensive statute, the *Criminal Code*. In so doing, Parliament hoped to reap the alleged advantages of codification mentioned above, including restricting judicial discretion in the criminal law. Since crimes were now clearly and authoritatively defined, judges would simply apply the law as Parliament had written it. It would no longer be necessary to refer to a vast and confusing system of precedent to apply the criminal law, or so it was hoped.

In fact, precedent and *stare decisis* quickly found their way back into the criminal law. Perhaps, as Parker has suggested, it was (and still is) impossible for judges and lawyers trained in the common law tradition to properly construe a code of law.[7] More likely the common law "habit" simply com-

---

[4] "The Institutional Character of the Judge," *Israel Law Review*, 7 (1972), p.341. Partially reprinted in Reading 12.2.

[5] Reprinted in Reading 3.1.

[6] *R. v. Paquette*,[1977] 2 S.C.R. 189; *McNamara Const. Western Ltd. v. The Queen*, [1977] 2 S.C.R. 654; and *Reference re Agricultural Products Marketing Act*, [1978] 2 S.C.R. 1198.

[7] Graham Parker, *An Introduction to Criminal Law*, 2nd ed. (Toronto: Methuen, 1983), p.43.

pounds a more serious problem — the ultimate ambiguity of statutory terminology itself. Try as they might, legislators will never be able to draft statutes that anticipate and encompass all possible future situations. This is due in part to the inherent tension between the generality of words and the specificity of reality, and in part to human ignorance of the future. As new situations inevitably arise, the applicability of the original wording of statutes becomes increasingly questionable. *Regina v. Ojibway* is a clever satire on the inadequacies of statutory language, and the occasional tendency of judges to exacerbate the problem. (Reading 9.5) The comical example of "Blue, J." notwithstanding, the only practical way to bridge this gap is through judicial discretion; and the traditional (if not the only) way to discipline the exercise of judicial discretion is through adherence to *stare decisis* — to decide like cases alike. In the final analysis, judicial interpretation of statutes is similar to the "reasoning by example" method of the common law.

The preceding argument notwithstanding, judicial discretion in interpreting statutes, including the Criminal Code, is much more circumscribed than in interpreting the common law. As Weiler says, judges can develop new torts, but not new crimes, and there are sound reasons for preferring this arrangement. As issues of tort law are rarely the subject of partisan political controversy, an innovative court cannot be accused of usurping the legislative function. The controversies over capital punishment and abortion show that the same is not true of the criminal law. In the area of tort law, judicial expertise is very high, relative to other policy-making institutions. Finally, judicial initiatives in substantive criminal law would pose the threat of punishing innocent persons. No comparable problem of "due process" arises in tort law.

While codification and statutes clearly circumscribe the limits of judicial law-making, there is still the element of judicial "choice" and its accompanying responsibility. This is especially true of the Criminal Code, which authorizes the continued use of common law defenses such as *mens rea*. Once again Weiler argues that judges should go beyond superficial resemblances of wording of facts and grasp the principles that animate this area of law. (Reading 9.6) The examples used appear to be contradictory decisions concerning the availability of the *mens rea* defense. Weiler suggests that these can be reconciled by reference to the underlying competition between the "crime control" and "due process" principles of criminal law. Different judges could reasonably reach different conclusions in these two cases. The essential point from Weiler's perspective is not so much what a judge decides, but how he decides the case. A final appellate court should explicitly ground its decision in the underlying principles, and explain why the particular circumstances of this case dictated favouring one over the other. Failure to do so is a failure to live up to the standards of judicial craftsmanship that can reasonably be expected from a final appellate court in an age of legal realism.

# 9.1

## STARE DECISIS: THE USE OF PRECEDENTS
G. Gordon Post

In the resolution of conflicts a court invokes and applies rules of law to proven facts. A question arises: Just where does a court find these rules?

There are two *chief* sources of law: *statutes* and *precedents*. The former, of course, come from the legislature which consists of the elected representatives of the people. The latter come from the courts; precedents are the products of earlier decisions. To the latter, we should add the decisions of an increasing number of administrative bodies and the precedents established thereby, but of this matter we shall speak later.

Most everybody knows what a statute is, but what is a precedent? In a general, non-legal way, precedent plays an important role in our lives. Often, we do things as our parents did them and cite their experience as precedent for what we do now; out of some continuing or repetitive situation there comes a rough rule of thumb. When a father is questioned as to why he spanked his son for some infraction of the household rules, he might reply that as a boy in like circumstances he had been spanked as had his father before him. He might go on to explain that such treatment was an application of the rule of experience, ''Spare the rod and spoil the child.''. . .

. . . In all of these instances, there is the application of a rule of experience to a given situation. These are homely examples. Clubs, business organizations, boards of trustees, student groups — all have their rules, some written, some unwritten, which are often invoked as precedent for doing, or not doing, one thing or another. And a precedent here is defined by Webster as ''something done or said that may serve as an example or rule to authorize or justify a subsequent act of the same or analogous kind.''

### Judicial Precedent

A judicial precedent is defined in the same dictionary as ''a judicial decision, a form of proceeding, or course of action that serves as a rule for future determinations in similar or analogous cases.''

The driver of a wagon loaded with buckskin goods stopped for the night at a certain inn. He was received as a guest and the innkeeper took charge of his property. During the night a fire broke out which resulted in the destruction of

---

*Introduction to Law.* Englewood Cliffs, N.J.: Prentice Hall, 1963, p.80. Reprinted with permission.

horses, wagon and goods. The owner of the property thus destroyed sued the innkeeper for damages.

Let us suppose that this was a case of first impression, that is, a situation which is before [Canadian] court for the first time. After hearing the evidence from both sides, the judge does not simply say "I decide for the plaintiff," or "I decide for the defendant." He decides for one or the other and gives his reasons. He will speak as follows: "An innkeeper is responsible for the safe keeping of property committed to his custody by a guest. He is an insurer against loss, unless caused by the negligence or fraud of the guest, or by the act of God or the public enemy." The judge looks to the English common law and finds that the liability of innkeepers was expressed tersely in *Cross v. Andrews*: "The defendant, if he will keep an inn, ought, *at his peril*, to keep safely his guests' goods," and at greater length by Coke in *Calye's Case*: "If one brings a bag or chest, etc., of evidences into the inn as obligations, deeds, or other specialties, and by default of the innkeeper they are taken away, the innkeeper shall answer for them."

The judge will go on to explain the reason for the rule. He will say that the rule has its origins in public policy.

Every facility should be furnished for secure and convenient intercourse between different portions of the kingdom. The safeguards, of which the law gave assurance to the wayfarer, were akin to those which invested each English home with the legal security of a castle. The traveller was peculiarly exposed to depredation and fraud . . . .

## Stare Decisis

Let us suppose that a year or so later, another driver with a wagon load of hides spends the night at an inn. Again, the horses, the wagon, and the hides, are turned over to the innkeeper; and again, a fire occurs during the night and the property of the guest is burned up. The owner of the property then sues the innkeeper for damages. The situation here is exactly the same as in the earlier case.

The judge in the second case, according to the theory, will apply the rule or principle (which is the precedent) and decide in favor of the plaintiff. The precedent or authority of the first case is precise and fits the facts of the second case very nicely. This application by courts of rules announced in earlier decisions is spoken of as *stare decisis*, which means "let the decision stand." This has been, and is, a fundamental characteristic of the common law, although . . . it is the practice upon occasion for a high court to overrule its own precedents.

Obviously, a legal system in which judges could decide cases any which way, manifesting prejudice, whimsy, ignorance and venality, each decision being a entity in itself unconnected with the theory, practices and precedents of the whole, would be a sorry system, or, one might say, no system at all, and a source of little comfort either to attorneys or litigants. Speaking of *stare decisis* many years ago, Judge Maxwell said: "In the application of the principles of the common law, where the precedents are unanimous in the support of a proposition, there is no safety but in a strict adherence to such precedents. If the court will not follow established rules, rights are sacrificed, and lawyers and litigants are left in doubt and uncertainty, while there is no certainty in regard to what, upon a given state of facts, the decision of the court will be.''

One concludes, after a little thought, that *stare decisis* is ''the instrument of *stability* in a legal system,'' that it ''furnishes a legal system with *certainty* and *predictability*,'' and ''clothes a legal system with *reliability*''; in addition, it ''assures all persons of *equality and uniformity of treatment*'' and judges with ''an instrument of *convenience and expediency*.'' In short, ''*Stare decisis* preserves the judicial *experience* of the past.''

After a little more thought, however, one also sees that *stare decisis* is an instrument of conservatism, of immobility, of eyes-in-the-back-of-the-head, of stultification. The application of the same rule, decade after decade, long after changed conditions have robbed the rule of its validity, makes the rule a troublesome fiction.

But, American high courts do not hesitate to overrule their own precedents when social, economic, or political change demand a corresponding change in the law. Cardozo has said that ''If we figure stability and progress as opposite poles, then at one pole we have the maxim of *stare decisis* and the method of decision by the tool of a deductive logic; at the other we have the method which subordinates origins to ends. The one emphasizes considerations of uniformity and symmetry, and follows fundamental conceptions to ultimate conclusions. The other gives freer play to considerations of equity and justice, and the value to society of the interests affected. The one searches for the analogy that is nearest in point of similarity, and adheres to it inflexibly. The other, in its choice of the analogy that shall govern, finds community of spirit more significant than resemblance in externals.'' ''Much of the administration of justice,'' says Pound, ''is a compromise between the tendency to treat each case as one of a generalized type of case, and the tendency to treat each case as unique.'' ''Each method,'' concludes Cardozo, ''has its value, and for each in the changes of litigation there will come the hour for use. A wise eclecticism employs them both.''

# 9.2

## THE DUTY OF A COURT

A.V. Dicey

The duty of the court — is not to remedy a particular grievance but to determine whether an alleged grievance is one for which the law supplies a remedy. . . . If Parliament changes the law, the action of Parliament is known to every man and Parliament tries in general to respect acquired rights. If the Courts were to apply to the decision of substantially the same case, one principle today and another principle tomorrow, men would lose rights which they already possessed; a law which was not certain would in reality be no law at all.

---

*Lectures on the Relation between Law and Public Opinion during the Nineteenth Century.* 2nd ed. London: MacMillan, 1948. Reprinted with permission.

# 9.3

## ARCHITECT OF THE COMMON LAW

Paul Weiler

I shall begin my analysis of the role and performance of the Supreme Court of Canada by reviewing some of its decisions in the area of tort liability for personal injuries. Perhaps some students of the judicial process will ask why bother with these rather insignificant cases? Let's get on to the attention-getting constitutional or civil liberties decisions. However, there are several reasons why I think tort law is a good starting point. First, we can fully understand much of the contemporary character of the judicial process only if we see how it is directed at the adjudication of private law disputes between

---

*In the Last Resort: A Critical Study of the Supreme Court of Canada.* Toronto: Carswell-Methuen, 1979, p.57. Reprinted with permission.

one individual and another. Moreover, most of this area of law is almost totally judge-made, the *common law*. Our Supreme Court is a useful vehicle for reflecting on the true range and complexity of the judicial function precisely because of the breadth of its jurisdiction. The Court regularly handles the garden variety tort case as well as the newsworthy public law dispute. We must not miss the opportunity to appraise the exercise of judicial creativity in a private law area where the Court is not distracted by the involvement of other institutions, whether legislative or administrative. Finally, as I shall try to demonstrate, these attitudes concerning the private law role of the Supreme Court of Canada are wrong. Tort cases do raise important issues of public policy, and it is critical that they be settled intelligently. Let us start with a typical motor vehicles action which reached the Court, and produced a not-so-typical response.

### The Curious Doctrine of Cattle Trespass

One sunny summer afternoon, Floyd Atkinson was driving a jeep along a gravelled country road in a farming district in Ontario. Suddenly, upon reaching the brow of a hill, he was confronted with a herd of cows belonging to a farmer named Leo Fleming. Although he applied his brakes and steered past some of the cows, Atkinson's jeep eventually struck three of the animals, killing two, and causing serious injuries to his own knee. The driver sued the farmer for his personal injuries and the latter responded with a claim for his two dead cows. Apparently Fleming took the attitude that he could let his cows wander where they wanted and they customarily pastured on the highway, strolling back and forth across the road. The trial judge found this to be negligence on his part and, given a certain lack of due care on the driver's part also, apportioned the relative responsibility 60% to the farmer and 40% to Atkinson.

This would seem to be a relatively straight forward case and easy to resolve in terms of the ordinary doctrines of negligence law. Unfortunately, hidden away in the nooks and crannies of the common law was a legal rule which absolved the farmer of any duty to prevent his cattle from straying on the highway and endangering its users. This rule owed its origin to two factors: (1) when highways were first created at the end of the medieval period in England, land was dedicated by the adjoining landowners subject to their own right of passage for their animals; (2) for a very long time this created no risk of danger from domestic animals such as cattle because traffic was so slow moving that the animals could easily be avoided. With the advent of automobiles, this factual situation was radically changed. However, the House of Lords, in its 1947 decision in *Searle v. Wallbank*, declined an invitation to revise the legal duties of the farmer to bring them into line with modern needs, and the Ontario Court of Appeal felt compelled to respect the authority of this common law precedent in its 1952 decision in *Nobel v. Calder*. The true wishes of the Ontario judges were expressed in these concluding passages from their own opinion in *Fleming v. Atkinson*.

I do not want to part with this case without expressing the hope that it may draw attention to the present unsatisfactory state of the law in this province as to civil liability for injuries sustained due to the present on our public highways of straying domestic animals. *The Courts cannot change the law; the legislature can.* The common law as applied by the House of Lords in England to the highways there is not adequate here, and yet the Courts of this province must follow those decisions. . . . [emphasis added].

. . . When the case reached the Supreme Court of Canada, one judge, Mr. Justice Cartwright, agreed that the English common law, as reflected in *Searle,* defined the duties of the cattle owner until and unless they were changed by legislation. In his view it was not the function of the judges to alter a legal doctrine when it no longer reflected reasonable social policies. Fortunately for Canadian law, and for Floyd Atkinson, Mr. Justice Judson for the majority took a wider view of the judicial mission. He did not consider himself bound by an English doctrine which originated in features which are not part of Canadian society and which was reiterated in a heavily-criticized House of Lords decision. The decision of the Supreme Court in *Fleming v. Atkinson* is important because it clearly expressed our judicial independence of the House of Lords, especially when that body adheres to such an irrational legal anomaly. It is even more important as a example of the style of legal reasoning which a truly independent Supreme Court, at the top of our judicial hierarchy, must exhibit.

A rule of law has, therefore been stated in *Searle v. Wallbank* and followed in *Noble v. Calder* which has little or no relation to the facts or needs of the situation and which ignores any theory of responsibility to the public for conduct which involves foreseeable consequences of harm. I can think of no logical basis for this immunity and it can only be based upon a rigid determination to adhere to the rules of the past in spite of changed conditions which call for the application of rules of responsibility which have been worked out to meet modern needs. It has always been assumed that one of the virtues of the common law system is its flexibility, that it is capable of changing with the times and adapting its principles to new conditions. There has been conspicuous failure to do this in this branch of the law and the failure has not passed unnoticed. It has been criticized in judicial decisions (including the one under appeal), in the texts and by the commentators. . . . My conclusion is that it is open to this Court to apply the ordinary rules of negligence to the case of straying animals and that principles enunciated in *Searle v. Wallbank,* dependent as they are upon historical reasons, which have no relevancy here, and upon a refusal to recognize a duty now because there had been previously no need of one, offer no obstacle.

Judson's opinion is almost a textbook illustration of the conception of legal reasoning I proposed in the preceding chapter. Judges should not just blindly follow a legal rule because it has been recognized in the law for a long time. If the rule appears to require unjust results in the immediate situation, the judge must ask why. He should have a sense of unease when asked to use a rule that does not fit comfortably into the basic principles of tort responsibility which condition a lawyer's perception of the area. Perhaps there will be good reasons for this exceptional doctrine: on investigation of the cattle trespass rule, its only support turns out to be ancient history. In such a situation the legal obligation of a judge is clearly the forthright elimination of the legal anomaly which produces that kind of injustice.

### The Need For Judicial Renovation

What are the lessons we can draw from *Fleming v. Atkinson* about when and how the Court should respond in the common law? The case is certainly an unprepossessing factual situation with which to lead off a detailed assessment of the work of the Supreme Court across the spectrum of Canadian law. The question of whether the farmer or the motorist should bear the losses caused by a cow does seem to be of a somewhat lesser order of importance than constitutional disputes, issues of civil liberties and due process, problems of administrative regulation of the economy, and other such issues which regularly appear before the Supreme Court. The legal situation in the *Fleming* case is typical of the private law disputes which still constitute the bulk of the Court's work and which many now advocate deleting from its jurisdiction.[8] I will leave my assessment of these proposals for later when we have a more detailed view of the kinds of problems involved in these cases. For the moment we must recognize that there was an issue of general law to be resolved in the case and that the Supreme Court of Canada still has final judicial authority in this area. As is typical of a great many private law doctrines, tort liability for escaping cattle will not affect very many people but when it does arise, the question of whether damages can be collected will be of vital importance to the person involved. There are many legal doctrines with precisely this impact and the cumulative quality of their policies tells a lot about the justice afforded to the individual in our society. Up to now, the judiciary has been primarily responsible for their development in Canada. It behooves us then to enquire into the Court's performance in this area and to suggest the standards by which it should govern itself.

As Mr. Justice Judson stated in *Fleming v. Atkinson*, there is a general *principle* of law firmly established in this area. A person is required to take reasonable care in his behaviour when it creates the risk of physical injuries to another. If he does not take care and his faulty behaviour causes losses to another, the law requires that he assume responsibility for payment of damages to make whole the innocent victim. This legal principle had been clearly and authoritatively established in the general law of torts in the case of *Donoghue v. Stevenson*, but had become embedded in the motor vehicle area some time earlier. Appraised in the light of this theory of liability, the special immunity for "cattle trespass" was an historical anomaly. As Judson J. showed in his opinion, there may have been some rationale for its original adoption in England several hundred years ago but there certainly was no valid argument which could be made for its retention in contemporary Canada.

---

[8] This is no longer true, as right of appeal in civil cases was abolished in 1975.

Mr. Justice Cartwright's dissent did raise some doubt whether the Court should leave it to the legislature to administer the *coup de grace* to the doctrine. To adopt the framework of analysis I sketched earlier, assuming there are good policy reasons for tort liability in this situation, are there countervailing legal values which should make a court wary of itself abolishing the immunity? In my view, the *Fleming* case is significant because when we assess in a realistic way the arguments against judicial innovation, they seem largely inapplicable here. In this respect *Fleming* is typical of tort law and, indeed, of much of the private law area.

What about the argument of predictability in the law and the possibility that judicial elimination of the immunity will defeat the expectations of those who relied on it being the law? Did the farmer rely on his immunity from tort liability when he failed to take reasonable care to control his cattle? If he did, is this the kind of expectation the legal system should be concerned to satisfy? Simply to ask these questions is to answer them. In tort law, at least as regards accidental injuries, the reliance interest of possible defendants enters primarily at the point of insurance planning against liability for the risk. Studies have indicated that special rules of tort immunity such as this one, especially when they are hedged in by equally anomalous exceptions, are irrelevant to insurance decisions. Indeed, if there are any reasonable expectations which will be frustrated in a situation similar to that of the *Fleming* case they will be those of the injured motorist when he consults his lawyer and finds that the farmer is protected by a special rule dating back to medieval England. If the farmer's lawyer (or that of his insurer) has any understanding of this whole area of tort law and the rationale for its evolution, he can estimate the shakiness of the farmer's immunity and anticipate its probable removal. For these reasons, the Supreme Court in *Fleming v. Atkinson* could quite confidently ignore the argument about the damage to the predictability of the law.

What about the competence of the Court to make an intelligent change in the law? The possible defects in judicial law reform seem irrelevant to this actual problem. There is no need for lengthy investigations, social science research, expert testimony, and so on, to decide about change. The issue is basically one of esoteric "lawyer's law" which can be resolved by careful analysis of the implications of the basic legal principles underlying the area. If the legislature were moved to reform in this area, it would have to rely on the same sort of appraisal and it would find it in the textbooks and law review articles which are equally available to the courts.

In fact, the "cattle trespass" rule is one in which the resources of the judicial forum are especially valuable. The issue is narrow in compass, occurs infrequently, and is only one of a very large number of such relatively independent tort problems. Yet there are a lot of judges in a lot of courts hearing such cases all the time. Each judge sees the human implications of the issue vividly portrayed in the concrete dispute before him. On the basis of the research and arguments prepared for him by opposing counsel, he can work out the solution which seems most rational in the light of the basic policies in the area.

This proposed rule, when reported, can become a piecemeal addition to the evolving common law of torts. The legislature seems much too bulky and unwieldy an instrument to solve the problem of cattle trespass. It operates at the wholesale level while so much of our private law requires retail treatment.

But at least the legislature is elected, one may suggest. Should not changes in the law be made by a representative body, rather than the appointed and tenured court? We must turn to the reasons for our qualms about judicial innovation and take a realistic view of their relevance to particular cases. The problem in *Fleming v. Atkinson* is not one which will figure in an election campaign. It is inconsistent with democratic values (though not always illegitimate for this reason) for a court to intervene and impose its own policies in an area where the popular will has been expressed in the political arena. If the legislature were moved to reform in this esoteric problem area, it would merely be ratifying a proposal worked out by an equally unrepresentative Law Reform Commission at as invisible a level as would be a judicial innovation.

Once more we find that not only is there no real argument against a judicial initiative, but there are positive reasons in favour of such an active role. Private law doctrines such as this often lead to a distortion of the legislative process. Pressure for reform is very diffuse and unorganized. There is no lobby of accident victims petitioning the government. Instead, there is usually only an academic who has shown how some legal relic is working a real injustice on the very few people who run afoul of it. However, there is often a narrow interest group which might be somewhat harmed by the change. The farmer's insurance premiums will go up a bit and he may have to answer for his negligence in a lawsuit. A politician might be a little worried about the farmers' votes if their organizations object, especially if there is no counter-vailing lobby pressing for the reform. It is extremely unlikely he would be moved to *create* the cattle trespass immunity, but he might be loath to come out in the open and remove it entirely. The safest course in his eyes is to "let sleeping dogs lie," allow the proposal to die on the legislative order paper, and rationalize this inaction on the grounds (often valid) that he is busy on too many other problems.

By contrast, the Supreme Court was duty-bound to reach a positive conclusion about this legal problem in order to resolve the concrete dispute between Fleming and Atkinson. It had to hear the arguments from both sides, decide which position was most persuasive, and justify its conclusion in a written opinion which is reported for others to see and criticize. If judges within such an institution are willing to exercise their power to develop our law in a rational way, then we can provide the individual litigant who has been hurt with a forum to which he can come as a one-man lobby looking for legal justice. There is something to be said in a democracy of an institution which will resolve such disputes on the basis of the quality of the arguments presented, rather than the number of votes represented.

On just about every dimension then, these legal or institutional values seem to favour *judicial* initiative in this area, and they certainly do not warn against it. In order to complete this picture, let me give an example of a tort law reform I do not think a court is entitled to make, even though the judges may be convinced of its substantive desirability. The basic principle underlying our current law of torts, the one appealed to in *Fleming v. Atkinson*, is that negligent fault is the basis of liability. More and more voices contend that this is too narrow a criterion. Especially in the motor vehicle accident area, we hear proposals for a market deterrence, etc. I think we are going to see some such doctrine adopted in Canada shortly but this reform should be the work of the legislature, not the court. Why is this so?

In the first place, this will introduce a very substantial change in the incidence of legal liability and it may require substantial increases in the premium level. To the extent that insurance companies have charged lower premiums in reliance on the fault doctrine, they can claim that this justifiable expectation should not be frustrated by retrospective judicial alteration of the law. I am not sure myself how compelling this argument is. It depends on the degree of increased recovery in the new system and the ability of the insurance industry to finance the extra payments for past losses out of future premiums.

The real point is that the court could not likely estimate this either, which brings us to a second and major objection against judicial adoption of strict liability. The court simply is not competent to set up a complete new scheme for compensating automobile accident victims. This is not a simple matter of eliminating an irrational anomaly like the cattle trespass doctrine and applying the established principle of fault. The objectives of a strict liability scheme require a complex series of adjustments in the kinds and level of damages recoverable, the relationship of tort liability to various other forms of liability compensation, the nature of the insurance which is to be used, and even the forum in which claims are to be made. To perform this job, we want royal commissions, legislative committees and research by a battery of experts. We cannot rely on the efforts of a few Supreme Court judges sitting in their chambers in Ottawa.

Finally, the Court does not have the authority to adopt such a scheme into law. Let us suppose that a Royal Commission had been appointed, had laboured for several years examining the issues and the various alternatives, and then worked out a detailed scheme. The expert work has been done but the legislature, for various reasons, has not gotten around to acting on it. Should the Court decide to implement this new scheme in substitution for the common law of fault-based tort liability on the assumption that it is indeed a better system? In my view, the answer is still no! As anyone who reads Canadian newspapers will realize, the desirability of compensation without fault is a matter of sharp political controversy in several Canadian provinces. It has figured prominently in several election campaigns and governments have teetered on the edge of defeat in trying to get schemes enacted. The various plans present important and ambiguous value judgments about such matters as social welfare, compulsory government insurance, administrative agencies, and the responsibility of the dangerous driver. The place where these controversial issues should be aired and inevitable compromises worked out is the public legislative arena where the participants can be held responsible for their judgments. The last place in which we would want the decision made is the sheltered, closed world of the judges who are in the process of resolving a private lawsuit. . . .

# 9.4

## BOUCHER v. THE KING

Supreme Court of Canada (1951)

Rand J.: - For the reasons given by me following the first argument, I would allow the appeal, set aside the verdict and conviction and enter judgment of not guilty.

(The reasons given by Mr. Justice Rand, following the first argument, read as follows).

This appeal arises out of features of what, in substance, is religious controversy, and it is necessary that the facts be clearly appreciated. The appellant, a farmer, living near the town of St. Joseph de Beauce, Quebec, was convicted of uttering a seditious libel. The libel was contained in a four page document published apparently at Toronto by the Watch Tower Bible & Tract Society, which I take to be the name of the official publishers of the religious group known as The Witnesses of Jehovah. The document was headed "Quebec's Burning Hate for God and Christ and Freedom Is the Shame of all Canada": it consisted first of an invocation to calmness and reason in appraising the matters to be dealt with in support of the heading; then of general references to vindictive persecution accorded in Quebec to the Witnesses as brethren in Christ; a detailed narrative of specific incidents of persecution; and a concluding appeal to the people of the province, in protest against mob rule and gestapo tactics, that through the study of God's Word and obedience to its commands, there might be brought about a "bounteous crop of the good fruits of love for Him and Christ and human freedom." At the foot of the document is an advertisement of two books entitled "Let God be True" and "Be Glad, Ye Nations," the former revealing, in the light of God's Word, the truth concerning the Trinity, Sabbath, prayer, etc., and the latter, the facts of the endurance of Witnesses in the crucible of "fiery persecution."

The incidents, as described, are of peaceable Canadians who seem not to be lacking in meekness, but who, for distributing apparently without permits, bibles and tracts on Christian doctrine; for conducting religious services in private homes or on private lands in Christian fellowship; for holding public lecture meetings to teach religious truth as they believe it of the Christian religion; who, for this exercise of what has been taken for granted to be the unchallengeable rights of Canadians, have been assaulted and beaten and their bibles and publications torn up and destroyed, by individuals and by mobs; who have had their homes invaded and their property taken; and in hundreds have been charged with public offences and held to exorbitant bail. The police are declared to have exhibited an attitude of animosity toward them and to have treated them as criminals in provoking, by their action of Christian profession and teaching, the violence to which they have been subjected; and public officials and members of the Roman Catholic Clergy are said not only to have witnessed these outrages but to have been privy to some of the prosecutions. The document charged that the Roman Catholic Church in Quebec was in some objectionable relation to the administration of justice and that the force behind the prosecutions was that of the priests of that Church.

The conduct of the accused appears to have been unexceptionable; so far as disclosed, he is an exemplary citizen who is at least sympathetic to doctrines of the Christian religion which are, evidently, different from either the Protestant or the Roman Catholic versions: but the foundation in all is the same, Christ and his relation to God and humanity.

The crime of seditious libel is well known to the Common Law. Its history has been thoroughly examined and traced by Stephen, Holdsworth and other eminent legal scholars and they are in agreement both in what it originally consisted and in the social assumptions underlying it. Up to the end of the 18th century it was, in essence, a contempt in words of political authority or the action of authority. If we conceive of the governors of society as superior beings, exercising a divine mandate, by whom laws, institutions and administrations are given to men to be obeyed, who are, in short, beyond criticism, reflection or censor upon them or what they do implies either an equality with them or an accountability by them, both equally offensive. In that lay sedition by words and the libel was its written form.

But constitutional conceptions of a different order making rapid progress in the 19th century have necessitated a modification of the legal view of public criticism; and the administrators of what we call democratic government have come to be looked upon as servants, bound to carry out their duties accountably to the public. The basic nature of the Common Law lies in its flexible process of traditional reasoning upon significant social and political matter; and just as in the 17th century the crime of seditious libel was a deduction from fundamental conceptions of government, the substitution of new conceptions, under the same principle of reasoning, called for new jural conclusions. . . .

. . . The definition of seditious intention as formulated by Stephen, summarised, is, (1) to bring into hatred or contempt, or to excite disaffection against, the King or the Government and Constitution of the United Kingdom, or either House of Parliament, or the administration of justice; or (2) to excite the

King's subjects to attempt, otherwise than by lawful means, the alteration of any matter in Church or State by law established; or (3) to incite persons to commit any crime in general disturbance of the peace; or (4) to raise discontent or disaffection amongst His Majesty's subjects; or (5) to promote feelings of ill-will and hostility between different classes of such subjects. The only items of this definition that could be drawn into question here are that relating to the administration of justice in (1) and those of (4) and (5). It was the latter which were brought most prominently to the notice of the jury, and it is with an examination of what in these days their language must be taken to mean that I will chiefly concern myself.

There is no modern authority which holds that the mere effect of tending to create discontent or disaffection among His Majesty's subjects or ill-will or hostility between groups of them but not tending to issue in illegal conduct, constitutes the crime, and this for obvious reasons. Freedom in thought and speech and disagreement in ideas and beliefs, on every conceivable subject, are of the essence of our life. The clash of critical discussion on political, social and religious subjects has too deeply become the stuff of daily experience to suggest that mere ill-will as a product of controversy can strike down the latter with illegality. A superficial examination of the word shows its insufficiency: what is the degree necessary to criminality? Can it ever, as mere subjective condition, be so? Controversial fury is aroused constantly by differences in abstract conceptions; heresy in some fields is again a mortal sin; there can be fanatical puritanism in ideas as well as in mortals; but our compact of free society accepts and absorbs these differences and they are exercised at large within the framework of freedom and order on broader and deeper uniformities as bases of social stability. Similarly in discontent, affection and hostility: as subjective incidents of controversy, they and the ideas which arouse them are part of our living which ultimately serve us in stimulation, in the clarification of thought and, as we believe, in the search for the constitution and truth of things generally.

Although Stephen's definition was adopted substantially as it is by the Criminal Code Commission of England in 1880, the latter's report, in this respect, was not acted on by the Imperial Parliament, and the *Criminal Code* of this country, enacted in 1891, did not incorporate its provisions. The latter omits any reference to definition except in section 133 to declare that the intention includes the advocacy of the use of force as a means of bringing about a change of government and by section 133A, that certain actions are not included. What the words in (4) and (5) must in the present day be taken to signify is the use of language which, by inflaming the minds of people into hatred, ill-will, discontent, disaffection, is intended, or is so likely to do so as to be deemed to be intended, to disorder community life, but directly or indirectly in relation to government in the broadest sense: Phillimore, J. in *R. v. Antonelli* "seditious libels are such as tend to disturb the government of this country. . . ." That may be through tumult or violence, in resistance to public authority, in defiance of law. The conception lies behind the association which the word is given in section 1 of chapter 10, C.S. Lower Canada (1860) dealing with illegal oaths:

To engage in any seditious, rebellious or treasonable purpose; and the corresponding section 130 of the *Criminal Code*:

To engage in any mutinous or seditious purpose.

The baiting or denouncing of one group by another or others without an aim directly or indirectly at government, is in the nature of public mischief: *R. v. Leese & Whitehead*; and incitement to unlawful acts is itself an offence.

This result must be distinguished from an undesired reaction provoked by the exercise of common rights, such as the violent opposition to the early services of the Salvation Army. In that situation it was the hoodlums who were held to be the lawless and not the members of the Army: *Beatty v. Gillbanks*. On the allegations in the document here, had the Salvationists been arrested for bringing about by unlawful assembly a breach of the peace and fined, had they then made an impassioned protest against such treatment of law abiding citizens, and had they thereupon been charged with seditious words, their plight would have been that of the accused in this case.

These considerations are confirmed by section 133A of the *Code*, which is as follows:

WHAT IS NOT SEDITION — No one shall be deemed to have a seditious intention only because he intends in good faith, —

(a) to show that His Majesty has been misled or mistaken in his measures; or

(b) to point out errors or defects in the government or constitution of the United Kingdom, or of any part of it, or of Canada or any province thereof, or in either House of Parliament of the United Kingdom or of Canada, or in any legislature, or in the administration of justice; or to excite His Majesty's subjects to attempt to procure, by lawful means, the alteration of any matters in the state; or,

(c) to point out, in order to their removal, matters which are producing or have a tendency to produce feelings of hatred and ill-will between different classes of His Majesty's subjects.

This, as is seen, is a fundamental provision which, with its background of free criticism as a constituent of modern democratic government, protects the widest range of public discussion and controversy, so long as it is done in good faith and for the purposes mentioned. Its effect is to eviscerate the older concept of its anachronistic elements. But a motive or ultimate purpose, whether good or believed to be good, is unavailing if the means employed is bad; disturbance or corrosion may be ends in themselves, but whether means or ends, their character stamps them and intention behind them as illegal.

The condemned intention lies then in a residue of criticism of government, the negative touchstone of which is the test of good faith by legitimate means toward legitimate ends. That claim was the real defence in the proceedings here but it was virtually ignored by the trial judge. On that failure, as well as others, the Chief Justice of the King's Bench and Galipeault, J. have rested their dissent, and with them I am in agreement.

# 9.5

# REGINA v. OJIBWAY

BLUE, J.: This is an appeal by the Crown by way of a stated case from a decision of the magistrate acquitting the accused of a charge under the Small Birds Act. R.S.O., 1960. c. 724, s. 2. The facts are not in dispute. Fred Ojibway, an Indian, was riding his pony through Queen's Park on January 2, 1965. Being impoverished, and having been forced to pledge his saddle, he substituted a downy pillow in lieu of the said saddle. On this particular day the accused's misfortune was further heightened by the circumstance of his pony breaking its right foreleg. In accord with current Indian custom, the accused then shot the pony to relieve it of its awkwardness.

The accused was then charged with having breached the Small Birds Act, s. 2 of which states:

> 2. Anyone maiming, injuring or killing small birds is guilty of an offence and subject to a fine not in excess of two hundred dollars.

The learned magistrate acquitted the accused, holding in fact, that he had killed his horse and not a small bird. With respect, I cannot agree.

In light of the definition section my course is quite clear. Section 1 defines "bird" as "a two-legged animal covered with feathers." There can be no doubt that this case is covered by this section.

Counsel for the accused made several ingenious arguments to which, in fairness, I must address myself. He submitted that the evidence of the expert clearly concluded that the animal in question was a pony and not a bird, but this is not the issue. We are not interested in whether the animal in question is a bird or not in fact, but whether it is one in law. Statutory interpretation has forced many a horse to eat birdseed for the rest of its life.

Counsel also contended that the neighing noise emitted by the animal could not possibly be produced by a bird. With respect, the sounds emitted by an animal are irrelevant to its nature, for a bird is no less a bird because it is silent.

Counsel for the accused also argued that since there was evidence to show accused had ridden the animal, this pointed to the fact that it could not be a bird but was actually a pony. Obviously, this avoids the issue. This issue is not whether the animal was ridden or not, but whether it was shot or not, for to ride a pony or a bird is of no offense at all. I believe that counsel now sees his mistake.

Counsel contends that the iron shoes found on the animal decisively disqualify it from being a bird. I must inform counsel, however, that how an animal dresses is of no concern to this court.

Counsel relied on the decision in *Re Chicadee*, where he contends that in similar circumstances the accused was acquitted. However, this is a horse of a different color. A close reading of the case indicates that the animal in question there was not a small bird, but, in fact, a midget of a much larger species. Therefore, that case is inapplicable to our facts.

Counsel finally submits that the word "small" in the title Small Birds Act refers not to "Birds" but to "Act", making it The Small Act relating to Birds. With respect, counsel did not do his homework very well, for the Large Birds Act, R.S.O., 1960, c. 725, is just as small. If pressed, I need only refer to the Small Loans Act, R.S.O., 1960, c. 727, which is twice as large as the Large Birds Act.

It remains then to state my reason for judgment which, simply, is as follows: Different things may take on the same meaning for different purposes. For the purpose of the Small Birds Act, all two-legged, feather-covered animals are birds. This, of course, does not imply that only two-legged animals qualify, for the legislative intent is to make two legs merely the minimum requirement. The statute therefore contemplated multilegged animals with feathers as well. Counsel submits that having regard to the purpose of the statute only small animals "naturally covered" with feathers could have been contemplated. However, had this been the intention of the legislature, I am certain that the phrase "naturally covered" would have been expressly inserted just as "Long" was inserted in the Longshoreman's Act.

Therefore, a horse with feathers on its back must be deemed for the purposes of this Act to be a bird, and *a fortiori*, a pony with feathers on its back is a small bird.

Counsel posed the following rhetorical question: If the pillow had been removed prior to the shooting would the animal still be a bird? To this let me answer rhetorically: Is a bird any less of a bird without its feathers?

Appeal allowed.

# 9.6

# THE ORACLE OF THE CRIMINAL CODE

Paul Weiler

The role of the Supreme Court in Canadian criminal law is more intricate and delicate than it is in tort law. The reason is that the criminal law is largely defined by a crisply worded statutory provision. . . . On the surface this would appear to place significant restrictions on the scope for judicial creativity. The freedom of a court in the face of an earlier legislative judgment is rightly more circumscribed than is the case with purely judicial authority. Yet, on further investigation, we can discern important similarities in the part played by our judges in the growth of each of these areas of law. The basic criminal law is expressed in a Code, a legislative enactment to be sure, but one intended to summarize the results of several centuries of common law development. The common law of both torts and crimes stemmed historically from the same source, the writ of trespass, and only gradually was differentiated in line with the differing objectives of the two kinds of legal remedy. This important judicial influence, both historical and contemporary, can be seen in many corners of the vast and complex structure of our criminal law. I can deal with only one, the doctrine of *mens rea*, summarizing the various excuses for criminal behaviour.

### Adhering to Principle in the War on Drugs

A natural starting point in examining the contribution of the Supreme Court of Canada is the decision in *Beaver v. R.,*. . . an important event in the evolution of the Canadian law of *mens rea*. Louis and Maxie Beaver were convicted of the possession and sale of heroin in a factual situation which alone would make me want to talk about the case. A Constable Tassie of the R.C.M.P., going under the alias of Al Demeter in his role as an undercover narcotics agent, was introduced to the Beaver brothers by one Montroy, a drug addict. At that meeting Montroy told the Beavers that Demeter wanted to buy some heroin, and eventually the defendants agreed to sell the agent a half ounce of heroin for $400. That afternoon, Louis and Maxie picked up Demeter in their car and drove to a point where Maxie got out, went to a lamp post, and picked up a parcel which he gave to Demeter in return for the $400.

---

*In the Last Resort: A Critical Study of the Supreme Court of Canada.* Toronto: Carswell-Methuen, 1974, p.91. Reprinted with permission.

Eventually the undercover agent surfaced, the Beavers were charged, and these facts emerged undisputed at trial. It is sufficient for our purposes to focus on the possession charge. The Opium and Narcotic Drug Act, R.S.C. 1952, c. 201, prohibited "possession" of heroin without a licence and prescribed penalties for the offence. There was no doubt that the Beavers were in actual possession of heroin and thus committed what the law calls the *actus reus* of the offence. If one believes this conduct is harmful and should be prohibited, then the defendants in fact engaged in unlawful, harmful behaviour. If they did this, why should they not be convicted? The reason is that there was further evidence in the case which the Beavers contended should be a legal excuse for their conduct.

Louis Beaver testified that the day before the meeting with Demeter and the sales of the heroin, Montroy had come to him and talked about Al Demeter. Montroy said that Demeter had double-crossed him in some way and that he wanted to get even. He proposed that Beaver should agree to sell Demeter heroin but in fact deliver him a package of powdered milk, which would look exactly the same as the drug. Beaver would get the $400 and pass it along to Montroy who would have his revenge. Beaver said that he agreed to this scheme because Montroy had done several favours for the two Beavers while they were in the penitentiary. However, someone must have slipped up in the plan to substitute the powdered milk for the heroin under the lamp post. When it turned out to be heroin instead, the Beavers were just as surprised as anybody.

Anyway, this was the story put forth by the defence. The Ontario trial judge did not put it to the jury and ask them whether they believed the Beavers (or at least had a reasonable doubt). Instead, following a decision of his own Court of Appeal, he held that a mistake as to the nature of the substance was not a defence to a charge of possession of a narcotic. At the time this case was appealed to the Supreme Court of Canada there were conflicting decisions about the issue in several provinces but no earlier decisions of its own. Nor did the legislation speak explicitly to the problem, although narcotic offences were created and defined by a fairly comprehensive statute. Section 4 of the Opium and Narcotic Drug Act prohibited the bare "possession" of a narcotic; it did not affirmatively require that this possession be "knowing" nor did it exclude this kind of excuse. The fact that the legislation was silent about the legal validity of such a mistake is as good an index as any that the legislature had never focused on the problem. The Canadian law for this problem would be settled by the Supreme Court of Canada in disposing of the Beavers' appeal. In a split decision the Court held in favour of the excuse.

Both the majority and the dissenting opinions began with the same legal assumption. The criminal law presumed that a person could not be convicted of a criminal law offence unless he had a wrongful intent. Like so many legal principles, this has a Latin phrasing: *actus non facit reum nisis mens sit rea.* The majority opinion of Mr. Justice Cartwright cites several authorities to this effect, which make the point that the doctrine is designed to protect the liberty of the citizen and to prevent punishment of the innocent. In the case of statutory offences, this doctrine can be over-ridden by a contrary legislative expression which the courts would be bound to follow. Judges have also allowed themselves the option of excluding *mens rea* in certain cases where this seems appropriate from the subject-matter of the statute. It is this rather vague doctrine which leaves the matter open for the judgment of the court and whose application generated the real controversy in this case.

First of all, Cartwright's majority opinion dismissed the authorities for strict liability in the criminal law as not really analogous to this situation. Those cases dealt basically with such offences as a butcher selling unwholesome meat, or a trader having imprecise scales. Here we have a very serious offence, the character of which is set by the fact that there is a minimum mandatory jail sentence of six months (plus a minimum fine). One senses that Cartwright's defence of the principle of *mens rea* in this case is very sketchy just because he believes the answer is obvious. He simply will not impute to Parliament the ''monstrous intention'' to impose a minimum sentence of six months on a defendant who is deemed to commit an offence if someone else gives him heroin when he honestly believes the substance to be baking soda. The elements of the case for *mens rea* can be discerned very dimly in this opinion which is the major effort of the Supreme Court in the area of so-called serious or ''real'' crime. It is rather unfortunate for the general development in this area of the law that the existence of this rare mandatory jail sentence relieved the Court of the need to articulate better arguments against the very powerful dissent of Mr. Justice Fauteux.

Fauteux J. starts with a rather different perception of the ''subject-matter'' of this Act:

> The plain and apparent object of the act is to prevent, by a rigid control of the possession of drugs, the danger to public health, and to guard against the social evils which an uncontrolled traffic in drugs is bound to generate.

When he reviews the statutory scheme to discover the setting in which his judgment is to be made, he again interprets the attitude of Parliament very differently from the majority.

> The enforcement sections of the Act manifest the exceptional vigilance and firmness which Parliament thought of the essence to forestall the unlawful traffic in narcotic drugs and cope effectively with the unusual difficulties standing in the way of the realization of the object of the statute.

This view was based on the existence of a great many sections in the Opium and Narcotic Drug Act which reversed traditional criminal law doctrines to ease the path of the police and prosecution even at the expense of the liberty of the citizen. More particularly, there were extension of police powers of search of both person and premises, by day and by night (section 19), the use of writs of assistance to avoid the necessity of individual search warrants (section 22), the alleviation of the burden of proof of the Crown and inroads on the presumption of innocence (sections 6, 11, 13, 16, 17 and 18), the creation of minimum mandatory sentences (sections 4 and 6), the mandatory deportation of convicted aliens (section 26) and the extension of the Identification of Criminal Act, R.S.C. 1952, c. 144 even to summary offences under the statute (section 27). "All of these provisions are indicative of the will of Parliament to give the most efficient protection" to the public from the use of heroin. In this setting, Fauteux J. reasons, why should judges be loath to create a similar exception in the traditional protection of the doctrine of *mens rea* which is their responsibility? He argues that the various provisions of the Act are,

> indicative of the intent of Parliament to deal adequately with the methods, which are used. . . . to defeat the purposes of the Act, ingenious as they may be. That enforcement of the provisions of the Act may, in exceptional cases, lead to some injustice, is not an impossibility. But, to forestall this result as to such possible cases, there are remedies under the law, such as a stay of proceedings by the Attorney General or a free pardon under the royal prerogative.

He concludes by holding that the bare language of the section creating the offence must be read literally, the conduct alone of the possession of heroin is an offence, and no further requirement of knowledge of the nature of the substance need be proved.

## The Value and the Burden of Mens Rea

*Beaver* is a very interesting case to me because we see exposed on the face of the opinions the two contrasting perspectives on the criminal justice system — which have been named the "crime control" and "due process" models. The confrontation between these two attitudes has shaped the evolution of the criminal law generally, and certainly determined the character of our law of *mens rea*. The ultimate positions are implicit in the opinions of Fauteux and Cartwright JJ. respectively. Fauteux J. states that the "efficient" achievement of the objectives of the narcotic laws will be furthered by the exclusion of legal excuses such as mistake. Cartwright J. states that the law must make these excuses available in order to protect the innocent. Each then focuses on the relevant elements in the setting of the narcotic laws to try to show that his preferred goal is more important. We must understand the rationale for each of these judicial starting points in order to appreciate the problems in the cases I will discuss in this chapter.

How would this kind of legal doctrine — one which allows Beaver to excuse his possession of heroin on the grounds he thought it was powdered milk — interfere with the efficient enforcement of the narcotic laws? After all, what is the point of convicting and sentencing someone who is not aware that his conduct is criminal? The particular defendant has not shown himself to be dangerous and in need of individual correction. Potential offenders who are in that stage of ignorance cannot be deterred by the threat of criminal punishment because they are not aware they are committing an offence. However, every time you permit a defendant to advance a new excuse which is available as a matter of law to those who merit it, you create the possibility of misuse of the doctrine by those who are not really entitled to it. If the law creates exceptions and qualifications in its general prohibitions in order to take account of the equities of individual situations, it creates loopholes whose existence may lessen the deterrent influence of the law on those who really are guilty.

This concern is particularly applicable to the requirement of a "wrongful intent." To decide at a trial some months later what a person thought is a much more tenuous matter than establishing the external, objective and verifiable facts of what he did. In both cases, the Crown must prove the element in the defendant's legal guilt beyond all reasonable doubt. Proof of *mens rea* is not impossible: we know that from the many convictions that are obtained in areas where it is required. However, prosecutors and police are always worried about such rules which permit defendants to dream up an ingenious excuse (and *Beaver* looks like a beautiful example of this) and hope it will have some plausibility for an inexperienced jury. The defendant has nothing to lose, and he merely has to be convincing enough to raise a reasonable doubt. Those who are primarily worried about crime control have an understandable concern about the impact of the doctrine of *mens rea*.

The defenders of *mens rea* are not willing to allow the objective of efficient enforcement of the criminal law to justify the sacrifice of certain unlucky individuals who do have a valid excuse. It is inevitable that some people will engage in criminal conduct accidentally or by mistake. To deny such a person his defence because of the dangers of creating a loophole for the guilty will involve very harsh consequences for an innocent person. This is most blatantly the case in *Beaver*, where his conviction would lead to a mandatory sentence of at least 6 months in jail. Even in the ordinary run of the criminal law, where his excuse might get him a suspended sentence, to suffer a conviction and a criminal record after a public trial is a very serious disability and harm. The point of the doctrine of *mens rea* is that we convict only those who have voluntarily chosen to commit an offence and so deliberately exposed themselves to the risk of punishment. Suppose that someone has not decided to forfeit his immunity by knowingly engaging in criminal process simply for the more efficient protection of the rest of us is offensive to the principle of justice. To subject him to the grossly unequal treatment of the criminal process simply for the more efficient protection of the rest of us is offensive to the principle of justice. It also entails a substantial loss in individual freedom from the state. A major point of the concept of *mens rea* is that it permits us to choose a way out of the clutches of the criminal law. If we eliminate it, we have no way of protecting ourselves against accidental involvement with the police, prosecutor, trial, etc. We are all subject to the risk that the unlucky defendant, singled out by fate, will be one of us.

The proponents of "crime control" respond that all of this concern is purely hypothetical. Police and prosecutors also care about these values of freedom and equality and they have enough good sense to proceed against only those defendants who have fabricated their excuses. They will informally dismiss those who are truly innocent of any "wrongful intent." If they don't, and a case of injustice does come to light in court, there is an opportunity for a discretionary pardon afterwards (as Fauteux J. pointed out). It is precisely here that the advocates of "due process" join issue. They don't really trust the officials administering our criminal justice system. They do not want to rely on the exercise of discretion by a prosecutor, who operates at a low level of visibility, and who is basically involved in one side of what he may see as the "war on crime." The thrust of the doctrine of *mens rea* is to allow the excuse as a matter of legal right, on the basis of evidence and arguments presented in open court, with conflicts resolved by an impartial judge or jury. If this requires some sacrifice in efficiency of enforcement, then so be it.

The *Beaver* case is a microcosm reflecting this basic confrontation in the criminal law between these two contrasting attitudes. Our criminal law treats neither objective as an absolute value. It assumes that without an effective criminal sanction, we will not have a viable society preserving the due process objectives of freedom and equality, but that there is also no point in permitting the criminal law to offend against the principles of the very society it is trying to protect. A workable compromise is necessary. We must look at different situations pragmatically, assessing the weight of the claims of each in con-crete situations. This is what the Court did in *Beaver*, and it reached the conclusion we have seen. In a recent decision in *Pierce Fisheries*, it reached the opposite conclusion, but again on a similar pragmatic basis.

### The Public Welfare Exception

*Pierce Fisheries* is an instructive contrast with *Beaver* because there was such a marked similarity in the surface legal elements of the situation. The accused firm was charged with the offence under the Fisheries Act R.S.C. 1952, c. 119, of having undersized lobsters in its "possession." Apparently some 50,000 to 60,000 lbs. of lobster had been delivered to the plant that day, by truck or boat, and the inspector found 26 undersized lobsters. There was no evidence that any of the officers of the responsible employees of the defendant firm knew of their size, and the firm had instructed its employees not to purchase lobsters which were in breach of the Regulations under the Act. As in *Beaver*, the term "possession" was not qualified by any reference to knowledge or intention, but again there was another provision of the same statute which did advert to this element. The question, then, was how the Court should construe the immediate offence in the light of this ambiguous direction from the legislature, read in the light of the basic principle of *mens rea*. Cartwright J., in a lone dissent, remained intransigently in favour of the position of the accused. He argued that *Beaver* laid down a binding legal rule for the construction of criminal offences — even conduct "not involving grave moral turpitude" — based on the activity of *possession*: "in a criminal case there is in law no possession without knowledge of the character of the substance." Perhaps the basis of his conclusion appears in a passage at the end of his opinion where he asks whether it may be in the "public interest" to allow absolute liability only where there are specific and unequivocal words from the legislature to that effect.

Mr. Justice Ritchie's opinion for the majority agreed that there was a common law presumption of *mens rea* as "an essential ingredient of all cases that are criminal in the true sense." However, he held that there is no such presumption for a "wide category of offences created by statutes enacted for the regulation of individual conduct in the interests of health, convenience, safety and general welfare of the public." The key to this category is that they "are not criminal in any real sense, but are acts which in the public interest are prohibited under a penalty." The Court must always ask whether it is faced with a "new crime added to the general criminal law," or "an act of a truly criminal character" for which a "stigma" attaches to any person convicted of it. In *Beaver*, the Court had found that it was a "*serious crime* to possess or deal in narcotics," as indicated also by the mandatory jail term. This Court could find little resemblance to the offence of possession of undersized lobsters, and did not believe the latter was a serious crime to which any stigma attached. Ritchie J. was concerned here that "if lack of knowledge by a responsible employee constituted a defence for a limited company. . . . it would in many cases be virtually impossible to secure a conviction." The Court could not apply the doctrine of "evil intent" because then "the statute, by which it was obviously intended that there should be complete control without the possibility of any leaks, would have so many holes in it, that in truth it would be nothing more than a legislative sieve."

The *Pierce Fisheries* opinion creates the impression, even more pronounced than was the case with *Beaver*, that while a decision may be right, no satisfactory rationale is provided. Mr. Justice Ritchie simply states that conviction for this offence is very different than it is for possession of heroin, and that the difficulties created by the *mens rea* doctrine could render the statute an unenforceable sieve. He may be right but he doesn't explain why. This pair of decisions is not like some of the horrible examples I described in the tort area of a legal distinction without any functional difference at all. There are plausible reasons for characterizing the *Beaver* offence in one way and the *Pierce Fisheries* offence in another. However, a final court has a duty to do more than reach the correct result in individual cases on an intuitive basis. It must articulate the reasons for its different conclusions in a way that gives meaningful guidance to the lower courts which must deal with this same problem recurring in so many different guises. Anyone who reads the flow of cases in this area will know the lower court judges have not been able to find such guidance in the decisions of the Supreme Court.

What are the distinctive characteristics of these "public welfare" offences, of which the regulation in *Pierce Fisheries* was representative, which could reasonably support a different conclusion as to *mens rea*? There are several reasons for believing that it will be much more difficult to prove knowledge or intent and, contrariwise, that it will be much easier to fabricate these excuses. The particular offence is merely one instance of a large number of similar transactions (28 lobsters out of over 50,000 lbs. that day); there is a fine line between legal and illegal situation (3 3/16 of an inch for a lobster); and because many different individuals in the firm or organization participate in the activity, it is hard to single out the one responsible. Management can just post signs in the area and then deny knowledge of what happened. I should note that these very same factors are also good reasons for believing that there will be many offences committed through legitimate mistakes. This must not obscure the fact that it is a lot more difficult for a court to separate the valid from the invalid excuses than in a case like *Beaver*, where a person is in the rather unusual situation of being in possession of and selling heroin.

This is merely one side of the equation, the problem of the prosecution. It is easy to see a similar shift on the other side, regarding the interests of the accused. Just as the Supreme Court judges, we all recognize, when we see it, the difference between conviction for possession of heroin and for possession of undersized lobsters, though we cannot always explain it. There are several factors in the background. Public welfare offences regulate conduct that is a considerable distance removed from any harm to any individual, and thus the retributive urges in the area are muted. The conduct is prohibited by laws of relatively recent origin and there is a relatively artificial line between illegal behaviour and legitimate business dealings. Hence, there is much less of an aura of popular moral attitudes surrounding the offence and little likelihood of public stigma in a conviction. This is reflected in the fact that the almost invariable sentence for the offence will be a fine imposed on the firm, not jail sentence on an individual. The firm has chosen to engage in the business where these regulatory laws apply. It can be required to treat the amount of these fines as a cost of doing business and made to adjust its affairs accordingly. The values of liberty and fairness to the individual, which underlie the principle of *mens rea*, are of considerably less weight for these offences while, as we saw before, the claims of crime control are much more insistent than for the unusual and isolated criminal conduct of *Beaver*. If we consider the doctrines of the criminal law as an expression of a pragmatic compromise between these sometimes competing objectives, then the different results in *Beaver* and *Pierce Fisheries* can be understood, and perhaps justified.

### The Judicial Function within our Criminal Law

Let us turn for the moment from analysis of the substantive issues in the Supreme Court decisions to the more basic question of the proper judicial role in this area. As we have seen, the Court has a great deal of legal flexibility in deciding whether particular statutes create strict liability or *mens rea* offences. I will discuss some cases which show how the Court must make similar judgments about the quality of *mens rea* for those offences for which it is required. What are the implication of *mens rea* for such distinct situations as drunkenness, insanity or duress? By what justification or authority does the Court have such a decisive impact on the character of this vital area of our criminal law?

First of all, there is the unusual circumstance that the Criminal Code provides an explicit legal source for the division of labour between legislature and court in developing our criminal law. By section 8 of the Code, common law offences are abolished. The legal values I sketched in Chapter 2 speak especially firmly in favour of the legislature as the sole source of new criminal offences. The legislature enacts its rules in definite language and through public procedures and makes them effective as of a fixed date in the future. This may reduce to some extent the elasticity of the criminal law and allow some ingenious individuals to find loopholes in the existing offences which enable them to achieve their dubious ends. However, to quote from the original Royal Commission Report which is the source of our Code, it is "better to run the risk of giving a temporary immunity to the offender than to leave any one liable to a prosecution for an act or omission which is not declared to be an offence by the . . . Code itself or some other Act of Parliament." Perhaps judges can develop new torts; they must not create new crimes. Society takes the risk that a few evil-doers may escape punishment when a new situation arises, and until legislation can be enacted, in order to avoid the unfairness of convicting those who thought they were behaving in an acceptably legal way but will be caught by the retrospective law-making of the judges.

The attitude of the Code is very different when it comes to the "defences." Section 7(3) reads:

> Every rule and principle of the common law that renders any circumstance a justification or excuse for an act or a defence to a charge continues in force and applies in respect of proceedings for an offence under this Act or any other Act of the Parliament of Canada, except in so far as they are altered by or are inconsistent with this Act or any other Act of the Parliament of Canada.

In this the Code again reflects the views of Mr. Justice Stephen and the Royal Commissioners who stated:

> In our opinion the principles of the common law on such subjects, when rightly understood, are founded on sense and justice . . . It is, if not absolutely impossible, at least not practicable, to foresee all the various combinations of circumstances which may happen, but which are of so infrequent occurrence that they have not hitherto been the subject of judicial consideration, although they might constitute a justification or excuse, and to use language at once so precise and clear and comprehensive as to include all cases that ought to be included, and not to include any case that ought to be excluded.

Hence, we have an authoritative statement in the Code of the view that the evolution of the law of *mens rea* should continue to be the work of the judicial process even though the rest of the criminal law was largely reduced to statutory form. What are the institutional factors which might justify this conclusion?

First of all, the defences are not matters of high political visibility and content, in contrast with definition (or repeal) of offences. The question whether an honest mistake should be an excuse for the possession of drugs is of a qualitatively different order than the question of what, if any, criminal offences we should have to deal with the problem of drugs. Secondly, most of the issues raised with respect to *mens rea* do not require detailed expertise or scientific research which may be needed for many other areas of criminal law reform. This is not universally true, as the example of the insanity defence demonstrates. However, even here much of the available research has been canvassed and appraised in ways which are usable by courts as well as legislatures. Moreover, a court has resources in the area which are not available to the legislatures. As we shall see, some of the key issues of *mens rea* require reflection on the implication of the basic values of the criminal law for very unusual situations. The legislature would not likely anticipate such cases in drafting and enacting general language; courts see the problem dramatically presented in a concrete, human context. Finally, the significance of "due process" for judicial reform of the criminal law is very different here than it was for the definition of new crimes. When a novel defence is raised, we cannot refuse to apply a new rule until the legislature gets around to adopting it. In the interim the innocent individual who should be excused because he was blameless will suffer the harsh injustice of criminal punishment. It is precisely because a court can and does make law retrospectively that the defendant should be able to appeal to it for a new rule to be applied to the old facts of his case.

These are the practical institutional factors which support the judgment that our law has made in favour of an active judicial role in developing criminal defences. Their operation, I suggest, is based on the assumption that the doctrine of *mens rea* is an established "legal principle" shaping this area of the law. Earlier in this book, I used this doctrine as an example of the concept of a legal principle when I was trying to show the significance of this instrument in my preliminary statement of the role of law in courts. Now that we have some appreciation of the content and use of the doctrine of *mens rea* itself, I can expand somewhat on what I mean by a legal principle.

Translated literally, *mens rea* means a "guilty mind." Obviously, there are innumerable sets of circumstances which could be relevant to the final judgement about whether the defendant's criminal conduct was as a result of a "blameworthy state of mind," and "evil intent," or whatever other synonym we can think of for the Latin phrase. Some have argued that the legal requirement of *mens rea* means that the judges or juries in the instant case should be asked to find whether the defendant was blameworthy, taking into account all of the facts in the immediate situation, without any further legal precision. This is certainly conceivable and practical; after all, that is how the law now deals with the defendant in a negligence action. Liability in tort depends upon the court's view as to whether the defendant showed reasonable care or was at fault in all of the circumstances of the accident. If the criminal law took a similar tack, the doctrine of *mens rea* would be a legal standard, not a legal principle. As stated earlier, principles are used in argument about the proper rules to be applied to the facts. However, for several reasons, the law has not conceived of the requirement of "blameworthiness" as a general standard to be applied directly to the events in an individual case. There is a greater need for precision, predictability, and even-handedness in the administration of the criminal law, and perhaps the controversial character of the issues generates greater emotional involvement about a situation than is common in tort law. Accordingly, the established scheme of our criminal law requires specific rules defining the various excuses, telling us for what offences they are available and the relevant facts in a situation for their application. The rules established in *Beaver* and in *Pierce Fisheries* are an example: we know that mistake as to the nature of a drug is an excuse under the narcotics laws but that mistake as to the size of one's lobsters is not an excuse under the Fisheries Act.

However, this branch of the law is not just a miscellaneous and apparently incoherent collection of such rules. The rules are developed primarily by the courts in adjudicating particular cases, and the judges do have some reasons for what they are doing. What is the role of the principle of *mens rea* in this process? I think it can be sketched in this way. In the early, formless state of the criminal law, the courts will be presented with the most obvious excuses for the infliction of criminal harms. The defendant may claim that he inflicted injuries on another through pure accident, or perhaps as a result of self defense. Acting on the common-sense view that it is unfair to convict some- one in a situation where he has shown himself no worse than persons who have complied with the law, judges begin to acquit the defendants. Reflection on the reasons for these decisions will suggest arguments to lawyers for the development of similar excuses for analogous but more difficult cases (such as insanity). Gradually a theory is articulated which shows how these various doctrines implement certain basic values of criminal justice. With a sharpened realization of the objectives that the law has been intuitively pursuing all along, the courts are ready to refine their doctrines to take account of unusual variations in the situation, or even to overturn earlier rules which appear no longer compatible with the overall thrust of the law (e.g., drunkenness). The fact that there is such an underlying theory in the law, based on the acceptance of certain values, is expressed in the legal principle of *mens rea*. Two final points may be made. First, it is in the relationship of rule and principle that we find "the genius of the common law." Because the process requires the judges to turn from immediate facts to basic theory and then back to the facts, the law can be kept pragmatic, functional, and oriented to the sense of the situation. It admits of exceptions to the availability of excuses (as we saw in *Pierce Fisheries*); it can admit of many qualifications to their operation, even where they are allowed. . . . Yet there is a guiding thread to the enquiry which channels the evolution of the law. The values on which *mens rea* is based are by no means self-evident. Eminent critics of the criminal law have called for the abolition of all such concepts of individual responsibility and blame. These arguments are properly addressed to the legislature, not the courts. We have a system of criminal law into which the notion of blameworthiness has been cemented as an integral part of a very complex structure. The Court can unravel on a case by case basis the strands of the existing system and can make necessary adjustments where this appears reasonable; it cannot create a new system based on a radically different view of the function of criminal punishment. Our judges are legally *bound* by the principle or presumption of *mens rea*.

# 9.7

# KEYTERMS

### *Concepts*

common law system
*stare decisis*
*ratio decedendi*
*obiter dicta*
precedent
"distinguishing a precedent"
"limiting a precedent"
"ignoring a precedent"
"overruling a precedent"
"prospective overruling"
statute
administrative rules and regulations
civil law system
codification
*mens rea*
*actus reus*
"Due process" and "crime control" models of criminal law

## *Institutions, Events, and Documents*

James Fitzjames Stephen, Draft Code of 1879
Criminal Code (1892)
*Beaver v. R.* (1957)
*Fleming v. Atkinson* (Cattle Trespass Case) (1959)
*R. v. Pierce Fisheries* (1971)

# 10

# Judicial Review and Federalism

## Constitutional Origins

The Constitution Act, 1867 united on a federal basis the separate colonies that had up to until that time constituted British North America. The federal form was essential to the act of union. None of the provinces, particularly Quebec, was willing to relinquish the degree of political autonomy and self-government to which they aspired, and to be subsumed under a single unitary state. At the same time the most influential leaders of the confederation movement, men like John A. Macdonald and George Brown, desired a strong central government based on ''legislative union,'' in order to avoid what they considered to have been the near fatal weakness of the central government in American federalism.[1]

The Constitution Act, 1867 represented an uneasy compromise between these conflicting goals. Provincial demands for preserving local autonomy and self-government were accommodated through a distribution of legislative powers between the newly created federal government and the provinces, primarily in sections 91 and 92 of the Act. The centralists' goals were recognized by a very broad wording of the federal government's section 91 law-making powers, and by the unilateral power to strike down provincial laws through the devices of disallowance (s. 56) and reservation (s. 90). The result was a written constitutional document establishing a highly centralized form of federalism. As it turned out, this original design was modified considerably by subsequent political developments, in which judicial review played a major role.

It is now accepted that judicial review is a necessary corollary to a federal form of government based on a written distribution of powers between two levels of government. For this distribution to be meaningful, there must be a

---

[1] This scepticism toward federalism appeared quite justified at the time. The Confederation process took place during and after the bloody American Civil War, which had pitted the ''states' rights'' advocates of the Southern slave-holding states against the national government.

mutually acceptable process for settling the inevitable disputes over where one government's jurisdiction ends and the other's begins. Neither level of government can be permitted to define unilaterally (and thus to redefine) the boundaries of federal-provincial jurisdiction, as this would violate the equal status of both levels of government, a central principle of federalism.[2] In practice the need for a "neutral umpire" of federal systems has been met through judicial review by a final court of appeal. This is true of the American and Australian political systems as well as Canada.

## Historical Origins

Originally, judicial review of the constitution came easily and without controversy in Canada. The Constitution Act took the form of an Imperial statute, and section 129 mandated the continuation of the existing legal regime. This meant that the Constitution Act was subject to the already existing Colonial Laws Validity Act, which required consistency of colonial law with British Imperial statutes. The Judicial Committee of the Privy Council was charged with the responsibility of enforcing this policy. The Judicial Committee had served as the final court of appeal for British North America prior to Confederation, and simply continued in this capacity after 1867. Any alleged violation of the federal division of powers set out in the Constitution Act could be challenged in the existing superior courts of the provinces, and appealed from a provincial court of appeal directly to the Judicial Committee in London.

The introduction of judicial review in Canada was made easier by the original absence of a national court of appeal. When the federal government moved to exercise its section 101 authority to create such a court, controversy quickly erupted. As Professor Smith explains, the attempt to create the Supreme Court of Canada became entangled in the already robust politics of federal-provincial competition. (Reading 10.1) This controversy was engendered in large part by the inclusion of the reference procedure as part of the Supreme Court Act. Some "provincial rights" advocates perceived the creation of a "federal" court of appeal and the simultaneous creation of a reference authority vested exclusively with the federal government as an ill-disguised attempt to refurbish the already controversial disallowance power by cloaking it with judicial legitimacy. This suspicion was supported by the original form of the reference procedure and the comments of centralists such as John A. MacDonald.[3]

---

[2] The disallowance and reservation powers violate the principle of parity, and for that reason it has been argued that Canada is not a "true" federal state. However, neither power has been exercised by Ottawa for over forty years. Although both powers still exist *legally*, it is generally accepted that a convention of non-use has been established, and that it is politically unacceptable for the federal government to re-activate either of these powers.

[3] The non-judicial characteristics of the original reference procedure are discussed in the introduction to chapter six.

Provincial fears of a centralizing Supreme Court notwithstanding, the Supreme Court Act was finally adopted in 1875. The newly created Supreme Court of Canada immediately began to exercise the power of judicial review, and did so without controversy. However, its decisions could be appealed to the Privy Council, and it could be avoided altogether by *per saltum* appeals directly from a provincial court of appeal to the Privy Council. Both of these routes of appeal were abolished by amendments to the Supreme Court Act in 1949, which established the Supreme Court of Canada as the final and exclusive court of appeal for Canada. Until 1949, however, the Supreme Court was decidely the junior partner in overseeing the judicial aspects of Canada's constitutional development. Its early decisions were frequently overturned by the Privy Council, and the doctrine of *stare decisis* meant that it was bound to follow the Privy Council's lead.

## Constitutional Interpretation

Constitutional interpretation raises problems that do not occur in common law or statutory interpretation. Because constitutional law regulates the powers of governments (rather than the private rights of individuals) it inevitably affects the making of public policy. Judicial review thus injects into the judicial process a political dimension that previously did not exist. As has already been explained, common law judges have been reluctant to acknowledge the policy-making function conferred on them by judicial review, as it seems to contradict and undermine so many of the traditional aspects of the judicial process.[4] As a result, Canadian, British, and Australian judges have tended simply to transfer the techniques of statutory interpretation to constitutional interpretation.

This was especially true of the Privy Council's approach to the Constitution Act. While this is easily explained by the unfamiliarity of British judges with the practice of a "written constitution" (indeed, to them it was just another Imperial statute!), it had the unfortunate effect of establishing this mode of constitutional interpretation as the standard for Canadian judges to follow. Significant discontent with the substance of the Privy Council's constitutional decisions (discussed below) led in turn to criticisms of its technique of interpretation. These critics called for an approach to constitutional interpretation that acknowledged the inherent policy dimensions of constitutional law, and reflected the need to adapt a written constitution to the changing needs and circumstances of the society it governs. William Lederman has summarized this issue as follows:

> There are principally two types of interpretation — literal or grammatical emphasizing of the words found in statutes and constitutional documents, and sociological, which insists that

---

[4] See introductions to chapters two, six, seven and eight.

constitutional words and statutory words must be carefully linked by judicially noticed knowledge and by evidence to the ongoing life of society.[5]

Examples of these two different approaches to constitutional interpretation are found in the excerpts from the Privy Council opinions of Lord Sankey (Reading 10.2) and Lord Atkin (Reading 10.3). Lord Sankey articulated his now famous "living tree" approach in his opinion in the well-known "Persons Case."[6] Henrietta Muir Edwards, a leader of the women's suffrage movement in the West, had been proposed for an appointment to the Senate from Alberta. At issue was whether any woman could be appointed to the Senate. Legally the case boiled down to whether the term used in section 24 of the Constitution Act, "qualified persons," included women. The Supreme Court of Canada ruled that it did not, basing its decision on internal evidence of the Constitution Act itself and the indisputable fact that at the time of Confederation, women did not have the right to vote, much less to hold public office. While this decision was arguably correct in a narrowly technical sense, it was overturned on appeal by the Privy Council. Lord Sankey stressed the necessity of interpreting constitutional language in light of society's changing beliefs and needs, and not just internal grammatical constructions.

Lord Atkin's very different approach to constitutional interpretation occurred in the 1937 *Labour Conventions Case.*[7] This case raised the issue of Parliament's authority to enact legislation implementing Canada's treaty obligations when the legislation involved matters that would normally have fallen under the provinces' section 92 jurisdiction. Despite the recent Statute of Westminster (1931), which had affirmed the sovereignty of Canada in the conduct of her foreign affairs, Lord Atkin ruled that the federal government's treaty-making power did not allow it to trench upon matters of provincial jurisdiction when implementing a treaty. This decision was widely perceived as a serious blow to the effective conduct of Canadian foreign policy, and was blamed on Lord Atkin's "watertight compartments" view of Canadian federalism. This view was widely condemned as being out of touch with the economic and political realities of twentieth-century Canada.

## Constitutional Politics

The Privy Council's decision in the *Labour Conventions Case* is only one in a long series of constitutional cases that progressively narrowed the scope of the federal government's section 91 powers while expanding the section 92

---

[5] W.R. Lederman, "Thoughts on Reform of the Supreme Court of Canada," *The Confederation Challenge*, Ontario Advisory Committee on Confederation, Vol. II (Toronto: Queen's Printer, 1970), p.295.

[6] *Re Meaning of the Word "Persons" in Section 24 of the B.N.A. Act* [1928], S.C.R. 276.

[7] [1937] A.C. 327; III Olmstead 180.

jurisdiction of the provinces. The federal government's broad residual power to make laws for the "Peace, Order, and good Government of Canada" was whittled away to almost nothing by the Privy Council's "emergency doctrine" test. The unrestricted power to make laws for the "Regulation of Trade and Commerce" was soon reduced to the narrow ambit of "interprovincial trade" by judicial interpretation. At the same time, the Privy Council's decisions expanded what originally appeared to be the rather meagre provincial powers to make laws in relation to "Property and Civil Rights in the Province" and "all matters of a merely local or private Nature in the Province." Throughout all of these decisions, the Privy Council adhered to the textually oriented, legalistic method of interpretation described above.

Mounting dissatisfaction with the Privy Council's performance as final constitutional arbiter for Canada manifested itself in the "judicial nationalism" discussed in chapter one. Following the recommendations of the 1939 O'Connor Report, Parliament abolished all appeals to the Privy Council in 1949. While Canadian critics of the Judicial Committee were unanimous in condemning the provincial bias of its decisions, they were far from agreed upon a diagnosis of the problem or a prescription for an acceptable "made in Canada" jurisprudence after 1949. One school of thought criticized the J.C.P.C. for being too textual and literal in its interpretation of the constitution, and thereby failing to make it a "living constitution," in accord with the changing times. The other principal group of critics accused the Judicial Committee of not following the obviously centralist bias of the text closely enough.[8] The inability of Canadian scholars, judges, and political leaders to agree on an appropriate constitutional jurisprudence has carried over into the post-1949 era. The latent pro-Ottawa attitudes of the old J.C.P.C. critics have not been acceptable to Quebec leaders or other "provincial rights" advocates. The result has been a continuing crisis in the authority of the Supreme Court whenever it acts as final arbiter of Canadian federalism.

The most important post-1949 federalism case has been the 1976 *Anti-Inflation Reference*.[9] (Reading 10.4) As Peter Russell recounts, this case seemed to present a perfect opportunity for the Supreme Court, led by its new chief justice, Bora Laskin, a known centralist, to repudiate once and for all the moribund "emergency doctrine" of the Privy Council. Several post-1949 decisions of the Supreme Court had silently ignored the old "emergency doctrine," and spoke instead of an "inherent national importance" test. Centralists anticipated that the time was ripe to institute this new and much broader basis for the exercise of the federal government's residual power. The public policy significance of the case was underscored by the large number of

---

[8] See Alan C. Cairns, "The Judicial Committee and its Critics," *Canadian Journal of Political Science*, 4 (September, 1971), p.301.

[9] [1976] 2 S.C.R. 373.

intervenors, consisting of both provincial governments and private groups. The Supreme Court itself tacitly acknowledged the policy dimensions of the case by devising new procedures to allow for the introduction of very untraditional, socio-economic evidence by both sides.[10] While the Supreme Court's final decision mildly increased the "Peace, Order, and good Government" authority of the federal government, it did not repudiate the work of the Privy Council. The "emergency doctrine" was preserved, although it now can be invoked in peace time situations. While this result was somewhat anticlimactic, the case itself is a picture-book example of the confluence of politics and law in the highest court of the land.

As it turned out, the *Anti-Inflation Reference* was the first in a series of Supreme Court decisions during the late seventies that dealt with federalism issues — all of which were won by Ottawa.[11] These decisions contributed to federal-provincial tensions on other fronts, and led to growing provincial suspicions about the dependence of the Supreme Court on the Liberal government in Ottawa. Shortly following several of these cases, an article appeared in the press suggesting that "the image of Chief Justice Laskin and his eight 'sober, grey men' acting as spear-carriers for the federal prime minister fails to add anything to one's hopes for improved national unity."[12]

The implications of these remarks so upset Chief Justice Laskin that he purposely went out of his way to respond publicly. At a hastily arranged "Seminar for Journalists" the same month, the late Chief Justice declared:

> I have to be more sad than angry to read of an insinuation that we are "acting as spear carriers for the federal prime minister" or to read of a statement attributed to a highly respected member of the academic community that "the provinces must have a role in the appointment of members of the Supreme Court in order to ensure that they have confidence that it can fairly represent the interests of the provincial governments as well as of any federal government."
>
> . . . The allegation is reckless in its implication that we have considerable freedom to give voice to our personal predilections, and thus to political preferences. . . . We have no such freedom, and it is a disservice to this Court and to the work of those who have gone before us to suggest a federal bias because of federal appointment.[13]

---

[10] See Introduction to chapter eight.

[11] The principal cases were two cases dealing with provincial regulation of broadcasting, *Capital Cities Communications v. C.R.T.C.*, [1978] 2 S.C.R. 141, and *Public Service Board v. Dionne*, [1978] 2 S.C.R. 191; and two cases dealing with provincial authority to tax and regulate the production of natural resources, *CIGOL v. Government of Saskatchewan*, [1978] 2 S.C.R. 545, and *Central Canada Potash v. Government of Saskatchewan*, [1979] 1 S.C.R. 42.

[12] Edwin R. Black, "Supreme Court Judges as Spear-Carriers for Ottawa: They need watching," *Report on Confederation* (Feb. 1978), p.12.

[13] Bora Laskin, "Judicial Integrity and the Supreme Court of Canada," *Law Society Gazette* (1978), pp. 118, 120.

There is no doubting the sincerity of the late Chief Justice's remarks, and he was factually vindicated by a subsequent law review article that effectively debunked the charge of any conscious federal bias in recent Supreme Court decisions.[14] But in politics, perceptions, not facts, usually carry the day, and the Supreme Court has a public image problem. The incident itself betrays a continuing lack of confidence in the Supreme Court among provincial elites, and a subsequent diminishing of its authority.[15] This problem takes on heightened significance in the 1980's, as the Supreme Court undertakes its new and broader mandate of interpreting the 1982 Charter of Rights and Freedoms. This is the subject of chapters eleven and thirteen.

---

[14] P.W. Hogg, "Is the Supreme Court of Canada Biased in Constitutional Cases?" *The Canadian Bar Review* (1979), p.722.

[15] A telling example of Western Canadian scepticism toward the Supreme Court was the front cover of a recent *Alberta Report*, an influential regional weekly news magazine. Refering to the federal Cabinet's decision to refer the legal issues of the French language dispute in Manitoba to the Supreme Court, the cover headlines read: "FRENCH ROULETTE — Manitoba is hauled into Ottawa's court over provincial language rights." (April 23, 1984).

# 10.1

# THE ORIGINS OF JUDICIAL REVIEW IN CANADA

Jennifer Smith

For many years students have been taught that the practice of judicial review in Canada is less important than it is in the United States. This is because it has had less scope, and it has had less scope because until recently Canada's written constitution, unlike the American Constitution, included no bill of rights. Whereas in both countries the courts, acting as "umpires" of their respective federal forms of government, have had the power to declare laws beyond the competence of the jurisdiction enacting them, the American courts have had the additional and, to many, fascinating power to enforce against governments the guarantees of the rights of citizens contained in the Bill of Rights. Obviously this line of comparison is outmoded now. After a prolonged and at times bitter debate, the federal government and nine of the

---

*Canadian Journal of Political Science*, 16 (1983), p. 115. Reprinted with permission.

ten provincial governments reached agreement last year on a set of amendments to the *British North America Act*, among them a Charter of Rights and Freedoms. As a result, the breadth of the courts' power of judicial review more closely approximates that possessed by their American counterparts. Is this development consistent with the nature of Canada's constitutional arrangements? Does the Charter provide the basis of the completion of an initially limited power?. . . .

. . . One of the most thorough studies available is B.L. Strayer's *Judicial Review of Legislation in Canada*. Strayer argues that the *BNA Act, 1867* and related acts did not vest explicitly in the courts the power of judicial review. Nor can our common law inheritance be held responsible for it. Instead, judicial review is a product of the British colonial system, "implicit in the royal instructions, charters, or Imperial statutes creating the colonial legislatures." Since these legislatures were bodies of limited power, the colonial charters establishing them typically included clauses prohibiting them from passing laws repugnant to Imperial statutes. . . .

. . . As early as the fifteenth century, it was customary for the King's Privy Council rather than English domestic courts to hear appeals arising out of colonial matters. This practice was regulated by the *Privy Council Acts* of 1833 and 1844, which established the Judicial Committee of the Privy Council, specified its membership and authorized it to hear appeals from colonial courts. Thus the Judicial Committee acted as the highest appellate court for the colonies. As Strayer points out, it showed no inclination to question its authority to review the validity of colonial legislation, undoubtedly because the colonies themselves possessed only limited or subordinate legislative powers. He attributes considerable importance to the precedent it set throughout the Empire for the exercise of a similar power by colonial courts. According to Strayer, we must look to the British colonial system, and especially its doctrine of judicial review of colonial legislation, for the origin of judicial review in Canada: "The constitutional law of the Empire in 1867 apparently embraced the convention that where legislative powers were granted subject to limitations the courts would enforce those limitations. The BNA Act was drafted and enacted in this context.". . .

. . . Thus he [Strayer] is faced with the fact that following Confederation, the Canadian courts took up the power of judicial review, and concludes that this was the result of both pre-Confederation practice and the federal character of the new constitution: "There was a continuity of judicial practice because the Imperial structure had not changed basically. . . . Colonial legislatures, whether Dominion or provincial, were limited legislatures, and courts could enforce the limitations." The inner logic of federalism with its distribution of legislative powers pointed to the need for something like the kind of judicial enforcement that pre-Confederation practice had established.

Strayer's search for an explanation of judicial review arises out of his insistence that it is not "absolute," that is, not fully guaranteed in the *BNA Act*. In his opinion, the relevant clauses of the Act gave Parliament and the local legislatures too much regulatory power over the courts to support such a view, power more in keeping with the principle of parliamentary as opposed to judicial supremacy. Indeed, according to W.R. Lederman, Strayer implies that an "element of judicial usurpation" figures in its establishment, an implication Lederman cannot accept. By contrast, Lederman reads into sections 96 to 100 of the Act an "intention to reproduce superior courts in the image of the English central royal courts." If he can demonstrate that these English courts had acquired a "basic independence" enabling them to withstand even the undoubted supremacy of the British Parliament, then courts deliberately modelled after them in Canada would assume a similar status. In "The Independence of the Judiciary," Lederman undertakes such a demonstration. . . .

. . . Strayer takes note of this argument and dismisses it by observing that the jurisdiction of Lederman's royal courts was subject to the British Parliament's control and that in any event it never included the power to review the validity of Parliament's acts "in spite of the pretensions of Coke and others." Canadian superior courts can hardly claim by inheritance an inviolable right of judicial review their English forebears never possessed. Lederman's rejoinder is that Canadian courts, both before and after 1867, have never faced legislatures equipped with the full supremacy of the British Parliament. Indeed, until 1931 they dealt with subordinate colonial legislatures, and while the Statute of Westminster substituted equality in the place of subordination, the constitution itself remained a British statute. Thus the power to review acts of subordinate bodies undertaken by Canadian courts before 1931 was well established by "history, custom, precedent and the need of federalism" and after 1931 merely continued as a matter of course. . . . Yet a closer examination of the framers' views may throw some light on this debate.

According to the records of the Quebec Conference edited by Joseph Pope, Macdonald alluded to the need for some form of judicial review in his initial argument on the desirability of federal union. Having put the case for a strong central government, he warned the delegates not so much of the importance of provincial governments per se but of the need of the people in each "section" to feel protected, that is, secure from the reach of an overweening central authority. One way of encouraging this feeling was to provide a guarantee of the test of legality against which centralist incursions on sectional matters might be measured. Since the new construction would take the form of a British statute, he continued, British courts could supply an answer to the question, "Is it legal or not?" The availability of some form of judicial arbitration might satisfy local partisans fearful of abandoning local autonomy to the mercies of a strong central power.

The issue was raised once more towards the end of the Quebec Conference, again in connection with the extent of jurisdiction appropriate to local governments. R.B. Dickey of Nova Scotia, expressing some sympathy for the opinion of E.B. Chandler of New Brunswick that the delegates were in danger of establishing a legislative rather than a federal union by insisting on reserving all unspecified subject matters to the central government, proposed a "Supreme

Court of Appeal to decide any conflict between general and state rights.'' He was supported by George Brown, leader of the "Grits" in Upper Canada, who suggested that provincial courts determine jurisdictional disputes, with provision for appeal to a superior court. Both men appeared to contemplate a Canadian court of last resort on constitutional questions. Jonathan McCully of Nova Scotia, however, disputed this proposal. Throughout the Conference, he had made no bones about his preference for a legislative over a federal union, although he was prepared to accept a highly centralized form of federalism. From this perspective, he succinctly stated the difficulty posed by a constitutional court: "Mr. Brown will land us in [the] position of [the] United States by referring [the] matter of conflict of jurisdiction to [the] courts. You thus set them over the General Legislature.''. . . .

. . . In the Maritime provinces, even less attention was paid to the issue despite the fact that a number of anti-Confederates were sorely exercised by what they deemed the insufficiently federal character of the proposed scheme. . . . Their major concern was the lack of any provision for the scheme's amendment, but in an aside they observed that the "wise framers" of the American Constitution had given the Supreme Court the "power to decide all questions of jurisdiction and authority, between the general Government and those of the several States.'' The Quebec scheme, by contrast, did not require the establishment of any such court. Indeed, in their view, it contained no safeguards at all for the provinces in the event of conflict between their legislatures and the central Parliament. Guided by the American example, they recommended establishment of a tribunal authorized to decide disputes arising out of the division of powers. In New Brunswick A.J. Smith, recently defeated by Tilley's pro-union party in a second election over the Confederation issue, similarly advocated "a court for the determination of questions and disputes that may arise between the Federal and Local governments as to the meaning of the Act of Union.''

Such clearly worded statements indicated a view of federalism rather more in line with the American example than that set out in the Quebec scheme. Taken together with the views expressed at the Quebec Conference and in the debate in the Parliament of Canada, they also suggest that no one had any illusions about the significance of judicial review, particularly as it related to the distribution of legislative powers between Parliament and the local legislatures. The point at issue was whether the type of federalism set out in the Quebec Resolutions required it. Under the Resolutions, the central government possessed the power to disallow local laws just as the British government retained the power to disallow Parliament's enactments, a parallel feature not unnoticed by critics of the scheme like Christopher Dunkin. Disallowance not only undermined the need for judicial arbitration, whether by the Judicial Committee or a national court, it also suited partisans of parliamentary supremacy like Jonathan McCully, who clearly understood the threat to this supremacy posed by a tribunal patterned after the American Supreme Court.

The question of whether to establish a final appellate court was settled eight years after Confederation when Parliament finally used the power it possessed under section 101 of the *BNA Act*. The debate at the time is illuminating, since in picking up the threads of the earlier arguments it does so in the light of some years experience of union. It also reveals an attitude towards the new court and its power of judicial review somewhat at variance with that held today. . . .

. . . While the constitutionality of the bill was generally accepted, there remained the question of members' understanding of the court's position in relation to the central government. Here opinions varied. In introducing the bill, Fournier stressed the need for a court to settle disputes arising out of conflicting jurisdictional claims, particularly when the extent of provincial powers was in question. In this sense he portrayed the proposed court as the completion of the "young construction" established at Confederation, citing earlier remarks by Cartier and Macdonald in support of this view. Along side the notion of the court as an impartial arbiter, however, there is present in his speech the rather different view of it as a substitute for the failing remedy of disallowance. As he explained, the government was required daily to "interfere" with provincial legislation considered ultra vires the provinces' jurisdiction, and it was falling behind in the task. The result was that the statute books were filled with an "enormous mass of legislation" of dubious constitutionality, leaving citizens uncertain about what was and was not law. In light of this definition of the problem, namely, the excesses of provincial legislatures, the suggestion that the new court could resolve it more speedily than the central government's power of disallowance must have struck his listeners as doubtful. Indeed, it quickly became clear he was seeking legitimacy, not speed. The governor general, he pointed out, could disallow provincial laws only on the advice of the federal cabinet, in turn advised by law officers of the Department of Justice, and this state of affairs, predictably, was "not satisfactory." What was needed was a tribunal whose decisions — especially those adverse to the provinces — were acceptable to all parties. Apparently Fournier viewed his "independent, neutral and impartial court" as an instrument of the central government. He contended that Ottawa needed "an institution of its own" in order to ensure proper execution of its laws because, however contrary to the spirit of Confederation, the time might come when "it would not be very safe for the Federal Government to be at the mercy of the tribunals of the Provinces."

Some members feared that the powers conferred on the court would conflict with the principle of parliamentary supremacy. An Ontario member, Moss, excused the length of his speech by emphasizing the gravity of establishing a tribunal whose power to determine jurisdictional disputes finally rendered it "paramount" to Parliament itself. Rejecting this view, Macdonald interpreted the court's role under the "Special Jurisdiction" clauses as one of informing the "conscience" of the government. It would function simply as an adviser to the government in much the same way as the Judicial Committee did when asked for advice by the British Crown. Macdonald's view was consistent with

Fournier's exposition of these clauses for, as noted earlier, the minister of justice had stated that the court's decisions in such instances were to have the same effect as its decisions in reference questions, namely, a kind of "moral weight." Since moral weight undoubtedly influences but does not command, it would appear that for both men the supremacy of Parliament remained unimpaired. Their position seemed well grounded for neither the reference case provision nor the special jurisdiction clauses gave the new court's opinions the status of legal judgments. Yet many of their colleagues assumed that it did, especially Robert Haythorne, a Liberal senator from Prince Edward Island, who warned members that "their power of interpretation [on constitutional matters] ceased when the bill passed."

Concern over the precise nature of the court's advisory function on constitutional questions surfaced again in discussion of the reference case clause. Moss thought it "extreme" that the Governor General in Council might ask the court for an opinion on any matter, since this would result in the governor general relying on others for the advice "he ought under our system of Government to obtain from his responsible advisers." However, he was persuaded that the practice was not incompatible with responsible government on the ground that the British, the greatest authorities on responsible government, used the Judicial Committee in the same manner. Others were not so easily persuaded. Senator Haythorne argued that a ministry under pressure to exercise its power of disallowance might be tempted to refer a provincial act to the court for an opinion on its constitutionality, thus relieving itself of the burden of taking a decision and defending it before Parliament. He also thought it unwisely mixed law and politics because it substituted judicial review for disallowance, that is, a judicial ruling in the place of a political decision. From this flowed his third objection, namely, that judicial review was a greater threat to the small provinces' legislative programme than the power of disallowance since any ministry advising the Crown to exercise the latter power was required to defend publicly its advice in the Commons and, more important, the Senate, the very institution in which the provinces could expect support. The court's opinion faced no such political test. . . .

. . . Yet while both the constitution and practical necessity apparently pointed in the same direction, members of parliament clearly entertained two different views of the role of the proposed court in the very area that was thought to stand most in need of its services, namely, jurisdictional conflicts. As is evident from the above, some saw in the court an instrument of the federal government that would enable it to deal more satisfactorily with provincial pretensions. How else to interpret Senator Scott's contention?: "The fact that so many of the Acts in the different Provinces were *ultra vires* showed that a bill of this kind was necessary." The raft of suspect provincial statutes, for Scott, posed a problem for which the central government was inadequately equipped. But why was it ill equipped when it possessed the power of disallowance? As noted earlier, for Fournier the central government's problem was its inescapable partisanship. Only a court and its long-standing reputation of nonpartisanship could tame the aggression of the provinces without provoking bitter controversy. Left unstated was the assumption that the central government, by contrast, was unlikely to experience the embarrassment of an adverse ruling in its exercise of legislative power. Thus the view of the court as a tribunal whose very impartiality would serve the federal cause ignored the obvious tension between that impartiality and the central government's partisanship. The opinion of men like Macdonald that the proposed bill must not and, indeed, did not affect the principle of parliamentary supremacy simply overlooked it in favour of the central government. Had he not said that the special jurisdiction clauses were "principally for the purpose of informing the conscience of the Government"? Despite his interest in setting up the court, he was obviously unwilling to relinquish ultimate determination of the constitution to it.

At the same time, as we have seen, many supposed that the new court did signal a shift from the central government's control over the distribution of legislative powers to judicial determination of disputes arising out of it. It might be objected that this view was as incorrect as Macdonald's on the grounds that the executive's control in this respect was only partial to begin with, limited to supervision of provincial enactments through its power of disallowance, and that Parliament's own enactments in turn were subject to disallowance by the British government. Moreover, the Judicial Committee, representing the judicial mode of constitutional arbitration, had retained its position as the highest court of appeal for the new colony at the outset of Confederation. Nevertheless, it is clear that for many participants in the debate, the court's institution spelled a retreat from the executive fiat of disallowance in favour of the judicial remedy. And they assumed, contrary to Macdonald's supposition, that its jurisdiction would extend to impugned federal as well as provincial enactments. Indeed, opponents of the court, such as Senator Kaulbach of Nova Scotia, criticized it precisely because it would "take from this Parliament the right to decide constitutional questions." . . .

. . . In the event it appears that those who subscribed to the second view were closer to the mark. Certainly the new Supreme Court agreed with them. As Strayer points out, in its first reported constitutional decision, *Severn v. the Queen* (1878), the court, "without showing any hesitation concerning its right to do so," found an Ontario licensing statute invalid on the ground that it interfered with Parliament's jurisdiction over trade and commerce. The following year, in *Valin v. Langlois*, it reviewed and upheld the *Dominion Controverted Elections Act*, 1874 as a valid exercise of Parliament's legislative power. In the latter case, Chief Justice Ritchie set out the court's power of judicial review with unmistakable clarity:

> In view of the great diversity of judicial opinion that has characterized the decisions of the provincial tribunals in some provinces, and the judges in all, while it would seem to justify the wisdom of the Dominion Parliament, in providing for the establishment of a Court of Appeal such as this, where such diversity shall be considered and an authoritative declaration of the

law be enunciated, so it enhances the responsibility of those called on in the midst of such conflict of opinion to declare authoritatively the principles by which both federal and local legislation are governed.

Commenting on Ritchies's declaration, Strayer states: "And so the Canadian courts were launched on a course from which they have never swerved. The ease with which they could take up judicial review of legislation after Confederation must have been the result of the situation existing prior to 1867." He nowhere suggests that the chief justice might have based his understanding of the court's role on the terms of the *Supreme Court Act* or the expectations of many of those who participated in its passage four years earlier. But then, as indicated earlier, Strayer pays little attention to the debate surrounding its passage. Thus he is open to Lederman's charge, namely, that his argument implies an assumption of judicial review on the part of the court, an assumption possibly unwarranted. Yet Lederman too ignores the very debate in the light of which Ritchie's view is surely intelligible. The Chief Justice clearly favoured the side of those who, like Moss, thought that the proposed court would be able "to determine the [constitutional] controversy finally, virtually therefore, the Supreme Court could overrule the decisions of this legislature."

Although the chief justice's generous conception of the court's role in constitutional matters reaffirmed both the hopes and fears of those who supposed its decisions would be as authoritative as he claimed they were, the notion of the court as an instrument of the central government was not wholly eliminated. There remained the reference case provision of the *Supreme Court Act* which obliged the court to advise the executive on any question referred to it. To the extent that this obligation is understood as an executive advisory function as opposed to a judicial one, it recalls Macdonald's view of the court as an aid to the government, or the "conscience" of the government. If so, it is hardly surprising that the provinces were uncomfortable with the comprehensiveness of the reference case provision, especially since it enabled the government to refer provincial laws to the courts for a ruling on their validity. In the event, Parliament's competence to enact it was tested before the Judicial Committee in *Attorney General for Ontario v. Attorney General for Canada* (1912). The provinces choosing to intervene argued that it imposed an executive function on the court and thereby violated section 101 of the *BNA Act* which permitted Parliament to establish a tribunal possessed of judicial powers only. In his judgment delivered on behalf of the Judicial Committee, Earl Loreburn, L.C., appeared to accept their contention that the court's task in the reference case was in essence merely advisory and therefore nonjudicial, but he did not consider this fatal to its judicial character as a whole.

The competing views of the court apparent at its inception have left their mark on it. For example, those who approve its role as umpire of the federal system are critical of the fact that its establishment was permitted rather than required under the terms of the *BNA Act*, that its members are appointed formally by one level of government rather than both, and that the reference case procedure remains. On the other hand, partisans of parliamentary supremacy, understandably less enamoured of the American Supreme Court whose example inspired the criticisms just mentioned, prize these very features as symbols of the court's ultimate dependence on the will of Parliament. This tension between the court's judicial independence and the claims of the executive figures in the debate between Lederman and Strayer. Lederman, seeking to strengthen and reaffirm its independence, prefers to locate the origins of its power of judicial review in both the tradition of the old English royal courts and the logic of federalism, that is, beyond the reach of Parliament. Thus the intentions of legislators who founded the court are of little interest to him. By ignoring them he avoids confronting not only the view of those who supposed they were withholding the full power of judicial review but, more important, the opinion of those who assumed that Parliament could confer it. As a result, he overlooks the possibility that judicial review was deliberately, if tentatively, advanced as a remedy for the failing power of disallowance. In short, since Lederman wishes to secure judicial review, he cannot derive it from anything so precarious as legislators' intentions. This leaves him open to the criticism implied in Strayer's thesis. Strayer, much more sensitive to the claims of the executive, highlights the limitations on the court's power to review legislative enactments. Yet he is left with the new court's easy assumption of the power, and since he too disregards the debate surrounding its establishment he looks beyond Parliament to past colonial practice. Thus he does not see the tension between judicial review and executive claims which he ably expands as a reflection of clashing legislative intentions.

Viewed in the light of the older controversy about the court, the debate culminating in the recent set of amendments contained in the *Constitution Act, 1982* took a familiar turn. In the earlier contest, both opponents and partisans of judicial review focussed attention on its implications for the distribution of legislative powers so critical to the shape of the country's federalism. While some saw in it a solution to conflicts arising out of competing jurisdictional claims, others interpreted it as a direct challenge to their presumption in favour of Parliament's control of the constitution. Over a century later, the issue of judicial versus parliamentary supremacy surfaced again in connection with the proposed Charter of Rights and Freedoms. Prime Minister Pierre Trudeau, a determined champion of the notion of a charter, often defended his cause without even referring to the task it necessarily imposes on the courts. Instead, he claimed that it would "confer power on the people of Canada, power to protect themselves from abuses by public authorities." A charter would liberate people by preventing governments from denying specified freedoms. On the other hand, opponents of the idea like the then premier of Saskatchewan, Allan Blakeney, attempted to counter the undeniable appeal of this claim by drawing attention to the role of the courts that it implied. According to Blakeney, including rights in a written constitution means transferring responsibility for them from duly elected legislatures, the democratic seat of governments, to nonelected tribunals. It amounts to requiring the courts to make "social judgments" in the course of interpreting a charter's clauses, judgments which, in his view, properly belong to "the voters and their representatives," In the event, a Charter of Rights and Freedoms now forms part of Canada's newly amended constitution. Are we entitled to conclude, then, that acceptance of the Charter, and the increased scope for judicial review that it entails, signals a resolution of the issue of parliamentary versus judicial supremacy in favour of the latter? The answer is not quite.

It is true, as Peter Russell points out, that section 52 of the *Constitution Act, 1982*, by declaring the Constitution of Canada to be the "supreme law" and any law inconsistent with its provisions to be of "no force or effect," gives the courts' power to invalidate unconstitutional laws an explicit constitutional footing for the first time. Further, under the provisions of the new amending formula, the composition of the Supreme Court is protected from easy change by the stringent requirement of unanimity on the part of the Senate, the House of Commons and provincial legislative assemblies. The court is also listed under section 42(1) as an item that can be amended only in accordance with the general formula set out in section 38(1). Thus the court is constitutionally entrenched. However, neither the federal government's power to appoint Supreme Court justices nor the nonjudicial advisory task required by the reference mechanism is affected. More important still is the fact that the Charter itself, to the disappointment of its partisans, contains a provision enabling the legislative bodies of both levels of government to override some of its guarantees, namely, those dealing with fundamental freedoms, legal rights and equality rights. The provision is qualified to the extent that legislatures choosing to avail themselves of it are required to declare expressly their intention and reconsider the matter every five years, and there has been speculation about the likely effect of these qualifications on politicians' willingness to resort to the "override." Nevertheless, its very appearance in the the context of the Charter strikes an incongruous note and is testimony to the strength of the lingering tradition of parliamentary supremacy. Finally, there is the first clause of the Charter which subjects its guarantees to "such reasonable limits prescribed by law as can be demonstrably justified in a free and democratic society." Ultimately it is up to the Supreme Court to stake out the "reasonable limits." In the meantime, we do know that they are held to exist, that there is thought to be something higher than, or beyond the Charter's guarantees to which appeal can be made in order to justify their denial or restriction. And the initiative in this regard is secured to governments. While the courts' power of judicial review has undoubtedly surmounted the rather narrow, partisan function envisaged for the new Supreme Court in 1875 by Macdonald, the principle of parliamentary supremacy persists.

# 10.2

## THE "LIVING TREE" APPROACH TO INTERPRETING THE BNA ACT

Lord Sankey, *The "Persons" Case*, Judicial Committee of the Privy Council, 1928.

. . . The British North America Act planted in Canada a living tree capable of growth and expansion within its natural limits. The object of the Act was to grant a Constitution to Canada. "Like all written constitutions it has been subject to development through usage and convention."

Their Lordships do not conceive it to be the duty of this Board — it is certainly not their desire — to cut down the provisions of the Act by a narrow and technical construction, but rather to give it a large and liberal interpretation so that the Dominion to a great extent, but within certain fixed limits, may be mistress in her own house, as the Provinces to a great extent, but within certain fixed limits, are mistresses in theirs.

# 10.3

## THE "WATERTIGHT COMPARTMENTS" APPROACH TO INTERPRETING THE BNA ACT

Lord Atkin, *Labour Conventions Case*, Judicial Committee of the Privy Council, 1937.

. . . It must not be thought that the result of this decision is that Canada is incompetent to legislate in performance of treaty obligations. In totality of legislative powers, Dominion and Provincial together, she is fully equipped. But the legislative powers remain distributed, and if in the exercise of her new functions derived from her new international status Canada incurs obligations they must, so far as legislation be concerned, when they deal with Provincial classes of subjects, be dealt with by the totality of powers, in other words by co-operation between the Dominion and the Provinces. While the ship of state now sails on larger ventures and into foreign waters she still retains the watertight compartments which are an essential part of her original structure. The Supreme Court was equally divided and therefore the formal judgment could only state the opinions of the three judges on either side. Their Lordships are of opinion that the answer to the three questions should be that the Act in each case is ultra vires of the Parliament of Canada, and they will humbly advise His Majesty accordingly.

# 10.4

# THE ANTI-INFLATION CASE: THE ANATOMY OF A CONSTITUTIONAL DECISION

Peter Russell

The Supreme Court of Canada's decision in July 1976 on the constitutional validity of the federal Anti-Inflation Act was probably the Court's most heralded decision since it became Canada's final court of appeal in 1949. For the first time since 1949 a major national policy, upon which the federal government placed the highest priority, was challenged before the Court. Also, this was the first clear test of whether the Supreme Court would "liberate" the federal Parliament's general power to make laws for the "peace, order and good government of Canada" from the shackles placed upon it by the Privy Council's jurisprudence and thereby provide the constitutional underpinning for a revolutionary readjustment of the balance of power in Canadian federalism. And it was the first major constitutional case for a Supreme Court headed by Chief Justice Bora Laskin, who during his academic career had earned a reputation as Canada's leading authority on constitutional law and as an articulate critic of the Privy Council. All in all, the case appeared to be a showdown.

The outcome may seem rather anti-climatic. The federal government's wage and price control policy escaped a judicial veto. But the Court's decision gave it only a temporary and conditional constitutional mandate. More importantly, the Court did not endorse the expansive interpretation of Parliament's general power which a generation of central-minded commentators had hoped for as much as a generation of provincially-minded Canadians had feared.

*Canadian Public Administration*, 1977, p.632. Reprinted with permission.

Instead, the Court as a whole could agree only on the Judicial Committee of the Privy Council's "emergency doctrine," while its majority appeared to endorse a novel and unLaskin-like way of interpreting the peace, order and good government clause.

To understand the significance of these results, the case must be placed in both its legal and political settings. By so doing we may learn something about the nature of judicial review in Canada. Among other things, the case demonstrates the limited importance of judicial review in the politics of Canadian federalism. The court's decision may signal that a constitutional revolution is not about to occur, but the decision itself is far from being the major factor in preventing such a centralizing shift in the balance of power. The case also reveals how paradoxically political the process of judicial review can be in Canada even though the end product — the opinions of the judges — is cast in a relatively legalistic style. Above all, the case teaches us a good deal about the interaction of law and politics. The main lesson is clear: politicians and interest groups will risk losses in terms of long-run constitutional doctrine in order to secure important short-run policy objectives, although in the process they may try their best to minimize or obscure their constitutional losses.

### The Constitutional Stakes

On 14 October 1975 the federal government unveiled the new anti-inflation program. The program had four main prongs, only one of which was highly controversial and required new legislation. This was a scheme to control prices and wages in certain key sectors of the economy. The Liberal party had vigorously opposed a Conservative party proposal for wage and price controls in the federal election fifteen months earlier. But now Mr. Trudeau's government was apparently convinced that this was a policy whose time had come. Legal authority for the wage and price control policy was contained in the Anti-Inflation Act which became law 15 December 1975 (with retroactive effect to 14 October 1975) and in the detailed regulations or "guidelines" promulgated on 22 December 1975.

It was clear from the start that there was a good deal at stake constitutionally in the enactment of this legislation. The Anti-Inflation Act purported to give the federal government regulatory authority over prices, profit margins and wages in selected areas of the private sector: construction firms with twenty or more employees, other firms with five hundred or more employees, and professionals. The Act applied directly to the federal public sector, and it authorized the government to enter into agreements with the provinces to apply the program to the provincial public sectors. Normally most of the economic relations which the federal Act purported to regulate in the private sector are under exclusive provincial jurisdiction. Since the *Snider* case in 1925, labour relations has been treated as a field of divided jurisdiction, with federal authority confined to the limited number of activities which can be brought under specific heads of federal power. A long series of judicial decisions, beginning with the *Parsons* case in 1881, gave the provinces the lion's share of regulatory power over business and commercial transactions in the province. The only earlier peacetime attempt to control prices and profit levels on a national basis had been ruled unconstitutional by the Judicial Committee of the Privy Council of the *Board of Commerce* case [1922].

On what constitutional basis then could the federal government hope to rest the Anti-Inflation Act? The federal trade and commerce power which would be the basis of federal authority for such legislation in the United States was not a very likely possibility in Canada. "Interprovincial or international" as the main criterion of the trade and commerce which the federal Parliament can regulate has been narrowly interpreted in Canada, and the Act made no gestures toward focusing its impact primarily on activities of an interprovincial or international character. Thus, it was the federal Parliament's general power "to make laws for the peace, order and good government of Canada" which appeared to be the only constitutional basis for the Act, and it was in the possibility of successfully invoking the general power for this purpose that a revolution in constitutional doctrine was in the making.

Constitutional case-law had produced two rival conceptions of what could sufficiently magnify legislative matter normally subject to provincial jurisdiction to bring them under the general or residual power of the national Parliament: the emergency doctrine and the test of inherent national importance. The emergency doctrine was authored by Viscount Haldane of the Judicial Committee of the Privy Council in the 1920s, and, with but one clear exception, consistently followed by that tribunal until the end of its regime as Canada's highest court. The doctrine's only positive application was to justify the virtually unlimited scope of national power in time of war and postwar transition. Beyond war, the Judicial Committee's vision of emergencies serious enough to set aside the normal distribution of powers and invoke the general power had been limited to such possibilities as "famines," "epidemics of pestilence" or a drastic outbreak of the "evil of intemperance." Economic crisis — even the need for a national scheme of unemployment insurance during the Depression — failed to meet the Judicial Committee's standard of necessity. Further, it appeared that the presumption of constitutionality which attached to war-related legislation did not apply to *permanent* peacetime measures. With the former, the onus of proof rested with the opponents of the legislation who would have to adduce ". . . very clear evidence that an emergency has not arisen, or that the emergency no longer exists . . .," whereas, with the latter, the supporters of the legislation would have to provide "evidence that the standard of necessity . . . has been reached."

In 1946 Viscount Simon in the *Canada Temperance Federation* case wrote an opinion which offered a much wider conception of peace, order and good government than Haldane's emergency test. In dismissing Ontario's attempt to have the Privy Council overrule *Russell v. The Queen* (the Privy Council's earliest decision finding federal legislation constitutional on the basis of peace, order and good government), Viscount Simon held that the Dominion Parliament could not legislate in matters which are exclusively within the competence of the provincial legislature "merely because of the existence of an emergency." The "true test" for determining whether the national legislature may assume jurisdiction over matters which are normally provincial " . . . must be found in the real subject matter of the legislation: if it is such that it goes beyond local or provincial concern or interest and must from its inherent nature be the concern of the Dominion as a whole. . . . , then it will fall within the competence of the Dominion Parliament as a matter affecting the peace, order and good government of Canada. . . ." This holding seemed to return the interpretation of peace, order and good government to the pre-Haldane formula of national dimensions of concern enunciated by Lord Watson in 1896, namely ". . . . that some matters, in their origin local and provincial, might attain such dimensions as to affect the body politic of the Dominion, and to justify the Canadian Parliament in passing laws for their regulation or abolition in the interest of the Dominion." On its face this inherent national importance or national dimensions conception of peace, order and good government appeared to offer the federal government a much wider opportunity to exercise regulatory power in peacetime on more than a temporary basis in areas normally reserved to the provinces.

Court decisions after 1946 were not conclusive as to whether the Haldane emergency doctrine had been superseded by the wider notion of national dimensions. On the two occasions after 1946 when the Privy Council dealt with peace, order and good government it ignored Simon's opinion. The Supreme Court's decision in the *Johannesson* case in 1952 provided the only strong endorsement of Viscount Simon's national importance test. On two subsequent occasions in the 1960s, the Supreme Court employed the vocabulary of "national importance" in upholding federal jurisdiction over the national capital and offshore mineral rights. But in neither case was the Court reviewing a major scheme of federal regulation in an area normally under provincial jurisdiction. Even in *Johannesson*, though the Court sustained the paramountcy of federal control over aeronautics in part on national importance grounds, it was dealing with a regulatory scheme which had been in place for several decades and which could find a large measure of constitutional support in other heads of federal power.

So, coming down to the *Anti-Inflation* case, a large question mark still hung over the peace, order and good government power. That for three decades there had been so little Court action on this issue had much to do with the fact that even during the most centralist years of this period the federal government had relied primarily on its spending power rather than regulatory schemes for carrying out policy initiatives in areas normally under provincial jurisdiction. But inflationary pressures in the 1970s might force the federal government to shift from spending programs to regulatory schemes. Such a shift, as several political scientists have suggested, would increase the occasions for judicial review. Thus, as the federal government in the fall of 1975 moved toward the implementation of a fairly comprehensive scheme of price and wage controls, the question in constitutional law of whether the peace, order and good government would provide a basis for national regulation of broad areas of economic and social activity took on more than academic importance.

### Political and Legal Strategies of the Parties

With these constitutional stakes in the background, it is interesting to examine the approach taken by the federal and provincial governments and the major interest groups to the constitutional implications of the anti-inflation program. Turning first to the federal government, we find a significant difference between the political and legal aspects of its behaviour. Politically, Prime Minister Trudeau endeavoured to present the program as an exercise in cooperative federalism. The day before the program was presented to Parliament, the ten provincial premiers came to Ottawa to discuss the program. That night, in his address to the nation on radio and television, Mr. Trudeau said that he had asked the premiers "to join as full partners in the attack upon inflation." During this period Mr. Trudeau tended to be somewhat on the optimistic side in referring to the extent to which the provinces supported federal wage and price controls. Following the first ministers meeting on 13 October, a number of premiers reserved any commitment of support for the program until they had reviewed the matter with their provincial cabinets. Ten days later federal and provincial finance and labour ministers met in Ottawa and following their meeting, Mr. Macdonald, the federal Minister of Finance, announced that "No province declared that it is opposed to the programme or will refuse to co-operate." The next day Mr. Macdonald reported in a more positive vein to the House of Commons: apparently all of the provincial governments were now "prepared to support the programme and co-operate."

While, on the political front, the federal government proceeded on the assumption that provincial cooperation was a political imperative, the Anti-Inflation Act was drafted as if the federal Parliament had full legislative power to proceed with such a program on its own. Section 3 of the Act authorizing the federal government to establish guidelines for the restraint of prices and wages in the private and public sectors made no concessions to any constitutional limitations on the scope of Parliament's regulatory power. It is true that the next section of the Act exempted a province's public sector unless the provincial government entered into an agreement to apply the Act to its public sector. But the implication was that this "opting in" device was entirely dependent on the will of the federal Parliament, and that Parliament, if it had preferred, could have applied the program directly to the provincial public sectors. This implication became explicit later on when the federal government came to defend Ontario's "opting in" Agreement before the Supreme Court. In the absence of any provincial legislation authorizing this Agreement, the only legislative authority for the Agreement was provided by the federal Act and, indeed, federal lawyers asserted the power of the federal Parliament to bind the provincial Crown and regulate the provincial public service.

More important than this is the evidence that the Anti-Inflation Act was drafted so as to preserve the possibility of basing the legislation on a constitutional foundation wider than the emergency doctrine. Nowhere did the Act speak the language of national emergency Instead, the preamble referred to inflation as "a matter of serious national concern," language clearly suggesting Viscount Simon's approach to peace, order and good government in the *Canada Temperance Federation* case. The only mark of emergency or crisis legislation on the face of the Act was its penultimate section limiting its duration to three years unless Parliament agreed to an extension. Statements by government spokesmen in Parliament made it clear that the omission of any reference to a state of emergency was deliberate. Both Mr. Diefenbaker for the Conservatives and Mr. Brewin for the NDP questioned the government on the constitutional propriety of proceeding without a declaration of an emergency. Mr. Trudeau answered this question with rather vague references to alternative constitutional bases for the Act such as "the banking power" and "the commerce power." Mr. Macdonald gave a much clearer picture of the government's constitutional assumptions in his evidence to the Standing Committee on Finance, Trade and Economic Affairs:

> The opinion of the government on constitutionality is based on some cases that were pleaded before the judicial committee on sic the privy council in 1946, for instance *The Canada Temperance Federation* case, and, since then before the Supreme Court, *Thamieson and St. Paul*, and *Munro* and the *National Capital Commission*. Accordingly, when we have a scheme that goes beyond reasons that are strictly local, provincial or private, when you have a national scheme like this one, there can be a federal jurisdiction under which to legislate on these matters.

Of course, by the "*Thamieson* case" Mr. Macdonald meant *Johannesson v. West St. Paul* in which the Supreme Court had made its most significant application of the "inherent national importance" test of peace, order and good government.

Now, with the federal government playing something of a double game, how did the provinces respond to the constitutional issue? Briefly, because they saw that it was not in their political interests at the time to oppose the federal program, they agreed not to raise the constitutional issue. However, because they wished to avoid conceding constitutional power to Ottawa, they were careful not to commit themselves to any particular view of the Act's constitutional validity. At this stage it was in the interests of both levels of government to suppress the constitutional issue. Apparently the constitutional issue was discussed at the federal-provincial meetings concerning the anti-inflation program, and the federal leaders felt free to declare after these meetings that the provinces would not challenge Parliament's jurisdiction to enact the Anti-Inflation Bill. But, as with so much that happens at meetings of this kind, we do not know in what terms the constitutional issue was discussed. My own guess is that the constitutional discussion was kept at a pretty vague level and that there was just enough reference to the temporary nature of the legislation and the provision of an opting in mechanism for the provinces to set aside, at least for the time being, any reservations of a constitutional nature.

The provinces kept their word. They did not exercise the right which all of them have to refer the question of the Act's constitutionality directly to the courts. All, in varying ways, took steps to bring their public sectors in the program. But, nonetheless, they kept their constitutional options open and, as we shall see, when the constitutional issue was forced before the Supreme Court, a number of them attacked the broad grounds upon which the federal government tried to defend this legislation. In the legal instrument authorizing provincial participation, it is notable that Quebec, of all the provinces, was most careful to concede as little as possible to federal legislative authority. Thus, Quebec's Agreement not only established the province's own Inflation Control Commission to administer guidelines for the public sector "in consultation with" the federal Anti-Inflation Board, but further gave the province's consent to have the guidelines apply to the private sector. Quebec's submission to the Supreme Court subsequently made it clear that in the province's view, even in the context of an emergency, federal regulation of the provincial private sector of the economy could not take effect without provincial consent.

If the federal and provincial governments were the only agencies for initiating judicial review, there would probably not have been an Anti-Inflation case. In Canada only the federal and provincial governments have access to the most direct means of bringing questions before the courts — the reference procedure. Private litigants can raise constitutional issues in the courts only when they are plaintiff or defendant in normal litigation, and Canadian courts have tended to be relatively stringent in granting "standing" to raise such issues. One of the interesting features of the *Anti-Inflation* case is that it was the persistence of private interest groups, namely a number of trade unions, in trying to challenge the constitutional validity of the anti-inflation program through normal litigation which eventually persuaded the federal government to resort to the reference device and bring the issue directly before the Supreme Court.

It is particularly interesting that organized labour rather than business interests were responsible for initiating the constitutional challenge to the anti-inflation program. Traditionally, organized labour has favoured strengthening rather than weakening the capacity of the federal government to deal with national and international economic forces. But once labour representatives perceived what in their view was the unjust character of the federal program they began to oppose it vigorously, and soon after its introduction officials of the Canadian Labour Congress announced their intention to challenge the program in the courts. There is no indication that union leaders had any qualms about the long-run constitutional consequences if their court action was successful. The attack through the courts was adopted as simply one of the means for conducting the anti-control campaign. However, it should be noted that the grounds upon which the CLC initially proposed to base its challenge were that the controls program was too selective to meet the national dimensions test and that provinces could not turn over their legislative jurisdiction to the federal authority by order-in-council. While these arguments did not so clearly threaten the scope of federal authority, those which union counsel subsequently used before the Supreme Court were much more anti-centralist.

It was not easy for those labour groups who wished to challenge the constitutional validity of the anti-inflation program to gain access to the courts. The most direct means of appealing an order of the Anti-Inflation Administrator to the Appeal Tribunal (and from there to the Federal Court of Canada) was available only to employers. This deficiency in the Act was eventually remedied but not until after the federal government had made the reference to the Supreme Court. The legal actions which eventually provoked the reference all involved unions in Ontario resisting the application of the controls to collective agreements they were in the process of negotiating. The most significant of these, in terms of bringing the constitutional issue before the courts, was that of the Renfrew County branch of the Ontario Secondary School Teachers Federation. In November 1975 the Renfrew teachers had signed a collective agreement with the Renfrew County Board of Education for an amount considerably in excess of the anti-inflation guidelines. This settlement was made pursuant to the result of binding arbitration under Ontario legislation. The arbitration award had been made two weeks after the introduction of the anti-inflation program. On 10 February 1976 the Anti-Inflation Board notified the teachers and the Board that the settlement should be reduced. Six days later the teachers' federation applied to the Divisional Court of the Supreme Court of Ontario for a declaration that Ontario's Agreement with the federal government bringing its public sector under the anti-inflation program was invalid on the ground that the Order-in-Council authorizing the Agreement had been made without the necessary legislation by the province. It is doubtful whether this legal strategy would have worked because the Federal Court of Canada has exclusive jurisdiction to grant declaratory relief. On the same day that the Renfrew teachers submitted their application to Ontario's Supreme Court, a Board of Arbitration in another Ontario labour dispute (this time involving the University of Toronto and a local of the Canadian Union of Public Employees representing the University's library technicians) ruled that it was not bound by actions of the Anti-Inflation Board.

Apparently it was these two developments which convinced the Attorney General of Ontario, Mr. Roy McMurtry, that in order to avoid a lengthy and uncertain period of litigation he should ask the federal Minister of Justice to refer the issue to the Supreme Court. There were possibly other factors which influenced Mr. McMurtry. The Ontario government had entered into its Agreement with the federal government without any approval from the provincial legislature. The Agreements of all the other provinces except Newfoundland's had some legislative sanction. The Davis government wished to avoid the legislature because it was in a minority there and both opposition parties indicated they would oppose the government on the controls issue. But by February of 1976, the Ontario Liberals under Mr. Stuart Smith's leadership had shown that they did not want an election in the near future and so for the time being they would not use their balance of power in the legislature to defeat the government. Thus, Mr. McMurtry had some assurance that if the Ontario Agreement was ruled invalid by the Supreme Court he could go back to the legislature and with support from a compliant Mr. Smith obtain the necessary approval for the Agreement. This assurance was important, as the validity of the Ontario Agreement was a much more dubious proposition than was the validity of the federal Act.

On 12 March, the federal Minister of Justice, Mr. Basford, announced that the federal cabinet had approved an order-in-council referring the question of the federal Act's constitutional validity and of the Ontario Agreement's validity to the Supreme Court of Canada. It was, he said, the Renfrew teachers' action which prompted this decision,

> Because the whole thing (the anti-inflation programme) is vulnerable to such challenges and because the work of the nation must go on we have decided to avoid time-consuming litigation over issues like this which ultimately would have to be decided by the Supreme Court anyway.

We might also speculate that Mr. Basford's government, with its program well in place and having secured the cooperation of all the provinces, could now contemplate judicial review of the Anti-Inflation Act with a fair degree of confidence.

### The Reference: the Parties and Their Submissions

The use of Canada's extraordinary reference procedure in the circumstances outlined above illustrates one of the advantages of this device. Once it was reasonably certain that judicial review would occur through private litigation, it was in the government's interest to remove as quickly as possible the legal clouds surrounding the program — especially a program which was encountering considerable resistance from those whose behaviour it was supposed to regulate. In the alternative, if the unions had found their access to the courts completely blocked, the reference would compensate for the relative disadvantage which citizens or private groups are under in obtaining judicial review in Canada and give the unions an opportunity to establish their constitutional rights before the country's highest tribunal.

But the disadvantages of the reference procedure have been advertised just as much as its advantages. The primary criticism has been that the procedure forces judges to make decisions about the constitutional validity of government policies in a highly abstract and hypothetical manner divorced from any consideration of the factual context which gave rise to the legislation and in which the real effect of the legislation may be revealed. Added to this is the fear that such a procedure, by bringing statutes to court ". . . . in the very flush of enactment, while the feelings that produced them were at their highest pitch. . . ." may unduly politicize the process of judicial review and force the judges to participate in a political controversy in a way which will ultimately weaken their authority. It is instructive to review the conduct of the *Anti-Inflation Reference* in the light of these criticism and concerns.

Certainly, the question submitted to the court by the Reference Order were presented in the barest possible way:

1. Is the Anti-Inflation Act *ultra vires* the Parliament of Canada either in whole or in part, and, if so, in what particulars and to what extent?
2. If the Anti-Inflation Act is *intra vires* the Parliament of Canada, is the Agreement entitled "Between the Government of Canada and the Government of the Province of Ontario," entered into on January 13, 1976 effective under the Anti-Inflation Act to render that Act binding on, and the Anti-Inflation Guidelines made thereunder applicable to, the provincial public sector in Ontario as defined in the Agreement?

The reference itself was not accompanied by any factual material describing the situation which gave rise to the legislation or details concerning the implementation of the Anti-Inflation program. However, procedures were soon set in motion to provide the basic ingredients of a law case — adversaries and their submissions — and make the decision-making process less like an academic seminar and more like the adjudication of a concrete dispute.

There was no difficulty in obtaining parties to argue all sides of both questions. The federal government, of course, would appear in support of the legislation. All the provinces were notified of the hearing but only five decided to participate: Ontario, Quebec, British Columbia and Saskatchewan in support of the legislation (although for the latter three this "support" turned out to be qualified indeed) and Alberta in direct opposition. Alberta would be joined by five unions (or groups of unions) who were considered to have distinct interests at stake in the proceedings. This labour representation included the Ontario teachers and public service unions which had been attempting to litigate the constitutional issues in Ontario courts, the Canadian Labour Congress which had been pressing for judicial review since the introduction of the Act and one major international union, the United Steel Workers of America. Thus, the reference procedure, compensating for the relatively cautious policy of Canadian courts in granting access to the judicial process, enabled the major political contestants to do battle in the judicial arena. But the Supreme Court was not prepared to go all the way in the "politicization" of its process and drew the line at political parties, declining to give permission to the Ontario NDP to appear as an interested party.

The material submitted by these parties compensated, in part, for the bareness of the reference questions. Some of it also posed a severe challenge to the Supreme Court's jurisprudential style. Non-legal material such as the "Brandeis brief" prepared by social scientists and designed to support propositions about the social or economic background and implications of legislation has not played an important role in the Canadian Supreme Court's decision-making. This is not because there is any rule formally prescribing such material. It has stemmed primarily from the character of jurisprudence favoured by

Canadian judges and lawyers. In constitutional interpretation, as in other areas, Canadian jurists have been most comfortable with a highly conceptual approach in which the focus is on applying definitions of legal categories to the words of the statute with little or no reference to the empirical meaning of this exercise. But in the *Anti-Inflation* case some of the counsel came from a younger generation of lawyers imbued with the example of modern American constitutional jurisprudence which has been far more receptive to social science material. The Chief Justice of the Court both as an academic and a judge had stressed the importance of empirical evidence in constitutional interpretation. Also, one of the basic questions in the case — whether inflation in Canada had become a matter of inherent national importance or a national emergency — seemed to be essentially an empirical issue. Thus, it is not surprising that the Court's reception and use of socio-economic material as an "extrinsic aid" to constitutional interpretation became one of the most significant features of the case.

About a month after the Reference Order was issued, Chief Justice Laskin met with counsel for the various parties to consider some of the procedural issues. On 6 April, at the conclusion of this hearing, the Chief Justice, made a number of rulings: application to join the proceedings as an interested party would be accepted up until 15 April; the Attorney General of Canada was to prepare the "case" (the material submitted by the appellant in an appeal which would normally include full documentation of the proceedings in the lower courts), which here was to include the federal government's White Paper and any other materials the Attorney General considered appropriate; the parties were to file their factums (the written briefs setting out each party's arguments on the various issues) by 10 May, and could "annex supplementary material" to their factums; parties would have a short period (until 21 May) in which to submit additional material in reply to material filed by other parties; the oral hearing of the case would begin on 31 May 1976. These rulings gave an opportunity to all the parties to submit whatever empirical argumentation they wished and met one of the traditional complaints against this type of material by giving the parties an opportunity to prepare written replies to their adversaries' submissions. However, the Chief Justice could not make any commitment as to weight which the Court would give any of this material in reaching its final conclusion.

It is interesting to see how the various parties responded to this opportunity. Only the Canadian Labour Congress annexed supplementary material to its factum. This took the form of a 64-page brief written by Richard G. Lipsey, professor of economics at Queen's University. A group of thirty-eight economists who had been attacking the controls program outside of the judicial arena supported the Lipsey brief. Their telegrams of support were added to the CLC material. Professor Lipsey's study advanced the argument that it was very far-fetched to regard the state of the Canadian economy when controls were introduced as an "economic crisis." This argument was supported both by absolute considerations (inflation is primarily redistributive in its effects so that *average* living standards are not lowered) and, perhaps more impressively, by comparative data showing, for instance, that compared both with other periods in Canadian history and with the economic situation of Canada's major trading partners the level of inflation in the fall of 1975 was not extraordinary. Professor Lipsey concluded that:

> It seems hard to believe that the inflation-unemployment problem is unique in its degree of seriousness. . . . If it is held that this problem constitutes an economic crisis, then it is hard to avoid the conclusion that economies are nearly always in states of "economic crises." If this kind of "economic crisis" justified the use of extraordinary measures, these extraordinary measures may be nearly always justified.

In the light of the Supreme Court's final holding, this is a very significant conclusion. Professor Lipsey's study also attacked the efficacy of the controls program in reducing inflation. Given the strict taboo in our legal tradition against courts reviewing the wisdom of legislation, this, I believe, was a serious tactical mistake and made it easier for the judges to discount the Lipsey brief.

The only other material of this kind was submitted by the federal government and the Province of Ontario. The "case" material prepared by the Attorney General of Canada included, in addition to the White Paper requested by the Chief Justice (which nowhere referred to the existence of a "crisis" or "emergency"), the monthly bulletin of Statistics Canada showing fluctuations in the consumer price index up to September 1975. In reply to the Lipsey brief, the Attorneys General of Canada and Ontario both submitted additional material. The federal submission was a copy of an after-dinner speech delivered by the Governor of the Bank of Canada, Gerald K. Bouey, a month before controls were introduced. The speech stressed the seriousness of inflation but was in no sense a counter-analysis to Professor Lipsey's brief. But Ontario's additional material, prepared by the province's Office of Economic Analysis, did attempt a direct rebuttal of Lipsey's main argument. It challenged neither the accuracy of his data nor his technical economics, but (on Galbraithian grounds) it questioned his judgment that the severity of Canada's existing economic problems could be expected nearly always to prevail from now on. Perhaps most significantly, it argued that the question of whether or not a "crisis" exists cannot be answered by technical economics but by public opinion polls (although it cited no actual poll results on this question).

While empirical considerations were more prominent than is usually the case in constitutional references, the arguments which predominated in both the written factums and the oral hearing were still essentially legal in character. These arguments were put to the Court by as impressive an array of legal talent as has ever been assembled for a constitutional case. Amongst the group of participating lawyers were the federal government's counsel, Mr. J.J. Robinette, whom many regard as the outstanding advocate currently practising in Canada, a number of constitutional scholars including a dean, an ex-dean, and a dean elect of law, some of the country's ablest labour and civil rights lawyers, perhaps the most dynamic Attorney General and Deputy Attorney General in Canada, as well as some of the leading members of the youngest generation of Canadian lawyers. Certainly it would be difficult to contend that the outcome of this case was influenced by the fact that one or the other side was badly argued. This is important because the strictly adversarial dimension of the proceedings is probably more significant in the Canadian Supreme Court than it is, for instance, in the United States Supreme Court, where the time allowed for oral argument is very limited. In typical Canadian fashion our Supreme Court procedure combines the written American brief (called factums in Canada) with the English emphasis on virtually unlimited time for oral argument. In this case the oral hearing ran for a full week and it is likely that the way in which the adversarial exchange in the courtroom structured the issues had more to do with the Court's final decision than would be the case in the United States.

The Ontario Agreement was defended only by counsel for Ontario and the federal government. The other provinces did not make submission on this question. The unions all vigorously attacked the Agreement's validity. The Ontario unions were able to use the concrete situations which had been the original basis for their litigation as illustrations of the extent to which the Agreement altered the basic law regulating collective bargaining in Ontario. This added considerable strength to their proposition that an executive Agreement without any legislative sanction which purported to set aside existing legislation was a clear violation of the principle of responsible government. The main defence of the Agreement did not contend that the federal Act had actually provided the legislative sanction for the Ontario Agreement. Instead it relied primarily on precedents of executive agreements and contracts for which there had been no specific legislative authorization. Nonetheless one of the Canadian Labour Congress counsel, P.W. Hogg, argued that in a federal system of dual sovereignty there must be a basic immunity of the Provincial Crown which would set some limit on federal authority to regulate the remuneration of the provincial civil service directly under ministers of the Crown — even in an emergency, and yes, even during a war. This contention clearly shocked a number of judges, and one was heard to exclaim that "if the argument had any validity it would ultimately deny the existence of a Canadian Nation."

On the issues associated with the first question concerning the Anti-Inflation Act's constitutional validity, the alignment of the parties was revealing. The federal position before the Court was the most predictable. It reflected the double game which the federal government had been playing from the start on the peace, order and good government issue. Ottawa was fairly confident that the Act could at the very least be sustained as emergency legislation and its counsel now put forward the emergency use of the general power as a basis for the legislation — *but only as a fall back position*. The primary argument advanced by federal counsel was that "because inflation is a subject matter going beyond local or provincial concern or interests and is from its inherent nature the concern of Canada as a whole," the Anti-Inflation Act should be upheld as a proper exercise of the peace, order and good government power. To this was added reference to several specific heads of federal power — trade and commerce, taxation, the power to borrow, currency, banking, interest, legal tender — all of which were closely related to the aims and effects of the anti-inflation program and hence, it was argued, provided evidence of the inherently national character of the legislation. Obviously, the primary federal argument was designed to do more than save the Act: if it were accepted by the Court it would consolidate the gains in constitutional law which the federal government hoped would flow from Viscount Simon's decision in the *Canada Temperance Federation* case. Surprisingly, Ontario endorsed the federal position. In fact, Mr. McMurtry in one respect went further in that he did not advance the emergency doctrine even as an alternative argument. For Ontario, Viscount Simon's test of inherent national importance was the only test for invoking peace, order and good government.

But the other provinces and the unions all argued that the only possible way of supporting such legislation was on emergency grounds. The constitutional issue which it had been convenient to suppress in October now came out in the open. The most important constitutional arguments were advanced by Mr. Lysyk, the Deputy Attorney General of Saskatchewan and Professor Lederman for the Renfrew teachers. They put forward a new thesis on the meaning of previous decisions dealing with peace, order and good government. The gist of this thesis was that outside of emergencies, peace, order and good government can be used only in a residual sense to support federal legislation in discrete, narrowly defined areas of legislation which clearly fall outside provincial jurisdiction. Legislation in an area defined as broadly as "inflation" and clearly intruding on matters which are normally subject to exclusive provincial jurisdiction fails to meet this test. This interpretation of peace, order and good government was a clear alternative to the views expressed by Chief Justice Laskin in his academic writings — views which his frequent interventions from the bench indicated he might still hold.

Even on emergency grounds the federal position received meager support from the provinces. Alberta along with the unions went all the way and argued (in the CLC's submission on the basis of the Lipsey brief) that the Act should be found unconstitutional as there was no economic emergency. Quebec, British Columbia and Saskatchewan remained on the federal government's side of the courtroom nominally in support of the legislation. But their support, at times, must have reminded federal counsel of the old saying, "With friends like that - who needs enemies?" In their factums, they were at best agnostic as to whether an emergency existed sufficient to justify the use of the general power. Mr. Vickers, the Deputy Attorney General for British Columbia, concluded his oral presentation by submitting that the burden of proof (on the existence of an emergency) lay with the federal government, and that "on the evidence now before the court I do not feel one could conclude that there was a national emergency." Counsel for the federal government did not try to meet this burden of proof nor parry the economic arguments of the Lipsey brief. Mr. Robinette's position was that the Court had only to find that it was not unreasonable for Parliament to believe that there was an emergency or "a generally apprehended crisis."

The submissions of the parties in the *Anti-Inflation* case contrast in some important ways with those of counsel in the New Deal references of the 1930s — the last occasion on which there was a serious challenge to federal power through judicial review. In those cases a foreign tribunal witnessed a strong provincial attack on federal legislation rather weakly defended by a government whose political opponents had actually introduced the legislation. Here, a Canadian court in the national capital was considering the constitutional validity of what at the time was the federal government's most important domestic policy initiative. The judges knew that all of the provinces had in fact agreed to cooperate with the federal program. In the courtroom they *saw* on the federal side four provinces (including the three largest) with governments covering the entire Canadian political spectrum supporting the legislation. But they also heard that the only common denominator of constitutional support was the emergency doctrine. In these circumstances it would have taken an exceptionally bold court either to have found the federal Act *ultra vires* or to have based its constitutional validity on a wider footing than the emergency use of peace, order and good government.

### The Court's Decision

Five weeks after the conclusion of the hearing the Supreme Court pronounced its judgement. The Court unanimously found that the Ontario Agreement did not render the Anti-Inflation program binding on the provincial public sector. On the question of the Anti-Inflation Act's constitutional validity, the Court split seven to two: seven judges found that it was constitutional on emergency grounds, but Justices Beetz and de Grandpre, both from Quebec and the most recently appointed judges, dissented. That is the bare bones of the decision, but, as is always the case with appellate decisions, the reasons of the judges are more important than their votes.

First, the Court's decision on the validity of the Ontario Agreement, while constituting a small portion of the judgment quantitatively, is not without its constitutional significance. Chief Justice Laskin wrote the Court's opinion on this question. Because the federal Act did not spell out precisely how the guidelines should apply to the provincial public sector, the Chief Justice found that the Act itself did not provide the necessary legislative sanction for the Ontario Agreement. The Agreement could not be regarded as sanctioned by conditional legislation for which action by the provincial government was merely a "triggering device." However, it is significant that in reaching this conclusion he went out of his way to indicate that he did not accept the view that it would have been beyond federal power to regulate the provincial public service. Assertions of immunity for the provincial public service, he wrote, "misconceive the paramount authority of federal legislative power . . . and the all-embracing legislative authority of the Parliament of Canada when validly exercised for the peace, order and good government of Canada.'' But, in the absence of federal or provincial legislation *clearly* authorizing the Agreement, he ruled that the executive agreement could not make new labour legislation binding on the citizens of the province. The Chief Justice seemed bent on de-emphasizing the constitutional significance of this holding: the issue, he said, did *not* engage ''any concern with responsible Government and the political answerability of the Ministers to the Legislative Assembly.'' Nonetheless, by holding that:

> There is no principle in this country, as there is not in Great Britain, that the Crown may legislate by proclamation or Order in Council to bind citizens where it so acts without the support of a statute of the Legislature: see Dicey, *Law of the Constitution,*

he at least confirms an essential element of our ''unwritten constitution.'' Those concerned about the increasing erosion of the role of the legislature and the trend in Canada toward policy-making within the closed confines of federal-provincial negotiations, should welcome this judicial recognition of an important constitutional principle.

The Court's decision on the primary question concerning the constitutional validity of the Anti-Inflation Act can be analysed by breaking the question into two components: (1) the interpretation of the peace, order and good government clause and (2) the judgment as to whether the Anti-Inflation Act could be upheld as emergency legislation. The court split in quite different ways on these two aspects of the question. Three opinions were written: Chief Justice Laskin's reasons were supported by three Justices, Judson, Spence and Dickson; Mr. Justice Ritchies' were concurred in by Justices Martland and Pigeon; Mr. Justice de Grandpre concurred in Mr. Justice Beetz's opinion. On the second aspect of the question, Chief Justice Laskin's group of four and Justice Ritchies' group of three formed the majority which found the Act *intra vires.* But on the first issue — the fundamental question of constitutional doctrine — the reasoning of Mr. Justice Beetz's dissenting opinion was adopted by the Ritchie threesome and so became, in effect, the majority position of the Court.

The short 5-page opinion of Mr. Justice Richie at least has the merit of highlighting the Court's division on the meaning of peace, order and good government. Ritchie rejects broad considerations of national concern or inherent national importance as the framework within which to test whether Parliament can exercise its peace, order and good government power in areas normally under provincial jurisdiction. For him the relevant precedent is not Viscount Simon's judgment in the *Canada Temperance Federation* case, but the decisions following it, especially the *Japanese Canadians* case, in which the Privy Council returned to the emergency doctrine. Since then, Justice Ritchie takes it to be established ''that unless such concern [i.e., national concern] is made manifest by circumstances amounting to a national emergency, Parliment is not endowed under the cloak of the 'peace, order and good government' clause with the authority to legislate in relation to matters reserved to the Provinces under s. 92.'' For more elaborate jurisprudential reasons he refers to Mr. Justice Beetz with whose reasons he is "in full agreement."

Justice Beetz provided a re-interpretation of previous judicial decisions on this constitutional issue. This re-interpretation followed the mainline of argument submitted to the Court by Mr. Lysyk and Professor Lederman. The essence of this approach is to draw a radical distinction between the "normal" and the "abnormal" uses of peace, order and good government. The normal use of the clause is as an national residual power to cover " . . . clear instances of distinct subject-matters which do not fall within any of the enumerated heads of s. 92 and which, by nature, are of national concern." Thus, it has been invoked successfully in the past to support such fields as radio, aeronautics, the incorporation of Dominion companies and the national capital, all of which in Justice Beetz's view display the requisite "degree of unity", "distinct identity" or "specificity." But the containment and reduction of inflation fails to meet this test of specificity: "It is so pervasive that it knows no bounds. Its recognition as a federal head of power would render most provincial powers nugatory." The normal applicaton of peace, order and good government has the effect of adding, by judicial process, new subject matters of legislation to the list of exclusive federal powers in Section 91 of the BNA Act. National concern, national dimensions are still relevant in determining whether such unforeseen, discrete, new subject matters should be brought under the federal residual power or under its counterpart on the provincial side, Section, 92(16) — "Matters of a merely local or private nature in the province." But the only constitutional basis for federal legislation cast in such broad terms as the Anti-Inflation Act is the abnormal use of peace, order and good government — the emergency doctrine. It is abnormal precisely because it "operates as a partial and temporary alteration of the distribution of power between Parliament and the provincial Legislatures." Once the Court agrees to apply this doctrine no longer is the power of Parliament limited by the identity of subject matters but solely "by the nature of the crisis."

This then was the new constitutional doctrine fashioned by Justice Beetz and supported by a bare majority of the Court. Against it — but by no means in total opposition to it — was Chief Justice Laskin's opinion supported by three other judges. The Chief Justice wrote a long review of all the major cases bearing upon peace, order and good government. While it is not always clear just where this review is going, it contains one basic point of contrast with the majority position. Instead of driving a wedge between the normal and abnormal use of the general power, Chief Justice Laskin tries to weave a single piece of cloth out of all the strands to be found in previous decisions. The key to this approach, the central idea which gives the multi-coloured fabric some shape and pattern, is Lord Watson's proposition in the *Local Prohibition* case that " . . . matters in origin local or provincial . . . might attain national dimensions." Since then Laskin sees the jurisprudence moving in two directions — under Viscount Haldane narrowing to the point of "studiously ignoring" Lord Watson's "national dimensions," but then returning to it, at first cautiously in judgments written by Lord Atkin and Chief Justice Duff followed by the more expansive views of Viscount Simon. The Chief Justice's response to this legacy of competing emphases is not to pick his own favourite strand and discard the others but to identify the extremes which clearly lie beyond the main body of jurisprudence. Thus, at one extreme, basing the use of peace, order and good government on the mere desirability or convenience of national regulation (a possible interpretation of the first Privy Council decision on this issue, *Russell v. The Queen*) is ruled out. But at the other extreme, a pure Haldane approach which ignores "national dimensions" and confines the use of peace, order and good government to war-related emergencies is equally beyond the pale. In between these extremes there are many possibilities, and the Chief Justice warns against fixing constitutional doctrine so tightly as to prevent the constitution from serving " . . . as a resilient instrument capable of adaptation to changing circumstances."

In the case at hand, because all of the parties accepted as constitutional doctrine the use of peace, order and good government to deal with a national emergency, " . . . it becomes unnecessary to consider the broader ground advanced in its support. . . ." So the Chief Justice was willing to rest his decision on the narrow ground of emergency (semantically softened to "crisis"). But unlike the majority he did not rule out the broader ground advanced by the federal government.

For those who have admired the Chief Justice's contribution to Canada's constitutional jurisprudence, the opaque, open-ended quality of his reasoning in this case may be a disappointment. But it is reasonable, I think, to regard his opinion as that of a Chief Justice endeavouring to build a majority around the widest common denominator on his Court without foreclosing jurisprudential possibilities which he personally favoured. That he failed is not too surprising. Since joining the Court in 1970 he has been its most frequent dissenter. The available statistical data (based on the *Supreme Court Reports* from 1970 to 1974 inclusive) reveal that of the 196 dissents recorded during this period more than half (109) were attributed to three justices: Laskin (45), Spence (34) and Hall (30). The relative isolation of these justices is not tied to issues of federalism. Between the time the present Chief Justice joined the Court and the Anti-Inflation Reference, the Court rendered 20 decisions on the division of powers in the BNA Act. Fifteen of them were unanimous, and although the Chief Justice was on the dissenting side in three of the split decisions, an examination of these cases does not suggest a division on provincial rights/centralist lines. Chief Justice Laskin's differences with a majority of his colleagues more likely stem from general questions of judicial philosophy and style. If there is a consistent pattern of division on matters of substance, it is more likely to be found in cases dealing with criminal law and the Bill of Rights.

Given the clear consensus both on the Court and amongst the litigants concerning the power of Parliament in a national emergency (or crisis) to override the normal division of powers, the second dimension of the constitutional question — whether in fact the Anti-Inflation Act was emergency legislation — may become more important than the general doctrinal issue of the meaning of peace, order and good government. The Supreme Court's handling of this issue indicates a significant shift to a more deferential attitude to the exercise of emergency powers in peacetime by the national government.

The Court's split on the issue — Chief Justice Laskin's group of four plus Justice Ritchie's group of three versus Justices Beetz and de Grandpre in dissent — did not turn on the empirical question of whether in fact there was an emergency. It concerned the prior question of whether emergency legislation must be clearly identified as such by Parliament. The dissenters took the position that a necessary but by no means sufficient test of valid emergency legislation is a clear, unambiguous indication by Parliament that it is enacting the legislation on an emergency basis. Justice Beetz emphasized that responsibility for declaring an emergency must lie with the "politically responsible body," not the courts. The courts' responsibility begins after the affirmation by Parliament that an emergency exists. In this case not only was there no acknowledgment on the face of the federal Act (as there had been with other recent exercises of the emergency power), but there was clear evidence to show that this was no accidental oversight. Breaking the convention which precludes Canadian judges from considering parliamentary history, Justice Beetz referred to the numerous passages in Hansard where government spokesmen refused to be pinned down on the constitutional basis of the legislation and refused to preface the Bill with a declaration of an emergency. Further, the large gaps in the Act's coverage — the omission of farmers and small businesses, the optional nature of the provincial public sector's inclusion — were, in Justice Beetz' view, not easily reconciled with an emergency characterization of the Act. He was also impressed by the lack of provincial support for the view that it was emergency legislation.

For the majority, Parliament's failure to declare an emergency or stamp "emergency" on the face of the Act was not fatal. The reference in the Act's preamble to a level of inflation "contrary to the interests of all Canadians" which had become "a matter of serious national concern," combined with similar statements in the government's White Paper, were enough to indicate how serious the situation must have appeared to Parliament. The omissions from the Act's coverage and the opting-in approach to the provincial public sector, in Chief Justice Laskin's view, could be accounted for in terms of administrative convenience and need not be regarded as indicating a lack of any sense of crisis. Since there were no formal deficiencies in the federal Act, the only grounds upon which its validity as emergency or crisis legislation could be impugned was the factual question: did an emergency exist? Here, for a least three of the justices, the onus of proof was placed squarely on the Act's opponents. The peacetime exercise of the federal emergency power was put on the same footing as its use in time of war. Justice Ritchie cited Lord Wright's statement in the *Japanese Canadians* case.

> But very clear evidence that an emergency has not arisen, or that the emergency no longer exists, is required to justify the judiciary, even though the question is one of ultra vires, in overruling the decison of the Parliament of the Dominion that exceptional measures were required or were still required.

In Justice Ritchie's opinion the evidence presented by the opponents of the legislation failed to meet Lord Wright's test.

Chief Justice Laskin approached the issue in terms of assessing the rationality of Parliament's judgment. The Court would be justified in overruling the Act as emergency legislation only if it found that:

> . . . The Parliament of Canada did not have a rational basis for regarding the *Anti-Inflation Act* as a measure which, in its judgment, was temporarily necessary to meet a situation of economic crisis imperilling the well-being of the people of Canada as a whole and requiring Parliament's stern intervention in the interests of the country as a whole.

In assessing rationality the Chief Justice did not place the burden of proof solely on the Act's opponents. He took into consideration statistics showing the rise in the consumer Price Index submitted by the federal government as well as the arguments advanced in Professor Lipsey's brief. He noted Professor Lipsey's candid admission that whether ''a problem is serious enough to be described as a crisis must be partly a matter of judgment,'' and added that the Court cannot be governed by the judgement of an economist however distinguished he may be in the opinion of his peers. Positive evidence of the rationality of Parliament's judgment could be found in the connection between rising inflation and Parliament's clear constitutional responsibilities in monetary policy and areas of trade and commerce which ''the extrinsic material does not reveal'' could be treated in isolation from those economic areas ordinarily beyond federal regulatory control.

Thus, the Chief Justice concluded that the Court would be unjustified in finding Parliament lacked a rational basis for its judgment that the legislation was needed to meet an urgent crisis. But we should note how in this part of his opinion he attempted to retain as close a link as possible between the emergency use of peace, order and good government and broad consideration of national dimensions or national aspects. With severe inflation impinging so heavily on areas of federal responsibility, the subject matter of the Anti-Inflation Act — the regulation of prices and wages — loses its ordinary parochial or local character and becomes a matter sufficiently urgent for the well-being of all Canadians as to require national action.

### The Significance of the Decision

Normally a judicial decision in our system of government ''settles'' one aspect — the judiciable aspect — of what is usually a larger dispute. In the context of this larger dispute a court's role is perhaps better described as "dispute processing" rather than "dispute settlement." In assessing the political importance of a judicial decision it is important to see how it affects the political interests involved in the larger area of conflict. The political impact of a constitutional decision by the national court of appeal will usually be felt much more in terms of the long-run significance of the new rules of law it produces than in terms of the immediate outcome of the adjudication.

This is certainly true of the Supreme Court's decision in the Anti-Inflation case. For the labour organizations which provoked the case as part of a general anti-controls campaign the immediate outcome was a loss. The controls would continue. Even that part of the decision which invalidated the Ontario Agreement was quickly overcome. The ink was scarcely dry on the Court's judgment when the Ontario government went back to the legislature and obtained retroactive legislative sanction for its participation in the anti-inflation program. The government's minority position in the legislature proved to be no problem, as Mr. Smith, the Liberal leader, was as compliant as predicted. But the "loss" for labour was probably not a very serious one. Labour opposition to the controls program, if anything, intensified rather than diminished after the decision. It is doubtful that the Supreme Corut's validation of the Anti-Inflation Act added to the program's political legitimacy. In fact, a judicial veto of the Anti-Inflation Act might have provided the immediate benefit to the Trudeau government of a politically safe exit from a potentially unpopular program. Besides, the ground of the Court's decision meant that the door was far from closed on future constitutional challenges to the program. If the inflationary situation significantly eased, it would always be possible to argue that the circumstances which made it reasonable to regard the Act as an emergency measure no long existed. Indeed, shortly after the Parti Quebecois took over in Quebec City, Mr. Parizeau, Quebec's Finance Minister, announced that he was considering a challenge on precisely those grounds.

The rules of law and the constitutional doctrine which emerge from the decision bear more directly on the interests of the two levels of government in the Canadian federation than upon the labour-capital axis. Indeed, one of the interesting features of the case is the apparent indifference of organized labour to the division of powers question. The federal and provincial governments cannot be indifferent because Supreme court rulings on the constitution directly increase or diminish their political resources. From this perspective, the Court's judgment on the Ontario Agreement entails a slight decrease in the resources of both levels of government. The decision reduces the freedom of provincial and federal governments to collaborate in making policy through the mechanisms of cooperative federalism without obtaining support from their respective legislatures. This modest restraint on "executive federalism" is a boon for citizens and interest groups (like labour unions), not to mention old-fashioned democrats who believe that major changes in the law should be approved by the legislature. But its significance must not be over-rated. Chief Justice Laskin's decision clearly implies that federal legislation upheld on emergency grounds could, if properly worded, regulate all aspects of a field normally under provincial jurisdiction and eliminate any need for provincial legislative sanction.

As for the meaning of the peace, order and good government clause in the BNA Act, the decision did not yield the particular benefit sought by federal legal strategists. The legislation was not sustained on broad grounds of inherent national importance or concern. Viscount Haldane was not put away in mothballs. The jurisprudence of Viscount Simon and the *Johannesson* case, which Mr. Macdonald said his government was counting upon, was not accepted by the Court's majority as the key to interpreting peace, order and good government. But the federal government did not come away from the decision empty-handed. To begin with, what I shall call the "Lederman doctrine" on peace, order and good government, adopted by Justice Beetz and supported by a majority of the judges, means that when new matters of legislation are considered distinct and specific enough to justify the residual or "normal" use of the peace, order and good government, they are added to the list of *exclusive* federal powers. The exclusiveness of federal jurisdiction in areas such as aeronautics and radio communications, which are cited as instances of this normal use, was not clear in the past. The Lederman doctrine, while apparently not as favourable to federal power as Viscount Simon's dictum, still is not necessarily unfavourable. While it may have seemed relatively easy to Justice Beetz and his colleagues to apply the criterion of "specificity" retrospectively, I would contend that it is not an easy test to apply prospectively. In the hands of a nationally-minded court it may be surprising what turns out to be specific enough to come under the federal residual power. Besides, it should be noted that considerations of national concern and importance have not been discarded by the Court. Under the Lederman doctrine, national concern is the test for determining whether a new subject with the requisite degree of specificity should be brought under the federal rather than the provincial residual power. Also, as I have tried to explain above, Chief Justice Laskin's opinion, which after all spoke for four of the Court's nine judges, kept Viscount Simon's jurisprudence alive and, in deciding whether the legislation was valid on emergency grounds, made the national dimensions of the economic crisis a prime consideraton.

But the Court's handling of the emergency question constitutes a more distinct gain for the federal authorities. The majority's ruling that Parliament does not have to proclaim an emergency or crisis in order to be able to defend legislation successfully in court as emergency legislation increases the maneuverability of federal government leaders. This is especially important with regard to crisis situations related to peacetime economic management when the open admission in Parliament that an emergency or urgent crisis exists might be politically embarrassing to the government. The majority's position means that the federal government does not have to pay the price of that embarrassment in order to secure the emergency argument as the basis for an Act's constitutional validity. To put the matter bluntly, temporary federal legislation may be upheld on emergency grounds if federal lawyers can persuade the Court that there is not enough evidence to conclude that it would have been unreasonable for Parliament to have regarded a matter as an urgent national crisis at the time it passed the legislation. Given the probable deference of most Supreme Court Justices to the judgment of Parliament, this is at least a small gain for federal authority.

It may, however, be a significant loss to those Canadians who care about maintaining parliamentary democracy and constitutionalism. For it must be remembered that all of the judicial decisions upholding federal legislation on emergency grounds (as well as those denying it on these grounds) indicate that "the rule of law as to the distribution of powers" is set aside for the duration of the emergency. One can understand the need for an overriding emergency power to protect the state against threats to its very survival, as well as the reluctance of judges to question a clear determination by Parliament that such an emergency exists. But the constitution as a limit on governmental authority will come to mean very little if it is set aside too easily. At the very least, the better constitutional policy might be to insist, with Justice Beetz, that it should be the responsibility of Parliament rather than the courts to proclaim an emergency.

Finally, what does the *Anti-Inflation* case indicate about the future of judicial review in Canada? First, I think it is likely that the frequency with which constitutional issues are brought before the court will increase rather than decrease. The Supreme Court's almost perfect record in upholding federal laws will not be a serious deterrent to those who wish to challenge federal legislation. For provincial governments, and even more, for private interest groups, constitutional litigation is just one weapon that can be used to fight a larger campaign. Even the Parti Quebecois, for instance, although it has no respect for the Supreme Court as an institution of national government, contemplates constitutional litigation as a tactic in its larger constitutional warfare. If it loses, it can portray the decison as yet further evidence of the hostility of federal institutions to Quebec's interests; if it wins this would vindicate the charge that the federal government is encroaching on areas of provincial jurisdiction. But private individuals and groups may be even more likely to provoke constitutional litigation. The rapid growth of the legal profession, more generous rules of standing, the influence of the American example and the new jurisdictional rules under which the Supreme Court's docket is shaped primarily by judicial selection of nationally important cases — all of these factors are likely to generate more privately-initiated constitutional cases. And, as labour's approach to the *Anti-Inflation* case indicates, when these pressure groups litigate constitutional issues they may be inclined to let the constitutional chips fall where they may for the sake of pursuing some short-run advantage on an immediate policy issue.

So the Supreme Court's decision in this case will not deter resort to judicial review in the future. Nor, despite the scant attention given Professor Lipsey's brief, should future litigants in constitutional cases be deterred from supporting their arguments with this kind of social science evidence. None of the judges denied that Professor Lipsey's brief was admissible evidence, and the Chief Justice explicitly acknowledged its relevancy even though he did not find it completely persuasive. Further, where the question of constitutionality turns on the reasonableness of regarding a situation as an urgent national crisis requiring national legislation, what other than empirical arguments can lawyers who wish to challenge the legislation use? I am not suggesting that there will be a sudden revolution in the Supreme Court's style of jurisprudence, but that we will likely see more lawyers using this type of material in future constitutional cases. One leading constitution scholar has suggested that ". . . the admission of social science briefs in constitutional cases where legislative facts are in issue. . . . may prove in the long run to be the most influential point of the case."

On a more fundamental plane, the Court's majority in subscribing to Professor Lederman's approach to peace, order and good government, rather than Professor Laskin's (as he once was), have opted to maintain a more traditional style of opinion-writing. The central concern apparent in this style of reasoning is "distilling the essences" of legal categories and characterizing the subject matter of legislation. It is basically the old game of sticking the legislation in the right pigeon-hole. Most of our judges (and probably, still most of our lawyers) find this a more congenial exercise than reasoning about legislative schemes in terms of the necessary requirements of effective national policy-making.

Judicial decisions based on the majority's approach have the *appearance* of being based on narrow, technical, purely legal considerations. But the preference for this style of jurisprudence is based on larger considerations of constitutional policy. Only Justice Beetz gave a clear expression of the underlying policy reason for rejecting the federal government's first submission that the Anti-Inflation Act should be sustained under peace, order and good government as a matter of inherent national importance. "It is not difficult to speculate," he wrote "as to where this line of reasoning would lead: a fundamental feature of the Constitution, its federal nature, the distribution of powers betweeen Parliament and the provincial legislatures, would disappear not gradually but rapidly." So, for policy reasons, a jurisprudential style which would make policy reasons more transparent, is rejected. As a result, Canadians cannot expect judicial reasoning to add very much to the country's stock of constitutional wisdom. The question remains whether this masking of judicial power is in itself a kind of constitutional wisdom.

# 10.5

## KEYTERMS

*Concepts*

federalism
judicial review
disallowance (s.56)
reservation (s.90)
"Peace, Order, and good Government"
residual power
"emergency doctrine"
"inherent national importance test"
"living tree" approach to constitutional interpretation
textual approach to constitutional interpretation

### *Institutions, Events, and Documents*

Judicial Committee of the Privy Council (1833)
Colonial Laws Validity Act (1865)
Constitution Act, ss. 91 and 92 (1867)
Supreme Court Act (1875)
*The Peace Case* (1928)
Statute of Westminster (1931)
*The Labour Conventions Case* (1937)
O'Connor Report (1939)
Amendments to Supreme Court Act (1949)
*Anti-Inflation Reference* (1976)

# 11
# Judicial Review and Civil Liberties

The practice of judicial review is unique to liberal democratic nations. The grounding principles of liberal democracy posit that good government is "limited government," and a written constitution enforced by judicial review is a means to that end. While all instances of judicial review are found in liberal democracies, not all liberal democracies use judicial review. Great Britain is certainly a liberal democracy, but it does not have a "written constitution," and consequently English judges do not exercise judicial review.

The absence of a written constitution and judicial review does not mean that the government of Great Britain is "unlimited." The doctrine of parliamentary sovereignty notwithstanding, Dicey makes it clear that political conventions of self-restraint and fair play, reinforced by public opinion, operate to protect the same fundamental freedoms of Englishmen as judicial review of the U.S. Bill of Rights does for Americans. Dicey clearly preferred the flexibility of an "unwritten constitution" and vesting primary responsibility for the preservation of liberty in a direct majoritarian legislature such as Parliament. But he does not rule out the possibility of codifying the fundamental freedoms of the English people. After enumerating the fundamental components of the "rule of law" — "the right to personal freedom; the right to freedom of discussion; the right of public meeting; the use of martial law; the rights and duties of the army; the collection and expenditure of the public revenue; and the responsibility of ministers" — Dicey concludes:

> If at some future day the law of the constitution should be codified, each of the topics I have mentioned would be dealt with by the sections of the code. (Reading 11.2)

In adopting the Charter of Rights and Freedoms in 1982, Canada did what Dicey merely speculated about some 100 years earlier — to entrench in a written constitution the rights and freedoms that had previously been preserved through the British-style tradition of an "unwritten constitution." The preamble of the Constitution Act, 1867, declares that Canada shall have "a Constitution similar in Principle to that of the United Kingdom." This declaration meant not just the Westminster system of parliamentary democracy, but also the entire "unwritten constitution" that accompanied it. During its first 93 years Canada indeed had such a constitution, with the one very important exception of federalism. In 1960, the Diefenbaker government enacted the Canadian Bill of Rights, thus beginning the transition away from the British approach to the protection of civil liberties toward the American approach. Twenty-two years later, the Trudeau government's enactment of the Charter of Rights completed this transition. Parliamentary supremacy was replaced by constitutional supremacy, enforced by judicial review — or nearly replaced. The last minute compromise leading to the section 33 "legislative override" power preserved a qualified form of parliamentary supremacy.

## Civil Liberties and the Courts prior to 1960

From Confederation until 1960, judicial protection of civil liberties was limited to two techniques. The first was the "interpretive avoidance" approach inherited from British judges.[1] When interpreting a statute of Parliament or one of the provinces, the courts always assumed that the legislature intended to respect traditional rights and liberties. If a statute was open to two interpretations, one of which infringed a right or freedom, judges would exercise their discretion to choose the other interpretation. This approach is consistent with parliamentary supremacy, in that the courts do not overrule the legislature by declaring statutes "of no force or effect." "Interpretive avoidance" simply sends a message to parliamentary lawmakers that until they indicate otherwise, by redrafting the statute in more explicit language, the courts will interpret it as indicated. While a determined majority in Parliament could easily override such judicial attempts at protecting civil liberties, in practice this was rare. The *Roncarelli* case (Reading 11.3) and the *Boucher* case (Reading 11.4) are both important examples of the Canadian judiciary's use of the "interpretive avoidance" technique to protect the traditional freedoms of individual Canadians.

The second method of judicial protection of civil liberties prior to 1960 was distinctively Canadian — the use of federalism limitations. Using this "power allocation" method, Canadian appeal court judges ruled intemperate or discriminatory provincial policies *ultra vires* on section 91-92 grounds, when the real issue appeared to be one of civil liberties. For example, in 1938 the Supreme Court struck down the euphemistically titled *Accurate News and Information Act*, which was an attempt by the Alberta Social Credit government to muzzle newpaper criticism of its economic policies. The Supreme Court ruled that this was legislation in relation to criminal law, and therefore

---

[1] The three related aproaches of interpretive avoidance, power allocation, and power denial are elaborated by E.E. Dais, "Judicial Supremacy in Canada in Comparative Perspective: A Critical Analysis of *Drybones*," Paper presented at the Annual Meeting of the Canadian Political Science Association, June 8, 1971.

beyond the legislative jurisdiction of any province.[2] Another well-known example of this technique was the 1953 case of *Saumur v. Quebec*.[3] This was one of a series of Jehovah's Witnesses' cases from Quebec, where both provincial and municipal governments were restricting the controversial religious sect. In this instance Quebec City had passed a bylaw prohibiting the distribution of pamphlets in the streets without permission of the Chief of Police. Saumar (and many other) Jehovah's Witnesses were arrested for violating this bylaw. While normally this type of legislation is clearly within the section 92 powers of the provinces, the punitive intentions behind it were equally clear. In striking down the Quebec bylaw, a number of Supreme Court judges argued that is was legislation in relation to religious freedom, and that this was denied to the provinces either by section 91 (criminal law) or section 93 (denominational rights) of the Constitution Act.

While the "power allocation" approach was successfully used on a variety of occasions to protect civil liberties, there were several drawbacks to this approach. First, whatever powers were denied to provincial governments were logically conceded to the federal government. While this had the disturbing implication that the federal government was free to enact the illiberal policies of the provinces, this never proved to be a practical problem. A more serious objection to this approach was that it forced the judges to use the language of federalism when dealing with the logic of civil liberties. This surreptitious method of reasoning tended to confuse the jurisprudence of both federalism and civil liberties.

There is a third strand of pre-Bill of Rights civil liberties jurisprudence that deserves mention, even though it has never been accepted by a Supreme Court majority. Known as the "implied Bill of Rights" approach, it argues that the provisions of the preamble of the Constitution Act — that Canada shall have "a Constitution similar in Principle to that of the United Kingdom" — imported into Canada the traditional rights and freedoms protected by Britain's "unwritten constitution." The previously cited passages from Dicey show the plausibility of this argument. In the *Alberta Press Case*, Justice Duff argued that "the right of public debate" was inherent in a parliamentary system, and that the preamble provided sufficient grounds to declare the Alberta Press bill inoperative. Similarly in the *Saumur* case, Justices Rand, Kellock, and Locke said that the preamble implicitly protected "freedom of religion" from both levels of government. The strength of this approach lies in its correct recognition of the civil liberties dimension of the "unwritten constitution" inherited from Great Britain. But this is also its weakness, since British judges never pretended to have the authority to enforce these freedoms directly against

---

[2] *Reference re Alberta Statutes*, [1938] S.C.R. 100, more commonly known as the *Alberta Press Case*.

[3] [1953] 2 S.C.R. 299.

Parliament. It is widely accepted that constitutional custom and convention are not judicially enforcable, and the strength of this tradition prevented the "implied Bill of Rights" approach from gaining any general acceptance.

## Civil Liberties and the Courts under the 1960 Bill of Rights

In the aftermath of the Second World War, growing awareness of the Stalinist and Nazi atrocities of the preceding decades alarmed Western democracies about the fragile nature of human rights and civil liberties in the mass societies of the twentieth century. This concern was shared by Canadian leaders, who were also troubled by their own harsh treatment of Japanese Canadians during the war years, and the government's harassment of the Jehovah's Witnesses in Quebec. After a decade of committee hearings and public discussion, the Diefenbaker government adopted the Canadian Bill of Rights in 1960. (Reprinted in the Appendix)

The 1960 Bill of Rights took the form of a statute of Parliament, not an amendment to the Constitution Act. It also applied only to the federal government. The provinces would not consent to additional restrictions on their legislative powers, and Ottawa lacked the authority to impose them unilaterally.

From the start the Bill of Rights was plagued by problems of interpretation. These problems stemmed principally from its legal status as an ordinary statute and the ambiguous wording of its second section. Canadian judges, including those on the Supreme Court, could not agree on what function the Bill of Rights assigned to the courts. Some argued that the Bill of Rights conferred new authority on the courts to declare Parliamentary statutes "of no force or effect," if they conflicted with enumerated rights. According to this interpretation, the Bill of Rights armed the Canadian courts with an American-style "power denial" function. Others thought that the Bill of Rights was essentially a canon of statutory interpretation, a codification of the traditional "interpretive avoidance" method. They pointed to the ambiguous wording of section 2, and the statutory as opposed to constitutional status of the Bill. Implicit in this position was the feeling that if Parliament had intended to terminate or substantially modify the tradition of parliamentary sovereignty in Canada, it would have said so in a much clearer manner.

The Supreme Court's landmark decision in the 1969 *Drybones* case put an end to this particular problem. (Reading 11.5) A majority of the Court took the position that the Bill of Rights did confer authority on the judges to declare offending statutes inoperative. The Court ruled that section 94(b) of the Indian Act denied Drybones his rights to "equality before the law," because it treated him more harshly for public intoxication than other Canadians would have been treated for the same offense, simply because he was an Indian. The *Drybones* decision was hailed as a major development in Canadian constitutional evolution. It seemed to signify an important new restraint on the tradition of parliamentary supremacy and an important new role for the Canadian judiciary in policing Bill of Rights violations.

The high expectations created by *Drybones* were short-lived. Subsequent Supreme Court decisions indicated that the judges were still inclined to defer to Parliament's judgement on substantive issues of criminal procedure. This trend culminated in the Supreme Court's 1974 decision of the *Lavell* and *Bedard* cases. (Reading 11.6) Lavell and Bedard were Indian women who had lost their Indian status pursuant to section 12(1)(b) of the Indian Act. This section provides that Indian women who marry non-Indians lose their status, but no similar disability is imposed on Indian men who marry non-Indians. Lavell and Bedard argued that this violated their right to ''equality before the law,'' since it discriminated against them on the basis of their sex. Based on the *Drybones* precedent, which appeared to prohibit discrimination in the laws based on explicitly prohibited categories such as race and sex, their case seemed very strong. The Supreme Court surprised almost everyone by finding otherwise. A majority of the Court ruled that the right to ''equality before the law'' meant ''equality in the application and administration of the laws.'' Since there was no question that section 12(1)(b) had been applied to Lavell and Bedard the same as it was applied to all other Indian women, there was no violation of the Bill of Rights. The dissenting justices protested the apparent inconsistency of this interpretation with the *Drybones* precedent, but to no avail.

## Civil Liberties and the Courts under the 1982 Charter of Rights

Events in the years immediately following the *Lavell* and *Bedard* decisions proved the truth of the old adage that ''politics makes strange bedfellows.'' Feminists and civil libertarian groups were increasingly disillusioned with the 1960 Bill of Rights as an effective legal instrument to achieve the kinds of decisions that they expected. At the same time Prime Minister Trudeau and his Liberal party had become increasingly interested in a constitutionally entrenched Bill of Rights as a potential ''nation-building'' device to counter the increasing intensity of conflict in federal-provincial relations. (Reading 11.7) Out of these seemingly diverse interests was born the political coalition responsible for the adoption of the Charter of Rights and Freedoms in 1982. (Reprinted in the Appendix)

The important elements of the Charter of Rights are adequately covered by the Russell and Knopff-Morton articles in reading 11.8 and 13.3. It suffices to point out here that the Charter is best understood as a compromise between the advocates and opponents of a greater role for the courts in Canadian politics and policy-making. The Liberal party-feminist-libertarian coalition succeeded in strengthening the role of the courts under the Charter in three specific ways, relative to the 1960 Bill of Rights. First and foremost, the Charter applies to both levels of government, provincial and federal. (s. 32) Second, the Charter is constitutionally entrenched, not just a statute as the Bill of Rights was. Third, the Charter explicitly authorizes the judges to review legislation for violations of enumerated rights (s. 24(1)), and to declare ''any law that is

inconsistent with the provisions of the Constitution . . . of no force or effect."
(s. 52)

The opponents of too great a role for the judges extracted two concessions from the government in return for their support. The first is the "reasonable limitations" clause of section 1, which makes explicit what was already understood to be implicit — that none of the enumerated rights are absolute. The second and much more important concession is the section 33 "legislative override," which essentially allows either level of government to "veto" a judicial decision to which they object, if it is based on the fundamental freedoms (s. 2), legal rights (ss. 7-14), or equality rights (s. 15) sections of the Charter. This "legislative review of judicial review," as Russell ironically labels it, is very important, because it preserves the principle of parliamentary sovereignty, albeit in a modified form. It also has the potential to undermine the effectiveness of the Charter, and for this reason is likely to influence judicial interpretation of the Charter.[4]

The Charter will significantly increase the policy-making role of Canadian courts, especially the Supreme court. As Russell correctly argues,

> [A] charter of rights guarantees not rights but a particular way of making decisions about rights, in which the judicial branch of government has a much more systematic and authoritative role. (Reading 11.8)

The Charter simply amplifies the rights that were already protected by the 1960 Bill of Rights, and the latter only codified the rights and freedoms that already existed as common law and as constitutional conventions. What is new about both the Bill of Rights and now the Charter is the growing transfer of the decision-making process from representative legislative assemblies to the courts. Russell has pithily summarized the net effect of this evolution as "its tendency to judicialize politics and to politicize the judiciary." The preceding chapters have elaborated what is meant by the first part of this statement, but the implications of what it means to "politicize the judiciary" need elaboration.

As we have already seen, a variety of interest groups are already willing and able to pursue their respective policy objectives through Charter litigation. The view that the Charter is a "redistributive mechanism" for "social justice issues" seems to be shared by certain influential members of the educational and legal elites, and by the press generally.[5] As a result, the courts will feel the pressure of such expectations to exercise their new-found power in a broad and "progressive" fashion. If American experience is an accurate indicator, these expectations are likely to begin to influence the judicial selection process as well. Groups interested in litigating their special causes before the

---

[4] This is the subject of the Knopff-Morton article in Reading 13.3.

[5] See Introduction to chapter seven.

courts will begin to maneuver in the recruitment and selection process to push appointees who are sympathizers or fellow-travelers.

This possible scenario must be juxtaposed to the traditional understanding of the ''rule of law'' and the role it entails for judges. Recall the late Chief Justice Laskin's response to the suggestions that judges are ''spokesmen for special interests'':

> I know of no better way to subvert our judicial system . . . than to give currency to the view that the judiciary must be a representative agency.

Such a view, he concluded would undermine the ''rule of law, without which we cannot maintain our free society.''[6] Likewise, William Lederman rejects the suggestion that judicial enforcement of the ''rule of law'' amounts to ''the personal supremacy of superior court judges.''

> It is basic to the rule of law that doctrines, ideas and principles are supreme, not persons . . . . Believing in the supremacy of law, [judges] must themselves scrupulously obey it . . . . Judicial restraint on these terms at the superior court level is the ultimate safeguard of the supremacy of law, enacted and unenacted.[7]

The Charter of Rights and Freedoms holds the potential for both positive and negative developments in Canadian society. The responsibility for maximizing the former and minimizing the latter falls on the shoulders of Canadian judges, especially those of the Supreme Court of Canada. How they exercise their new authority — whether they can meet the challenge of judicial statesmanship — is the subject of the last chapter.

---

[6] ''Judicial Integrity and the Supreme Court of Canada,'' *Law Society Gazette*, 1978, p.121.

[7] Reading 5.2.

# 11.1

# ON THE EXTENT OF THE LEGISLATURE POWER

John Locke, *The Second Treatise* (1690)

This excerpt is reprinted as Reading 1.2.

# 11.2

## THE RULE OF LAW
A.V. Dicey (1885)


This excerpt is reprinted as Reading 1.4.


# 11.3

## RONCARELLI v. DUPLESSIS
Supreme Court of Canada (1959)


This case is reprinted as Reading 1.1.


# 11.4

## BOUCHER v. THE KING
Supreme Court of Canada (1951)


This case is reprinted as Reading 9.4.

# 11.5

## DRYBONES v. THE QUEEN
Supreme Court of Canada (1969)

CARTWRIGHT, C.J. (dissenting) — The relevant facts, which are undisputed, and the course of the proceedings in the courts below, are set out in the reasons of my brothers Ritchie and Pigeon which I have had the advantage of reading.

There is no doubt that, on the facts, the respondent was guilty of a breach of sec. 94 (b) of the *Indian Act*, RSC, 1952, ch. 149, and the question to be decided is whether that provision is rendered inoperative by the terms of the *Canadian Bill of Rights*, 1960, ch. 44, hereinafter referred to as "the Bill."

In approaching this question I will assume the correctness of the view that sec. 94 (b) infringes the right of the respondent to equality before the law declared by clause (b) of sec. 1 of the Bill, in that because he is an Indian it renders him guilty of a punishable offense by reason of conduct which would not have been punishable if indulged in by any person who was not an Indian. . . .

. . . In these circumstances the choice open to us is to give effect to the section according to its plain meaning or to declare it inoperative, that is to say, to declare that the *Indian Act* is *pro tanto* repealed by the Bill.

In *Robertson and Rosetanni v. Reg., supra*, I had to deal with a similar question as in my view the *Lord's Day Act* did infringe the freedom of religion. At pp. 661 and 662 I used the following words:

> It remains to consider the reasons for judgment of Davey, J.A. in *Reg. v. Gonzales* (1962) . . . . At page 239 of the C.C.C. Reports the learned Justice of Appeal says:
>
> "In so far as existing legislation does not offend against any of the matters specifically mentioned in clauses (a) to (g) of s. 2, but is said to otherwise infringe upon some of the human rights and fundamental freedoms declared in s. 1, in my opinion the section does not repeal such legislation either expressly or by implication. On the contrary, it expressly recognizes the continued existence of such legislation, but provides that it shall be construed and applied so as not to derogate from those rights and freedoms. By that it seems merely to provide a canon or rule of interpretation for such legislation. The very language of s. 2, 'be so construed and applied as not to abrogate' assumes that the prior Act may be sensibly construed and applied in a way that will avoid derogating from the rights and freedoms declared in s. 1. If the prior legislation cannot be so construed and applied sensibly, then the effect of s. 2 is exhausted, and the prior legislation must prevail according to its plain meaning."

With the greatest respect I find myself unable to agree with this view. The imperative words of s. 2 of the *Canadian Bill of Rights*, quoted above, appear to me to require the courts to refuse to apply any law, coming within the legislative authority of Parliament, which infringes freedom of religion unless it is expressly declared by an Act of Parliament that the law which does so infringe shall operate notwithstanding the *Canadian Bill of Rights*. As already pointed out s. 5 (2), quoted above, makes it plain that the *Canadian Bill of Rights* is to apply to all laws of Canada already in existence at the time it came into force as well as to those thereafter enacted. In my opinion where there is irreconcilable conflict between another Act of Parliament and the *Canadian Bill of Rights* the latter must prevail. . . .

. . . After a most anxious reconsideration of the whole question, in the light of the able arguments addressed to us by counsel, I have reached the conclusion that the view expressed by Davey, J.A., as he then was, in the words quoted above is the better one.

The question is whether or not it is the intention of parliament to confer the power and impose the responsibility upon the courts of declaring inoperative any provision in a statute of Canada, although expressed in clear and unequivocal terms, the meaning of which after calling in aid every rule of construction including that prescribed by sec. 2 of the Bill is perfectly plain, if in the view of the court it infringes any of the rights or freedoms declared by sec. 1 of the Bill.

In approaching this question it must not be forgotten that the responsibility mentioned above, if imposed at all, is imposed upon every justice of the peace, magistrate and judge of any court in the country who is called upon to apply a statute of Canada or any order, rule or regulation made thereunder.

If it were intended that the question should be answered in the affirmative there would, in my opinion, have been added after the word "declared" in the seventh line of the opening paragraph of sec. 2 of the Bill some such words as the following "and if any law of Canada cannot be so construed and applied it shall be regarded as inoperative or *pro tanto* repealed."

What now appears to me 'to have been the error in my reasoning in the passage from *Robertson and Rosetanni v. Reg.* quoted above is found in the statement that the Bill requires the courts to refuse to apply any law of Canada which is successfully impugned as infringing one of the declared rights or freedoms, whereas on the contrary, as Davey, J.A. had pointed out, the Bill directs the courts to apply such a law, not to refuse to apply it.

For these reasons I would dispose of the appeal as proposed by my brother Pigeon.

FAUTEUX, J. concurs with Ritchie, J.

ABBOTT, J. (dissenting) — The relevant facts, which are undisputed, are set out in the reasons of my brothers Ritchie and Pigeon which I have had the advantage of reading.

The interpretation of the *Canadian Bill of Rights*, 1960, ch. 44, adopted by the courts below, necessarily implies a wide delegation of the legislative authority of parliament to the courts. The power to make such a delegation cannot be questioned but, in my view, it would require the plainest words to impute to parliament an intention to extend to the courts such an invitation to engage in judicial legislation. I cannot find that intention expressed in sec. 2 of the Bill. On the contrary, I share the opinion expressed by the chief justice, by my brother Pigeon and by Davey, J.A., . . . that, with respect to existing legislation, the section provides merely a canon or rule of interpretation for such legislation.

I would dispose of the appeal as proposed by my brother Pigeon.

MARTLAND and JUDSON, JJ. concur with Ritchie, J.

RITCHIE, J. — This is an appeal brought with leave of this court from a judgment of the court of appeal for the Northwest Territories (1967) 61 WWR 370, dismissing an appeal by the crown from a judgment of Morrow, J. (1967) 60 WWR 321, of the territorial court of the Northwest Territories by which he had acquitted Joseph Drybones of being "unlawfully intoxicated off a reserve" contrary to sec. 94 (b) of the *Indian Act*, RSC, 1952, ch. 149, after having heard an appeal by way of trial *de novo* from a judgment of Anderson-Thompson, P.M. who had convicted the respondent of this offence and sentenced him to be fined $10 and costs and in default to spend three days in custody. The full charge against Drybones was that he:

"On or about the 8th of April, 1967 at Yellowknife in the Northwest Territories, being an Indian, was unlawfully intoxicated off a reserve, contrary to s. 94 (b) of the Indian Act."

The respondent is an Indian and he was indeed intoxicated on the evening of April 8, 1967, on the premises of the Old Stope Hotel in Yellowknife in the Northwest Territories, where there is no "reserve" within the meaning of the *Indian Act*.

When he was first arraigned before Anderson-Thompson, P.M., Drybones, who spoke no English, pleaded guilty to this offence, but on appeal to the territorial court, Morrow, J. found that there was some serious doubt as to whether he fully appreciated his plea in the lower court and he was allowed to withdraw that plea, whereafter the appeal proceeded as a trial *de novo* with a plea of not guilty. Sec. 94 of the *Indian Act* reads as follows:

"94. An Indian who

(a) has intoxicants in his possession,

(b) is intoxicated, or

(c) makes or manufactures intoxicants

"off a reserve, is guilty of an offence and is liable on summary conviction to a fine of not less than ten dollars and not more than fifty dollars or to imprisonment for a term not exceeding three months or to both fine and imprisonment."

I agree with the court of appeal (at p. 374) that the use of the words "off a reserve" creates

" . . . an essential element to be proved in any charge laid under sec. 94. But once it is proved, as it was in the present case, that the offense was not committed upon a reserve, the requirement of the section was satisfied. The fact that there are no reserves in the Territories is quite irrelevant.''

The important question raised by this appeal has its origin in the fact that in the Northwest Territories it is not an offence for anyone except an Indian to be intoxicated otherwise than in a public place. The *Liquor Ordinance*, RONWT, 1957, ch. 60, sec. 19(1), which is of general application in the Territories provides that: ''No person shall be in an intoxicated condition in a public place . . .'' but unlike sec. 94 of the *Indian Act*, there is no provision for a minimum fine and the maximum term of imprisonment is only 30 days as opposed to three months under the *Indian Act*.

The result is that an Indian who is intoxicated in his own home ''off a reserve'' is guilty of an offence and subject to a minimum fine of not less then $10 or a term of imprisonment not exceeding three months or both, whereas all other citizens in the Territories may, if they see fit, become intoxicated otherwise than in a public place without committing any offence at all. And even if any such other citizen is convicted of being intoxicated in a public place, the only penalty provided by the Ordinance is ''a fine not exceeding $50 or. . . . imprisonment for a term not exceeding 30 days or. . . . both fine and imprisonment.''

The argument which was successfully advanced by the respondent before Morrow, J. and before the court of appeal was that because of this legislation, Indians in the Northwest Territories, by reason of their race, are denied ''equality before the law'' with their fellow Canadians, and that sec. 94 (b) of the *Indian Act* therefore authorizes the abrogation, abridgement or infringement of one of the human rights and fundamental freedoms recognized and declared as existing in Canada without discrimination by reason of race, pursuant to the provisions of the *Canadian Bill of Rights*, 1960, ch. 44 (hereinafter sometimes referred to as ''the *Bill of Rights*'' or ''the Bill'') which provides, *inter alia*:

''1. It is hereby recognized and declared that in Canada there have existed and shall continue to exist without discrimination by reason of race, national origin, colour, religion or sex, the following human rights and fundamental freedoms, namely,
. . .

''(b) the right of the individual to equality before the law and the protection of the law;
. . .

''2. Every law of Canada shall, unless it is expressly declared by an Act of the Parliament of Canada that it shall operate notwithstanding the *Canadian Bill of Rights*, be so construed and applied as not to abrogate, abridge or infringe or to authorize the abrogation, abridgment or infringement of any of the rights or freedoms herein recognized and declared. . . .
. . .

''5. (2) The expression 'law of Canada' in Part I means an Act of the Parliament of Canada enacted before or after the coming into force of this Act, any order, rule or regulation thereunder, and any law in force in Canada or in any part of Canada at the commencement of this Act that is subject to be repealed, abolished or altered by the Parliament of Canada.''

The court of appeal agreed with Morrow, J. that sec. 94 (b) of the *Indian Act* is rendered inoperative by reason of this legislation and the notice to appeal to this court is limited to the single ground:

"That the Court of Appeal in the Northwest Territories in upholding the decision of the Territorial Court of the Northwest Territories erred in acquitting the respondent of 'an offense contrary to s. 94 (b) of the Indian Act, R.S.C. 1952 Ch. 149 on the ground that s. 94 of the Indian Act is rendered inoperative by reason of the Canadian Bill of Rights, Stat. Can. 1960 Ch. 44." . . .

. . . The question of whether sec. 94 of the *Indian Act* is rendered inoperative by reason of the provisions of the *Bill of Rights* on the ground that it abrogates, abridges or infringes the right of Canadians of the Indian race to "equality before the law" was considered by the court of appeal of British Columbia in *Re Indian Act; Reg. v. Gonzales* (1962) . . . where Tysoe, J.A., speaking for the majority of the court, concluded that:

"Sec. 94 (a) of the *Indian Act* does not abrogate or infringe the right of the appellant to "equality before the law" as I understand it. Sec. 2 of the *Canadian Bill of Rights* does not therefore affect it."

In reaching the same conclusion, Davey, J.A., as he then was, who wrote separate reasons for judgment from the other two members of the court, took the view that sec. 1 of the *Bill of Rights* should be treated as merely providing a canon of construction for the interpretation of legislation existing at the time when the statute was enacted. . . .

. . . This proposition appears to me to strike at the very foundations of the *Bill of Rights* and to convert it from its apparent character as a statutory declaration of the fundamental human rights and freedoms which it recognizes, into being little more than a rule for the construction of federal statutes, but as this approach has found favour with some eminent legal commentators, it seems to me to be important that priority should be given to a consideration of it.

I will hereafter refer to *Robertson and Rosetanni v. Regina* [1963], but in the present context I mention it only to say that, like the courts below, I agree with what was said by the present chief justice in his dissenting reasons for judgment when commenting on the above view expressed by Davey, J.A. He there said,

"With the greatest respect I find myself unable to agree with this view. The imperative words of s. 2 of the *Canadian Bill of Rights*, quoted above, appear to me to require the courts to refuse to apply any law, coming within the legislative authority of Parliament, which infringes freedom of religion unless it is expressly declared by an Act of Parliament that the law which does so infringe shall operate notwithstanding the *Canadian Bill of Rights*. As already pointed out s. 5 (2), quoted above, makes it plain that the *Canadian Bill of Rights* is to apply to all laws of Canada already in existence at the time it came into force as well as to those thereafter enacted. In my opinion where there is irreconcilable conflict between another Act of Parliament and the *Canadian Bill of Rights* the latter must prevail."

I do not find that this expression of opinion in any way conflicts with the reasoning of the majority of this court in *Robertson and Rosetanni v. Reg., supra*, which held that there was no conflict between the impugned section of the *Lord's Day Act*, RSC, 1952, ch. 171, and the *Bill of Rights*.

I am, however, with respect, of the opinion that Davey, J.A.'s reasoning is untenable on another ground. The result of that reasoning is to conclude that any law of Canada which can only be "construed and applied sensibly" so that it offends against the *Bill of Rights*, is to operate notwithstanding the provisions of that Bill. I am unable to reconcile this interpretation with the opening words of sec. 2 where it is provided that:

"Every law of Canada shall, *unless it is expressly declared by an Act of the Parliament of Canada that it shall operate notwithstanding the Canadian Bill of Rights*, be so construed and applied as not to abrogate. . . ." [The italics are my own].

If Davey, J.A.'s reasoning were correct and the *Bill of Rights* were to be construed as meaning that all laws of Canada which clearly offend the Bill were to operate notwithstanding its provisions, then the words which I have italicized in sec. 2 would be superfluous unless it be suggested that parliament intended to reserve unto itself the right to exclude from the effect of the *Bill of Rights* only such statutes as are unclear in their meaning.

It seems to me that a more realistic meaning must be given to the words in question and they afford, in my view, the clearest indication that sec. 2 is intended to mean and does mean that if a law of Canada cannot be "sensibly construed and applied" so that it does not abrogate, abridge or infringe one of the rights and freedoms recognized and declared by the Bill, then such law is inoperative "unless it is expressly declared by an Act of the parliament of Canada that it shall operate notwithstanding the *Canadian Bill of Rights*."

I think a declaration by the courts that a section or portion of a section of a statute is inoperative is to be distinguished from the repeal of such a section and is to be confined to the particular circumstances of the case in which the declaration is made. The situation appears to me to be somewhat analogous to a case where valid provincial legislation in an otherwise unoccupied field ceases to be operative by reason of conflicting federal legislation.

I think it is desirable at this stage to deal with the submission made on behalf of the appellant to the effect that the rights and freedoms recognized and declared by the *Bill of Rights* must have reference *and be circumscribed by* the laws of Canada as they existed on August 10, 1960, when the Bill was passed, which laws included sec. 94 of the *Indian Act*. This submission is based in large measure on the following paragraph from the reasons for judgment of this court in *Robertson and Rosetanni v. Reg., supra*, where it was said:

"It is to be noted at the outset that the *Canadian Bill of Rights* is not concerned with 'human rights and fundamental freedoms' in any abstract sense, but rather with such 'rights and freedoms' as existed in Canada immediately before the statute was enacted. (See also s. 5 [1]). It is therefore the 'religious freedom' then existing in this country that is safe-guarded by the provisions of s. 2. . . ."

What was at issue in that case was whether the *Lord's Day Act*, in providing that "it shall be unlawful for any person on the Lord's Day . . . to carry on or transact any business of his ordinary calling . . . abrogated, abridged or infringed the right to "freedom of religion," and it was contended on behalf of the appellant (at p.657) that the phrase "freedom of religion" as used in the *Bill of Rights* meant "freedom to enjoy the freedom which my own religion allows without being confined by restrictions imposed by Parliament for the purpose of enforcing the tenets of a faith to which I do not subscribe." In considering this contention, it became necessary to examine the decided cases in order to determine what was the accepted meaning of "freedom of religion" as it existed in Canada immediately before the *Bill of Rights* was enacted and the last-quoted excerpt from the reasons for judgment must, in my view, be read in this sense. This appears to me to be confirmed by the succeeding paragraph of these reasons where it is said at p. 655:

"It is accordingly of first importance to understand the concept of religious freedom which was recognized in this country before the enactment of the *Canadian Bill of Rights* and after the enactment of the *Lord's Day Act* in its present form. . . ."

If it had been accepted that the rights to "freedom of religion" as declared in the *Bill of Rights* was circumscribed by the provisions of the Canadian statutes in force at the date of its enactment, there would have been no need, in determining the validity of the *Lord's Day Act*, to consider the authorities in order to examine the situation in light of the concept of religious freedom which was recognized in Canada at the time of the enactment of the *Bill of Rights*. It would have been enough to say that "freedom of religion" as used in the Bill must mean freedom of religion subject to the provisions of the *Lord's Day Act*. This construction would, however, have run contrary to the provisions of sec. 5 (2) of the Bill which makes it applicable to every "Act of the Parliament of Canada enacted before or after the coming into force of this Act."

In any event, it was not necessary to decide this question in *Robertson and Rosetanni v. Reg.* because it was found that the impugned provisions of the *Lord's Day Act* and the *Bill of Rights* were not in conflict, and I accordingly do not consider that case to be any authority for the suggestion that the *Bill of Rights* is to be treated as being subject to federal legislation existing at the time of its enactment, and more particularly I do not consider that the provisions of sec. 1 (b) of the *Bill of Rights* are to be treated as being in any way limited or affected by the terms of sec. 94 (b) of the *Indian Act*.

The right which is here at issue is "the right of the individual to equality before the law and the protection of the law." Tysoe, J.A., who wrote the reasons for judgment on behalf of the majority of the court of appeal of British

Columbia in the *Gonzales* case, *supra*, expressed the opinion (at p. 264) that as these words occur in the *Bill of Rights* they mean:

> ". . . a right in every person to *whom a particular law relates or extends*, no matter what may be a person's race, national origin, colour, religion or sex, to stand on an equal footing with every other person to whom that particular law relates or extends, and a right to the protection of the law." [The italics are Tysoe, J.A.'s]

Like the members of the courts below, I cannot agree with this interpretation pursuant to which it seems to me that the most glaring discriminatory legislation against a racial group would have to be construed as recognizing the right of each of its individual members "to equality before the law," so long as all the other members are being discriminated against in the same way.

I think that the word "law" as used in sec. 1 (b) of the *Bill of Rights* is to be construed as meaning " the law of Canada" as defined in sec. 5 (2) (i.e., Acts of the parliament of Canada and any orders, rules or regulations thereunder) and without attempting any exhaustive definition of "equality before the law" I think that the sec. 1 (b) means at least that no individual or group of individuals is to be treated more harshly than another under the law, and I am therefore of opinion that an individual is denied equality before the law if it is made an offence punishable at law, on account of his race, for him to do something which his fellow Canadians are free to do without having committed any offence or having been made subject to any penalty.

It is only necessary for the purpose of deciding this case for me to say that in my opinion sec. 94 (b) of the *Indian Act* is a law of Canada which creates such an offence and that it can only be construed in such manner that its application would operate so as to abrogate, abridge or infringe one of the rights declared and recognized by the *Bill of Rights*. For the reasons which I have indicated, I am therefore of opinion that sec. 94 (b) is inoperative.

For the purpose of determining the issue raised by this appeal it is unnecessary to express any opinion respecting the operation of any other section of the *Indian Act*.

For all the above reasons I would dismiss this appeal. . . .

. . . HALL, J. — I agree with the reasons of my brother Ritchie and wish only to add some observations regarding the decision in *Re Indian Act; Reg. v. Gonzales* (1962) 37 WWR 257, 37 CR 56, 132 CCC 237, affirming (1961) 35 WWR 703, 35 CR 320, 130 CCC 400.

The concept that the *Canadian Bill of Rights*, 1960, ch. 44, is operative in the face of a law of Canada only when that law does not give equality to all persons within the class to whom that particular law extends or relates, as it was expressed by Tysoe, J.A. at p. 264:

> "Coming now to sec. 1 (b) of the *Canadian Bill of Rights*. The meaning of the word 'equality' is well known. In my opinion, the word 'before' in the expression 'equality before the law,' in the sense in which that expression is used in sec. 1 (b) means 'in the presence of.'

It seems to me this is the key to the correct interpretation of the expression and makes it clear that 'equality before the law' has nothing to do with the application of the law equally to everyone and equal laws for everyone in the sense for which appellant's counsel contends, namely, the same laws for all persons, but to the position occupied by persons to whom a law relates or extends. They shall be entitled to have the law as it exists applied equally and without fear or favour to all persons to whom it relates or extends."

is analogous to the position taken by the Supreme Court of the United States in *Plessy v. Ferguson* (1896) 163 US 537, 16 S Ct 1138, 41 L Ed 256, and which was wholly rejected by the same court in its historic desegregation judgment, *Brown v. Board of Education of Topeka* (1953) 347 US 483, 74 S Ct 686, 98 L Ed 873.

In *Plessy v. Ferguson* the court had held that, under the "separate but equal" doctrine, equality of treatment is accorded when the races are provided substantially equal facilities even though these facilities be separate. In *Brown v. Board of Education* the court held the "separate but equal" doctrine to be totally invalid.

The social situations in *Brown v. Board of Education* and in the instant case are, of course, very different, but the basic philosophic concept is the same. The *Canadian Bill of Rights* is not fulfilled if it merely equates Indians with Indians in terms of equality before the law, but can have validity and meaning only when, subject to the single exception set out in sec. 2, it is seen to repudiate discrimination in every law of Canada by reason of race, national origin, colour, religion or sex in respect of the human rights and fundamental freedoms set out in sec. 1 in whatever way that discrimination may manifest itself, not only as between Indian and Indian, but as between all Canadians, whether Indian or non-Indian.

SPENCE, J. concurs with Ritchie, J.

PIGEON, J. (dissenting) — . . . The question before us is essentially whether, in respect of existing federal legislation, sec. 2 of the Bill enacts a canon of construction or casts upon the courts the task of removing therefrom, whenever the question is raised, every provision that may be considered as being in conflict with the enumerated rights and freedoms. . . .

In considering the provisions just quoted, one must observe that the Bill itself begins by a solemn declaration by parliament in the form of an enactment that, in Canada, the enumerated rights and freedoms "have existed and shall continue exist. . . ." This statement is the essential element of the very first provision of the Bill and it is absolutely unqualified. It is the starting point of that legislation and I have great difficulty in reconciling it with the contention that in fact these rights and freedoms were not wholly and completely existing but were restricted by any number of statutory and other provisions infringing thereon.

There can be no doubt that in enacting legislation parliament is presumed to be aware of the state of the law: *Walker v. Reg.* 1939. *A fortiori* must it be so when the enactment itself has reference thereto. Where is the extent of existing human rights and fundamental freedoms to be ascertained if not by reference to the statute books and other legislative instruments as well as to the decisions of the courts?

It must also be considered that the rights and freedoms enumerated in sec. 1 are not legal concepts of precise and invariable content. If those words were to be taken by themselves, a great deal would be left undefined. However, by declaring those rights and freedoms as they existed a large measure of precision was supplied. Is this not an important purpose of sec. 1 and a very effective way of defining some key words of the enactment?

In the instant case, the question whether all existing legislation should be considered as in accordance with the nondiscrimination principle cannot fail to come immediately to mind, seeing that it arises directly out of head (24) of sec. 91 of the *B.N.A. Act, 1867*, whereby parliament has exclusive legislative authority over "Indians, and lands reserved for the Indians." As was pointed out by Riddell, J. in *Rex v. Martin* (1917), this provision confers legislative authority over the Indians *qua* Indians and not otherwise. Its very object, in so far as it relates to Indians, as opposed to lands reserved for the Indians, is to enable the parliament of Canada to make legislation applicable only to Indians as such and therefore not applicable to Canadian citizens generally. This legislative authority is obviously intended to be exercised over matters that are, as regards persons other than Indians, within the exclusive legislative authority of the provinces. Complete uniformity in provincial legislation is clearly not to be expected, not to mention the fact that further diversity must also result from special legislation for the Territories. Equality before the law in the sense in which it was understood in the courts below would require the Indians to be subject in every province to the same rules of law as all others in every particular, not merely on the question of drunkenness. Outside the Territories, provincial jurisdiction over education and health facilities would make it very difficult for federal authorities to provide such facilities to Indians without "discrimination" as understood in the courts below.

If one of the effects of the *Canadian Bill of Rights* is to render inoperative all legal provisions whereby Indians as such are not dealt with in the same way as the general public, the conclusion is inescapable that parliament, by the enactment of the Bill, has not only fundamentally altered the status of the Indians in that indirect fashion but has also made any future use of federal legislative authority over them subject to the requirement of expressly declaring every time "that the law shall operate notwithstanding the *Canadian Bill of Rights*." I find it very difficult to believe that parliament so intended when enacting the Bill. If a virtual suppression of federal legislation over Indians as such was meant, one would have expected this important change to be made explicitly, not surreptitiously, so to speak. . . .

. . . The meaning of such expressions as "due process of law," "equality before the law," "freedom of religion," "freedom of speech," is in truth largely unlimited and undefined. According to individual views and the evolution of current ideas, the actual content of such legal concepts is apt to expand and to vary as is strikingly apparent in other countries. In the traditional

British system that is our own by virtue of the *B.N.A. Act, 1867*, the responsibility for updating the statutes in this changing world rests exclusively upon parliament. If the parliament of Canada intended to depart from that principle in enacting the Bill, one would expect to find clear language expressing that intention. On the contrary, what do we find in sec. 1 but an apparent desire to adhere to the traditional principle and to avoid the uncertainties inherent in broadly-worded enactments by tying the broad words to the large body of existing law and in effect declaring the recognized human rights and fundamental freedoms to be as existing in the laws of Canada.

I fail to see how it can be considered that by taking this to be the fundamental intention, the apparent character of the Bill is not fully recognized. I also fail to see how it can be said that to read sec. 2 as little more than a rule of construction is to fail to give effect to the Bill. On what basis is it assumed that anything else was intended in an Act that is not of a constitutional character?

That canons of construction are of less importance than constitutional rules does not mean that they are of minimal importance. For instance, in our legal system, the rule against retrospective operation of enactments as well as the principle that a criminal offense requires *mens rea* are nothing more than canons of construction. It certainly does not mean that they are of secondary importance. Decisions such as *Beaver v. Reg.* [1957], clearly show how far-reaching such principles are. If the Canadian parliament should consider it desirable to enshrine them in a statute, would it be contended that those who subsequently read it as not altering their fundamental nature and letting them remain canons of construction are failing to give it effect?

On the whole, I cannot find in the *Canadian Bill of Rights* anything clearly showing that parliament intended to establish concerning human rights and fundamental freedoms some overriding general principles to be enforced by the courts against the clearly expressed will of parliament in statutes existing at the time. In my opinion, parliament did nothing more than instruct the courts to construe and apply those laws in accordance with the principles enunciated in the Bill on the basis that the recognized rights and freedoms did exist, not that they were to be brought into existence by the courts.

For those reasons I would allow the appeal, reverse the judgments of the court of appeal and of the territorial court of the Northwest Territories, and re-establish the conviction and sentence. In view of the terms of the order granting leave to appeal, it is presumed that suitable arrangements have been made for the costs of representation of the respondent and, therefore, no order requires to be made in that regard.

Since writing the above I have had the advantage of reading the reasons of the chief justice and I wish to add that I agree with his observations entirely.

# 11.6

## ATTORNEY-GENERAL OF CANADA v. LAVELL AND BEDARD

Supreme Court of Canada (1974)


FAUTEUX, C.J.C., concurs with RITCHIE, J.

ABBOTT, J. (dissenting): — The facts which are not in dispute are set out in the reasons of Ritchie and Laskin, JJ., which I have had the advantage of reading. I am in agreement with the reasons of Laskin, J., and wish to add only a few observations.

I share his view that the decision of this Court in *R. v. Drybones* (1969), cannot be distinguished from the two cases under appeal although in these two appeals the consequences of the discrimination by reason of sex under s. 12(1)(b) of the *Indian Act*, R.S.C. 1970, c. I-6, are more serious than the relatively minor penalty for the drinking offence under s. 94 of the Act which was in issue in *Drybones*.

In that case, this Court rejected the contention that s. 1 of the *Canadian Bill of Rights* provided merely a canon of construction for the interpretation of legislation existing when the Bill was passed. With respect I cannot interpret "equality before the law" as used in s. 1(b) of the Bill as meaning simply "the equal subjection of all classes to the ordinary law of the land as administered by the ordinary courts" to use the language of Dicey which is quoted in the reasons of Ritchie, J. . . . .

. . . In my view the *Canadian Bill of Rights* has substantially affected the doctrine of the supremacy of Parliament. Like any other statute it can of course be repealed or amended, or a particular law declared to be applicable notwithstanding the provisions of the Bill. In form the supremacy of Parliament is maintained but in practice I think that it has been substantially curtailed. In my opinion that result is undesirable, but that is a matter for consideration by Parliament not the Courts. . . .

MARTLAND AND JUDSON, JJ., concur with RITCHIE, J.

RITCHIE,J.: — . . . These appeals, which were heard together, are from two judgments holding that the provisions of s. 12(1)(b) of the *Indian Act*, R.S.C. 1970, c. I-6, are rendered inoperative by s. 1(b) of the *Canadian Bill of Rights*, R.S.C. 1970, App. III, as denying equality before the law to the two respondents.

Both respondents were registered Indians and "Band" members within the meaning of s. 11 (b) of the *Indian Act* when they elected to marry non-Indians and thereby relinquished their status as Indians in conformity with the said s. 12(1)(b) which reads as follows:

12(1)  The following persons are not entitled to be registered, namely,
   (b)  A woman who married a person who is not an Indian, unless that woman is subsequently the wife or widow of a person described in section 11.

It is contended on behalf of both respondents that s. 12(1)(b) of the Act should be held to be inoperative as discriminating between Indian men and women and as being in conflict with the provisions of the *Canadian Bill of Rights* and particularly s. 1 thereof which provides:

1.  It is hereby recognized and declared that in Canada there have existed and shall continue to exist without discrimination by reason of race, national origin, colour, religion or sex, the following human rights and fundamental freedoms, namely,
   (b)  the right of the individual to equality before the law and the protection of the law; . . . .

. . . The contention which formed the basis of the argument submitted by both respondents was that they had been denied equality before the law *by reason of sex*, and I propose to deal with the matter on this basis. . . .

. . . In my view the meaning to be given to the language employed in the *Bill of Rights* is the meaning which it bore in Canada at the time when the Bill was enacted, and it follows that the phrase "equality before the law" is to be construed in light of the law existing in Canada at that time.

In considering the meaning to be attached to "equality before the law" as those words occur in s. 1(b) of the Bill, I think it important to point out that in my opinion this phrase is not effective to invoke the egalitarian concept exemplified by the 14th Amendment of the U.S. Constitution as interpreted by the Courts of that country: see *R. v. Smythe* (1971). I think rather that, having regard to the language employed in the second paragraph of the preamble to the *Bill of Rights*, the phrase "equality before the law" as used in s. 1 is to be read in its context as a part of "the rule of law" to which overriding authority is accorded by the terms of that paragraph.

In this connection I refer to *Stephen's Commentaries on the Laws of England*, 21st ed., vol. III (1950), where it is said at p. 337:

Now the great constitutional lawyer Dicey, writing in 1885 was so deeply impressed by the absence of arbitrary . . . governments present and past, that he coined the phrase "the rule of law" to express the regime under which Englishmen lived; and he tried to give precision to it in the following words which have exercised a profound influence on all subsequent thought and conduct.
"That the 'rule of law,' which forms a fundamental principle of the constitution has three meanings, or may be regarded from three different points of view."

The second meaning proposed by Dicey is the one with which we are here concerned and it was stated in the following terms:

It means again equality before the law or the equal subjection of all classes to the ordinary law of the land administered by the ordinary courts; the "rule of law" in this sense excludes the idea of any exemption of officials or others from the duty of obedience to the law which governs other citizens or from the jurisdiction of the ordinary courts.

"Equality before the law" in this sense is frequently invoked to demonstrate that the same law applies to the highest official of Government as to any other ordinary citizen, and in this regard Professor F.R. Scott, in delivering the Plaunt Memorial Lectures on *Civil Liberties and Canadian Federalism* (1959), speaking of the case of *Roncarelli v. Duplessis* (1959), had occasion to say:

> . . . it is always a triumph for the law to show that it is applied equally to all without fear or favour. This is what we mean when we say that all are equal before the law.

The relevance of these quotations to the present circumstances is that "equality before the law" as recognized by Dicey as a segment of the rule of law, carries the meaning of equal subjection of all classes to the ordinary law of the land *as administered by the ordinary Courts*, and in my opinion the phrase "equality before the law" as employed in s. 1(b) of the *Bill of Rights* is to be treated as meaning equality in the administration or application of the law by the law enforcement authorities and the ordinary Courts of the land. This construction is, in my view, supported by the provisions of paras. (a) to (g) of s. 2 of the Bill which clearly indicate to me that it was equality in the administration and enforcement of the law with which Parliament was concerned when it guaranteed the continued existence of "equality before the law.". . .

. . . These were the provisions that were at issue in the case of *R. v. Drybones* (1969), 9 D.L.R. (3d) 473, [1970] 3 C.C.C. 355, [1970] S.C.R. 282, where this Court held that they could not be construed and applied without exposing Indians as a racial group to a penalty in respect of conduct as to which the Parliament of Canada had imposed no sanctions on other Canadians who were subject to Canadian laws regulating their conduct, which were of general application in the Northwest Territories where the offence was allegedly committed and in which there are no Indian reserves.

In that case the decision of the majority of this Court was that the provisions of s. 94(b), as it then was, could not be enforced without bringing about inequality between one group of citizens and another and that this inequality was occasioned by reason of the race of the accused. It was there said, at pp. 484-5:

> . . . I am . . . of opinion that an individual is denied equality before the law if it is made an offence punishable at law, on account of his race, for him to do something which his fellow Canadians are free to do without having committed any offence or having been made subject to any penalty.

> It is only necessary for the purpose of deciding this case for me to say that in my opinion s. 94(b) of the *Indian Act* is a law of Canada which creates such an offence and that it can only be construed in such manner that its application would operate so as to abrogate, abridge or infringe one of the rights declared and recognized by the *Bill of Rights*. For the reasons which I have indicated, I am therefore of opinion that s. 94(b) is inoperative.

> For the purpose of determining the issue raised by this appeal it is unnecessary to express any opinion respecting the operation of any other section of the *Indian Act*. . . .

Having regard to the express reservations contained in these passages, I have difficulty in understanding how that case can be construed as having decided that any sections of the *Indian Act*, except s. 94 (b) are rendered inoperative by the *Bill of Rights*.

The *Drybones* case can, in my opinion, have no application to the present appeals as it was in no way concerned with the internal regulation of the lives of Indians *on* reserves or their right to the use and benefit of Crown lands thereon, but rather deals exclusively with the effect of the *Bill of Rights* on a section of the *Indian Act* creating a crime with attendant penalties for the conduct by Indians *off* a reserve in an area where non-Indians, who were also governed by federal law, were not subject to any such restriction.

The fundamental distinction between the present case and that of *Drybones*, however, appears to me to be that the impugned section in the latter case could not be enforced without denying equality of treatment in the administration and enforcement of the law before the ordinary Courts of the land to a racial group, whereas no such inequality of treatment between Indian men and women flows as a necessary result of the application of s. 12(1) (b) of the *Indian Act*.

To summarize the above, I am of opinion:

1. that the *Bill of Rights* is not effective to render inoperative legislation, such as s. 12(1)(b) of the *Indian Act*, passed by the Parliament of Canada in discharge of its constitutional function under s. 91(24) of the *British North American Act, 1867*, to specify how and by whom Crown lands reserved for Indians are to be used;

2. that the *Bill of Rights* does not require federal legislation to be declared inoperative unless it offends against one of the rights specifically guaranteed by s. 1, but where legislation is found to be discriminatory, this affords an added reason for rendering it ineffective;

3. that equality before the law under the *Bill of Rights* means equality of treatment in the enforcement and application of the laws of Canada before the law enforcement authorities and the ordinary Courts of the land, and no such inequality is necessarily entailed in the construction and application of s. 12(1)(b) . . . .

HALL and SPENCE, JJ., concur with LASKIN, J.

PIGEON, J.: — I agree in the result with Ritchie, J. I certainly cannot disagree with the view I did express in *R. v. Drybones* (1969), that the enactment of the *Canadian Bill of Rights* was not intended to effect a virtual suppression of federal legislation over Indians. My difficulty is Laskin, J.'s strongly reasoned opinion that, unless we are to depart from what was said by the majority in *Drybones*, these appeals should be dismissed because, if discrimination by reason of race makes certain statutory provisions inoperative, the same result must follow as to statutory provisions which exhibit discrimination by reason of sex. In the end, it appears to me that, in the circumstances, I need not reach a firm conclusion on that point. Assuming the situation is such as Laskin, J., says, it cannot be improper for me to adhere to what was my dissenting view, when a majority of those who did not agree with it in respect of a particular section of the *Indian Act*, R.S.C. 1970, c. I-6, now adopt it for the main body of this important statute. . . .

LASKIN, J. (dissenting): — . . .In my opinion, unless we are to depart from what was said in *Drybones*, both appeals now before us must be dismissed. I have no disposition to reject what was decided in *Drybones*; and on the central issue of prohibited discrimination as catalogued in s. 1 of the *Canadian Bill of Rights*, it is, in my opinion, impossible to distinguish *Drybones* from the two cases in appeal. If, as in *Drybones*, discrimination by reasons of race makes certain statutory provisions inoperative, the same result must follow as to statutory provisions which exhibit discrimination by reasons of sex.

The issues in both appeals are, in the main, as simple as that. They focus on s. 12(1)(b) of the *Indian Act*, R.S.C. 1970, c. I-6, which is as follows:

12(1)  The following persons are not entitled to be registered, namely,
    (b) a woman who married a person who is not an Indian, unless that woman is subsequently the wife or widow of a person described in section 11.

There are other provisions of the Act to which I will refer later in these reasons but for the moment it is enough to say that no similar disqualification is visited upon an Indian man who marries a non-Indian woman. . . .

. . . The contentions of the appellants in both cases in appeal, stripped of their detail, amount to a submission that the *Canadian Bill of Rights* does not apply to Indians on a reserve nor to Indians in their relations to one another whether or not on a reserve. This submission does not deny that the effect of s. 12(1)(b) of the *Indian Act* is to prescribe substantive discrimination by reason of sex, a differentiation in the treatment of Indian men and Indian women when they marry non-Indians, this differentiation being exhibited in the loss by the women of their status as Indians under the Act. It does, however, involve the assertion that the particular discrimination upon which the two appeals are focused is not offensive to the relevant provisions of the *Canadian Bill of Rights*; and it also involves the assertion that the *Drybones* case is distinguishable, or, if not, that it has been overcome by the re-enactment of the *Indian Act* in the Revised Statutes of Canada, 1970, including the then s. 94 (now s. 95) which was in issue in that case. I regard this last-mentioned assertion, which is posited on the fact that the *Canadian Bill of Rights* was not so re-enacted, as simply an oblique appeal for the overruling of the *Drybones* case.

The *Drybones* case decided two things. It decided first — and this decision was a necessary basis for the second point in it — that the *Canadian Bill of Rights* was more than a mere interpretation statute whose terms would yield to a contrary intention; it had paramount force when a federal enactment conflicted with its terms, and it was the incompatible federal enactment which had to give way. This was the issue upon which the then Chief Justice of this Court, Chief Justice Cartwright, and Justices Abbott and Pigeon, dissented. Pigeon, J., fortified his view on this main point by additional observations, bringing into consideration *inter alia*, s. 91(24) of the *British North American Act, 1867*. The second thing decided by *Drybones* was that the accused in that case, an Indian under the *Indian Act*, was denied equality before the law, under s. 1(b) of the *Canadian Bill of Rights*, when it was made a punishable offence for him on account of his race, to do something which his fellow Canadians were free to do without being liable to punishment for an offence. Ritchie, J., who delivered the majority opinion of the Court, reiterated this basis of decision by concluding his reasons as follows:

> It appears to me to be desirable to make it plain that these reasons for judgment are limited to a situation in which, under the laws of Canada, it is made an offence punishable at law on account of race, for a person to do something which all Canadians who are not members of that race may do with impunity . . .

It would be unsupportable in principle to view the *Drybones* case as turning on the fact that the challenged s. 94 of the *Indian Act* created an offence visited by punishment. The gist of the judgment lay in the legal disability imposed upon a person by reason of his race when other persons were under no similar restraint. If for the words ''on account of race'' there are substituted the words ''on account of sex'' the result must surely be the same where a federal enactment imposes disabilities or prescribed disqualifications for members of the female sex which are not imposed upon members of the male sex in the same circumstances.

It is said, however, that although this may be so as between males and females in general, it does not follow where the distinction on the basis of sex is limited as here to members of the Indian race. This, it is said further, does not offend the guarantee of ''equality before the law'' upon which the *Drybones* case proceeded. I wish to deal with these two points in turn and to review, in connection with the first point, the legal consequences for an Indian woman under the *Indian Act* when she marries an non-Indian.

It appears to me that the contention that a differentiation on the basis of sex is not offensive to the *Canadian Bill of Rights* where that differentiation operates only among Indians under the *Indian Act* is one that compounds racial inequality even beyond the point that the *Drybones* case found unacceptable. In any event, taking the *Indian Act* as it stands, as a law of Canada whose various provisions fall to be assessed under the *Canadian Bill of Rights*, I am unable to appreciate upon what basis the command of the *Canadian Bill of Rights*, that laws of Canada shall operate without discrimination by reason of sex, can be ignored in the operation of the *Indian Act*. . . .

. . . Section 12(1)(b) effects a statutory excommunication of Indian women from this society but not of Indian men. Indeed, as was pointed out by counsel for the Native Council of Canada, the effect of ss. 11 and 12(1)(b) is to excommunicate the children of a union of an Indian woman with a non-Indian. There is also the invidious distinction, invidious at least in the light of the *Canadian Bill of Rights*, that the *Indian Act* creates between brothers and sisters who are Indians and who respectively marry non-Indians. . . .

. . . I do not think it is possible to leap over the telling words of s. 1, "without discrimination by reason of race, national origin, colour, religion or sex," in order to explain away any such discrimination by invoking the words "equality before the law" in para. (b) and attempting to make them alone the touchstone of reasonable classification. That was not done in the *Drybones* case; and this Court made it clear in *Curr v. The Queen* (1972), 26 D.L.R. (3d) 603, 7 C.C.C. (2d) 181, [1972] S.C.R. 889, that federal legislation, which might be compatible with the command of "equality before the law"· taken alone, may none the less be inoperative if it manifests any of the prohibited forms of discrimination. In short the proscribed discriminations in s. 1 have a force either independent of the subsequently enumerated paras. (a) to (f) or, if they are found in any federal legislation, they offend those clauses because each must be read as if the prohibited forms of discrimination were recited therein as a part thereof. . . .

. . . In my opinion, the appellants' contentions gain no additional force because the *Indian Act*, including the challenged s. 12(1)(b) thereof, is a fruit of the exercise of Parliament's exclusive legislative power in relation to "Indians, and Lands reserved for the Indians" under s. 91(24) of the *British North American Act, 1867*. Discriminatory treatment on the basis of race or colour or sex does not inhere in that grant of legislative power. The fact that its exercise may be attended by forms of discrimination prohibited by the *Canadian Bill of Rights* is no more a justification for a breach of the *Canadian Bill of Rights* than there would be in the case of the exercise of any other head of federal legislative power involving provisions offensive to the *Canadian Bill of Rights*. The majority opinion in the *Drybones* case dispels any attempt to rely on the grant of legislative power as a ground for escaping from the force of the *Canadian Bill of Rights*. The latter does not differentiate among the various heads of legislative power; it embraces all exercises under whatever head or heads they arise. . . .

. . . I would dismiss both appeals with costs.

# 11.7

# A CONSTITUTIONAL DECLARATION OF RIGHTS

Pierre Elliot Trudeau (1967)

Of all the problems that Canadian public opinion is currently concerned with, the one that is most frequently debated, the one that brings forth the strongest expressions of view, is that of constitutional reform.

Although the subject is one of serious proportion, it is nevertheless one on which I should like to express some thoughts to you.

. . . We must recognize that the constitution is the country's fundamental law, the law on which our entire judicial system is based. If the constitution of a country collapses, or if its authority is seriously challenged, ordinary law loses its power to command and society itself is propelled toward anarchy.

For this reason men who are free — and who are anxious to remain so — do not lightly undermine the constitutional framework of a democratic country. They only approach it "with fear and trembling." For this reason, among others, I have personally resisted what, if it has not become a mania, might be termed a fashion of constitutional iconoclasm. . . . While I wished to reflect upon the matter, it was not the possibility of change itself that displeased me. On the contrary, I have always been convinced that we, men of the law, should not only advocate respect for the constitution, but also encourage its development.

In a submission presented to the Tremblay Commission in 1955, I wrote:

> The Province [of Quebec] could well declare herself ready to accept the incorporation of a declaration of human rights in the constitution on the condition that the rights of disallowance and reservation be done away with. The Province could suggest a precise plan for repatriating the Canadian constitution, including in it a method of amendment, on the condition that the Senate be turned into a body more federalist and less unitary and on condition that the organization of the Supreme Court be made to depend directly on the Canadian constitution rather than solely on federal law.

Six years later, in *Social Purpose of Canada*, I again took up the same kind of propositions. And ten years later, at the beginning of 1965, in a paper prepared for eventual presentation to the Committee of the Quebec Legislature set up to examine the constitution, I made similar suggestions, adding:

*Federalism and the French Canadians.* Toronto: MacMillan, 1968, p.52. Reprinted with permission.

I do not accord an absolute and eternal value to the political structures or the constitutional forms of states. . . . With the exception of a certain number of basic principles that must be safeguarded, such as liberty and democracy, the rest ought to be adapted to the circumstances of history, to traditions, to geography, to cultures and to civilizations.

As Thomas Jefferson said about the Constitution of the United States: "Nothing then is unchangeable but the inherent and unalienable rights of man.". . .

. . . And this is what prompts me to say a few words about the policy of the present Liberal government in constitutional matters. . . .

. . . We have not confined our activities in the constitutional field to these studies. While this work has been going on, ministers and officials have been looking for the best basis on which to begin a dialogue on constitutional reform between the federal government and the provincial governments. We have reached the conclusion that the basis most likely to find a wide degree of acceptance, and one that is in itself a matter calling for urgent attention, is a constitutional Bill of Rights — a Bill that would guarantee the fundamental freedoms of the citizen from interference, whether federal or provincial, and that would have a high degree of permanence in that neither Parliament nor the Legislatures would be able to modify its terms by the ordinary legislative process.

As lawyers, you will appreciate that the adoption of a constitutional Bill of Rights is intimately related to the whole question of constitutional reform. Essentially, we will be testing — and, hopefully, establishing — the unity of Canada. If we reach agreement on the fundamental rights of the citizen, on their definition and protection in all parts of Canada, we shall have taken a major first step toward basic constitutional reform. . . .

. . . Much useful work has already been done in the field of civil rights in Canada, particularly in connection with the enactment of the Canadian Bill of Rights in 1960. We are now aiming at a new Bill which will be broader in scope and will be firmly entrenched in the constitution. The Canadian Bill of Rights sets out the legal rights of the citizen in respect of life, liberty, and the security of the person, and such basic political rights as freedom of speech and of the press, freedom of religion, and freedom of assembly. There are also various provincial statutes affording protection against discrimination and invasions of human rights. All of these measures are, however, statutory in character and they do not preclude future encroachments on these rights by Parliament or the Legislatures. They may be amended in the same way as any other statute. Moreover, they do not cover certain rights which are of special concern to a country like Canada, founded on two distinct linguistic groups.

Accordingly, we envision a Bill of Rights that will be broader in scope than the existing legislation. We all agree on the familiar basic rights — freedom of belief and expression, freedom of association, the right to a fair trial and to fair legal procedures generally. We would also expect a guarantee against discrimination on the basis of race, religion, sex, ethnic or national origin.

These are the rights commonly protected by bills of rights. They are basic for any society of free men.

But there are rights of special importance to Canada arising, as I have said, from the fact that this country is founded on two distinct linguistic groups. While language is the basic instrument for preserving and developing the cultural integrity of a people, the language provisions of the British North America Act are very limited. I believe that we require a broader definition and more extensive guarantees in the matter of recognition of the two official languages. The right to learn and to use either of the two official languages should be recognized. Without this, we cannot assure every Canadian of an equal opportunity to participate in the political, cultural, economic, and social life of this country. I venture to say that, if we are able to reach agreement on this vital aspect of the over-all problem, we will have found a solution to a basic issue facing Canada today. A constitutional change recognizing broader rights with respect to the two official languages would add a new dimension to Confederation.

If we agree on the general content of a constitutional Bill of Rights, a number of important questions will remain to be resolved. These will be important for everyone but, from a technical point of view, they will be of special concern to those who, like ourselves, are trained in the law. Should the rights be declared generally, or defined precisely with exceptions clearly specified? For example, if we guarantee freedom of speech without qualification, will this invalidate some of our laws which deal with obscenity, sedition, defamation, or film censorship? Is freedom of religion compatible with compulsory Sunday-closing legislation? What of a constitutional guarantee of "due process of law"? In the United States, this phrase has, in the past, created many problems because of its vagueness. At times, the courts have construed it so broadly as to invalidate some social legislation which we would now accept as essential. Should we avoid the possibility of such an interpretation of "due process" in Canada by using a more precise term to guarantee the rule of law? What of the right to counsel? Should this "right" impose a duty on the government to provide counsel for those who cannot afford it? If we recognize the right of every person to use and to be educated in either of the two official languages, should we limit the exercise of this right to places where there is a concentration of one or the other language group?

These are some of the questions which will arise as we try to develop a constitutional Bill of Rights. I mention them here, not because I expect immediate answers, but to illustrate the complexities involved in any basic constitutional reform. . . .

. . . I envision a Bill of Rights that will not only be broader in scope than the existing legislation but will also be firmly entrenched constitutionally. The Canadian Bill of Rights of 1960 is a statute binding only at the federal level of government. Even at that level, the courts have shown some reluctance to interpret it as having an overriding effect. Also, it obviously does not apply to the exercise of provincial powers. Moreover, the effect of most existing human rights legislation in Canada is rendered uncertain by the present division of legislative powers. It is not clear to what extent Parliament or the Legislatures can validly act in the protection of human rights. We will face this problem as long as we try to protect human rights by ordinary legislation. It is for these reasons that I believe the time has come to place the necessary safeguards in the constitution.

I am thinking of a Bill of Rights that will be so designed as to limit the exercise of all governmental power, federal and provincial. It will not involve any gain by one jurisdiction at the expense of the other. There would be no transfer of powers from the federal Parliament to the provincial Legislatures, or from the provincial Legislatures to the federal Parliament. Instead, the power of both the federal government and the provincial governments would be restrained in favour of the Canadian citizen who would, in consequence, be better protected in the exercise of his fundamental rights and freedoms. . . .

. . . We shall also face other constitutional issues. A constitutional Bill of Rights would modify even further the concept of parliamentary sovereignty in Canada. Once fundamental rights are guaranteed, they will be beyond the reach of government at all levels. This will confer new and very important responsibilities on the courts, because it will be up to the courts to interpret the Bill of Rights, to decide how much scope should be given to the protected rights and to what extent the power of government should be curtailed. This will inevitably bring us to consideration of the system of final adjudication in the constitutional field by the Supreme Court of Canada, as the latter is presently constituted.

A Bill of Rights entrenched by an amending formula that "brings home" the constitution, and applied throughout Canada by our supreme constitutional tribunal, will open the door to further constitutional reform. For example, will not the powers of reservation and disallowance of provincial legislation lose their meaning once a Bill of Rights has been entrenched in the constitution? Are there not other antiquated features of the British North America Act which might well be reconsidered at that time? . . .

. . . If the Fulton-Favreau formula for the amendment and repatriation of the constitution has failed, it is probably because what was sought was unanimous agreement on the technical details rather than on the substance. Today, we are beginning with the substance. We say to all Canadians, from all provinces: let us first agree on the basic freedoms, on the fundamental rights that we wish to guarantee. After that, we will deal with the mechanism. . . .

# 11.8

## THE EFFECT OF THE CHARTER OF RIGHTS ON THE POLICY-MAKING ROLE OF CANADIAN COURTS

Peter Russell

### The Charter's Impact on Judicial Power

It now seems almost certain that a charter of rights will be added to the Canadian constitution. This Charter will add a new dimension to judicial review of the constitutional validity of governmental actions. Whereas up to now the courts in assessing constitutionality have focused almost exclusively on the division of powers between the two levels of government, they will now be at least equally concerned with the constitutional rights of citizens against both levels of government. The consequences of finding legislation unconstitutional because it violates an individual's constitutional rights would appear, particularly where the legislative override does not apply, to be more drastic than finding legislation unconstitutional because it violates the federal division of powers. The former means that, unless the constitution is amended, no government may legislate in the proscribed area, whereas with the latter, what is excluded from one level of government will normally be within the jurisdiction of the other.

On the face of it, this looks like a major change in the constitutional role of the courts. But we should be careful to keep the significance of this change in perspective. The first part of this paper has endeavoured to show how judicial participation in policy-making is a built-in feature of our system of government. Policy-making in Canada involves a complex set of interactions amongst the three branches of government — the legislature, the executive and the judiciary — whose roles cannot be accounted for adequately by the textbook theory that the legislature makes the laws, the executive gives them practical effect, and the judiciary applies them to individual cases. In many areas the real core of policy is shaped not by a decisive act of the cabinet or the legislature but by the way in which administrators and judges gradually give substance to laws day by day and case by case.

Still, it must be acknowledged that the new basis of judicial review could involve a significant shift in policy-making authority from the other branches of government to the courts, especially to the Supreme Court of Canada. The

*Canadian Public Administration*, 25 (1982), p. 1. Reprinted with permission.

extent of this shift will depend on the terms of the Charter, the use which litigants make of it and perhaps, most of all, the way in which the courts (above all, the Supreme Court) interpret it.

## The Response of Judges, Lawyers and Litigants

So far as the Supreme Court is concerned, it would be rash to predict its approach solely on the basis of its treatment of the statutory Canadian Bill of Rights. Ambiguities in the wording of that bill provided a fertile bed for the seeds of doubt which judges had about their mandate to use the bill as a basis for even a temporary judicial veto of policies endorsed by Parliament. But now section 52 of the Constitution Act, by injecting an explicit constitutional supremacy clause into the Canadian constitution, will surely remove any doubts about what judges should do if they find an inconsistency between any law and the Charter (or, for that matter, any other provision of the Constitution of Canada): they must declare such a law, "to the extent of the inconsistency, of no force or effect." Also it is important to recall that the Supreme Court of Canada has on occasion played an aggressive role in imposing civil liberty principles on at least provincial administrations. The most notable examples occurred in the 1950s when the Supreme Court, in a series of decisions involving the interpretation of statutory law, common law and the BNA Act, rejected policies and actions of the Duplessis administration in Quebec that were restrictive of the rights of dissenting policial and religious minorities. Much more recently, the Supreme Court gave a fairly clear signal that it is prepared to render a much broader interpretation of constitutionally entrenched rights than of rights enshrined in an ordinary statute. In the *Blaikie* case, in finding that sections of Quebec's Charter of the French Language dealing with the language of legislation and the courts were unconstitutional, the Court justified its expansive interpretation of the language rights in section 133 of the BNA Act by referring to the need to avoid "overly-technical" interpretations of constitutional guarantees so as to give them "a broad interpretation attuned to changing circumstances." This opinion, it should be noted, took the unusual form of an anonymous "opinion of the Court" — giving it the aura of an institutional policy.

There is a more general consideration which should caution us against making predictions of judicial behaviour — especially long-run predictions — on the basis of recent experience. Judicial culture is dynamic, not static. The English-speaking democracies over the past century or so have witnessed large changes in the attitudes of judges to their legislative role. Logically, or at least sociologically, this is what we should expect. Judges, like other participants in the process of governing, are not immune from the conditioning influence of changes in political culture. There are developments in the Canadian political culture which, at least for a while, may foster a judicial predisposition to give broad effect to a constitutional charter of rights. Amongst these influences is a growing recognition of the limited extent to which elected officials can be held accountable for their decisions and of the limited extent to which decisions formally endorsed by elected officials represent "the will of the majority." This "sophistication" of our democratic culture is apt to reduce the qualms of judges about their mandate to veto decisions of the executive or legislature. Another factor is the education of the lawyers who become judges. A generation of Canadian lawyers has been exposed to the influence of professors who have contrasted unfavourably the Supreme Court of Canada's restrained treatment of the Canadian Bill of Rights with the much more activist approach of the U.S. Supreme Court, particularly during the era of the Warren Court. As a result of such influences I think we are likely to see persons with a much more activist philosophy appointed to the Supreme Court and other courts of appeal.

The response of litigants and lawyers to the Charter is more predictable than the response of judges. In the period immediately following the Charter's enactment there is likely to be a flurry of claims presented in the lower courts as there was in the first three years following the enactment of the Canadian Bill of Rights. The volume of early Charter litigation is apt to be considerably greater than twenty years ago. Civil liberties organization and special interest groups are better organized and financed and their leadership has become more experienced in the use of litigation to promote policies they favour. Indeed, numerous of these groups will resort to Charter litigation to overcome their lack of strength in the legislative and executive arenas. Further, the availability of lawyers, indeed of hungry lawyers looking for business, has also increased. The Canadian legal profession has been expanding rapidly over the past decade. Legal aid which scarcely existed in 1960 is now available for criminal cases throughout Canada and for civil cases in most provinces. Litigation will be heaviest in the criminal courts. The Charter is weighted toward criminal justice procedures and a natural tactic of defence counsel will be to toss in a Charter of Rights claim or two — especially in the first year or so before the Supreme Court has declared its position on the breadth of the Charter's key terms or police supervisors have been able to adapt police practices to the Charter's requirements.

Supreme court decisions in the 1970s significantly expanded the private sector's access to constitutional litigation. Very early in Canadian history, the federal and provincial governments gave themselves virtually an unconditional right to put constitutional questions to the courts. The Supreme Court's decision in *Thorson* and *McNeil* extended the right of individuals to have courts examine the constitutional validity of laws which affect them as part of a larger public (for example as taxpayers or movie-goers). Quite independently of this judicial expansion of the citizen's right to "standing" in constitutional cases, section 24 of the Charter appears to extend a very broad right of standing to "Anyone whose rights or freedoms, as guaranteed by this Charter have been infringed or denied" to apply to a court of competent jurisdiction for "such remedy as the court considers appropriate and just in the circumstances."

The litigation which will begin at the lower court level will, fairly quickly, generate appeals to the Supreme Court of Canada. The unitary nature of Canada's judicial system means that there are fewer steps here than in the United States between local trial courts and the highest court in the land. The centralized character of our judicial system increases the prospects of lower court compliance with Supreme Court rulings. Coherence in judicial interpretation of the new Charter should also be fostered by the fact that the judges of all the higher provincial and federal courts are appointed by the same authority. Thus the potential for effective Supreme Court control of the process of Charter interpretation is quite high. In this sense, the Charter will likely have a strong centralizing impact, especially where it affects policies over which provincial governments normally have primary control.

### Implications for Judicial Review of Legislation

The clearest policy-making challenge to the courts is posed by the first section of the Charter which states that all the rights and freedoms set out in the Charter are ''subject only to such reasonable limits prescribed by law as can be demonstrably justified in a free and democratic society.'' This general qualifying clause recognizes the obvious point that no right or freedom is to be enjoyed in an absolute sense at the expense of all other individual rights or social interests. Perhaps the most difficult and important decisions a democratic society must make are precisely those involving the competing claims of diversity and order, equality and liberty, welfare and economy. Section 1 invites the Supreme Court (and lower courts, too) to participate more systematically in making these decisions.

The provision for a legislative override inserted in the Charter in order to reach an accommodation with those provinces opposed to the entrenchment of rights makes the judiciary's role in these areas of policy-making less final and decisive than it would otherwise have been. By virtue of section 33 (the so-called notwithstanding clause), the federal Parliament and provincial legislatures may expressly exempt a legislative provision from the fundamental political freedoms in section 2, the legal rights in sections 7 to 14 and the equality rights in section 15 of the Charter. Such an exemption expires after five years but can be renewed. In relation to judicial decision-making, this legislative override can be used prospectively to preclude a judicial veto of legislation for five years or retrospectively to overcome, for five years at a time, an adverse judicial ruling.

The effect of the legislative override in diminishing judicial power should not be over-estimated. Legislators who contemplate recourse to the notwithstanding clause will face some powerful political disincentives. Experience with judicial interpretation of statutes and judicial development of the common law demonstrates how difficult it may be for a legislature to counter the policy fall-out of judicial decisions. Access to the crowded agenda of modern legislatures is never easy and may be especially difficult when influential groups have a vested interest in a position adopted by the judiciary. In proposing a legislative override, government will be committing itself to a policy position which is almost bound to be labelled by the media as "subverting civil liberties." This is bad politics, even for a government with a clear legislative majority.

It is instructive to consider what the federal government would have to do to take advantage of the override in relation to the War Measures Act. Legislation would have to be introduced specifying the rights and freedoms which could be set aside when an emergency is proclaimed under the act. Proposing such legislation when international and domestic security conditions are relatively tranquil will provoke an unwelcome political row and suspicions that the government has something awfully sinister up its sleeve. In the past both Conservative and Liberal administrations have been reluctant to take such an initiative in relation to the Canadian Bill of Rights. Future federal governments are unlikely to be any keener than their predecessors to sponsor such a proposal.

On the other hand, the notwithstanding clause may make the judiciary more activist and less self-restrained in enforcing the Charter. In deciding cases where the legislative override is available but has not been used, some judges may, with the burden of finality removed from their shoulders, be less reluctant to overturn legislation enacted by elected legislators or orders-in-council or regulations endorsed by politicians responsible to the legislature.

I believe that federal and provincial governments are more likely to rely on section 1 than on the legislative override as protection against judicial vetoes. While section 1 may be read as placing the onus of proof on government to demonstrate that limits on rights are "reasonable" and "justified in a free and democratic society," this burden of proof may be fairly easily discharged where a federal law allegedly restricting some right or freedom has been recently enacted following extensive public debate. For instance, if capital punishment is restored in Canada after being an issue in several general elections and after a great deal of discussion in Parliament, Supreme Court judges, even if a majority are personally abolitionists, may well be reluctant to second-guess this popular legislative process and may hesitate to conclude that capital punishment is an unreasonable and unjustifiable limit on the right under section 12 of the Charter not to be subjected "to any cruel and unusual treatment or punishment." Similarly, if something like the scenario of October 1970 is repeated and the War Measures Act is proclaimed to be in force following a request for its invocation from a province and a municipality experiencing serious terrorist incidents, a two-day discussion of the reasons for its invocation in the federal Parliament, approval by a very substantial bi-partisan majority of MP's and indication of overwhelming public support, I think it highly unlikely that the Supreme Court would hold that restrictions on rights and freedoms imposed by the orders issued under the act were unreasonable and unjustifiable. Those who have advertised the Charter as a way of preventing repressive wartime or emergency measures are unrealistic. A handful of judges chosen by the government likely lack the will and the power to restrain representatives of an aroused national majority which believes the nation's security requires restrictions on civil liberties. On the other hand, when provincial laws are challenged, another consideration will come into play — namely, the maintenance of uniform standards across the country. This consideration may make the Supreme Court more inclined to override recently enacted legislation of a "maverick" province.

## Implications for Judicial Review of Executive Activities

Another factor which may diminish the impact of the override clause is that many of the claims made under the Charter will be aimed not at legislation but at the activities of government officials and policemen that are alleged to fall short of Charter standards. It is with regard to these activities that the Charter may have its greatest and most welcome effect. Judges who may be disinclined to second-guess decisions of elected legislators may feel much less restrained in assessing the reasonableness of actions or inactions of bureaucrats, policemen or security agents that are not clearly mandated by law. In applying the requirements of a constitutional charter in this context, instead of vetoing elected legislators, the judiciary is more likely to be compensating for the weakness of legislative bodies in our system of parliamentary government in monitoring and sanctioning the activities of the executive.

One feature of the Charter which substantially reduces the scope of judicial review of executive actions is the removal of any reference to property rights. The Charter contains no general due process of law clause. Section 7, with its reference to "the principles of fundamental justice," is the only section which might be taken to embrace general standards of fair procedure. But it applies only to deprivations of "the rights to life, liberty and security of the person." It excludes any reference to property. This, of course, is not an accidental omission. It is one of the concessions made to gain support for the Trudeau proposals from the NDP who, as democratic socialists, were wary of encumbering government regulation of economic activity with uncertain constitutional requirements. The omission of property from the "principles of fundamental justice" section, together with the confinement of the detailed procedural rights in section 11 to the criminal justice process may immunize the procedures followed in most areas of public administration from *constitutional* judicial review. However, as earlier noted, Canadian judges have already carved out for themselves a strong role in reviewing administrative procedures, a role which recently has been reinforced by federal and provincial statutes. This non-constitutional judicial review will likely be more flexible and certainly more decentralized than the Supreme Court's application of the Charter's constitutional requirements. Public administrators in Canada may be grateful for both these features.

The Charter has very different implications for the administration of criminal justice. Here again political manoeuvering played a big role in shaping the Charter. It was originally drafted in a manner calculated to maximize provincial support. Many of the provinces were opposed to charters in general and members of departments of the Attorney General who figured prominently in early negotiations were especially wary of imposing tough constitutional requirements on the process of obtaining criminal prosecutions. As a result, at first the Charter's criminal justice safeguards were extremely weak. They required only that searches and seizures, detention and imprisonment be carried out according to law. There were no requirements for the laws that govern these procedures nor were any particular remedies provided for enforcement of rights in this area. However, once it became clear that most of the provinces were opposed to even a weak charter and Ontario's support was publicly secured, then the Trudeau government, which was determined to proceed with the Charter despite substantial provincial opposition, could move to meet the criticisms of civil liberties groups and obtain much-needed vocal political support for its program of unilateral constitutional reform by putting some teeth in the criminal justice sections of the Charter. Thus, sections 8 and 9 were amended so that there would be the right to be secure not simply from *unlawful* search or seizure, detention or imprisonment but from *unreasonable* search or seizure and *arbitrary* detention or imprisonment. Perhaps more importantly, a new remedy and sanction for enforcing these provisions was added in the form of a qualified exclusionary rule in section 24(2).

Section 24(2) directs judges to exclude evidence "obtained in a manner that infringed or denied rights or freedoms guaranteed by this Charter . . . if it is established that, having regard to all the circumstances, the admission of it in the proceedings would bring the administration of justice into disrepute." It must be emphasized that this is a qualified, not an absolute, exclusionary rule. It would put Canadian judges in a position more akin, in principle, to that of Australian and Scottish judges than that of American judges, and would restore to Canadian judges a power they have denied themselves by faithfully following English precedents. It would require Canadian judges to weight in the scales of social justice the risk, on the one hand, of permitting police blundering to result in the acquittal of guilty persons, against the risk, on the other hand, that courts by appearing to condone police lawlessness and wrongdoing will engender disrespect for the criminal justice system. The coupling of this remedy with, *inter alia*, the requirement that searches be reasonable, detentions not arbitrary and that detained persons be able to instruct counsel without delay is apt to be a fertile source of police station bargaining and court house litigation.

American experience with a broader, judicially constructed, exclusionary rule has not demonstrated that excluding unconstitutionally obtained evidence necessarily deters police wrongdoing. But in Canada, evidence given to the McDonald Commission by the RCMP disclosed that the silence of Canadian judges when confronted in criminal trials with evidence of questionable police practices has been taken by the police to amount to judicial approval of these practices. Section 24(2) would at least put an end to this silent and surely unintended judicial policy-making on police practices.

Assessing the requirements of fair, civilized, yet effective law enforcement is an area of policy-making for which judges, by virtue of their experience and aptitudes, may be reasonably well prepared. Still, it would be unfortunate if we came to rely on judicial enforcement of constitutional guarantees as the primary way of supervising police activities. Again, the recent inquiry into certain activities of the RCMP has shown that the same government which so proudly proclaims the new Charter of Rights as a "guarantee" of our liberties had little knowledge of the policies governing the investigative activities of our national security force and, even worse, had adopted the mistaken constitutional theory that it was not politically accountable for those operational policies. The first line of defence against improper police or security activity should not be episodic judicial monitoring but democratically accountable approval of investigative policies and practices.

## The Challenge of Equality Rights

The other part of the Charter which may eventually become a close rival to the criminal justice sections in generating litigation is section 15 which incorporates equality rights. I say eventually, because this section will not take effect until three years after the Constitution Act comes into force. During those three years federal and provincial officials will have the daunting task of ascertaining how their statutes, regulations, programs and practices should be altered to meet the new egalitarian standards of the constitution. Then the judiciary will be called upon to grade their work.

It is evident that in the drafting of the equality rights care was taken to benefit from American experience with the equal protection clause of the 14th Amendment and from Canadian experience with the vaguely and ambiguously worded equality section of the Canadian Bill of Rights. For instance, affirmative action programs which have as their object "the amelioration of conditions of disadvantaged individuals or groups" are explicitly exempted from the ban against discrimination based on race, national ethnic origin, colour, religion, sex, age or mental or physical disability. Further, these aforementioned categories are given as explicit examples of ways in which the law must not discriminate. The right to the "equal benefit of the law" has been added to the "equal protection of the law," and now everyone is to be equal "under the law" as well as "before the law."

These changes, while removing some ambiguity, by no means relieve the courts of a difficult burden of interpretation. The wording of section 15 may prevent the Supreme Court from reducing the constitutional requirement of equality to a procedural requirement in the administration of laws — the position a majority arrived at in *Lavell* in relation to the equality before the law provision in the Bill of Rights. Still, the specification of prohibited forms of discrimination will require judges to distinguish reasonable from unreasonable forms of discrimination in the law. It is simply inconceivable that judges will treat all of these prohibited forms of discrimination as absolutes. Nowhere is this more evident than in relation to age which is frequently used (and not unreasonably) as a basis for legal classification. Moreover, the nine prohibited classifications (race, national origin, ethnic origin, colour, religion, sex, age, mental disability and physical disability) do not exhaust the bar against legal discrimination. Section 15 requires that there be *no* discrimination in the protection or benefits provided by law. This requirement if taken literally would condemn most of the contents of federal and provincial statute books to the shredder, as one of the prime purposes of law is to redistribute wealth and opportunity in ways that favour some and penalize others.

Nevertheless, I do not think that our statute books will produce the heaviest or most challenging burden for section 15 adjudication. By the 1980s most of the discriminatory laws which are really offensive in our egalitarian culture — laws, for instance, discriminating against racial groups or against women — have been repealed. The courts, however, may frequently be asked to review the extent to which facilities, programs and employment in the public sector are equally available to all. Here judges, in considering the reasonableness of limitations, will have to indulge in what amount to cost/benefit analyses. How far, for example, should public buildings be required to go in providing equal access to the disabled? Washroom facilities on every floor? Elevators in all buildings over two stories high? Over three stories? etc. Nor is it clear where the public sector ends and the private begins. Should the property of private clubs that practise racial discrimination enjoy the protection of law? What about religious schools? Or a will that benefits a particular faith or ethnic group? Should these private forms of discrimination enjoy the protection and benefits of the law?

Canada's judges are less well prepared for their new policy-making role under section 15 than they are for their additional responsibilities in relation to criminal justice policy. Most will lack familiarity with the social and economic programs that are likely to be challenged on section 15 grounds. The adjudicative process as it is now conducted in Canada is not well designed to enable judges to obtain a good understanding of the factual setting in which their decisions take place. But even if our judges produce policy results which coincide with our political preferences, I worry about what this judicialization of the resolution of equality issues will do to the quality of our political life. Deciding questions of distributive justice is an essential responsibility of political man. Political life, as Aristotle taught, rises above the organization of animal herds when it is characterized by man's distinctive capacity of expressing and exchanging ideas about right and wrong.

I would be much happier about section 15 if its adoption as part of the law of our constitution had followed a widespread public and parliamentary discussion about the principles and practice of equality. But that is not the case.

Section 15 was developed primarily on public relations grounds as a means of co-opting highly visible and vocal interest groups into supporting the Trudeau government's unilateral constitutional restructuring. The public and legislative discussions concerning it provide little guidance to our judges as to how far or how fast it is desirable to eliminate all forms of discrimination in Canadian society. Leaving these matters to our judges may have the unfortunate consequence of relieving ourselves as citizens from the responsibility of reasoning together about acceptable answers to these questions of social justice in our municipal, provincial and federal political life.

Most certainly, Supreme Court enforcement of section 15 will have a centralizing effect on social policy in Canada. This could produce an important change in the workings of our federal system because, whereas criminal justice policies have always been primarily national in nature, many of the social, economic and cultural policies to which the Supreme Court will apply egalitarian norms have been subject to determination at the provincial level. This centralizing effect is not likely to be significantly reduced by the legislative override clause. While some provinces may resort to the legislation override for a five-year period in relation to a specific piece of legislation, in the meantime the Supreme Court will be making authoritative rulings on the meaning of the constitutional guarantee of equality. Provincial governments will find it difficult politically to resist adapting their policies to these judicially established national standards of social justice.

## Fundamental Freedoms

Section 2 of the Charter setting out "fundamental freedoms" is badly cluttered with extravagant phrases. This has the unfortunate result that the section fails to distinguish between those freedoms which are essential to the workings of a parliamentary democracy and those which are not. Constitutional entrenchment of the former is more compatible with democracy, as it invites courts to consider whether the democratic process has been interfered with rather than whether the judges approve of laws resulting from the democratic process. For that reason, I believe Chief Justice Duff was on the right track back in 1938 when he held that provisions of the BNA Act establishing parliamentary government in Canada rendered unconstitutional Alberta legislation controlling newspaper commentary on government policies. Regrettably, a majority of Supreme Court judges never accepted (nor, in my view, understood) Duff's position, and more recently the Court's majority has laid it to rest.

But now the Charter, instead of asking our judges to identify the boundaries of political freedom requisite for the practice of parliamentary democracy, asks them to uphold guarantees of "freedom of conscience and religion," "freedom of thought, belief, opinion and expression, including freedom of the press and other media of communication," "freedom of peaceful assembly" and "freedom of association" without any direction as to the purposes for which this vast range of human activities should be constitutionally protected.

Among other things, this section may soon plunge the Supreme Court into a review of the reasonableness of provincial censorship practices and federal broadcasting regulations. The inclusion of "freedom of conscience" will likely bring forward claims urging the Court to reconsider the position it adopted nearly twenty years ago in *Robertson and Rosetanni* that the concept of religious freedom does not entail an immunity to secular laws offensive to an individual's religious scruples. If the Court accepts this invitation, it will take on the challenging task of deciding whose conscience or religious beliefs have constitutional status and whose do not. I believe our liberal democratic system would have been quite secure without issuing this particular invitation to judicial policy-making.

## Distinctive Canadian Rights

Besides the more universal, fundamental rights, the Charter has sections concerning rights more specific to the Canadian experience: language rights, mobility rights, multiculturalism and aboriginal rights. These sections are not subject to the legislative override clause.

The most important of these sections in terms of dealing the courts into contentious policy issues is section 23 entrenching minority-language school rights. This section will probably generate an early challenge to that part of Quebec's Language Charter (Bill 101) designed to prevent newcomers to the province from having access to its English schools. As a concession to the Quebec government, the only provincial government whose premier refused to sign the Constitutional Accord of November 5, 1981, section 23 will not fully apply to Quebec until the Quebec legislature assents to it. Until then, parents who did not receive their own English education in Canada and who have had none of their children attending English schools in Canada will not have a constitutional right to place their children in Quebec's English schools. Still, some Quebec parents will qualify right away for the new constitutional right. Their attempt to exercise this right will provide an early test of the problems there may be in enforcing Canada's new constitution against the one province whose government has not endorsed it. In the process Canadians may learn first-hand about some of the difficulties entailed in securing local compliance with constitutional rulings of courts, such as the United States experienced a quarter of a century ago at Little Rock.

Equally important for the long run is the continuous monitoring the Supreme Court will be required to carry on of minority-language facilities throughout Canada. In carrying out this function its work will be analogous to that of the U.S. Supreme Court in supervising the enforcement of racially integrated education. It is a pity we have not taken the opportunity in Canada to reflect more creatively about the difficulties of U.S. courts in acting as education supervisors. A national education commission staffed by federal and provincial appointees with experience in education policy and with the capacity to carry out in-depth inquiries into local school situations might have been a far more sensitive and effective instrument for implementing the ideal of education in the official language of one's choice. One of the problems with a Bill of Rights is that it applies a single methodology — judicial enforcement of constitutional guarantees — to a variety of policy problems which may be most effectively dealt with by a variety of mechanisms.

Of all the rights entrenched in the new Charter, language rights embody the substantive policy objective of greatest importance to the Trudeau government. In addition to the school rights, the Charter gives explicit constitutional recognition, for the first time, to English and French as Canada's two official languages. The Charter extends the right to use the official languages in government considerably beyond the existing requirements of section 133 of the BNA Act. For communications with all levels of government in New Brunswick and with central offices of the federal government, statutory rights become constitutional rights — a change which the Ontario government refused to accept for the province with Canada's second-largest francophone community. Where the use of the official languages is constitutionally entrenched, the judiciary take on the authoritative role in determining the adequacy of bilingualism. This responsibility will challenge our courts' capacity to make accurate and prudent judgments about social and administrative situations. This is especially true in relation to the new constitutional right to communicate in English or French with the executive branch of the federal government, a right which depends on the existence of "a significant demand" for the service or on the "nature of the office" being such as to make it "reasonable" to have service in both languages.

The "mobility rights" in section 6 have been much heralded as a means of breaking down provincial barriers to the operation of a Canadian common market. But the section has been cast in very narrow terms. It is only the right "to reside" or "to pursue the gaining of a livelihood" in any province that is entrenched. It does not appear to affect provincial power (upheld by the Supreme Court in the *Morgan* case) to restrict the rights of out-of-province Canadians to own property in a province. As a result of changes made to obtain provincial support for the Charter, even these limited mobility rights will not apply to discriminatory programs designed to benefit the residents of any province experiencing above-average unemployment. Other limitations attached to this right appear to rule out a successful section 6 challenge to laws such as the Quebec Language Charter which impose requirements on participation in business or professions which, although difficult for out-of-province Canadians to meet, are not discriminatory on their face. Generally, despite the fanfare about mobility rights, I do not expect section 6 to create many opportunities for judicial policy-making or, for the matter, to do much for the Canadian common market.

Section 27 on multiculturalism does not purport to create any new constitutional rights but simply to serve as a direction to the judiciary to interpret other sections of the Charter "in a manner consistent with the multicultural heritage of Canadians." This section at least has the merit of recognizing the necessity of judicial interpretation and of giving some direction to the courts as to the principles which should guide their judgement in marginal cases. Such direction might be relevant, for example, in deciding how far to extend the right to freedom of religion or association.

The rights of native people are recognized in the Charter only to the extent that section 25 stipulates that any rights they have enjoyed in the past or may acquire through future land settlements are not to be jeopardized by the enforcement of any other Charter rights. Outside of the Charter, Part II of the Constitution Act, which was surreptitiously dropped by the First Ministers in negotiating their final accord and then restored under public pressure, recognizes and affirms "the existing aboriginal and treaty rights of the aboriginal peoples of Canada." However, there is no commitment to preserving these rights and no clause requiring the consent of native peoples as a condition for modifying or extinguishing these rights. Further, the Constitution Act contains no clarification of the meaning of aboriginal rights. That the definition of the constitutional rights of Canada's original peoples is still very much an unfinished business is shown by the inclusion in Part IV of the Constitution Act of a provision specifying that "constitutional matters that directly affect the aboriginal peoples of Canada, including the identification and definition of the rights of those peoples to be included in the Constitution of Canada" must be on the agenda of a constitutional conference to take place within one year after Part IV comes into force. In the meantime native peoples will not be able to make much use of the aboriginal rights provisions of the Constitution Act to challenge in court the government's approval of development projects on the lands to which they claim aboriginal title. However, the provisions, and more importantly the political negotiations which produced them, might increase the political leverage of native leaders by threatening to embarrass the government when its actions so sharply contradict its rhetoric.

## Conclusion

I shall conclude by commenting briefly on how the new constitutional charter through both its substantive provisions and the shift of power it entails to the national judiciary is likely to affect public participation in government decision-making — the central theme of the 1981 annual meeting of the Institute of Public Administration of Canada at which the original version of this paper was presented.

There are certainly a few ways in which the Charter may enhance public participation. The free speech provisions of section 2 might remove a few of the remaining legal constraints on participation in the political process and compensate for the contemporary Supreme Court's repudiation of earlier jurisprudence recognizing the freedom to publish political opinions as implicit in the BNA Act's entrenchment of parliamentary government. For example, local by-laws restricting political posters such as the Vancouver by-law recently upheld by a provincial court judge may be found unconstitutional under the

Charter. The Supreme Court might even be persuaded to invoke section 2 as grounds for overruling its own recent decision on the law of libel making newspaper publishers liable for defamatory comments contained in letters to the editor. The guarantee in section 3 of the right to vote in federal and provincial elections might be regarded as enhancing participation, but I doubt that this right has been seriously in jeopardy anywhere in Canada for some time. One other section that might have a slight effect on public participation in the criminal justice system is section 11(f) which establishes a constitutional right to trial by jury in the case of offences liable to five years or more punishment.

What is perhaps of greater importance than the consequences of the Charter's specific provisions is the general effect of the Charter on our system of government and politics. The central thesis of this paper is that a constitutional charter of rights guarantees not rights but a particular way of making decisions about rights in which the judicial branch of government has a much more systematic and authoritative role. For some members of our society this system will increase the opportunity to influence public policy. This is true for those individuals and groups who will obtain more direct leverage on policy-making through Charter litigation than they could through the legislative process. These opportunities will be especially important for groups who are devoted to a single issue, particularly an issue that politicians are afraid to touch (for example, gay rights or either side of the abortion issue). However, transferring the policy-making focus from the legislative to the judicial arena also has a negative side. It represents a further flight from politics, a deepening disillusionment with the procedures of representative government and government by discussion as means of resolving fundamental questions of political justice. The attempt to settle differences in our society on issues such as obscenity, Sunday closing, abortion, the rights of the elderly and the benefits available to the disabled through the judicial process entails the danger, however the courts resolve these issues, of transforming these matters into technical legal questions and of making the answers to these questions hinge on the outcome of a contest between legal adversaries rather than on a political process more likely to yield a social consensus.

It may be that the legislative override clause, the quintessential Canadian compromise, will mitigate this danger. It does hold out the possibility of an interesting interchange between the judicial and the legislative process. Perhaps only Canada, still teetering uncertainly between British and American models of government, could come up with legislative review of judicial review. Weird as such a system may seem to the purists on both sides, it just might help us wring the best that can be hoped for from a charter of rights without totally abandoning our reliance on the processes of parliamentary government to settle difficult issues of social policy.

One other contribution a charter is almost bound to make concerns the focus of my own interest — the policy-making role of courts. The Charter, however it is interpreted, will sharpen public understanding of the policy-making capacity of courts, which our prevailing theories of government do not acknowledge. As a result there is no informed discussion of the policy matters which in a democracy are properly the concern of judges nor of the factors which may properly influence the decisions of judges in shaping our laws. The decisions of Canadian courts interpreting a constitutional charter of rights and freedoms will provide Canadians with a crash course in judicial policy-making. Among other things we may learn through this course how to improve the adjudicative process so that judges can give adequate consideration to all of the societal facts relevant to deciding whether laws are reasonable. We may also come to care much more about the representative quality of those who are to do our judging. This may not be a bad thing, providing the learning process does not take too long nor, while it is going on, do too much damage to the democratic quality of our political life.

# 11.9

## KEYTERMS

### Concepts

constitutional convention
constitutionally entrenched
canon of statutory interpretation
"interpretive avoidance"
"power allocation"
"power denial"
"equality in the application and administration of the laws"
"equal laws"
legislative override clause

### Institutions, Events, and Documents

1960 Bill of Rights
*Drybones v. the Queen* (1969)
*A.-G. Canada v. Lavell and Bedard* (1974)
Charter of Rights and Freedoms (1982)

# 12

# Judicial Decision-making

The subject of this chapter is the decision-making processes of appeal courts, and specifically the Supreme Court of Canada. The practicing bar and the general public are interested only in the practical "product" of courts — the final judgement and opinion. However, the character and even the quality of the final "product" are influenced by the internal procedures and jurisdiction of a court — how a court goes about its business. To better understand the judicial process, we must go behind the institutional facade of courts, and examine how appeal court judges actually decide cases and write opinions. (Reading 12.1)

As we have seen throughout this book, courts, like other institutions, have a particular institutional logic formed by and around their purpose. The traditional adjudicatory function of courts has moulded the internal decision-making procedures of courts in all common law countries. The notion that the judicial function is "to find the law" led to the practice of *seriatim* opinion-writing, in which each judge gives his own reasons for his judgement. *Seriatim* opinions reflect and reinforce the tradition of judicial independence, which is an independence of the judges not just from "outside" influences, but from each other as well.

Whatever the merits of *seriatim* opinions in the traditional realm of private law, the practice is open to criticism in the realm of public law, particularly constitutional law, where the public policy-impact of judicial decisions is greater. The two principal criticisms of *seriatim* opinions are that they are often confusing and that they erode the authority of the court. The first criticism can be warmly appreciated by any student who has had to wade through the multiple opinions in such Supreme Court decisions as *Saumur* or *Johannesson*, both from the 1950's. In constitutional law cases, it is typical to have a number of public and private policy "actors" looking to the Supreme Court's decisions for guidance as to what is or is not permissible government policy, and what can reasonably be expected in the future. A decision that gives five different reasons for the majority decision is obviously not as helpful as a single "opinion of the court." The multiplicity of opinions also saps the authority of the court. If a final appellate court hands down a single unanimous opinion in a potentially controversial case, it sends a subtle but important message to the "losing" side that continued litigation or resistance to the decision would be futile.[1] Multiple reasons for the same result send a very different message.

Predictably it was the American Supreme Court that first abandoned the practice of *seriatim* opinion writing. John Marshall, considered the greatest and most influential of all American chief justices, persuaded his colleagues that a single "opinion of the court" expressing the majority view would enhance the authority and prestige of the then fledgling court. This practice remained intact until 1937. Since the so-called "constitutional revolution" of that year, concurring and dissenting opinions have steadily multiplied to the point where it is inaccurate to describe contemporary American practice as still being a single "opinion of the Court."

Notwithstanding these recent developments, American Supreme Court opinions still tend to be more coherent — if simply because they are less diverse — than the Canadian Supreme Court's continuing practice of *seriatim* opinions. There have been recommendations for the Canadian Supreme Court to adopt the single "opinion of the court" approach, and some of the late Chief Justice Laskin's procedural reforms were designed to increase the collegiality of the court, which is certainly a step toward fewer separate opinions. (See below)

There is some evidence that these reforms have begun to affect the opinion-writing procedures of the Court. Since 1978 there have been six cases where the decision has been delivered simply as the opinion of "The Court." Prior to this there had only been one such case, the 1969 *Offshore Minerals Reference*. These decisions are unanimous and there is no indication of who wrote the opinion. Most of these cases have dealt with politically volatile issues — minority language rights in Quebec[2] and Manitoba,[3] Quebec's claim to a unilateral veto over constitutional amendments,[4] the federal government's claim to unilateral authority to reform the Senate,[5] and Newfoundland's jurisdictional claim to the offshore Hibernia oil fields.[6] It is tempting to speculate that the Supreme Court, aware of the political sensitivity of the

---

[1] The textbook example of this was the U.S. Supreme Court's decision in the 1954 *School Desegregation Case*. Then Chief Justice Warren spent several years "negotiating" with reluctant members of the Court in order to produce a unanimous opinion for a decision that he knew would incite controversy and opposition in the American South.

[2] *A.-G. Quebec v. Blaikie*, [1979] 2 S.C.R. 1016.

[3] *A.-G. Manitoba v. Forest*, [1979] 2 S.C.R. 1032.

[4] [1982] 2 S.C.R. 792.

[5] [1980] 1 S.C.R. 54.

[6] Released March 8, 1984, unreported.

issues raised in these cases, may have consciously borrowed the U.S. Supreme Court's tactic in the *School Desegregation Case* of a "united front." While this trend is potentially significant, such decisions remain rare. However, even in the more typical cases the Supreme Court seems to have abandoned the classical *seriatim* style of each judge writing his own opinion. There has been an increase in the tendency of the judges simply to concur with the written opinion of another judge. There has also been an instance of "group authorship" of single majority and dissenting opinions.[7] Taken together, these developments are yet another indicator that the Supreme Court is a court in transition.

Another important procedural difference between final appellate courts is the relative importance that they assign to oral and written argument. In Great Britain, written argument is limited to a brief one or two page outline of issues and precedents, while oral argument is unlimited, and typically lasts several days. This practice represents the extension of the adversary process into the appeal courts, and reflects a very adjudicative view of the appellate process. At the other extreme is the American practice of strictly limited oral argument but lengthy and detailed written "briefs." In the U.S. Supreme Court oral argument is strictly limited to thirty minutes, with a system of flashing lights to warn counsel that time is almost over. Prior to this, however, the American justices will typically have received written briefs of twenty to one hundred pages, detailing not just the legal arguments and precedents, but often relevant socio-economic evidence as well. After *amici curiae* have submitted similar written briefs, a typical case will have hundreds of pages of written legal arguments and supporting documentation. Canadian practice falls somewhat in between the American and British approaches. Unlike their British counterpart, the Canadian Supreme Court does accept substantial written argument known as factums. Unlike the Americans, however, the Canadian justices allow unlimited oral argument, typically running two days. This eclectic compromise between British and American practice is an accurate reflection of the Supreme Court's centre position on the ajudicatory — policy-making spectrum.

There have been a number of recent changes in Supreme Court procedure that reflect its transition from a strictly adjudicatory function to what Laskin has called the "supervisory function" appropriate to a final appellate court. It should be noted that many of the institutional aspects of the Supreme Court that Laskin criticized in his 1972 article on the "institutional character of the judge" were subsequently changed during his tenure as Chief Justice from 1973 to 1984. (Reading 12.2) This can hardly be attributed to coincidence, and is testimony to the strength of intellect and influence of the late Chief Justice.

One important change was the abolition in 1975 of appeals as of right in civil cases with a value over $10,000. This has permitted the Supreme Court

---

[7] See *Re Exported Natural Gas Tax*, [1982] 1 S.C.R. 1006.

to control its own docket, to pick and choose which cases raise sufficiently important questions of law or policy to merit the Supreme Court's time and energy. The impact of this change has been dramatic. Between 1970 and 1975, 72% of the Supreme Court's docket came from appeals as of right, and only 23% by its own decision to grant leave to appeal. This situtation was reversed after 1975. Between 1976 and 1980, 75% of its cases were chosen by granting leave to appeal, while only 20% were heard as a matter of right.[8]

An important consequence of the Court's control of its docket has been a dramatic increase in the number of constitutional law cases it hears annually. Between 1950 and 1975, the Court heard only two to three constitutional cases a year. Beginning in 1975, this number began to increase, reaching an annual rate of ten or more in recent years. The additional constitutional litigation generated by the Charter of Rights is just beginning to reach the Supreme Court, and will at least double the 1975-1982 rate. At the beginning of the third year of the Charter, May, 1984, there were 31 Charter cases waiting to be decided or heard by the Supreme Court. This changing composition of the Supreme Court's case load is transforming it more and more into a "constitutional court," with all the political implications that this entails.

Another important change in the internal procedures of the Supreme Court has been the trend to sit as a full nine judge bench, rather than in panels of five. The practice of five judge panels has long been followed, and has been defended on the grounds of efficiency. After the Supreme Court assumed final responsibility for overseeing the legal dimensions of Canada's constitutional development in 1949, this practice began to be criticized as introducing a haphazard element into the court's decisions. A case might be decided differently depending on how the five judge panel was selected, a matter totally at the discretion of the Chief Justice. This was considered particularly inappropriate in constitutional cases, which have steadily increased as a percentage of the court's workload. Even before his appointment as Chief Justice, Laskin had publicly disapproved of the five judge panels for important cases, and he quickly exercised his new administrative prerogative to implement his preferred policy of nine judge panels. The results have been significant. In the three terms preceding his appointment, nine judge panels heard only 10% of the cases argued before the Supreme Court. In the eight years following Laskin's elevation to the chief justiceship, the average increased to 36%, and since 1976 there have been more nine judge panels than five judge panels.[9] The cumulative effect of this trend is to increase the authority of the Supreme Court's pronouncements on constitutional issues, and so to make it a more influential participant in the process of constitutional politics.

---

[8] S.I. Bushnell, "Leave to Appeal Applications to the Supreme Court of Canada: A Matter of Public Importance," *Supreme Court Law Review*, 3 (1982), p. 479.

[9] Ibid.

A final reform of recent years, again at the initiative of Bora Laskin, has been to increase the potential for collegiality among the nine Supreme Court justices. Collegiality is an intangible matter, but it has a cumulative effect on the opinion-writing of final appellate courts. Early on in the American republic, Chief Justice Marshall initiated the practice of formal conferences as a means for the judges to share their opinions, to discover common ground as well as differences, and so to facilitate the production of a single "opinion of the court." During his tenure as chief justice, Laskin formalized the judges' conferences by scheduling them on a regular basis. He rearranged the Court's schedule so that during their three annual sessions they hear cases for only two out of every three weeks, and no cases are scheduled for Fridays. Last, but in his own opinion not least, he had a private dining room installed, so that the judges could have lunch together and confidentially continue discussing the business before the court that day. All of these changes contribute in their own ways to enhancing that elusive quality of judicial collegiality.

The greater opportunity for informal interaction and discussion among the justices is calculated to enhance the coherence of the Supreme Court's opinion-writing style. While nobody pretends that it will lead overnight to the adoption of a single "opinion of the court" approach, it will facilitate a more integrated set of opinions. The justices will know ahead of time one another's positions, and be inclined to acknowledge points of agreement and disagreement in their respective opinions. This is certainly a first step toward the Court's speaking with a more unified if not a single voice, and thus speaking more authoritatively.

While Bora Laskin was well aware of the political advantages that accrue to a court that speaks with one voice, he was equally aware of the advantage of the dissenting opinion. One of the secondary but important consequences of the demotion of *stare decisis* is the new significance that this gives to dissenting opinions. Under a strict regime of *stare decisis*, judicial dissents were equivalent to "crying in the wilderness." With the Supreme Court's new freedom to reverse precedent, a dissenting judge can now hope to appeal to a future court majority on the strength of his dissenting argument. Ironically, Laskin was a frequent dissenter on the very court he presided over, so much so that he was sometimes referred to as the "Great Dissenter." While he would no doubt have preferred to be in the majority, Bora Laskin was well aware of the pattern in American constitutional law whereby the great dissents of one era have come to form the basis of a new majority in the following generation. Anyone familiar with the late Chief Justice's dissenting opinions knows that they were not just written for the day that they were delivered.

# 12.1

# TWO MODELS OF JUDICIAL DECISION-MAKING

Paul Weiler

. . . It is now a truism that personal relationships on a court are going to have some effect on its product, even if individual members feel compelled to make all decisions in the light of relatively objective (or neutral) rules and principles. One's perceptions of the preferable solutions to ambiguous problems will be affected by the way those whom we respect, or are attracted to, react to the same problem. "Small group" analysis deepens our level of understanding of these intuitively sensed propositions and shows us, in particular, the importance of leadership. . . .

. . . Small group psychology may also have fruitful implications for the "judicial strategy" of a member of the court interested in implementing his own policy preferences. For instance, it is obvious that a single judge can attempt to obtain the necessary majority for his position either by appealing to a colleague's intellectual premises or his emotional affinities. As such, it is in his interest to work to obtain a position of relative intellectual eminence and of affection in the eyes of his colleagues. Again the Chief Justice of the court is in a better strategic position for obtaining such a position of influence, although probably only marginally so.

Of much greater interest are the implications of economic analysis, and in particular of game theory, for the process of negotiation, or bargaining, to reach a group decision. The conditions for bargaining are present because all the participants are agreed on the necessity for reaching a group decision and each has an effective bargaining counter in his vote and the threat of writing a separate opinion (especially a dissent). It is obvious that the individual judge who is most effective at bargaining has a great advantage over his fellow in (1) achieving a favourable majority vote, (2) obtaining the most favourable operative doctrines in any institutional opinion, and (3) minimizing the likelihood of any majority adopting against him an opinion which is radically harmful to his policy interests.

The fact that the court is a collective group introduces important complications. The structure of the institutional decision is an important factor determining the nature of the bargaining which must be undertaken. Because there are several members of the court and a majority must be attracted to a position,

---

*Canadian Bar Review*, 1968, p. 406. Reprinted with permission.

the development of sub-groups or blocs in the court is facilitated. Obviously the nature of the majority required is also important. If, as in Canada, only a majority vote for a decision is needed, and seriatim opinions are issued, bargaining may not be intensive. By comparison, in the United States Supreme Court, where a general opinion creates authoritative policy only if it is accepted by a majority of the court, instances of "legislative" maneuvering are well-documented.

Suppose, for example, it appears to a judge in a case that he is not going to be in the majority. He has at least three alternative strategies. First, he can try to bargain with the majority by offering his silent concurrence, in exchange for some dilution of the general doctrine in the opinion. His concurrence may have some marginal value because of the desirability of maintaining the image of a unified court and the extra precedential value which is given to a unanimous or near-unanimous decision. Of course, the marginal cost to the majority of weakening the doctrine may outweigh any damage which could be done by a dissent from the minority judge. Second, a judge could just dissent alone (or with any other who join him fortuitously) and appeal in his opinion to the bar of history. Such a tactic has little real cost to the dissenter, although it may also be of little effect (but then it may not be, depending on the configuration of political forces which the court faces).

However, the opportunity costs of such a tactic may be great if there is a viable alternative, the use of one's vote and opinion, to create and maintain a bloc of several judges (in political terms, an informal "party") who may be in the minority in this case. A bloc in a small group can have tremendous leverage if the rest of the members are distributed randomly (although this will rarely be the case) and, in any event, will dispose of much more effective power than an individual judge. The formation and maintenance of a bloc over time requires much the same talent and effort as has been indicated above for an individual majority. Economic analysis and game theory can show the theoretical implications of different sized blocs within different sized groups. . . .

. . . There have been several recent calls for greater collaborative work by the Canadian Supreme Court, especially by Professor McWhinney. He suggests the American practice of a formal judicial conference about a case, where the differing analyses by the judges are thrashed out, and a common authoritative opinion of the court agreed-to, if possible. Obviously, even within the adjudication model, this is a much more preferable mode of elaborating the law than the practice of writing and delivering individual, seriatim opinions which do not even refer to each other. However, the alternative institutional system, which can be viewed as a variant of a legislative forum voting on possible outcomes, is much more amenable to frankly political strategies, an informal party system, and the like. Presumably, it would be made use of in this way as the Supreme Court's work became overtly political.

# 12.2

# THE INSTITUTIONAL CHARACTER OF THE JUDGE

Bora Laskin

I do not propose to speak directly of judicial performance, of the ingredients of judgment, of the agonies of decision. It is more than fifty years ago that Cardozo delivered the lectures entitled ''The Nature of the Judicial Process'' and they are as fresh for today as they were in 1921. When I took my seat on the Supreme Court of Canada I told my colleagues and others who attended the induction ceremony that (1) I had no expectations to live up to save those I placed upon myself; (2) I had no constituency to serve save the realm of reason; (3) I had no influences to dispel unless there was a threat to my intellectual disinterestedness; and (4) I had no one to answer to save my own conscience and my personal standards of integrity. The euphoria of the occasion was my excuse for a touch of hyperbole. My previous judicial experience had already taught me better; what I said was not the whole story. I am not certain that I can tell it now, but I shall try.

The principle of judicial independence, both in its internal and in its external application, may serve as my touchstone. The paradox of this principle is that in securing the individual responsibility of each judge of a court once he is appointed, as against subservience to any fellow judge and as against external interference by others, it at the same time gives cohesion to the court as an institution distinct from other units of government. I do not shrink from describing a court in the Anglo-American-Canadian tradition as a unit of government. The models which each of these countries present reflecting differences of organization, of operation and of function, at least in their ultimate appellate tribunals, only certify to the depth of their governmental character; they do not deny it. In each, the courts are concerned among other things, with the lawful limits of the exercise of public power whether it be by the executive or by an administrative body or by an official of a local or central government. In Canada and in the United States they are, additionally, concerned with the lawful exercise of power by the Legislatures under the respective Constitutions of those countries. In all this there is a balance struck between public authority and private claims. . . .

. . . Appellate courts, and especially final appellate courts, project their institutional character — their structure, composition, jurisdiction and organization

---

*Israel Law Review*, 7 (1972), p. 329. Reprinted with permission.

for the dispatch of their judicial business — into their writing of opinions. I know, from personal experience, that the scope of appellate jurisdiction, the volume of appellate work within the compass of jurisdiction and the internal procedures adopted by a court for disposing of its case load are mirrored in that court's opinions, in how they are written and in how much they say. The Supreme Court of the United States, always sitting in a full complement of nine (save in case of vacancies or occasional self-disqualification or indisposition), copes with its work only by a ruthless sifting and discriminating selection of cases for hearing from the thousands of application for *certiorari*, that is, for leave to appeal; the number of such applications has been running to some 3,000 or more annually over the past three years. Dealing in the main with constitutional issues, which take it into the very heart of American political, social and economic organization, its decisions are bound to be often those of a closely divided court. The writing, whether in majority or in concurrence or in dissent, has been generally strong. It is, after all, addressed to the nation in a sense that has no parallel, except occasionally, in the judgments of the Supreme Court of Canada or of the House of Lords. It is the style as well as the nature of the jurisdiction that gives the opinions of the Supreme Court of the United States this focus; and I believe that what influences the style is the greater hospitality that is shown by that Court to extrinsic materials than is the case in either the Supreme Court of Canada or the House of Lords.* That, however, is largely accounted for by the constitutional Bill of Rights jurisdiction that now engages so much of the time of the Supreme Court of the United States. There is no such jurisdiction in Canada or in the United Kingdom.**

It is not surprising, therefore, that the American Supreme Court should have a more fixed and formal internal procedure for decision-making than the other two ultimate Courts that I have mentioned, and that, of necessity, oral argument should be rigidly limited, and be merely a supplement to or gloss upon comprehensive written briefs. By contrast, it is still true to say that in the Supreme Court of Canada where oral argument on appeals proper is not, or not yet, subject to any prescribed time limitations, the written brief, or factum, is reflected in the oral argument and, generally, is not something that overwhelms it; indeed, the factum is often very subservient. The oral and the written overlap more than they complement each other.

A quorum in the Supreme Court of Canada is five judges; and although the full nine sit frequently (as in constitutional or other public law cases and in capital cases) and seven-judge courts are also constituted from time to time,

---

*Editor's note: This was written before the Supreme Court's innovative use of extrinsic evidence in the 1976 *Anti-Inflation Reference*. See Reading 10.4 and Introduction to chapter eight.

**Editor's note: This was written before the adoption of the Charter of Rights and Freedoms in 1982.

most of the cases are adjudicated by a panel of five judges; and in different combinations of the nine judges of the Court, so as to equalize the work load.* It is not only the national character of the Court, as already explained, and the wide jurisdiction that it has under its governing statute that justifies this course; it is also the fact that the larger proportion of the appeals heard by the Court come before it as of right rather than by leave.** The appeal as of right in civil cases is controlled in general by a monetary limit of $10,000, so long as the question involved is not one of fact alone. This is not a very tight control, and results in many cases being brought to the Court which are of interest only to the litigants, without wider ramifications. In my opinion, they have a cluttering effect which would be even worse if each was heard by the full complement of judges. . . .

. . . No appellate court can operate without some organized conferring. The Supreme Court of Canada does have scheduled conferences on cases reserved for judgment, but without rigid patterns save that conferences of the whole Court are invariably held prior to the opening of a term of the Court (there are three terms per year) and prior to the close of a term; and there are conferences also, in relation to each case reserved for judgment, by the members of the Court who heard the case. The fact that the Court may sit in panels of five, seven or nine, and that on the five and seven judge panels there may be different combinations of judges, dictates flexibility and informality in the procedures for arriving at a judgment and for agreeing (or disagreeing) on the reasons in support of (or against) the judgment. But this practice also raises important questions, in the minds of academic writers and in the minds of counsel, about the relation of the particular decision to the particular composition of the Court (especially where only five judges sit), and about the extent to which a decision of a five judge court should be invariably regarded as the judgment of the Court. Formally, of course, it is. There have been cases however, which, argued first before a five judge court, have been reargued before a full court. . . .

. . . I understand that the decision-making procedures in the House of Lords, which generally sits as a five judge court although three is a quorum, are no less flexible and informal than those of the Supreme Court of Canada. The House of Lords too has more than five judges to call on, and hence there may be differently constituted panels for different cases. The workload does not appear to be as heavy as that of the other two final appellate courts that have mentioned. In general, appeals to the House of Lords lie by leave only; in civil cases, by leave of the relevant court of appeal of the House of Lords and in criminal cases by leave of the latter only. There is therefore no such compulsory obligation to entertain appeals at the instance of litigants as exists in relation to the Supreme Court of Canada, at least in civil cases. . . .

---

*Editor's note: This has changed. See Introduction.

**Editor's note: This has changed. See Introduction.

. . . The methods of disposition of applications for leave to appeal are, of course, of institutional importance to any appellate court to which recourse for leave must be had. In the Supreme Court of Canada, such applications must be heard by at least three judges; there was a time when they were heard by only one. The applications are supported by oral argument on which there is now a time limit, and are disposed of on the spot or after a short reserved period; and, also, without written reasons, except where the Court's jurisdiction is an issue and it is considered advisable, for future guidance, that that issue should be put to rest. The question whether reasons for granting or refusing leave (and, particularly, reasons for refusing) should be given in other cases has been considered from time to time, but the Court, overall, has not favoured such a course. Apart from overburdening the members and having to draw possibly arbitrary lines in determing which applications deserve reasons and which do not, there is the concern that what should be a matter of special indulgence, based on the individual merits of the case and the ripeness of its issues for adjudication, should not become enmeshed in case law that would rob the application for leave of its special character. What makes this position questionable is the differentiation, of which I have already spoken, between appeals in civil cases and appeals in criminal cases. It would have more cogency if the Court's jurisdiction was in the main one that depended on leave. In any event, it cannot be reasonably urged that there should be reasons in all applications for leave; but there should be room for discriminating selection of cases in which it would be appropriate to give reasons.

Speedy disposition of applications for leave reacts upon the deliberations of the three judge panel which hears them. Since the issue is generally whether there is an arguable question of sufficient importance to deserve a hearing on the merits before a larger body, the panel is not so much concerned with rigid majority views on an application for leave as with threshing out the significance of the point or points at issue on the application. The approach is less majoritarian than principle-oriented. It may happen therefore that leave, if given, may be for an appeal at large or upon specific questions which the panel will frame.

This procedure differs from that followed by the Supreme Court of the United States in treating applications for *certiorari*. They are generally disposed of on the written submissions of the parties, without opportunity for oral argument; and it is the practice to grant the application if at least four of the nine justices are in favour of so doing. Occasionally, short reasons are given for dispositions that are made; and, occasionally too, a dissenting opinion on an application for *certiorari* will be filed. . . .

. . . Time pressure upon judges is bound to result in opinions of poorer quality. If the case load is heavy, the tendency will be for judges to concentrate their limited time and their energy on opinions that have been assigned to them; and to show generous institutional faith in opinions in other cases prepared by others, unless strong conviction induces the preparation of a concurring opinion or of a dissent, where either in general or private conference the opinion writer cannot be persuaded to meet objections or suggestions for change.

Of course, much depends on the kinds of cases in which appeals lie. There is, generally speaking, small point in separate concurrences or dissents in cases turning on facts; and no less a waste of energy, better spent otherwise, to write in concurrence or even in dissent on contested applications of well-known principles of law; if a dissent must be filed, it can be terse and brief. Complaisance in such cases is not a matter of inertia; the prudent conservation of judicial energy is also a value of our adjudicative system. In one other respect, at least judges may be expected to show largeness of spirit toward their fellows. Each judge has or develops his own writing style; and collegiality dictates that one be generous enough in concurrence to tolerate literary compositions that are different from one's own, and hence to join in another's opinion where the only reason for writing separately would be a preference for a different literary style.

Silent concurrence in a majority opinion may often have to be bought by compromise in the drafting of that opinion. There is nothing necessarily ignoble about this. It is always open to the judge who drafts the opinion to conclude that too high a price is being exacted; he may prefer to insist on his elaboration of principle rather than find refuge in the facts. Marginal cases, where this dilemma is generally met, are bound to produce varying reactions among independent-minded judges. There must be an effective disposition of an appeal; and although this does not depend on concordant reasoning, there is an institutional preference to support a majority result by reasons acceptable to a majority. The late Justice Frankfurter, reminiscing put it this way:

> When you have to have at least five people [out of nine] to agree on something, they can't have that comprehensive completeness of candor which is open to a single man, giving his own reasons untrammelled by what anybody else may do or not do if he put that out.

It is obvious, I may add, that a judge never writes more freely than when he writes in dissent.

I have spoken of the monitoring function of ultimate appellate courts in their supervision of courts below them in the hierarchy. But who monitors the monitors? The answer is easy; they are self-monitoring, thus expressing one aspect of their judicial independence. It has been for them to say whether they would be faithful to their own previous decisions or reject adherence to *stare decisis*. The stamp of a final court in the present Anglo-American-Canadian judicial tradition is that finality of decision in the immediate case is all that is invariably guaranteed; finality of legal principle is not.

Indeed, a final court can no more bind its successor members than a parliament or a congress. The institution is what its members from time to time make it. Save as constitution or statute enjoins particular processes or procedures (and Israel offers an illustration of a statutory treatment of *stare decisis* under which the Supreme Court is left free to change its views), contemporary obedience to patterns of predecessors is not a duty imposed from without. New members give no guarantees of fidelity to the decisions of the past, either in courts or in legislative assemblies. What *stare decisis* has stood for in the past was a generalization of experience raised to a self-limiting rule; and yet final appellate courts, even though dealing with marginal cases, were never under such continuing pressures to change course so frequently as to require reliance on a standardized rule of *stare decisis* to save their balance. In one sense, therefore, *stare decisis* has been a convenience, even in the House of Lords until it was formally dispatched by the policy announcement of July 26, 1966. It is no longer an article of faith in the Supreme Court of Canada, but it still remains a cogent principle there. It must be remembered, however, that until the abolition of appeals to the Privy Council in 1949, the Supreme Court of Canada was a captive court, subject to the binding effect of Privy Council decisions, and by the latter's dictate to the decisions of the House of Lords.

Now that both the House of Lords and the Supreme Court of Canada have given themselves the elbow room for unabashed re-examination of doctrine that has long been characteristic of the Supreme Court of the United States, the dissenting judgment becomes more than merely a personal avowal of the dissenter. He may hope, by persistence, to bring enough of his colleagues to his point of view so as to remake the law. But equally, as a signal illustration in the Supreme Court of Canada reveals, a dissenter may repent and recant upon later reconsideration of his dissenting opinion. . . .

# 12.3

## KEYTERMS

### Concepts

*seriatim* opinion writing
"opinion of the court"
majority opinion
dissenting opinion
concurring opinion
plurality decision
judicial collegiality
five and nine judge panels

# 13

# Reconciling Judicial Review and Constitutional Democracy

The readings in this final chapter raise and address some of the fundamental questions about the practice of judicial review. Donald Smiley's contribution emphasizes that the real question raised by an entrenched Charter of Rights is not whether Canadians shall have civil liberties or not, but *who* decides what is and is not a civil liberty. The principal effect of the Charter is to transfer the primary, although not exclusive, responsibility for such decisions to the courts, or more specifically, to Canadian judges. Smiley expresses scepticism over the judges' ability to make these kinds of decisions better than Canadian parliamentary legislatures. In effect, Smiley asks what special competencies do judges have that elected legislators lack? (Reading 13.1)

The late Alexander Bickel, the leading American constitutional scholar of his generation, has elaborated this question and also provided an answer. He described the requirements for a justification of judicial review on principle, rather than habit and tradition, as follows:

> The search must be for a function which might (indeed, must) involve the making of policy, yet which differs from the legislative and executive functions; which is peculiarly suited to the capabilities of the courts; which will not likely be performed elsewhere if the courts do not assume it; which can be so exercised as to be acceptable in a society that generally shares Judge Learned Hand's satisfaction in a "sense of common venture"; which will be effective when needed; and whose discharge by the courts will not lower the quality of the other departments' performance by denuding them of the dignity and burden of their own responsibility.[1]

---

[1] *The Least Dangerous Branch: The Supreme Court at the Bar of Politics* (Indianapolis: Bobbs-Merrill, 1962), p.24.

The potentially unique contribution of judicial review, according to Bickel, is the defense and articulation of a society's fundamental political and ethical principles. In the name of individual liberty, the pursuit of self-interest is given wide range in Western democracies. The executive and legislative branches are purposely made responsive to the resulting clash of interests and groups that is the stuff of democratic politics. Amidst the welter of competing self-interests, the rush and crush of practical affairs, and the ensuing short-term perspective on all matters, it is prudent to have one institution, purposely distanced from the fray, to guard the principles that preserve the justice and dignity of that society. Judicial review offers this potential.

The contribution by then Justice Brian Dickson, now the new Chief Justice of the Supreme Court of Canada, elaborates one dimension of Bickel's defense of judicial review. It does not do to say that judicial review is "undemocratic" simply because it sometimes replaces the decisions of a representative assembly with the judgement of nine, non-elected judges. In many instances the principles that the court intervenes to protect — freedom of political speech and press, freedom of association and thought — are the very processes that constitute liberal democracy. (Reading 13.2)

The Knopff-Morton contribution focuses on one of the most controversial aspects of the Charter — the section 33 "legislative override" — and suggests that while it was the product of political expediency and compromise, it can still be defended on principle. It is argued that section 33 only formalizes the limiting conditions of judicial authority in all circumstances — public opinion. The sources and dynamics of judicial authority are briefly explored, particularly with respect to judicial review. The essay concludes that to build up the authority and effectiveness of the Charter, less may be more for the early years. (Reading 13.3)

# 13.1

## COURTS, LEGISLATURES, AND THE PROTECTION OF HUMAN RIGHTS

Donald Smiley

This paper examines in a Canadian context the appropriateness of judicial as against legislative decision in the definition and ranking of human rights. The issue is often put within the framework of proposals for the further entrenchment of human rights in the Canadian constitution. . . . Most provisions related to human rights. . . . would necessarily be expressed in general language conferring on the courts of law the responsibility of defining and ranking rights in an ongoing process of judicial review of the constitution. . . .

. . . Most discussions of legislative as against judicial decision with respect to human rights proceed according to conflicting views of what I call democratic fundamentalism.

The first view asserts that in terms of democratic theory elected officials have better claims than courts to define and rank human rights as well as to make other important decisions about public policy. Democracy in this view is government in accord with the will of the governed, and the organs of government best able and most likely to act in accord with this will are composed of people who have successfully contested popular elections - and act in anticipation of future elections. I do not find this argument completely convincing. If we look at the operative constitution of any developed political system — the constitution in action as against the constitution of the textbooks of law or civics — we find a complex allocation of discretionary powers. Powers are wielded in various kinds of matters by judges and juries, by political executives and career bureaucrats, by elected legislatures and political parties, by the electorate, by the groups who effect constitutional amendment. And we also find different kinds of procedural rules for reaching various kinds of decisions — unanimous consent in jury verdicts, certain motions in the House of Commons and the most crucial of constitutional amendments, consensual decision-making at federal-provincial conferences and, perhaps, in cabinets, pluralities, bare majorities and extraordinary majorities as so defined, different provisions for quorums, and so on. On this basis, I would see no a priori reason stemming from democratic theory which would prevent a democratic community from conferring decisions involving human rights on the

*Courts and Trials: A Multidisciplinary Approach.* Edited by M.L. Friedland. Toronto: University of Toronto Press, 1975, p.89. Reprinted with permission.

courts or from enacting provisions respecting such rights other than those which prevail in respect to ordinary lawmaking . . . .

. . . It seems to me,. . . . that the connection between the preferred procedures for protecting human rights and natural law is historical and psychological rather than logical in the sense that if the imperatives of natural law are binding surely they bind legislatures as much as courts. Which of the two sets of institutions will better protect such rights is thus a matter of prudential political judgment rather than political philosophy. . . .

. . . Perhaps some will agree with most of this but still maintain that, on balance, courts will be wiser and more zealous than elected bodies in defining and ranking human rights. In much of the argument for entrenchment there is the underlying premise that the community needs to be saved from the inherently liberal tendencies of public opinion because these create irresistible pressures on elected legislatures. Perhaps. It is my own impression, however, that in Canada the elected political elites are considerably more liberal than are the prevailing sentiments in their respective local, provincial, and national electorates. Again, it is my impression that when we begin to inquire carefully into those institutions of Canadian society under the direct control of the bar and the bench we will find less than a total commitment to humane values. There is a strain of absolutism in recent Canadian proposals for an entrenched Bill of Rights. Prime Minister Trudeau said in 1969, "To enshrine a right in a constitutional charter is to make an important judgment, to give to that right of the individual a higher order of value than the right of government to infringe it." This argument proceeds on the assumption that encroachments on human rights are always unequivocal and disinterested and liberal people will always be able to agree when such encroachments are made. Again, if we take Mr. Trudeau's statement literally, there is the assumption that under all conceivable circumstances entrenched rights are to prevail over other considerations. These absolutist premises are in practice indefensible. In the sphere of human rights there is indeed an economy, and rights have what economists call "opportunity costs," in the sense that to get something of value it is necessary to give up something else of value.

As a non-lawyer, it seems clear to me that if Canadian courts are to assume a more active role in the ranking and defining of human rights there must be profound changes in the Canadian legal culture. Canadian jurists are profoundly in the positivist tradition. But the determination of human rights in particular circumstances is in Peter Russell's terms the "delicate balancing of social priorities." I confess not to know the shape of the new jurisprudence or how judges and legal scholars are going to get us to realize it while maintaining the continuity with past traditions and lines of judicial interpretation that is surely necessary in our kind of polity. I confess also that the break proposed by Atkey and Lyon is too radical for me. But perhaps there should be a warning to enthusiasts for a socially relevant jurisprudence. This approach by its nature downgrades the technical nature of the law, and when members of bar and bench set up shop to articulate the political need and political ideals of the community they enter a world in which others make the same claims. To be blunt: as piety does not make a theologian or pugnacity a military strategist, an increasing social sensitivity among lawyers and judges is no substitute for intellectual discipline in the social sciences and political philosophy.

To return to the main argument of this paper, I quote what I said on a previous occasion:

> Apart from those times where public opinion is inflamed, the democratic legislature is uniquely equipped to make sound judgements about human rights. In my view Parliament has been at or near its best in some of the debates about human rights in the past decade - debates in respect to capital punishment, divorce, abortion, hate literature, official languages. Although the determination of the scope and nature of human rights usually involves some technical considerations, the technical content of reasoned discussion and decision is characteristically not as high as in regard to, say, defence policy or environmental pollution. Thus the major considerations in respect to human rights ordinarily involve the clash of human values, the sense of the community about what is acceptable and the broadest judgements of where society is going. Further, questions involving human rights tend not to be as localized in their incidence as is true of many other public policies and the Member of Parliament may well be more free to act primarily as a member of a deliberative body rather than a voice of particularized constituency interests. Elected politicians working within an environment of public discussion and debate are well equipped to deal wisely with questions of human rights. It is yet to be demonstrated that the Canadian judiciary can do better. . . .

# 13.2

# THE DEMOCRATIC CHARACTER OF THE CHARTER OF RIGHTS

The Honourable Mr. Justice Brian Dickson, Supreme Court of Canada

It has sometimes been said that the *Charter* marks an "Americanization" of the Canadian Constitution. It has not always been clear to me whether this is meant as praise, as criticism, or simply as a neutral statement of fact, but however it is intended I think it is only partly true at best. . . .

. . . The American Constitutional system is sometimes described as one of "judicial supremacy." Whether or not this characterization is strictly accurate in political science terms, there is no doubt that in a real sense the American judiciary always has the last word. American legislation must conform to the

---

Lecture at the University of Calgary, Faculty of Law, September 13, 1983. Reprinted with permission.

Constitution including the *Bill of Rights*, and once the Supreme Court has ruled that a given enactment violates the *Bill of Rights* the legislature's only recourse is to the lengthy and difficult process of constitutional amendment.

The Anglo-Canadian tradition, by contrast, is one of parliamentary sovereignty. A British Parliament is free to pass any legislation it wishes and no court has jurisdiction to invalidate a regularly enacted statute. The only constraints on Parliament in its legislative capacity are political ones. In Canada this concept of parliamentary sovereignty was modified to the extent that the distribution of powers under the *British North America Act* necessitated giving the courts a mandate to rule on whether a given enactment was within the legislative competence of the enacting parliament. But assuming that the distribution of powers in ss. 91 and 92 of the *British North America Act* was respected it was generally thought that there was no other limit on parliamentary sovereignty.

It seems clear that the very concept of a bill of rights which would act as a further constraint on Parliament's legislative freedom is in serious conflict with the assumptions of such a theory. The history of the Canadian *Bill of Rights* perhaps illustrates some of the consequences of this conflict. It is true that in the *Drybones* decision the Supreme Court of Canada held that the Canadian *Bill of Rights* did provide a mandate to strike down legislation inconsistent with the fundamental freedoms enumerated in the *Bill*, but that mandate was always controversial. . . . It is sufficient to note that despite the *Drybones* decision the Canadian judiciary proved itself to be very cautious about using the *Bill of Rights* to override the enactments of democratically-elected legislatures or to expand the ambit of judicial review. . . .

. . . Much of this caution is no doubt to be attributed to the fact that in contrast to the American *Bill of Rights*, the Canadian *Bill* was simply an ordinary statute, or at most — in the words of Chief Justice Laskin — a "quasi-constitutional document." The *Charter of Rights and Freedoms* is, of course, an entrenched constitutional document. Given s. 52, there can be no doubt as to the legitimacy of judicial review. . . .

. . . In the result, while I do not think we have moved to an American model of judicial supremacy, it does seem clear that we have moved some-what away from pure parliamentary sovereignty. That we have not moved that far away is made clear by s. 33, a provision unique to our constitution which allows for a time-limited legislative override of rights and freedoms guaranteed in sections 2 and 7 through 15 of the *Charter*. Without in any way denying the provisions of s. 52, s. 33 provides a way for the legislature directly to abrogate constitutionally-entrenched rights. Provided that the proper formalities have been complied with, the only effective constraint on a legislature so-minded to do is a political one, based on its perception of the electoral consequences of legislating directly in the face of the supreme law of the land. And, of course, the principle of democratic control has always been the theoretical basis underlying the notion of parliamentary sovereignty.

This does not mean, however, that without s. 33 or insofar as it does not apply to any parts of the *Charter*, there is anything necessarily undemocratic about a constitution in which legislative power is constrained by a judicially-enforced *Charter of Rights.* In this regard I commend to you a statement by the Committee on the Constitution of the Canadian Bar Association:

> A democracy is the basis and prerequisite for the operation of the supremacy of Parliament. That being so, it would seem justifiable to entrench in a constitution principles which are prerequisite to the existence of democracy. Democracy is the periodic determination of the common will by the free expression of the genuine and informed will of the individual. There must be freedom of thought, conscience and opinion, or there can be no expression of the genuine will of the individual. There must be freedom of information, assembly and association, or there can be no expression of an informed will of the individual. There must be freedom of speech, or there can be no ''expression'' of the will of the individual at all. There must be universal suffrage and free elections, representation by population and required sittings and elections of legislative institutions, or there can be no ''expression of the common will.'' The right to privacy is a prerequisite to freedom of speech, expression, thought, conscience, opinion, assembly and association. It is inconsistent to guarantee these rights directly when a person's knowledge that his privacy may be violated will indirectly inhibit the exercise of the guaranteed rights. All the above rights are prerequisites to the proper exercise of democracy, which in turn, is a prerequisite to the proper operation of the principle of the supremacy of parliament. There is, therefore, no conflict between the entrenchment of these rights and the principle of the supremacy of parliament.

In addition to its commendable eloquence, this statement is noteworthy for its approach to the *Charter* as a purposive document rather than simply as a text to be analyzed. I think that this is the proper approach to take.

# 13.3

# JUDICIAL STATESMANSHIP AND THE CHARTER OF RIGHTS AND FREEDOMS

Rainer Knopff and F.L. Morton

Canada's new Charter of Human Rights was born in controversy concerning the proper role of the courts in formulating civil liberties ''policy.'' The document which emerged was a compromise between the advocates of judicial activism and restraint (including those who would have preferred no Charter at all). On the one hand, entrenchment of the Charter, and the wording of many of its clauses, were intended to remedy defects in the existing

Paper presented at 1982 Annual Meeting of the Canadian Political Science Association, June 7-9, 1982. Reprinted with permission.

statutory Bill of Rights which were thought to contribute to an excessive restraint on the part of Canadian courts. On the other hand, the first clause, which subjects the entrenched rights and freedoms ''. . . to such reasonable limits prescribed by law as can be demonstrably justified in a free and democratic society,'' and the thirty-third clause, which provides for a legislative override, bespeak a wariness of the extremes of activism. This paper argues that the middle ground staked out by the Charter is defensible not only on the ground of political compromise, but on the basis of principle as well. Further, we suggest the establishment of this middle ground is, for both theoretical and institutional reasons, a task of delicate statesmanship — a statesmanship which is necessary always, but especially at the outset, and particularly with regard to certain of the specified rights and liberties. Finally, in light of these considerations, we elaborate some of the forces which will influence the effective judicial enforcement of the Charter.

> We hold these truths to be self-evident, that all men are created equal, that they are endowed by their Creator with certain unalienable Rights, that among these are Life, Liberty and the pursuit of Happiness. That to secure these rights, Governments are instituted among Men, deriving their just powers from the consent of the governed.

Although an entrenched Bill of Rights is not essential to the enterprise of liberal democracy, it underscores the liberalism of such a democracy, for liberalism insists that government is established for, and limited to, the protection of rights. These rights derive from political equality: because there is no natural or divinely revealed right to rule, each is naturally free to rule himself. To the extent that this condition of natural freedom is insecure, it may have to be replaced by civil society, which constitutes an artificial inequality constructed on the foundation of, and intended to serve, natural equality. In a word, government is not by nature but by consent. That consent is given only better to secure natural equality and freedom, and government remains legitimate only to the extent that it respects this purpose. This is what we mean by limited, or constitutional government.

The requirement of consent in the institution of government need not entail the forms of political democracy in its day to day operation. Even the Declaration is more of a liberal than a democratic document. Among liberal *democrats*, however, consent is satisfied only through the rule of public (which is to say majority) opinion. Thus the equality which lies at the heart of liberal democracy points in two directions: to rights and freedoms as the end of government, and to consent (understood as majority opinion) as the procedure of government. These are allied in the sense that the political power of majority opinion prevents minority tyranny, but they may also be opposed whenever majority opinion denies the equality and freedom of minorities.

It is this tension which constitutes the problem of statesmanship in a liberal democracy. As Abraham Lincoln understood, a majority which denies the equal rights of a minority denies the very political equality which is the ground of government by consent, and hence of the principle of majority rule. The fact that such a majority opinion was self-contradictory, on the other hand, was, for Lincoln, no warrant for ignoring it. To dismiss public opinion would require the statesman either to retire from active politics or to abandon *democratic* politics. But to resort to oligarchy to enforce equality was an insupportable irony. The task of statesmanship, therefore, was to steer a middle course.

The founders of the first self-conscious liberal democracy, the United States, were acutely aware of the need to hold this middle ground between majority rule and minority rights. While recognizing the role of elevated statesmanship in solving the problem, they considered it imprudent to rely on its timely emergence, and proposed instead a more reliable institutional solution. More precisely, they constructed a number of institutional devices designed both to reduce the need for statesmanship and to encourage the emergence of the more limited form of it which remained necessary. Judicial review must be understood as a component of this institutional strategy. . . .

. . . Those who thought that this balance was still tipped too far in the direction of consent found in judicial review an additional precaution against democratic abuse of power. It is true that the Constitution does not explicitly provide for judicial review, and it is arguable that a written constitution can perform a restraining function without it. Yet the ratification debates disclose that both Federalists and Anti-Federalists expected the Supreme Court to exercise such a power. Through the statesmanship of Chief Justice John Marshall, this expectation was realized in the landmark case of *Marbury* v. *Madison*.

The exercise of such a politically significant power by appointed judges with life tenure clearly represents the ultimate in independence from public opinion. If all forms of such "political distance" were intended to give weight to the "rights" side of the rights/consent dilemma, the judiciary exercising judicial review is particularly well equipped to do so, not only because of its greater independence, but also by virtue of its training. Indeed, were it not for the fact that the judiciary is the "least dangerous" as well as the most independent branch, one might be tempted to suggest that these characteristics point more to a tyranny of rights over consent than to a proper balance between the two. In fact, the unarmed character of the court under- scores the impossibility of such judicial tyranny because, in the most decisive sense, judgements must generate consent to be effective.

It might be thought that the impossibility of judicial tyranny supports the case for judicial activism: given the court's inability to do permanent damage, why should it not stand firm in its contest with unwise power? Yet the lack of judicial force points just as strongly in the opposite direction. If it is true that judicial pronouncements cannot be effective without consent, it is equally true that the hallowed judicial independence, which supports judicial capacity to concentrate on principle, is just as dependent on consent. Stated differently, judicial independence is a convention. It exists not so much as a matter of law as by virtue of public consent. In the final analysis, the courts are dependent upon the other branches of government for the appointment of their members, the boundaries of their appellate jurisdiction, and even compliance with their decisions. Any of these powers could be used to subvert their independence. In a democratic age the required public support is forthcoming only to the extent that the non-elected judiciary is perceived as non-political (or at least as much less political than the other branches). A court which too often and too easily thwarts majority opinion cannot long maintain this perception.

The destiny in store for a "politicized" court is foreshadowed by the fate of the indirect selection of the American President and Senate — those "distancing" devices which most closely approximated judicial independence at the political level. Unlike the judiciary, the President and Senate came to be perceived as political, and this ensured the demise of their original methods of selection. In 1913, the Seventeenth Amendment "democratized" the Senate by providing for direct popular election. Similarly, the intended non-partisan character of the Presidency did not outlast its first occupant, George Washington. The emergence of organized national political parties in the early nineteenth century short-circuited the non-partisan elements of the electoral college, and the rise of the "stewardship" model of presidential leadership in the twentieth century completed the transformation. What hope is there that a politicized court, less representative than either of these institutions, could long escape a similar fate? Furthermore, while democratization actually increased the power of the Senate and the Presidency, a court which was merely a political "rubber stamp" would cease to be significant.

In a word, a judiciary reviewing a written constitution remains subject to the demand of liberal democratic statesmanship to strike a prudent balance between rights and consent. Institutional capacity inclines the court to principle, and this is what makes it valuable, but the maintenance of that institutional capacity involves some deference to consent. Whatever one thinks of the manner in which it is effected, the compromise between activism and restraint in the new Canadian Charter is justifiable on principle.

To strike the proper balance, the court must remember that in a democratic age the capacity of appointed judges to stand against the public will depends upon a general perception that they are not speaking merely in their own name — i.e., imposing on the nation their particular policy preferences — but in the name of long-range principles enshrined in the constitution. Furthermore, the perception that judges speak in the name of the constitution is an improvement upon the belief that they speak in their own name only if the constitution is itself an object of respect. As James Madison observed, an effective constitution depends on ". . . that veneration which time bestows on everything, and without which perhaps the wisest and freest governments would not possess the requisite stability." Such respect is neither self-generating nor self-sustaining. Whether or not a constitution comes to enjoy it depends largely on the court's skill in choosing and handling its battles with the legislature, especially at the beginning. The extremes of either activism or restraint will almost certainly undermine it.

The extreme of judicial restraint is most closely associated with parliamentary democracy and is fueled by positivist jurisprudence. It was the approach of the Canadian court to the 1960 Bill of Rights. Such excessive deference to the legislature leads a court to interpret entrenched rights to fit the legislation in order to avoid striking down the latter. As the post-*Drybones* interpretation of the 1960 equality clause shows, this leads to a series of irreconcilable precedents which can hardly enhance the reputation of the judiciary or of the document it is interpreting. In effect, a judiciary which abandons principle to consent will not long retain public confidence.

The extreme of activism, on the other hand, has characterized recent American jurisprudence, especially that of the Warren Court. Just as extreme restraint neglects principle, so this unchastened activism ignores the limits placed on institutional capacity by consent. It forgets that the judiciary wields neither sword nor purse, and that the more popular branches are required to enforce a ruling of unconstitutionality against themselves. Needless to say, such voluntary acquiescence is not automatic. A Bill of Rights is not self-interpreting, which is to say that the practical implication of its provisions are almost never perfectly clear, and that decent (non-tyrannical) opinion can usually be found on either side of an issue. A court which indiscriminately and frequently opposes decent majorities on such issues will almost certainly come to be seen as narrowly partisan, and in its frustration the majority will tend to lose respect either for the court, the constitution it interprets, or both. An unrestrained activism, then, is as likely to undermine the constitutional veneration of which Madison spoke as is the muddying of constitutional principle produced by undue judicial deference.

This does not mean that the Court cannot successfully defend constitutional rights against hostile majority opinion. But its ability to do so depends on its having created and sustained a high degree of moral capital in the form of veneration for the constitution, and in spending that capital carefully. The American Court is the beneficiary of such an inheritance. The Canadian Court is not.

At first glance the ability of the American Supreme Court to make one controversial decision after another, often with minimal textual support, and frequently overturning established and popular law or practice, tends to obscure the fragile basis of judicial authority and to depreciate the case for judicial statesmanship. The apparent triumph of American activism, in other words, implies the irrelevance, if not the cowardice, of restraint. Perhaps nothing so dramatically illustrates the power and independence of the American Court as the *Watergate Tapes Case*, where a single stroke of the judicial pen accomplished what the combined strength of the House and Senate could not. It was not always thus. The first exercise of judicial review involved a similar confrontation of the Court and the President, and the outcome was not nearly so predictable. A comparison of *Marbury* v. *Madison* and *U.S.* v. *Nixon* reveals the dramatic difference between the authority of a court before and after the convention of judicial review is firmly established. More importantly, the former case illustrates the kind of statesmanship which made the latter possible.

Much like the Burger Court in the *Watergate Tapes Case*, the Court of Chief Justice John Marshall was confronted with a fairly clear case of executive malfeasance. The Secretary of State, James Madison, had refused to deliver a commission for a federal judgeship to William Marbury. Precedent and practice supported Marbury's legal claim to the commission, but, unlike the Burger Court, Marshall knew full well that he could not issue a mandamus and expect automatic compliance. To the contrary, he had every reason to believe that Jefferson and Madison would ignore such an order, and would be supported in so doing by both Congress and public opinion.

Marshall was acutely aware of the dilemma confronting the Court. If it ordered Madison to deliver the commission, it would not be obeyed. Not only would such disobedience deny justice to Marbury and humiliate the Court, but it would establish a precedent of discretionary compliance with Court decisions. Agreeing with Alexander Hamilton that limited government depended on the Court's ability to enforce a written constitution, Marshall thought such a precedent would threaten not only the court but constitutionalism itself.

The alternative of denying Marbury's petition was no better. Since the legality of Marbury's claim was generally accepted, the Court would be perceived as abandoning integrity for political expedience. In addition to an obvious breach of justice, there would again be the broader implication that the executive is "above the law," because of its ability to subdue to the courts.

Marshall's ingenious escape from this dilemma is now well known. Deferring the issue of jurisdiction, he held that Madison had violated Marbury's legal right to the commission, and that his position in the executive branch did not exempt him from the rule of law as interpreted by the courts. Marshall was thus able to publicly upbraid Madison and Jefferson for their action, and to serve notice that their newly acquired positions of authority did not exempt them from the law of the land. A disastrous confrontation was avoided, however, by the subsequent "finding" that the statute purporting to grant the Court the power to issue writs of *mandamus* was an unconstitutional addition to its original jurisdiction, and that the Court could not, therefore, issue the writ to which Marbury was entitled! In declining this power, Marshall claimed for the Court the much greater power of judicial review, and exercised it here for the first time.

While Jefferson and Madison were happy to have prevailed in their dispute with Marbury, they were furious with Marshall's successful claim to and exercise of judicial review. But as Marshall had so keenly anticipated, there was nothing Jefferson or Madison could do to block or annul the decision. Since it commanded nothing requiring executive compliance, it could not be disobeyed.

This successful first exercise of judicial review was the necessary precondition for the convention of "automatic" compliance with Supreme Court decisions. The dispute could easily have issued in a very different result, establishing the opposite covention of discretionary compliance. John Marshall has long been memorialized for initiating the practice of judicial review in unlikely circumstances. Less emphasized has been the implicit lesson that in establishing judicial authority, less may sometimes be more.

The relevance of *Marbury* v. *Madison* to judicial review of the new Canadian Charter may be questioned. After all, judicial review is already firmly established in Canada. Moreover, a battle for its legitimacy never had to be fought; it began as a function of colonialism and lingered on as the relatively unquestioned requirement of federalism. True, judicial review of a Bill of Rights is more controversial, but one would expect the Canadian court to begin this jurisprudence with a greater fund of legitimacy than the American court enjoyed before the legitimation of judicial review *per se*.

On reflection, however, the differences do not appear so great. One must remember that the American Court's civil rights jurisprudence did not begin until after a century devoted primarily to issues of federalism. Furthermore, despite *Dred Scott*, the Civil War, and the New Deal Crisis, it has been suggested that it was the Court's success in handling federalism that built up the moral capital (a process begun but certainly not completed in *Marbury*) necessary to sustain its later succession in the civil rights field. In Canada, to the contrary, it is arguable that the Court's work in federalism has depleted rather than enhanced the moral capital available for a Bill of Rights jurisprudence. Certainly the opposition of some of the provinces to a Charter was fueled by their perception of a federally biased court. Even the traditional justification of judicial review in the hitherto unproblematic area of federalism itself has recently come under attack. We may thus be closer to the situation of *Marbury* v. *Madison* than first appears. At any rate, the kind of statesmanship required to establish judicial review in that case is also necessary to sustain it.

What made *Marbury* v. *Madison* such a *tour de force* was Marshall's ability to avoid a direct confrontation which he was likely to lose, without creating the impression that the court was simply yielding to political pressure. Successful enforcement of the new Charter will require a similar strategy. . . .

. . . When the Court does make active use of its new power, it must ensure that citizens can see the *constitution* speaking through its decision. To do this, it should base its judgements as closely as possible on the concrete language of the Charter and avoid the kind of latitudinarian interpretation that has embroiled the American Court in political warfare. Judicial discoveries of a right to "freedom of contract" or a "right of privacy" lurking somewhere in the "penumbras" of the constitution are not persuasive and can only buttress the dangerous perception that the constitution is merely what the judges say it is. When the Court uses such penumbral rights to strike down existing laws in 48 of 50 states, as it did in the 1973 *Abortion Case*, it is hardly surprising that it should become the focus of sustained and growing political attack.

This is not to suggest that the Court should strike down only the "clear mistake" — i.e., the mistake which is clear to any reasonable man. Judicial statesmanship is not identical to strict constructionism or what Ely calls interpretivism. Almost all of the rights and liberties protected in a Charter are open to reasonable differences of interpretation, and the courts must make choices. Still, it is one thing to make a disputed ruling on freedom of religion or speech, about which the constitution clearly has something to say, and quite another to discover and *then* interpret a right which is not so obviously present. In the former case it is much easier, even for the losing side, to rationalize the decision as one required by the constitution, and not simply by the preferences of the judges. It goes without saying that the Court must attempt to provide reasons for its decision which appear to the losing side to be principled rather than capricious, and such as a reasonable (even if mistaken) man might give. Paul Weiler's admonition of several years ago is still valid. If the Court is to fulfill its new responsibility, it must avoid the practice of formalistically reciting numerous (often conflicting) precedents and then concluding with a quick, unelaborated ruling.

The example of what happens when these standards of prudence are ignored is the United States where, despite a great fund of legitimacy for judicial review, serious court-curbing is now under way. In Canada, where the fund of legitimacy is yet to be built, such imprudence could kill the Charter, especially since easy court-curbing is explicitly provided for in the form of the *non-obstante* clause.

# APPENDIX

# CONSTITUTION ACT, 1867, ss. 91-92

## VI — Distribution of Legislative Powers

### *Powers of the Parliament*

91. It shall be lawful for the Queen, by and with the Advice and Consent of the Senate and House of Commons, to make Laws for the Peace, Order, and good Government of Canada, in relation to all Matters not coming within the Classes of Subjects by this Act assigned exclusively to the Legislatures of the Provinces; and for greater Certainty, but not so as to restrict the Generality of the foregoing Terms of this Section, it is hereby declared that (notwithstanding anything in this Act) the exclusive Legislative Authority of the Parliament of Canada extends to all Matters coming within the Classes of Subjects next herein-after enumerated; that is to say, —

1. The amendment from time to time of the Constitution of Canada, except as regards matters coming within the classes of subjects by this Act assigned exclusively to the Legislatures of the provinces, or as regards rights or privileges by this or any other Constitutional Act granted or secured to the Legislature or the Government of a province, or to any class of persons with respect to schools or as regards the use of the English or the French language or as regards the requirements that there shall be a session of the Parliament of Canada at least once each year, and that no House of Commons shall continue for more than five years from the day of the return of the Writs for choosing the House: provided, however, that a House of Commons may in time of real or apprehended war, invasion or insurrection be continued by the Parliament of Canada if such continuation is not opposed by the votes of more than one-third of the members of such House. (39)

1A.  The Public Debt and Property. (40)
2.   The Regulation of Trade and Commerce.
2A.  Unemployment insurance. (41)
3.   The raising of Money by any Mode or System of Taxation.
4.   The borrowing of Money on the Public Credit.
5.   Postal Service.
6.   The Census and Statistics.
7.   Militia, Military and Naval Service, and Defence.
8.   The fixing of and providing for the Salaries and Allowances of Civil and other Officers of the Government of Canada.
9.   Beacons, Buoys, Lighthouses, and Sable Island.
10.  Navigation and Shipping.
11.  Quarantine and the Establishment and Maintenance of Marine Hospitals.
12.  Sea Coast and Inland Fisheries.
13.  Ferries between a Province and any British or Foreign Country or between Two Provinces.
14.  Currency and Coinage.
15.  Banking, Incorporation of Banks, and the Issue of Paper Money.
16.  Savings Banks.
17.  Weights and Measures.
18.  Bills of Exchange and Promissory Notes.
19.  Interest.
20.  Legal Tender.
21.  Bankruptcy and Insolvency.
22.  Patents of Invention and Discovery.
23.  Copyrights.
24.  Indians, and Lands reserved for the Indians.
25.  Naturalization and Aliens.
26.  Marriage and Divorce
27.  The Criminal Law, except the Constitution of Courts of Criminal Jurisdiction, but including the Procedure in Criminal Matters.
28.  The Establishment, Maintenance, and Management of Penitentiaries.
29.  Such Classes of Subjects as are expressly excepted in the Enumeration of the Classes of Subjects by this Act assigned exclusively to the Legislatures of the Provinces.

And any Matter coming within any of the Classes of Subjects enumerated in this Section shall not be deemed to come within the Class of Matters of a local or private Nature comprised in the Enumeration of the Classes of Subjects by this Act assigned exclusively to the Legislatures of the Provinces. (42)

### Exclusive Powers of Provincial Legislatures

92. In each Province the Legislature may exclusively make Laws in relation to Matters coming within the Classes of Subject next herein-after enumerated; that is to say, —

1.   The Amendment from Time to Time, notwithstanding anything in this Act, of the Constitution of the Province, except as regards the Office of Lieutenant Governor.
2.   Direct Taxation within the Province in order to the raising of a Revenue for Provincial Purposes.
3.   The borrowing of Money on the sole Credit of the Province.

4. The Establishment and Tenure of Provincial Offices and the Appointment and Payment of Provincial Officers.

5. The Management and Sale of the Public Lands belonging to the Province and of the Timber and Wood thereon.

6. The Establishment, Maintenance, and Management of Public and Reformatory Prisons in and for the Province.

7. The Establishment, Maintenance, and Management of Hospitals, Asylums, Charities, and Eleemosynary Institutions in and for the Province, other than Marine Hospitals.

8. Municipal Institutions in the Province.

9. Shop, Saloon, Tavern, Auctioneer, and other Licences in order to the raising of a Revenue for Provincial, Local, or Municipal Purposes.

10. Local Works and Undertakings other than such as are of the following Classes: —

    (a) Lines of Steam or other Ships, Railways, Canals, Telegraphs, and other Works and Undertakings connecting the Province with any other or others of the Provinces, or extending beyond the Limits of the Province;

    (b) Lines of Steam Ships between the Province and any British or Foreign Country;

    (c) Such Works as, although wholly situate within the Province, are before or after their Execution declared by the Parliament of Canada to be for the general Advantage of Canada or for the Advantage of Two or more of the Provinces.

11. The Incorporation of Companies with Provincial Objects.

12. The Solemnization of Marriage in the Province.

13. Property and Civil Rights in the Province.

14. The Administration of Justice in the Province, including the Constitution, Maintenance, and Organization of Provincial Courts, both of Civil and of Criminal Jurisdiction, and including Procedure in Civil Matters in those Courts.

15. The Imposition of Punishment by Fine, Penalty, or Imprisonment for enforcing any Law of the Province made in relation to any Matter coming within any of the Classes of Subjects enumerated in this Section.

16. Generally all Matters of a merely local or private Nature in the Province.

# CANADIAN BILL OF RIGHTS

(1960), 8-9 ELIZ. II, c. 44 (Can.)

An Act for the Recognition
and Protection of Human Rights
and Fundamental Freedoms

[Assented to 10th August, 1960.]

The Parliament of Canada, affirming that the Canadian Nation is founded upon principles that acknowledge the supremacy of God, the dignity and worth of the human person and the position of the family in a society of free men and free institutions;

Affirming also that men and institutions remain free only when freedom is founded upon respect for moral and spiritual values and the rule of law;

And being desirous of enshrining these principles and the human rights and fundamental freedoms derived from them, in a Bill of Rights which shall reflect the respect of Parliament for its constitutional authority and which shall ensure the protection of these rights and freedoms in Canada;

THEREFORE Her Majesty, by and with the advice and consent of the Senate and House of Commons of Canada, enacts as follows:

## PART I
## BILL OF RIGHTS

1. It is hereby recognized and declared that in Canada there have existed and shall continue to exist without discrimination by reason of race, national origin, colour, religion or sex, the following human rights and fundamental freedoms, namely,

(a) the right of the individual to life, liberty, security of the person and enjoyment of property, and the right not to be deprived thereof except by due process of law;

(b) the right of the individual to equality before the law and the protection of the law;

(c) freedom of religion;

(d) freedom of speech;

(e) freedom of assembly and association; and

(f) freedom of the press.

2. Every law of Canada shall, unless it is expressly declared by an Act of the Parliament of Canada that it shall operate notwithstanding the Canadian Bill of Rights, be so construed and applied as not to abrogate, abridge or infringe or to authorize the abrogation, abridgment or infringement of any of the rights or freedoms herein recognized and declared, and in particular, no law of Canada shall be construed or applied so as to

(a) authorize or effect the arbitrary detention, imprisonment or exile of any person;

(b) impose or authorize the imposition of cruel and unusual treatment or punishment;

(c) deprive a person who has been arrested or detained

(i) of the right to be informed promptly of the reason for his arrest or detention,

(ii) of the right to retain and instruct counsel without delay, or

(iii) of the remedy by way of *habeas corpus* for the determination of the validity of his detention and for his release if the detention is not lawful;

(d) authorize a court, tribunal, commission, board or other authority to compel a person to give evidence if he is denied counsel, protection against self crimination or other constitutional safeguards;

(e) deprive a person of the right to a fair hearing in accordance with the principles of fundamental justice for the determination of his rights and obligations;

(f) deprive a person charged with a criminal offence of right to be presumed innocent until proved guilty according to law in a fair and public hearing by an independent and impartial tribunal, or of the right to reasonable bail without just cause; or

(g) deprive a person of the right to the assistance of an interpreter in any proceedings in which he is involved or in which he is a party or a witness, before a court, commission, board or other tribunal, if he does not understand or speak the language in which such proceedings are conducted.

3. The Minister of Justice shall, in accordance with such regulations as may be prescribed by the Governor in Council, examine every proposed regulation submitted in draft form to the Clerk of the Privy Council pursuant to the *Regulations Act* and every Bill introduced in or presented to the House of Commons, in order to ascertain whether any of the provisions thereof are inconsistent with the purposes and provisions of this Part and he shall report any such inconsistency to the House of Commons at the first convenient opportunity.

4. The provisions of this Part shall be known as the *Canadian Bill of Rights*.

## PART II

5.(1) Nothing in Part I shall be construed to abrogate or abridge any human right or fundamental freedom not enumerated therein that may have existed in Canada at the commencement of this Act.

(2) The expression "law of Canada" in Part I means an Act of the Parliament of Canada enacted before or after the coming into force of this Act, any order, rule or regulation thereunder, and any law in force in Canada or in any part of Canada at the commencement of this Act that is subject to be repealed, abolished or altered by the Parliament of Canada.

(3) The provisions of Part I shall be construed as extending only to matters coming within the legislative authority of the Parliament of Canada.

6. Section 5 of the *War Measures Act* is repealed and the following substituted therefor:

6.(1) Sections 3, 4, and 5 shall come into force only upon the issue of a proclamation of the Governor in Council declaring that war, invasion or insurrection, real or apprehended, exists.

(2) A Proclamation declaring that war, invasion or insurrection, real or apprehended, exists shall be laid before Parliament forthwith after its issue, or, if Parliament is then not sitting, within the first fifteen days next thereafter that Parliament is sitting.

(3) Where a proclamation has been laid before Parliament pursuant to subsection (2), a notice of motion in either House signed by ten members thereof and

made in accordance with the rules of that House within ten days of the day the proclamation was laid before Parliament, praying that the proclamation be revoked, shall be debated in that House at the first convenient opportunity within the four sitting days next after the day the motion in that House was made.

(4) If both Houses of Parliament resolve that the proclamation be revoked, it shall cease to have effect, and sections 3, 4 and 5 shall cease to be in force until those sections are again brought into force by a further proclamation but without prejudice to the previous operation of those sections or anything duly done or suffered thereunder or any offence committed or any penalty or forfeiture or punishment incurred.

(5) Any act or thing done or authorized or any order to regulation made under the authority of this Act, shall be deemed not to be an abrogation, abridgement or infringement of any right or freedom recognized by the *Canadian Bill of Rights*.''

# CANADIAN CHARTER OF RIGHTS AND FREEDOMS

Whereas Canada is founded upon principles that recognize the supremacy of God and the rule of law:

### *Guarantee of Rights and Freedoms*

1. The *Canadian Charter of Rights and Freedoms* guarantees the rights and freedoms set out in it subject only to such reasonable limits prescribed by law as can be demonstrably justified in a free and democratic society.

### *Fundamental Freedoms*

2. Everyone has the following fundamental freedoms:
    (a) freedom of conscience and religion;
    (b) freedom of thought, belief, opinion and expression, including freedom of the press and other media of communication;
    (c) freedom of peaceful assembly; and
    (d) freedom of association.

### *Democratic Rights*

3. Every citizen of Canada has the right to vote in an election of members of the House of Commons or of a legislative assembly and to be qualified for membership therein.

4.(1) No House of Commons and no legislative assembly shall continue for longer than five years from the date fixed for the return of the writs at a general election of its members.

(2) In time of real or apprehended war, invasion or insurrection, a House of Commons may be continued by Parliament and a legislative assembly may be continued by the legislature beyond five years if such continuation is not opposed by the votes of more than one-third of the members of the House of Commons or the legislative assembly, as the case may be.

5. There shall be a sitting of Parliament and of each legislature at least once every twelve months.

## *Mobility Rights*

6.(1) Every citizen of Canada has the right to enter, remain in and leave Canada.

(2) Every citizen of Canada and every person who has the status of a permanent resident of Canada has the right

    (a) to move to and take up residence in any province; and

    (b) to pursue the gaining of a livelihood in any province.

(3) The rights specified in subsection (2) are subject to

    (a) any laws or practices of general application in force in a province other than those that discriminate among persons primarily on the basis of province of present or previous residence; and

    (b) any laws providing for reasonable residency requirements as a qualification for the receipt of publicly provided social services.

(4) Subsections (2) and (3) do not preclude any law, program or activity that has as its object the amelioration in a province of conditions of individuals in that province who are socially or economically disadvantaged if the rate of employment in that province is below the rate of employment in Canada.

7. Everyone has the right to life, liberty and security of the person and the right not to be deprived thereof except in accordance with the principles of fundamental justice.

8. Everyone has the right to be secure against unreasonable search or seizure.

9. Everyone has the right not to be arbitrarily detained or imprisoned.

10. Everyone has the right on arrest or detention

    (a) to be informed promptly of the reasons therefor;

    (b) to retain and instruct counsel without delay and to be informed of that right; and

    (c) to have the validity of the detention determined by way of *habeas corpus* and to be released if the detention is not lawful.

11. Any person charged with an offence has the right

    (a) to be informed without unreasonable delay of the specific offence;

    (b) to be tried within a reasonable time;

    (c) not to be compelled to be a witness in proceedings against that person in respect of the offence;

    (d)  to be presumed innocent until proven guilty according to law in a fair and public hearing by an independent and impartial tribunal;

    (e)  not to be denied reasonable bail without just cause;

    (f)  except in the case of an offence under military law tried before a military tribunal, to the benefit of trial by jury where the maximum punishment for the offence is imprisonment for five years or a more severe punishment;

    (g)  not to be found guilty on account of any act or omission unless, at the time of the act or omission, it constituted an offence under Canadian or international law or was criminal according to the general principles of law recognized by the community of nations;

    (h)  if finally acquitted of the offence, not to be tried for it again and, if finally found guilty and punished for the offence, not to be tried or punished for it again; and

    (i)  if found guilty of the offence and if the punishment for the offence has been varied between the time of commission and the time of sentencing, to the benefit of the lesser punishment.

12. Everyone has the right not to be subjected to any cruel and unusual treatment or punishment.

13. A witness who testifies in any proceedings has the right not to have any incriminating evidence so given used to incriminate that witness in any other proceedings, except in a prosecution for perjury or for the giving of contradictory evidence.

14. A party or witness in any proceedings who does not understand or speak the language in which the proceedings are conducted or who is deaf has the right to the assistance of an interpreter.

### Equality Rights

15.(1) Every individual is equal before and under the law and has the right to the equal protection and equal benefit of the law without discrimination and, in particular, without discrimination based on race, national or ethnic origin, colour, religion, sex, age or mental or physical disability.

(2) Subsection (1) does not preclude any law, program or activity that has as its object the amelioration of conditions of disadvantaged individuals or groups including those that are disadvantaged because of race, national or ethnic origin, colour, religion, sex, age or mental or physical disability.

### Official Languages of Canada

16.(1) English and French are the official languages of Canada and have equality of status and equal rights and privileges as to their use in all institutions of the Parliament and government of Canada.

(2) English and French are the official languages of New Brunswick and have equality of status and equal rights and privileges as to their use in all institutions of the legislature and government of New Brunswick.

(3) Nothing in this Charter limits the authority of Parliament or a legislature to advance the equality of status or use of English and French.

17.(1) Everyone has the right to use English or French in any debates and other proceedings of Parliament.

(2) Everyone has the right to use English or French in any debates and other proceedings of the legislature of New Brunswick.

18.(1) The statutes, records and journals of Parliament shall be printed and published in English and French and both language versions are equally authoritative.

(2) The statutes, records and journals of the legislature of New Brunswick shall be printed and published in English and French and both language versions are equally authoritative.

19.(1) Either English or French may be used by any person in, or in any pleading in or process issuing from, any court established by Parliament.

(2) Either English or French may be used by any person in, or in any pleading in or process issuing from, any court of New Brunswick.

20.(1) Any member of the public in Canada has the right to communicate with, and to receive available services from, any head or central office of an institution of the Parliament or government of Canada in English or French, and has the same right with respect to any other office of any such institution where

(a) there is a significant demand for communications with and services from that office in such language; or

(b) due to the nature of the office, it is reasonable that communications with and services from that office be available in both English and French.

(2) Any member of the public in New Brunswick has the right to communicate with, and to receive available services from, any office of an institution of the legislature or government of New Brunswick in English or French.

21. Nothing in sections 16 to 20 abrogates or derogates from any right, privilege or obligation with respect to the English and French languages, or either of them, that exists or is continued by virtue of any other provision of the Constitution of Canada.

22. Nothing in sections 16 to 20 abrogates or derogates from any legal or customary right or privilege acquired or enjoyed either before or after the coming into force of this Charter with respect to any language that is not English or French.

## Minority Language Educational Rights

23.(1) Citizens of Canada

(a) whose first language learned and still understood is that of the English or French linguistic minority population of the province in which they reside, or

(b) who have received their primary school instruction in Canada in

English or French and reside in a province where the language in which they received that instruction is the language of the English or French linguistic minority population of the province,

have the right to have their children receive primary and secondary school instruction in that language in that province.

(2) Citizens of Canada of whom any child has received or is receiving primary or secondary school instruction in English or French in Canada, have the right to have all their children receive primary and secondary school instruction in the same language.

(3) The right of citizens of Canada under subsections (1) and (2) to have their children receive primary and secondary school instruction in the language of the English or French linguistic minority population of a province

- (a) applies wherever in the province the number of children of citizens who have such a right is sufficient to warrant the provision to them out of public funds of minority language instruction; and
- (b) includes, where the number of those children so warrants, the right to have them receive that instruction in minority language educational facilities provided out of public funds.

### Enforcement

24.(1) Anyone whose rights or freedoms, as guaranteed by this Charter, have been infringed or denied may apply to a court of competent jurisdiction to obtain such remedy as the court considers appropriate and just in the circumstances.

(2) Where, in proceedings under subsection (1), a court concludes that evidence was obtained in a manner that infringed or denied any rights or freedoms guaranteed by this Charter, the evidence shall be excluded if it is established that, having regard to all the circumstances, the admission of it in the proceedings would bring the administration of justice into disrepute.

### General

25. The guarantee in this Charter of certain rights and freedoms shall not be construed so as to abrogate or derogate from any aboriginal, treaty or other rights or freedoms that pertain to the aboriginal peoples of Canada including

- (a) any rights or freedoms that have been recognized by the Royal Proclamation of October 7, 1763; and
- (b) any rights or freedoms that may be acquired by the aboriginal peoples of Canada by way of land claims settlement.

26. The guarantee in this Charter of certain rights and freedoms shall not be construed as denying the existence of any other rights or freedoms that exist in Canada.

27. This Charter shall be interpreted in a manner consistent with the preservation and enhancement of the multicultural heritage of Canadians.

28. Notwithstanding anything in this Charter, the rights and freedoms referred

to in it are guaranteed equally to male and female persons.

29. Nothing in this Carter abrogates or derogates from any rights or privileges guaranteed by or under the Constitution of Canada in respect of denominational, separate or dissentient schools.

30. A reference in this Charter to a province or to the legislative assembly or legislature of a province shall be deemed to include a reference to the Yukon Territory and the Northwest Territories, or to the appropriate legislative authority thereof, as the case may be.

31. Nothing in this Carter extends the legislative powers of any body or authority.

## Application of Charter

32.(1) This Charter applies
  (a) to the Parliament and government of Canada in respect of all matters within the authority of Parliament including all matters relating to the Yukon Territory and Northwest Territories; and
  (b) to the legislature and government of each province in respect of all matters within the authority of the legislature of each province.

(2) Notwithstanding subsection (1), section 15 shall not have effect until three years after this section comes into force.

33.(1) Parliament or the legislature of a province may expressly declare in an Act of Parliament or of the legislature, as the case may be, that the Act or a provision thereof shall operate notwithstanding a provision included in section 2 or sections 7 to 15 of the Charter.

(2) An Act or a provision of an Act in respect of which a declaration made under this section is in effect shall have such operation as it would have but for the provisions of this Charter referred to in the declaration.

(3) A declaration made under subsection (1) shall cease to have effect five years after it comes into force or on such earlier date as may be specified in the declaration.

(4) Parliament or a legislature of a province may re-enact a declaration made under subsection (1).

(5) Subsection (3) applies in respect of a re-enactment made under subsection (4).

## Citation

34. This Part may be cited as the *Canadian Charter of Rights and Freedoms*.

# AMERICAN BILL OF RIGHTS

## AMENDMENTS TO THE
## CONSTITUTION OF THE UNITED STATES

First Ten Amendments passed by Congress September 25, 1789.
Ratified by three-fourths of the States December 15, 1791.

### ARTICLE I

Congress shall make no law respecting an establishment of religion, or prohibiting the free exercise thereof; or abridging the freedom of speech, or of the press; or the right of the people peaceably to assemble, and to petition the government for a redress of grievances.

### ARTICLE II

A well regulated militia, being necessary to the security of a free State, the right of the people to keep and bear arms, shall not be infringed.

### ARTICLE III

No soldier shall, in time of peace be quartered in any house, without the consent of owner, nor in time of war, but in a manner to be prescribed by law.

### ARTICLE IV

The right of the people to be secure in their persons, houses, papers, and effects, against unreasonable searches and seizures, shall not be violated, and no warrants shall issue, but upon probable cause, supported by oath or affirmation, and particularly describing the place to be searched, and the persons or things to be seized.

### ARTICLE V

No person shall be held to answer for a capital, or otherwise infamous crime, unless on a presentment or indictment of a grand jury, except in cases arising in the land or naval forces, or in the militia, when in actual service in time of war or public danger; nor shall any person be subject for the same offense to be twice put in jeopardy of life or limb; nor shall be compelled in any criminal case to be a witness against himself, nor be deprived of life, liberty, or property, without due process of law; nor shall private property be taken for public use without just compensation.

## ARTICLE VI

In all criminal prosecutions, the accused shall enjoy the right to a speedy and public trial, by an impartial jury of the State and district wherein the crime shall have been committed, which district shall have been previously ascertained by law, and to be informed of the nature and cause of the accusation; to be confronted with the witnesses against him; to have compulsory process for obtaining witnesses in his favor, and to have the assistance of counsel for his defense.

## ARTICLE VII

In suits at common law, where the value in controversy shall exceed twenty dollars, the right of trial by jury shall be preserved, and no fact tried by a jury shall be otherwise reexamined in any court of the United States, than according to the rules of the common law.

## ARTICLE VIII

Excessive bail shall not be required, nor excessive fines imposed, nor cruel and unusual punishments inflicted.

## ARTICLE IX

The enumeration in the Constitution of certain rights shall not be construed to deny or disparage others retained by the people.

## ARTICLE X

The powers not delegated to the United States by the Constitution, nor prohibited by it to the States, are reserved to the States respectively, or to the people.

## ARTICLE XIII

Passed by Congress January 31, 1865. Ratified December 6, 1865.

SECTION 1.  Neither slavery nor involuntary servitude, except as punishment for crime whereof the party shall have been duly convicted, shall exist within the United States, or any place subject to their jurisdiction.

SECTION 2.  Congress shall have power to enforce this article by appropriate legislation.

## ARTICLE XIV

Passed by Congress June 13, 1866. Ratified July 9, 1868.

SECTION 1. All persons born or naturalized in the United States, and subject to the jurisdiction thereof, are citizens of the United States and of the State wherein they reside. No State shall make or enforce any law which shall abridge the privileges or immunities of citizens of the United States; nor shall any State deprive any person of life, liberty, or property, without due process of law; nor deny to any person within its jurisdiction the equal protection of the laws. . . .

SECTION 5. The Congress shall have power to enforce, by appropriate legislation, the provisions of this article.

## ARTICLE XV

Passed by Congress February 26, 1869. Ratified February 3, 1870.

SECTION 1. The right of citizens of the United States to vote shall not be denied or abridged by the United States or by any State on account of race, color, or previous condition of servitude.

SECTION 2. The Congress shall have power to enforce this article by appropriate legislation.

## ARTICLE XIX

Passed by Congress June 4, 1919. Ratified August 18, 1920.

The right of citizens of the United States to vote shall not be denied or abridged by the United States or by any State on account of sex.

The Congress shall have power by appropriate legislation to enforce the provisions of this article.

## ARTICLE XXIV

Passed by Congress August 27, 1962. Ratified January 23, 1964.

SECTION 1. The right of citizens of the United States to vote in any primary or other election for President or Vice President, for electors for President or Vice President, or for Senator or Representative in Congress, shall not be denied or abridged by the United States or any State by reason of failure to pay any poll tax or other tax.

SECTION 2. The Congress shall have the power to enforce this article by appropriate legislation.

## ARTICLE XXVI

Passed by Congress March 23, 1971. Ratified June 30, 1971.

SECTION 1. The right of citizens of the United States, who are eighteen years of age or older, to vote shall not be denied or abridged by the United States or any state on account of age.

SECTION 2. The Congress shall have the power to enforce this article by appropriate legislation.